The Shaping
of the
American High School
1920–1941

The Shaping of the

AMERICAN HIGH SCHOOL

Volume 2

1920–1941

EDWARD A. KRUG

THE UNIVERSITY OF WISCONSIN PRESS

MADISON, MILWAUKEE, AND LONDON

Published 1972
The University of Wisconsin Press
Box 1379, Madison, Wisconsin 53701

The University of Wisconsin Press, Ltd.
70 Great Russell Street, London, WC1B 3BY

First printing

Printed in the United States of America
NAPCO, Inc.
Milwaukee, Wisconsin

ISBN 0-299-05980-4; LC 64-12801

Contents

Acknowledgments

*I*t was in 1964 that I began this journey through the high schools of the 1920s and 1930s. Since 1966 the School of Education of the University of Wisconsin has helped make the work possible through research provisions in the professorship established in memory of Virgil Herrick, Professor in the Department of Education from 1948 to 1963. The Graduate School Research Committee made grants available for the summer sessions of 1965, 1967, and 1970. For the inspiration and opportunity to do the work, I am indebted to the climate of scholarship established over many years by the Deans of our School of Education, Charles Anderson, John Guy Fowlkes, Lindley Stiles, and at present Donald McCarty.

Librarians, archivists, and curators in a number of places have enabled me to find and use a variety of materials. I am especially grateful for the patience and helpfulness of Marguerite Christensen and her colleagues in the Reference Department of the Memorial Library of the University of Wisconsin, who obtained much material for me on interlibrary loan, and of Josephine Harper, Manuscripts Curator, State Historical Society of Wisconsin, who made available to me the Michael Vincent O'Shea Papers and other collections.

I also owe thanks to Katherine W. Kridl of the Teachers College Library, Columbia University; Nancy Prewitt of the Western Historical Manuscript Collection, State Historical Society Manuscripts, University of Missouri; Jane F. Smith and Joseph Howerton of the Social and Economic Branch, Office of Civil Archives, National Archives and Record Services; Professor Robert B. Sutton, Director, Educational Archives, College of Education, Ohio State University; Maynard Brichford, University Archivist, University of Illinois Library; Maxine B. Clapp, University Archivist, and Clodaugh Neiderheiser, Assistant Archivist, University of Minnesota Libraries; and Ann Colley, Special Collections, University of Chicago Library. I am especially indebted to Barbara Bergan and to the late Professor Archibald Anderson, both of the College of Education, University of Illinois, for their help to me in my use of the university's collection of unpublished documents of the Progressive Education Association.

For copies of hard-to-get documents of local schools, I am grateful to the public school system of Appleton, Wisconsin, and to its Secondary Curriculum Coordinator, Orlyn Zieman; and to the systems of Oshkosh, Wisconsin; Seattle, Washington; Kalamazoo, Michigan; Fort Wayne, Indiana; St. Louis, Missouri; and Joliet, Illinois.

I appreciate the kindness of Homer P. Rainey, former Director of the American Youth Commission, in granting me permission to read portions of his papers on deposit with the Western Historical Manuscript Collection, State Historical Society Manuscripts, University of Missouri, and of William Beard and Mrs. Miriam B. Vagts for permission to read correspondence written by their father, Charles A. Beard, on deposit in the August C. Krey Papers, University of Minnesota Archives. My appreciation goes also to Harcourt Brace Jovanovich, Inc., for permission to quote from Carl Sandburg's poem "The People, Yes."

E. A. K.

Madison, Wisconsin
July 1971

Abbreviations in Footnotes

Bur Ed	U.S. Bureau of Education, Washington, D.C.
EA&S	*Educational Administration and Supervision*
ER	*Educational Review*
EJ	*English Journal*
High Points	*Bulletin of High Points in the Work of the High Schools of New York*
High School Conference	*High School Conference* (Illinois), *Proceedings*
J Ed	*Journal of Education*
NEA J	*Journal of the National Education Association*
NEA Proc	National Education Association, *Addresses and Proceedings*
NC Proc	North Central Association of Colleges and Secondary Schools, *Proceedings*
Off Ed	U.S. Office of Education, Washington, D.C.
Prog Ed	*Progressive Education*
S&S	*School and Society*
Sch R	*School Review*
Superintendence *Report*	Department of Superintendence, *Official Report*
TCR	*Teachers College Record*

In the text, the abbreviation NEA is used for National Education Association, and *NEA Journal* for its journal.

Changes in the Names of Magazines

*T*he names of many of the magazines referred to in the footnotes have changed in the years since 1920. In citing these magazines I have used the names in use at the times to which the footnotes refer: *Historical Outlook* rather than *Social Studies* is used for footnotes referring to the years between 1920 and 1934, for example. The following is a list of magazines with the new names adopted in the 1920s and 1930s:

American Educational Digest. School Executives Magazine Jan. 1929, *School Executive* Sept. 1935.

Bulletin of the Department of Secondary School Principals. See *Bulletin of the National Association of Secondary School Principals.*

Bulletin of the National Association of Secondary School Principals. Bulletin of the Department of Secondary School Principals April 1928, back to the original name Oct. 1939.

California Journal of Secondary Education. See *California Quarterly of Secondary Education.*

California Quarterly of Secondary Education. California Journal of Secondary Education Oct. 1935.

Clearing House. See *Junior High School Clearing House.*

Curriculum Journal. See *News Bulletin of the Society for Curriculum Study.*

Educational Method. See *Journal of Educational Method.*

Frontiers of Democracy. See *Social Frontier.*

General Science Quarterly. Science Education May 1929.

Harvard Educational Review. See *Harvard Teachers Record.*

Harvard Teachers Record. Harvard Educational Review Jan. 1937.

Historical Outlook. Social Studies Jan. 1934.

Junior High Clearing House. See *Junior High School Clearing House.*

Junior High School Clearing House. Junior High Clearing House April

1928, *Junior-Senior High School Clearing House* Sept. 1929, *Clearing House* Sept. 1932.

Junior-Senior High School Clearing House. See *Junior High School Clearing House.*

Journal of Educational Method. Educational Method Oct. 1929.

Michigan Education Journal. Michigan Journal of Education June 1937.

Michigan Journal of Education. See *Michigan Education Journal.*

News Bulletin of the Society for Curriculum Study. Curriculum Journal Jan. 1935.

Occupations. See *Vocational Guidance Magazine.*

School Executive. See *American Educational Digest.*

School Executives Magazine. See *American Educational Digest.*

Science Education. See *General Science Quarterly.*

Social Frontier. Frontiers of Democracy Oct. 1939.

Social Studies. See *Historical Outlook.*

Vocational Guidance Magazine. Occupations June 1933.

Introduction

$\mathcal{T}$his book is a continuation of *The Shaping of the American High School 1880–1920*. It carries the story of the public high school* through two decades of peace and up to our direct involvement in the Second World War. The end of one war marked the beginning of this period, the beginning of another war marked its end.

As a comprehensive and nonselective institution, the American high school of 1920 had been in the process of development over the course of at least forty years, with its major doctrinal formulation set forth in the decade before 1920. Enrolling some two million students by the end of that decade, it had moved toward universal enrollment. One question before the people in 1920 was whether the high school should remain as comprehensive as it had become. Another was whether the claim to custodianship of all American youth made by some leaders in secondary education should be accepted or rejected.

The ordeal through which the high school passed in the two decades after 1920 had two phases. Before 1929 the high school was not taken seriously enough. After that it was taken too seriously. Prosperity fostered a climate in which scholarship gained little more than amused toleration. The academic tradition persisted, nonetheless, and in spite of the assault mounted against it by the social efficiency educators through their programs of curriculum revision. It was in part the quest for custodianship that prompted this anti-academic drive, reflecting the idea that large numbers of students would be incapable of scholarship.

Prosperity may have been, and for many people probably was, an illusion, but there could be no doubt of the reality of the depression that followed. Social and economic upheaval called all tradition into question

---

* Throughout the book, the term *high school* will be used to mean public high school, although I have sometimes included the modifier as a reminder to myself. When private schools are referred to they are explicitly so designated.

and helped promote the vigorous pedagogical debate about social recon-struction through the schools. Mass unemployment not only increased the population of the high schools, thereby approaching universal cover-age, but raised questions about the best national policy for youth.

Just as the depression seemed on the verge of establishing the high school as the universal custodian, a new set of factors appeared in the creation of national youth agencies under the New Deal. Social efficiency, it seemed, was about to triumph, but under which king? Schoolmen were determined that the kingship should be theirs. Their seesaw struggle with the New Deal ended in victory, but to achieve this victory they had to portray themselves as anti-academic enough to be trusted with the custodial task.

Whether their victory was a good thing or not is debatable. From the point of view of what Thomas H. Briggs called the investment theory of education, which seemed to preclude even the existence of private schools, it was a very good thing indeed, predicated as the theory was on the need for social control and the stern adjustment of the individual to the group. The theory of the schoolmen also furthered ideas that had already appeared in the 1930s and that later emerged as the familiar triad of life-adjustment education: academic or so-called college prepara-tory work serving one group of students, vocational another, and a new, as yet undefined, curriculum serving a third.

From the point of view of those who today consider all schooling repressive or an instrument of establishment control, the victory of the schoolmen was disaster. It nailed down firmly the proposition that the high school was to be what the elementary school had already become and what in some future time the college or some institution of adult education might become, an institution of custodianship. Whether the national government, through agencies like the National Youth Admin-istration and the Civilian Conservation Corps, might have developed into a better custodian is another question, as is that of avoiding such custodianship altogether. In any case, the victory of the schoolmen tended to process youth on a vast assembly line into the high school and in many cases into the college, at least the junior college, a state of affairs preceding the explosion of the youth culture in the decade of the 1960s.

Since my position on this matter affects the way I have told the story of this book, I should state it here. I believe in a public high school open to all youth, not for social efficiency or control but for the opportunity for advancement, enrichment, and welfare. Such a high school would identify itself with and make available what might broadly be termed the human intellectual, moral, and cultural estate.

Following Charles W. Eliot, however, I do not believe there is any specified portion of this estate, at least as represented by its subject packages, through which all students must necessarily proceed. I do believe, like Eliot, that every human being has some quality at which he can excel, for himself and in his own terms. Were such a thing as a perfect high school ever achieved, its main characteristic would be a curriculum broad and diversified enough for every student to find and to develop this unique quality in himself. Something reasonably close to this might yet be achieved, and with this hope I still believe that the victory of the schoolmen in the early 1940s was a desirable thing. I should add also my personal conviction that the development of the intellect cannot be detached from human relationships and human interaction based on individuality and freedom, the old doctrines of progressive education. The tragedy of war nullified this aspect of progressivism, and the schools committed themselves anew to status, authority, and force. My hope for the future is a high school where the intellectual function is reflected in decent social behavior, sensitivity to the rights and feelings of others, and a desire at all times to see that social justice is achieved.

The Shaping
of the
American High School
1920–1941

Chapter 1

Visions of the future

> "Personal liberty is a fine thing provided it is accompanied by a full recognition of the supremacy of the State as a whole."
>
> —FRANK HERBERT PALMER,
> OCTOBER, 1922.

*T*he war is won—marvelously and completely won," proclaimed Horace A. Eaton, Professor of English at Syracuse University, to a group of teachers at nearby Utica on November 16, 1918, "and we stand on a new Pisgah looking into the future." Past systems of "autocracy, nationalism, and industrialism" would vex humankind no more. To his own question of what this "splendid hope" had to do with education, he answered, "Everything."[1]

As this Wilsonian vision faded, other spokesmen for education offered their own versions of the future. They too saw a promised land, but one not quite like Eaton's. In theirs the schools would equip each young citizen to function in a society whose touchstone would be orderly and efficient management. The institution favored for this purpose was the public high school: not the allegedly narrow, academic school of the past, but a comprehensive high school housing a variety of curricula and enrolling youth of diverse abilities and interests. This meant getting and keeping all youth in school, and the National Education Association at its Milwaukee convention in 1919 recommended state laws that would require full-time attendance until the age of sixteen and at least part-time attendance until eighteen.[2] Secondary schools, public and private,

---

1. "English Problems after the War," *EJ* 8 (May 1919), 308–9.
2. "Report of the Committee on Resolutions," *NEA Proc*, 1919, p. 25.

enrolling in 1919–20 only one-third of the youth, fell far short of the ideal.[3]

The concept of the high school as a universal custodian of youth was an aspect of pedagogical doctrines preached since the turn of the century and reflecting the national impulse for reform. Popularized by William C. Bagley in his book *The Educative Process* (New York, 1905), the term *social efficiency* had become the militant and easily repeated slogan of those who sought a larger role for themselves than the teaching of academic subjects to a fraction of American youth. Fostered by school surveys and finding major expression in the campaigns for vocational education and the creation of the junior high school, the movement constituted the driving force behind the volume of controversy about high schools after 1910.

It persisted, moreover, through the war years, with an intensification of those aspects leaning toward heavy-handed social control, and survived beyond 1920 as well. "As a public agency," said Charles A. Prosser in 1923, "the schools of this democracy have in every age reflected the current political and social philosophy, the dominant social theory and aim of the day. However it may be phrased, that aim today is social efficiency through mass conservation. Consequently, layman and educator alike are no longer defining education in terms of personal accomplishment or political rights, but in terms of social necessity, social efficiency, social conservation, social adjustment." The aim of the secondary school, said Professor Thomas H. Briggs of Teachers College, Columbia, in 1922, was "to fit each person to contribute better to the state." Free public education was "a wise investment," and the school "just as truly as a manufacturing plant . . . must work up all its raw material so as to make it maximally useful."[4]

Like other slogans, such as progressive education and education for life adjustment, education for social efficiency had no precise definition. It represented a style of thought and action from which interpretations could be developed. Those flowing from social efficiency were hostile to the academic high school of the past, particularly to the doctrine of

3. Kenneth A. Simon and W. Vance Grant, *Digest of Educational Statistics*, 1967, Off Ed 10024–67, p. 29, table 32.

4. "Preparation for Leadership in Vocational Education," *TCR* 24 (May 1923), 225; "What Next in Secondary Education?" *Sch R* 30 (Sept. 1922), 524–25, 528.

mental discipline. Intelligence was not disparaged, particularly since it could contribute heavily to efficient social enterprise, but by a slight shading of the term, those aims identified as "intellectual" were another matter. Intellectual education, if not wrong, was from this point of view at least inadequate.

To sociologist Charles A. Ellwood of the University of Missouri, writing in 1921, intellectual education constituted a "halfway" place in the progress of the school toward broader social functions. As social evolution progressed, education would become "a more systematized, rationalized, and controlled social process, for the sake of greater social control over the whole of human life." This was not to mean the neglect of linguistic or intellectual training, but the real work of the school was to fit the individual "to play well his part as a producer, as a husband or wife, a father or mother, a friend and neighbor, a creator of public opinion, and a servant of the public will."[5]

Such traditional subjects as Latin and Greek obviously presented little attraction to the advocates of social efficiency, and the modern academic subjects needed special adaptation. Ross L. Finney contended, for example, that "history teaching, whatever it may be in graduate seminars, in the tenth grade is frankly propaganda, in the interests of the common good." Stephen G. Rich, principal of the high school of Essex Falls, New Jersey, found in educational sociology the criteria for course-of-study construction and called for "a rapid remodelling of courses to eliminate all that can not be shown to contribute toward these aims" and for the introduction of "new matter that does lead toward them."[6]

Neither did strictly vocational or industrial training constitute the ideal, although the powerful campaign in support of it had been part of the social efficiency movement. Vocational education was too narrow, and guilty in the same way as academic education of neglecting aspects of personality that needed direction and control. Even the Smith-Hughes Act for Vocational Education (1917) evoked opposition from some efficiency educators on the grounds that it fostered separateness by granting funds exclusively for vocational education. Comprehensive high schools, on the other hand, provided an environment for common enterprise, with

5. "The Educative Nature of the Social Process," *TCR* 22 (May 1921), 229–31.

6. "Course in General History from the Sociologist's Standpoint," *Historical Outlook* 11 (June 1920), 226; "A Claim for New Procedures in Education," *ER* 68 (June 1924), 19.

all the curricula, including the vocational, under one pedagogical roof.

In a prophetic utterance, Professor Walter McNutt of the Tallahassee, Florida, State College for Women moved to the farther reaches of the doctrine by calling for a view of all education as human engineering. "It is the place of the human engineer," said McNutt, "to discover the laws of human nature, and then to engineer life in the conservation, creation and perpetuation of human values. This the engineer achieves through his knowledge of life, human tendencies and institutions as agencies of development and control."[7] This was a vision not to be realized in the 1920s. While awaiting the sophisticated technologies of the future, the schoolmen of the immediate postwar period were left with the more primitive devices of the Americanization campaign and the expansion of the high school.

II

Although by the end of the war the goal of universal secondary schooling was far from achieved, even it was not enough for the most strenuous advocates of the systematic channeling of youth into society. Besides advocating state laws for more schooling, the NEA in 1919 called upon the national government to provide a full year of additional "instruction, training, and discipline" in accordance with "civic responsibility and vocational efficiency" for every man and woman between seventeen and one-half and twenty years of age. This national civic year would supplement, but not replace, the work of the secondary school. Superintendent Frank E. Spaulding of Cleveland, Ohio, proposed a variant plan, a compulsory national year for boys only that would include military training and be under the joint direction of the War Department and a Department of Education still to be established.[8]

Recommendations for the national year of training did not take hold, however, and the idea lay dormant until its revival in the late 1930s. This left the secondary school, especially the public high school, to be the custodian of youth, and the most numerous resolutions of the 1919 NEA convention were those calling for compulsory attendance beyond

7. "Some Objectives in Twentieth-Century Education," *Education* 45 (Nov. 1924), 155.

8. *NEA Proc*, 1919, p. 23; "Educating the Nation," *Atlantic* 75 (April 1920), 533–34.

age fourteen in schools provided by the states through local districts.

Contrary to a widespread impression, the expansion of the high school before 1920 had not been a result of compulsory schooling; the laws of the period did not compel most children to even start high school. The overwhelming majority of states fostered full-time attendance directly only until the age of fourteen or through the eighth grade, and even their requirements were modified by the common practice of issuing work permits. In 1917–18 there were thirty states with general requirements of full-time attendance until sixteen, eight until fifteen, nine until fourteen, and one until twelve. All the states, however, issued work permits, and of the thirty-eight with limits at fifteen or sixteen, all but five issued them to children fourteen or younger. The other five states set fifteen as the age for work permits, but one of these, Michigan, provided exemption, without stipulating age, for those who had completed elementary school. Besides Michigan, twenty-three other states granted educational exemptions for completion of elementary school or less, with no age stipulations beyond fourteen.[9] The result of work permits and of educational exemptions for elementary work or less was that only two states, Idaho and Ohio, unconditionally required full-time attendance until fourteen or older and then only until fifteen.

The fact was that despite the more than two million students enrolled in high schools in 1920, there were still more than four million youth not enrolled. This state of affairs was most unsatisfactory to those who wanted the secondary school to guide all young people into adult life, and they campaigned to raise the age limits of compulsory schooling.

A new law in Utah, passed in March 1919, three months before the summer resolutions of that year's NEA convention, furnished a promising start. It required part-time attendance until eighteen, with only high school graduates exempted. The law was less satisfactory on full-time attendance, since it permitted the part-time option to those under sixteen who were employed and had completed the eighth grade. (*Laws of Utah*, 1919, ch. 92, sec. 1). Representing the spirit of the NEA resolutions, the Utah program evoked applause throughout the country. As enthusiastically viewed by the NEA, it meant "the constant supervision of boys and girls to their eighteenth year."[10]

9. H. R. Bonner, "Compulsory Attendance Laws," *American School Board Journal* 60 (Jan. 1920), 39; (Feb. 1920), 46.
10. "Educational Advance," *NEA J* 10 (March 1921), 54.

Utah clearly pointed the way to the future, but the road ahead proved uncertain and slow, particularly on the matter of full-time attendance until sixteen. Hailed as the next great advance, the Ohio law of 1921 permitted only high-school graduates to leave school before sixteen and restricted the part-time option after sixteen to those who had completed the seventh grade.[11] Even by the mid-1920s there were only four states that unconditionally required children to be sixteen before they could leave school with work permits.[12]

Inconclusive results of the campaign did not diminish the drive to get and to keep all youth in school. What they did was to stimulate efforts to persuade youth and their parents of the value of secondary education, or, as it was often expressed, to "sell" the high school to its prospective clients. So long as high school was not "the paramount demand," said the principal of Central High School, Okmulgee, Oklahoma, it would be "imperative for the high school principal to continue as the head salesman of this gigantic organization." In Cleveland, Ohio, the board of education initiated a many-sided campaign to get more youth into high school, a campaign including a forty-eight-page book *Give Yourself a Fair Start*, distributed to all graduating from the eighth grade. In 1921 Superintendent J. Minor Gwinn of New Orleans sent his eighth-grade graduates a persuasive letter entitled "Go to High School." Editor Albert E. Winship of the *Journal of Education* wrote a brochure, *Why Graduate?*, distributed in thousands of copies throughout various school systems. (Five thousand were ordered by the Junior Chamber of Commerce of Dallas, Texas.)[13]

If the welfare of society depended upon universal secondary education, high schools could no longer be permitted the luxury of the academic exclusiveness of which they were accused. Serving all youth in the community was to take precedence over serving scholarship and high stand-

11. *State of Ohio: Legislative Acts Passed and Joint Resolutions Adopted by the 84th General Assembly at Its Regular Session Which Began January 3, 1921* (Springfield, 1921), 109:381, 387–90.

12. Bur Ed, *A Manual of Educational Legislation*, bull. 1926, no. 22, p. 46.

13. Cecil K. Reiff, "The Modern High School Principal," *National Association of Secondary School Principals Sixth Yearbook*, 1922, p. 10; Clyde R. Miller, "Persuading Cleveland Children To 'Stay in School through High School,'" *S&S* 16 (Nov. 11, 1922), 557–58; Reported in "Educational Forum," *J Ed* 94 (Sept. 22, 1921), 271; see *J Ed* 93: "Why Graduate" (Feb. 17, 1921), 171–75, "High Spots for High Schools" (March 24, 1921), 318, and (May 5, 1921), 492n.

ards.[14] To Winship it was "of far greater importance to keep under the influence of the schools a larger number of pupils who otherwise would leave to go to work" than it was "to turn out a very high type of graduate."[15]

At least as far back as 1900, the efficiency educators had called upon the high schools to adjust themselves to increasing numbers of students of allegedly low ability who were storming the doors. Now in the early 1920s high schools were being asked to change themselves so that more youth would storm them.

III

Also involved in custodianship was the emphasis on schooling as a force for national unity and cohesion. Calls for education to build common loyalties and convert immigrants to American ideals had been familiar enough in nineteenth-century oratory. Stimulated by the "new" immigration after 1900 and the pressures of the European war, they developed in 1915 into an intensive drive for Americanization involving all aspects of national life, but particularly and inevitably the schools. Eager as usual for cosmic mission, educators not only accepted their roles in this process but found many opportunities to expand them. For the advocates of efficiency and social control, these roles constituted an ideal application of doctrinal commitment.

In some ways the pursuit of national cohesion intensified during the immediate postwar years. It appeared in education not only in the form of much speaking and writing and such absurdities as the exclusion of German as a school subject, but also through bureaus and offices of Americanization in state departments of public instruction and city school systems, and in the Department of Immigrant Education in the NEA created in 1921. During these first postwar years, the Americanizers broadened the scope of their efforts to include groups besides the foreign born. "It must not be forgotten," declared a staff member of the Americanization department of the Alameda, California, schools, "that we must also undertake the assimilation of the Negro, the Indian, the Creole, the Filipino, the Porto Rican, the Alaskan, the natives of Haiti, San Domingo, Virgin Islands, Hawaii, in addition to Mexicans,

14. Philip W. L. Cox, "What is Scientific Management?" *NC Proc*, 1920, p. 28.
15. Quoted in news note, *Utah Educational Review* 15 (Oct. 1921), 12.

Chinese and other Asiatics, the isolated whites of Kentucky and West Virginia, and the decadents and defectives of the New England Hinterland."[16] When even the American Indians were viewed as subjects for Americanization, few indeed could hope to escape the campaign.

Yet educators did not accept the arguments for restrictive immigration —based largely on doctrines of Nordic superiority—which won out more or less successfully in the immigration acts of 1921 and 1924. One expression of such doctrine denounced immigrants of Alpine, Mediterranean, Semitic, and Asiatic stocks and called for a policy that would admit Nordics only.[17] Similarly, an editorial in the *Saturday Evening Post* entitled "Americanski" proposed "rigid limitation to selected individuals from those races who are biologically fitted for assimilation" and declared that many of the recent immigrants could never become Americans. "They will always be Americanski," said the *Post*, "near Americans with un-American ideals" (193 [May 14, 1921], 20).

Educators on the other hand believed, and necessarily so, in the power of conversion with all immigrants, including those characterized as new. There were some educators, however, who favored temporary immigration restriction to provide a breathing spell. The Department of Superintendence for example, in 1922, endorsed the closing of the doors "for the present" so that the schools might "more effectively remove illiteracy and more thoroughly Americanize and assimilate the foreign-born elements in this country." Although Secretary James W. Crabtree of the NEA believed that the new immigrants had come from "lower classes" in "less enlightened countries" than the old, he favored temporary restriction only until the country had learned how to Americanize the immigrants already here. The melting pot, he thought, was "too full to stir." Dean Ellwood Cubberley of Stanford's School of Education also defended temporary restriction as a breathing spell and thought the problem not insurmountable.[18]

Some educators, like Charles A. Prosser, director of Dunwoody Institute at Minneapolis, tended to be more hereditarian, but on the basis of

16. Robert F. Gray, "Americanism and Americanization Movement," *Sierra Educational News* 16 (Oct. 1920), 488–89.

17. Prescott F. Hall, "The Present and the Future of Immigration," *North American Review* 213 (May 1921), 607.

18. "Resolutions of the Department of Superintendence," *NEA Proc*, 1922, p. 1464; "Education the Foundation of Democracy," *S&S* 16 (Dec. 2, 1922), 620; "The American School Program from the Standpoint of the Nation," *NEA Proc*, 1923, p. 181.

individuals rather than ethnic groups. If the country excluded aliens with "low mentalities" and "diseased bodies," we could hope to do a better job with others. "The immigrants unfit for parenthood and citizenship," said Prosser, "should be stopped in Europe, and those immigrants finally admitted, after their ancestry and records have been carefully looked up, should be admitted to full citizenship or be returned to Europe."[19]

In the drive for national cohesion, great faith was placed in the use of English as the common American tongue; the NEA as well as other groups called for its use as the universal medium of school instruction.[20] Still, English as English was not enough. It too needed to be Americanized or revealed in its American aspects. In his presidential address at the National Council of the Teachers of English in 1921, James F. Hosic of the Chicago Normal College recommended the use of American authors, "not merely because they are more interesting and perhaps in spite of the fact that in some cases they are less effectively written than others, but *because they are* American."[21] An editorial in the *English Journal* strove to resolve the matter by pointing out that English was a body of ideals presented through literature. "In this sense," it concluded, " 'English' is for us truly American, as indeed, it is now often called. The supreme function of it is to orient and develop young Americans. . . . English is not English which does not result in a finer, truer, and larger Americanism on the part of those who study it" (9 [Dec. 1920], 600). Spoken English presented fewer problems, and the National Council of the Teachers of English frankly set up what it called the Committee on American Speech, a group that fostered American Speech Week in 1919.[22]

It was also proposed that a change in graduation standards would promote national cohesion. The demand that standards be adjusted to the alleged shortcomings of students was a familiar one, but what was now being proposed was that traditional standards be supplemented or replaced by "American" standards. An editorial in the *Ohio Educational Monthly* deplored the tendency of colleges to make scholarship the sole requisite for graduation. "How long, O Lord," asked the writer, "before

19. Quoted in Ruth A. Smart, "Notes from the Southern Section Meeting, *Sierra Educational News* 18 (Feb. 1922), 67.

20. "Report of the Committee on Resolutions," *NEA Proc*, 1921, p. 28.

21. "The National Council of the Teachers of English," *EJ* 10 (Jan. 1921), 8–9.

22. Claudia E. Crumpton, "American Speech Week throughout the Nation," *EJ* 8 (May 1919), 279–86.

they learn that worthy citizenship transcends mere scholarship, important as that is?" (72 [Dec. 1923], 348). More explicitly, a committee on American Citizenship of the American Bar Association declared that "America should no more consider graduating a student who lacks faith in our government than a school of theology should consider graduating a minister who lacks faith in God."[23]

The most spectacular and tumultuous of all the mechanisms for national cohesion through the schools was American Education Week. Probably suggested by the earlier Public Schools Week of the Masonic Lodges of California, the first of these took place in December 1920 by proclamation of the United States Commissioner of Education, Philander P. Claxton. Under Claxton's leadership, American Education Week in 1920 emphasized such comparatively modest goals as more pay for teachers and more money for school buildings and equipment.

In 1921, however, the NEA accepted the invitation of the American Legion to a kind of joint sponsorship of the week. Companion resolutions of the NEA in that year expressed its satisfaction in cooperating with the Legion "in the establishment of a universal requirement of English as the only basic language of instruction in all schools—public, private, and parochial" and commended heartily the Legion's demand "that thorough-going instruction in American history and civics be required of all students for graduation from elementary and secondary schools."

Beyond this the NEA welcomed the cooperation of the Legion "in the establishment of a longer school year, and in the enforcement throughout the United States of compulsory education to the end of the high school period" (*NEA Proc*, 1921, pp. 27–28). Presumably the NEA accepted President Harding's proclamation for American Education Week that year with its observation that the war had revealed "vast elements" of the population to be "illiterate, physically unfit, or unfamiliar with American ideals and traditions."[24] This proclamation so moved William Randolph Hearst that he wired instructions to all his editors for massive editorial treatment of the importance of education during the entire week.[25]

Throughout that week of December 4–10, 1921, school systems in all parts of the country involved their communities in an almost obsessive

23. Quoted in Robert E. L. Saner, "The Schools Must Save America," *NEA J* 12 (Dec. 1923), 395.
24. Quoted in "The President's Proclamation," *J Ed* 94 (Dec. 15, 1921), 597.
25. "Education Week," *J Ed* 95 (Jan. 19, 1922), 71.

concentration on the subject of education. In New Orleans, where "a great electric sign" hung across the main business street to proclaim American Education Week, Superintendent Gwinn itemized the local accomplishments, a list which included 12,509 visitors to the schools, 402 school exercises, and 287 addresses made by Legion representatives and others. Nationally Secretary Crabtree reported, as "a low estimate," the involvement of 200,000 merchants, 20,000 moving picture theatres, 9,000 Legion posts, 1,500 chambers of commerce, 14,500 newspapers, 2,000 women's clubs, and 50,000 "local fraternal, civic, commercial, and religious organizations," with a total of 25,000,000 people directly or indirectly reached.[26]

American Education Week came and went during the following two years, with similar enthusiasms and without dissent. *School Life* claimed a million sermons and addresses for the observance in 1923. In 1924, however, according to the magazine, the week ran into trouble. The program for that year lumped revolutionists, communists, and "extreme pacifists" together as "a menace" to our constitutional guarantees, and described the red flag as a symbol of "death, destruction, poverty, starvation, disease, anarchy, and dictatorship."[27] An editorial in the *Nation* objected to the program as "offensively nationalistic and illiberal" and quoted a statement by Charles W. Eliot that denouncing the red flag did not seem appropriate for American Education Week, even though in some places such a flag symbolized the evils set forth (119 [Nov. 19, 1924], 532).

Further controversy followed in the press, and a stream of letters, many of them critical, came to John J. Tigert, who as Claxton's successor in the office of commissioner of education represented the program, along with the Legion and the NEA. According to John Haynes Holmes, writing in his capacity as acting chairman of the American Civil Liberties Union, the program was an attack against progressive politics and industry masquerading as a fight against radicalism. Holmes blamed the American Legion and protested against their joint sponsorship of American Education Week. Writing on behalf of the Council of Church Boards of Education, Robert L. Kelly, the executive secretary, objected to the inclusion of pacifists with revolutionists and communists and felt that

26. "How We Are Selling the Public Program to Our City," *NEA Proc*, 1922, pp. 1456–57; "The Secretary's Annual Report," *ibid.*, p. 99.
27. "American Education Week Successful," 9 (Jan. 1924), 101; "American Education Week, November 17–23, 1924," 9 (June 1924), 245.

the program was phrased in the language not of intelligence but of violence. Kelly assured Tigert of the cooperation of his council in the program, adding, however, that the council, through its publication *Christian Education,* would try to undo some of the damage.

Letters of protest also came from schoolmen. Superintendent S. R. Logan of Hardin, Montana, wrote that the program preached class hatred, and he defended those who objected to the stirring of antagonisms against the teachings of peace. Even Superintendent H. B. Wilson of Berkeley, California, an ardent promoter of efficiency, suggested to Tigert that American Education Week should be marked by seriousness rather than boastfulness about our country.[28]

Startled by these reactions, Tigert sought to mollify his critics, pointing out to Holmes, for example, that 125 national organizations besides the American Legion were involved. This could not, however, obscure the role of the Legion as one of the three main sponsors. Tigert thanked Superintendent Wilson for his constructive criticism and said that it would be helpful in organizing next year's program.

To Editor Winship, who had written a defense of the program, Tigert said that a little patriotism had aroused some people to excitement.[29] Tigert's role and views remain unclear. In a letter of sympathy to him, Secretary James Crabtree of the NEA identified the points attacked as those neither Tigert nor the NEA had wanted.[30] Although Tigert had been denounced at the time of his appointment as a militarist, he had spoken early in 1922 for limitation of armaments and for the study of this as a topic for American Education Week.[31] In any case, he and the other sponsors gave some heed to the outburst, and the program for 1925 and succeeding years was free of these offending aspects. The connection with the Legion, however, was maintained. A decade later Crabtree expressed warm appreciation of the Legion for its cooperation with the NEA in this and in other matters involving the promotion of education as a national enterprise.[32]

28. Holmes to Tigert, Oct. 9, 1924; Kelly to Tigert, Oct. 23, 1924; Logan to Tigert, Nov. 7, 1924; Wilson to Tigert, Nov. 13, 1924. Commissioner's Office American Education Week and Peace Conferences, 1924–28, National Archives, Record Group 12.
29. Tigert to Holmes, Oct. 13, 1924; to Wilson, Nov. 24, 1924; to Winship, Nov. 17, 1924. Commissioner's Office, NA, RG 12.
30. Oct. 23, 1924. Commissioner's Office, NA, RG 12.
31. Cited in "Education and War," *J Ed* 95 (Feb. 2, 1922), 130.
32. *What Counted Most* (Lincoln, Neb., 1935), pp. 95–110.

In the view of the NEA, national unity in the domain of pedagogy was an indispensable element in developing national cohesion. The NEA set as its goal nothing less than the enrollment of all persons working in the schools and the inclusion and coordination in the organization of all state associations and groups still outside, such as the National Association of Secondary School Principals. In 1921 the state associations of Minnesota and Wisconsin came into the fold, and only Rhode Island, true perhaps to its traditional recalcitrance toward national organization, remained outside.

It was at the Des Moines convention in 1921 that President Frederick M. Hunter, superintendent of the Oakland, California, city schools, issued a strongly worded call for "complete enlistment of the profession." Utah led the states not only in compulsory education but also in the enrollment of its teachers in the NEA—83 percent. Hunter warned his audience in this address against unidentified "interests" seeking to fragment the profession by setting teachers, principals, and superintendents against one another. In conclusion he testified to his faith in the NEA as "the fundamental organization in this country behind the great American public school system, its defender, its leader, a militant protagonist of a program that stands fully and completely for American ideals." The Des Moines convention evoked from *Educational Review* the comment that the theme of Americanization "seemed rather threadbare and platitudinous before the end of the fifth day."[33]

IV

In making their case for the nationalizing mission of the schools, educators during this period leaned heavily on the argument that the country was in a situation of crisis. "The National Education Association," said the resolutions of the Milwaukee convention in 1919, "desires to outline at this time of crisis an American program of education" (*NEA Proc,* 1919, p. 22). Educators did not have to invent this sense of crisis; it was already shared by many of their fellow citizens, stimulated as they were by discussion of threats of radical ideologies from abroad. It was reflected in the anti-Bolshevik drives of the Attorney General's

33. "Report of the President on the Program and Development of the Association," *NEA Proc,* 1921, pp. 190–91, 194, 198, 207, 208; "The NEA Meeting at Des Moines," 62 (Sept. 1921), 173.

Office in 1919–20. Educators applied this sense of crisis to expansion of their own roles in American life. Whether or not they convinced their fellow citizens of the need for more education to meet the crisis, they did convince themselves.

Besides immigration and radicalism, the public was alarmed about crime, strikes, poverty, personal and public morals, economic depression, and interracial strife. The impression left from the writings of the time is one not merely of crisis but of disaster. Overwrought as some of this may have been, there were genuine tragedies indeed, such as the race riot in Chicago, the state of public health, poverty, child labor, and the wave of unemployment in 1920–21. With a million people still unemployed in 1922, even the *New Republic* accepted, although with great reluctance, the restriction of immigration on the grounds of protecting American labor.[34] It should be noted also that this was a time of crisis not only for the United States, but for Europe and many other parts of the world.

Much of the sense of crisis tended to focus on radicalism and subversion. Ross L. Finney, Professor of Educational Sociology at the University of Minnesota, saw the "menace of radicalism" as the great fact of the times and declared that the menace was real, not psychological. Russian bolshevism, for example, had not collapsed. The attitude of labor at home, he feared, was becoming "insolent and aggressive." Radicalism could be offset by social reform and by progress in solving social problems. For the distribution of knowledge needed to bring this about, the elementary school could no longer suffice, and "universal secondary education must be accepted as the American slogan."[35]

Finney's discussion was moderate in comparison with NEA president Hunter's reference in 1921 to bolshevism as "an organization of three hundred and fifty thousand paid-up members" spreading propaganda "to overthrow our government." Like Finney, he considered schooling beyond fourteen essential, declaring that "the radical propagandist and soap-box orator get their following from those leaving school early without adequate training in American ideals and good citizenship." In further testimony to the role of the high school, the director of research in the Pittsburgh public schools charged his audience at a section meeting of the Pennsylvania State Education Association to make the high

34. "No Immigrant Flood," 33 (Dec. 13, 1922), 58–59.
35. *Causes and Cures for the Social Unrest: An Appeal to the Middle Class* (New York, 1922), pp. 1–3, 236–38.

school pupil "such a pillar of Democracy that Trotzky or Lenin could not budge his devotion to the Stars and Stripes with a whole battery of Bolshevism."[36]

For the most part, educators stopped short of the extreme antiradical formulations of the times, such as the Lusk Laws of New York, named after Senator Clayton R. Lusk, chairman of the legislative committee investigating sedition in the state. Among the laws' provisions was a requirement that public school teachers obtain certificates of loyalty and character from the state commissioner of education. Although an editorial in the *Journal of Education* (93 [June 9, 1921], 643) defended the laws, while granting that they may have gone too far as "reforms" were likely to do, other journals and writers were sharply critical of them. Among protesters from Columbia's Teachers College were William C. Bagley, John Dewey, William H. Kilpatrick, and Edward L. Thorndike.[37] Educators praised Governor Alfred E. Smith for his efforts in bringing about the repeal of the laws in 1923.

The response of educators in this instance might be interpreted as self-interest, but not that of the superintendent of schools in Auburn, New York, who in his address to the Rotarians on American Day, 1920, warned against the term *Americanization* as one of national arrogance, called for recognition of the brotherhood of man, and pointed out that while we could deport reds we could not deport their ideas. Nor that of an NEA editorial approving the turn of public opinion against the Ku Klux Klan. While the psychology of war tended to encourage intolerance, the intelligence of the people, thought this editorial writer, could discriminate between disloyalty in war and "sincere differences of opinion and belief in times of peace," and the editorial concluded with the observation that schools could "well claim some of the credit for this intelligence."[38]

36. "The Most Important Thing in American Education," *NEA Proc*, 1921, p. 275; J. Freeman Guy, "The Intelligence of the High School Pupil," *Pennsylvania School Journal* 70 (Nov. 1921), 87.

37. "Educators Demand Repeal of Lusk 'Loyalty' Law for New York Teachers," *S&S* 15 (June 3, 1922), 605.

38. Henry D. Hervey, "Americanization," *J Ed* 91 (June 24, 1920), 712–13; "Ku Kluxism and the Schools," *NEA J* 10 (Dec. 1921), 194.

Chapter 2

The hammers of curriculum revision

"The curriculum movement now holds the center of the educational stage."
—CLYDE B. MOORE,
NOVEMBER, 1926.

By 1924 the sense of crisis was over. President Coolidge in his July 4 address to the NEA comforted the delegates by observing that "on this day, of all days, it ought to be made clear that America has had its revolution."[1] The nation was moving into the golden years of good feeling, good business, good Americanism, and what local boosters liked to refer to as good schools.[2]

Schoolmen eagerly followed the business model. William McAndrew, then associate superintendent of the New York City schools, rejoiced in his view of the superintendent "as a captain of big business" and in the invitations received by superintendents to join Rotary and Kiwanis clubs.[3] When Vierling Kersey became state superintendent in California, the pedagogical press noted with approval that he had made his way into the Optimists Club, the upper reaches of the Masonic hierarchy, and the Los Angeles Chamber of Commerce.[4] Nor was the business model confined to the adult world. An alert high school principal in Wisconsin prepared his students for life by organizing them into school managed replicas of the Lions, Kiwanis, and Rotary clubs of the community,

1. "New Importance Is Attaching to the Cause of Education," *School Life* 10 (Sept. 1924), 1.
2. "Education during 1924," *NEA J* 14 (Jan. 1925), 22.
3. "The Schoolman's Loins," *ER* 64 (Sept. 1922), 114.
4. "Our New Superintendent of Public Instruction," *Sierra Educational News* 25 (March 1929), 12.

"conducted as nearly as possible," approvingly noted the *Wisconsin Journal of Education*, "along the lines of their adult namesakes."[5]

Although this age was not the first to proclaim the interdependence of business and education, it cherished the idea with loving care and proclaimed it as a perfect marriage. Education, said State Superintendent Francis G. Blair of Illinois, created markets, and he contrasted the lack of markets in North America when "the Indian, the savage" held sway with the richness of demand brought about by "civilized man, educated man." Beyond this, said Blair, education inculcated in youth the respect for property on which all business depends.[6] From the President's cabinet came the conclusion of Hubert Work, Secretary of the Interior, that this was a business age in which the "business of educators" was to educate for business by "trying to speed up the public intellect."[7] Perhaps the highest praise came from Andrew Mellon, Secretary of the Treasury, who saw as the fruits of a long educational process the tendency of the American people to lose their fear of stocks, Wall Street, banks, and large corporations, with even women "finding that the symbols of the ticker tape are not Sanskrit after all."[8]

It was, moreover, a new kind of business age. Success, according to an *American Mercury* article, was no longer a matter of hard work, but rather of optimistic shrewdness that cashed in on a high demand for goods. The new businessman lived in a world of golf, long vacations, spectacular pronouncements, and convention pageantry. Does this help account for the outcry against hard teachers and hard subjects in high schools? If not, it at least suggests the model behind the graduation exercises of the high schools of Pasadena, California, in 1924, held in the Rose Bowl before an audience of 50,000, with the stadium arrayed as "a corner of old Holland where a winding canal curved its way through a flower-covered meadow and upon its shores a Dutch windmill turned its great vanes in the breeze."[9]

The image of the folk hero of the period, however, was not the

5. "An Adventure in Citizenship," 62 (May 1930), 434.

6. "Achievements of American Education—Public Relations," *Superintendence Report*, 1930, pp. 93–94.

7. "Prosaic Purpose of Education Is To Live More Comfortably," *School Life* 11 (April 1926), 141.

8. Quoted in Albert W. Atwood, "The Great Bull Market," *Saturday Evening Post* 201 (Jan. 12, 1929), 7.

9. William Feather, "The King of Loafers," 10 (Oct. 1924), 147; "Pasadena's Colorful Graduation Pageant," *American Educational Digest* 44 (Oct. 1924), 58.

businessman at his ease. Of the four major heroes, Henry Ford, Luther Burbank, Thomas Edison, and Charles Lindbergh, only Ford represented business, and he was a throwback to an older model. All four, however, did symbolize service, another aspect of business given much stress in this period, and they were all practical men who did tangible things. Educators and the public followed the pattern set by such magazines as the *Saturday Evening Post* in extolling the virtues of these heroes and setting them up as examples for youth.

Lindbergh outshone all the others. He provided a flash of romantic adventure, an escape, perhaps, from business—even business punctuated by conventions. (George Gershwin, in the psychology of the times, was called the Lindbergh of American music by some of his admirers.)[10] It is little wonder that Lindbergh became the standard in education as well, especially with the discovery that his mother was a high school teacher. The Department of Superintendence brought Lindbergh to its Boston convention as a speaker in March 1928, partly to get his advice on aeronautics in the curriculum, and in a special ceremony for his mother presented her with a life membership in the NEA.

A project in the English classes of the Harvard, Illinois, high school symbolized the blending of ideals in the hero worship of this period. Seeking as part of their work on *Idylls of the King* to equip a contemporary round table with appropriate knights, the students chose Lindbergh, Richard E. Byrd, Alvin York, Herbert Hoover, John Philip Sousa, John J. Pershing, Jane Addams, Lorado Taft, Edna St. Vincent Millay, Andrew Carnegie, Edison, Burbank, Ford, Calvin Coolidge, and John D. Rockefeller, a selection representing adventure, patriotism, business, social service, and the arts. They voted for Hoover as King Arthur, Lindbergh as Lancelot, and Edison as Merlin.[11]

Whether or not educators could claim much credit for molding the heroes of the period, schools, on the surface, enjoyed their share of general tranquility and goodwill. According to Albert E. Winship of the *Journal of Education*, the year 1926 had gone by without a single retirement under fire by a superintendent in the 50 largest cities of the country, and with only four such cases in the other 1,800 cities. Furthermore, he noted, anti-education candidates for governor had suffered defeats in four states during the preceding two years. Purged of its

10. "Jazzed Homesickness in Paris," *Literary Digest* 100 (Jan. 5, 1929), 23.
11. Veve Marquis, "Modern Knights of King Arthur," *EJ* 19 (June 1930), 486–87.

violent language and the shudders of crisis, American Education Week proceeded with majestic dignity through the communities of the nation in these serene years.[12] "No one who understands the force of education," concluded Secretary James W. Crabtree of the NEA in 1929, "need be pessimistic about the days that are ahead."[13]

Still, this did not all ring quite true. Even in this booster age, editorial and feature writers in the press and clergy in the pulpit denounced what they saw as trouble spots in American life. For the most part these were not the criticisms made by intellectuals who derided George F. Babbitt, or by nonconformists who called prosperity a sham and exposed injustices in American social and economic life. The popular and conventional targets were crime, political corruption, the alleged decadence of youth, and, but to a lessening degree, the immigrants and radicals who had figured in the immediate postwar years. Schoolmen directed their observations along the same lines. No generation of American educators had ever resigned itself to placidity, nor did this one. There was still work to be done in the world, and evils to be expunged from the American scheme of things.

As the mouthpiece of its supporting body, the *Journal of the National Education Association* sustained the prevailing optimism in American life, but also sounded the proper notes of alarm. Possibly in defense of the *Journal* against those who wanted undiluted positive thinking, William C. Bagley of Columbia's Teachers College said that it would be unfortunate "if the future historian should look at our appalling record of murder, assault, robbery, and other serious crimes, and then examine the files of our official professional journal and find that we had not even concerned ourselves with the situation."[14]

Some of the Jeremiads from educators carried forward the earlier rhetoric of crisis. Professor Calvin O. Davis of the University of Michigan, for many years one of the leaders in the North Central Association of Colleges and Secondary Schools, compared the times to those of Louis XV and asked, "Is a similar great political, social and moral deluge forming for America?" In his inaugural address as president of the University of Idaho, Frederick James Kelly suggested that the American faith in education was being undermined by crime, divorce, political corruption, widespread disrespect for law, and, a point not often made

12. "Public School Achievements," *J Ed* 105 (Jan. 3, 1927), 6.
13. "The Secretary's Report," *NEA Proc*, 1929, p. 1152.
14. "Report of the Editorial Council," *NEA Proc*, 1926, p. 241.

in such utterances, maldistribution of wealth. An editorial in the *American Educational Digest* expressed the fear that crime was fostered by excluding religion from public schools. "Without religion," said this editorial, "the nation cannot endure. It would be better for the country at large, if legislatures and courts would concern themselves more devotedly to the common weal, in regard to this matter of education and crime, rather than to try to avoid treading upon the prejudices of individuals and sects."[15]

Prohibition was already a matter of debate, although educators, with the notable exception of Nicholas Murray Butler, who had opposed it all along, tended to be optimistic about its accomplishments and future. Intoxication among undergraduates, said the president of Hamilton College, had "come to be counted in very bad form." Educators even claimed the credit for having brought prohibition about. "The teachers of the nation of a few decades ago," said Crabtree of the NEA in 1926, "are entitled to a large share of the credit for the passage of the 18th amendment. They taught the injurious effects of narcotics and stimulants and prepared a generation to stand against the existence of the saloon." Such teaching, he added, needed to be continued against a future when "that which required fifty years and more to achieve" might be undone in a day.[16]

Besides drink, according to the educators, there were other corrupting influences on youth, such as jazz, movies, lurid magazines and novels, and the sensationalist press. A professor at the University of Chicago reported a survey in which the concepts found most familiar to sixth-grade children of that city were bootlegging, divorce, alimony, sheriff, juvenile court, and jail and jury. "Now you may say," he observed, "of course they would, in Chicago, but the same examination was given to the children of Salem, Oregon . . . where sixty-three per cent of the people own their own homes. The result was exactly the same."[17]

Jazz had replaced ragtime as the major musical object of apprehension. A high school teacher of Harvey, Illinois, blamed jazz for what

15. "None Is So Blind," *High School Quarterly* 14, (April 1926), 147; "The University in Prospect," *S&S* 28 (Nov. 24, 1928), 634; "Education and Crime," 144 (Dec. 1924), 169.
16. Frederick C. Ferry, "Are the Colleges Safe for the Undergraduates?" *New York State Education* 14 (March 1927), 431; "Report of the Secretary," *NEA Proc*, 1926, p. 1131.
17. W. H. Burton, quoted in "Bootlegging Best Known," *J Ed* 107 (April 30, 1928), 537.

she considered to be a general looseness in speech, morals, dress, and conduct. In Wisconsin, the county superintendents at their convention condemned jazz by formal vote. At the University of Minnesota, the dean of women proudly reported, the students themselves had taken action against jazz and improper dancing. In the Sunlight Dances sponsored by the Women's Self-Government Association, couples who offended were handed cards saying, "We do not dance cheek to cheek, shimmy, or dance other extreme dances. You must not. A second notice will cause your public removal from the hall. Help keep up the Minnesota standard."[18]

Movies, at least most of those being made at the time, were considered as bad as jazz, and they reached many more children and youth. In one survey of children's ways of spending time, the investigators were shocked to find movie-going a practically universal form of indulgence, and noted the availability of cheap melodrama, vulgar comedy, and movies of crime, with titles such as *Sinners in Silk, Unguarded Women, A Perfect Flapper, The Gilded Butterfly,* and *The Untamed Lady.*[19]

On materials in print, it was reported in the *English Journal* in 1927 that the six leading "confessional" magazines were selling thirty-nine million copies a year. "The literature of lust," declared *Educational Review*, "is openly displayed on the book stalls. Lascivious clergymen, incontinent physicians, polygamous businessmen are the heroes of the current novels."[20]

There was a kind of defense of youth as well as of themselves implied in these observations made by educators. For the most part they considered youth good, but felt that it was very difficult to be fifteen or sixteen years old in the American culture of the mid-twenties. Even the flapper, thought a teacher in Salina, Kansas, was "human, square, and frank if you met her on the level."[21] The "ailments of youth," concluded a professor at the College of Emporia, Kansas, were the ailments of "our present civilization," and there was hope that with transformation of home,

18. Edith L. Hilderbrant, "Music Memory Contests," *Sch R* 30 (April 1922), 300; "News Notes," *American School* 8 (Feb. 1922), 49b; Jessie S. Ladd, "Recreation and the University Mixer," *NEA Proc,* 1922, p. 735.

19. Harvey Lehman and Paul Witty, "Education and the Moving-Picture Show," *Education* 47 (Sept. 1926), 43.

20. Arthur McKeogh, "The Truth about the 'True' Story," *EJ* 16 (June 1927), 419; "A Review of Matters of Moment" 74 (April 1927), 177.

21. Florence Healey, "What Is the High School Doing for the Flapper?" *J Ed* 97 (Feb. 22, 1923), 214.

church, school, and press the present generation would "land right-side up."[22] In this the educators had the support of such popular writers as Judge Benjamin B. Lindsey of the Denver Juvenile Court, who in his book written with Wainwright Evans, *The Revolt of Modern Youth* (New York, 1925), saw a younger generation dissatisfied with the adult life of the times and pronounced youth's failures to be "the failures of the age."

The culture of the mid-1920s, then, embraced both boosterism and guilt, the guilt underscored by a sense of having failed to achieve all the promised benefits of business success. Adults in this period took great satisfaction in the comforts of prosperity, especially when appropriately glossed by the idea of service, but they could not accept, in themselves or in youth, some of the newer folkways that accompanied it. As at all times, some adults enjoyed deploring the behavior of youth. Wayward youth furnished a good conversation piece and good copy for the press, and provided educators an opportunity to stress the importance of their own roles.

II

It was in this mixed context of national self-congratulation and national concern that educators began their movement for curriculum revision. Their leading spokesmen called for a major overhaul on all levels. In part this represented a continuation of the movement for social efficiency and scientific management and reflected the nineteenth-century idea of progress as the constant development of new techniques.

For those involved with high schools, the movement represented an intensified desire to carry into effect the immediate postwar vision of custodianship of youth. High schools, according to the critics, were still too centered in what had come to be known as college-preparatory subjects, and there were too many students enrolled in the academic or precollege programs. Curricula in the rural high schools of Oklahoma, said the U.S. Bureau of Education's *Public Education in Oklahoma*, based on a survey of that state in 1922, were "poorly adapted to the needs of the students. The favorite subjects are Latin, ancient history, mediaeval and modern history, English, and mathematics." Those in charge of the Texas Educational Survey in 1924 were appalled by high registrations in algebra, Latin, and ancient history. "In the matter of

22. Guy V. Price, "The Younger Generation," *Education* 46 (April 1926), 489–93.

the high school curriculum," said the surveyors, "Texas needs an awakening."[23]

So apparently did Chicago. Assistant Superintendent William J. Bogan of that city denounced its high schools and extended this by implication to the national domain. High schools in Chicago and elsewhere, said Bogan, were college preparatory schools and eliminated the great majority of students. He pointed to a failure rate in Chicago's high schools of 16 percent and contrasted this with 9 percent in the elementary schools of that city, concluding that "the high school does not appear to be part of the public school system."[24]

Implied in such statements and explicit in others was the idea that in failing to meet youth needs high schools were partly responsible for the shortcomings of youth. The principal of Brooklyn's Alexander Hamilton High School saw potential criminals being made "through forced subjection to hateful and impossible courses of study." Professor H. A. Hollister of the University of Illinois and the state high school visitor for that institution called upon his audience of teachers at the 1925 Illinois High School Conference to weigh their subjects "on the scales of the urgent needs of modern life in a great republic—a nation fighting against time to save itself from rottenness and death that seem imminent largely because of an unbalanced and outgrown system of education."[25]

Many of these critics derived their inspiration from the seven objectives of education in *Cardinal Principles of Secondary Education* (Bureau of Education bulletin 1918, no. 35), issued by the NEA Commission on the Reorganization of Secondary Education, under the chairmanship of Clarence Kingsley. The report advocated many things, among them universal secondary education and the comprehensive high school, but popular fancy settled on the seven aims—health, citizenship, vocation, worthy use of leisure, worthy home membership, ethical character, vocation, and command of fundamental processes.

High schools, feared the critics, were making little or no progress toward the realization of these aims, in spite of the fact that the Cardinal Principles Report, with some 110,000 copies sold through the Bureau of

23. Bur Ed bull. 1923, no. 14, p. 64; "The Texas Survey," *Sch R* 32 (Oct. 1924), 564–65.
24. "Is the High School a Part of the Public School System?" Superintendence *Report*, 1926, pp. 71–72.
25. Gilbert Raynor, quoted in *American Educational Digest* 48 (Dec. 1928), 158; "Interrelationships of High Schools and University," *High School Conference*, 1925, p. 14.

Education by 1929, enjoyed the largest sale of any bulletin ever issued through the bureau. The seven objectives, said Principal Merle Prunty of Tulsa Central High School in 1926, were the most comprehensive ever written or conceived, but "their transforming possibilities" were "but feebly felt" in the "fettered traditional high school." Practice had not followed faith, and "two generations of high school students have already come and gone since 1918."[26]

Prunty was directing his remarks to the 1926 national convention of the Department of Superintendence, an affiliate of the NEA. It was in 1926 also that the Department of Superintendence, through the Commission on Curriculum created at its Cleveland convention three years before, decided to move into the thorny domain of secondary school curriculum change.

In creating the commission in 1923 and naming its membership in 1924, the department reflected the increasing sense of corporate identity among school superintendents, and the high sense of professional pride.[27] The commission occupied itself first with elementary and junior high schools, clearing the way for a main assault against the conventional high school program. Involved in this project were the commission itself, with twenty-five members, and twenty-three subcommittees dealing with the separate subjects and other topics. The product of these diverse efforts was the sixth yearbook of the department, *The Development of the High School Curriculum* (Washington, D.C., 1928), presented at the Boston convention in 1928.

Judged as a clarion call, the sixth yearbook was a disappointment. The reports on separate subjects, largely compilations of research, seemed feeble compared to those of the Cardinal Principles Commission and the earlier Committee of Ten. Progress toward the seven aims of the Cardinal Principles Report was treated almost entirely as the adding of practical subjects and the discarding of those called academic, especially foreign languages, ancient and modern, and mathematics of the algebra-geometry sequence. Perhaps the most disconcerting news in the yearbook was that 255 high school principals in a sample of 1,228 had never heard of the Cardinal Principles Report (pp. 176–77).

26. "Bulletin No. 35, 1918," *High School Quarterly* 18 (Jan. 1930), 51; "Educational Objectives of the Senior High School," Superintendence *Report*, 1926, p. 143.
27. Department of Superintendence Third Yearbook, *Research in Constructing the Elementary School Curriculum* (Washington, D.C., 1925), p. 2.

The absence of specific recommendations in the sixth yearbook, in fact, reflected one of the main principles of the curriculum revision movement, local autonomy. National programs had come to be viewed with suspicion. After resolving in 1924 to accept as its "paramount duty" the preparation of an American public school curriculum "based on American needs and ideals," the department soon retreated from this lofty position.[28] A year later Chairman Edwin C. Broome, superintendent of the Philadelphia public schools, disclaimed any desire on the part of the commission to write a national course of study. "We believe, therefore," said Broome, "that the proper agencies for reconstructing the curriculum are the superintendents of schools and their assistants in the several communities of the United States."[29]

Even as the Commission on Curriculum took up the assault on the high school, Broome made it clear this would not result in a specific program. "Do not expect from us," he warned in his 1927 address on plans for the sixth yearbook, "as I believe you have already learned not to expect, a ready-made course of study like the courses that were handed down by the famous Committee of Ten twenty-five [sic] years ago."[30] There were some who did not agree with this department position, notably Charles H. Judd, head of the Department of Education at the University of Chicago, who had been one of the main voices in creating the Commission on Curriculum. Judd expressed his disagreement in 1927, not to the department but to the National Association of Secondary School Principals, hoping perhaps to find there a new sponsoring agency for his views. "The new curriculum of American high schools is coming," said Judd. "It is for such a body as this to choose whether the next ten or twenty years shall be spent in isolated individual experimentation or in well-ordered concerted attack on the problem."[31]

III

To Bagley in 1924, the movement for curriculum revision had been just another craze that would burn itself out in two or three years. He was wrong, and the bandwagon rolled triumphantly into the latter half

28. Quoted in "Superintendents' Official Review," *ER* 68 (Sept. 1924), 103.
29. "The Commission on the Curriculum," *NEA Proc*, 1925, p. 804.
30. "Report of the Commission on Curriculum," Superintendence *Report*, 1927, p. 319.
31. "Is There a National System of Secondary Education?" *Proceedings of the National Association of Secondary School Principals*, 1927, p. 96.

of the decade. It was, declared one writer in 1926, an "epidemic" and an example of mob psychology. According to State Commissioner Frank P. Graves of New York in 1927, "A school system which has not organized at least a committee for this purpose is now held by leading schoolmen to be hopelessly out of step and behind the times." In 1928, George D. Strayer of Teachers College found curriculum revision "in full blast." The fruits of these labors, or of portions of them, were gathered by the college's Curriculum Laboratory, with some thirty thousand local courses of study collected there by 1931.[32]

Local initiative and its presumed diversity did not mean that the movement was formless. It had overwhelming commitment, not only to improving the elementary school and recasting the high school but to a platform governing the curriculum enterprise itself: to curriculum revision as a science, as a formalized procedure following a series of steps, and as a cooperative effort involving the classroom teacher.

Scientific curriculum-making had been explicitly heralded by Franklin Bobbitt of the University of Chicago in his book *The Curriculum* (Boston, 1918), a book that made him the prophet of this aspect of curriculum revision. "An age of science," said Bobbitt, "is demanding exactness and particularity." His definition of curriculum, however, was rhetorical, not scientific. Bypassing the use of the term as a list of school subjects, and the use reflected in the Cardinal Principles Report as a list of subjects arranged in a program for a given group of students (the commercial curriculum, the academic curriculum), Bobbitt claimed for curriculum "the entire range of experiences, both undirected and directed, concerned in unfolding the abilities of the individual," including the "consciously directed training experiences used by schools" (p. 43).

With this as the working stuff, contended Bobbitt, objectives necessarily took in "the total range of human abilities, habits, systems of knowledge, etc., that one should possess." Scientific process would determine these objectives, and the first task was "to discover the total range of habits, skills, abilities, forms of thought, valuations, ambitions, etc.," that members of any particular class, or classification, of people would

32. "Professionalism in Education," *TCR* 26 (Sept. 1924), 8; W. C. McGinnis, "Curriculum Revision," *J Ed* 104 (Nov. 8, 1926), 431; "Editorial Comment," *New York State Education* 15 (Nov. 1927), 204; "School Administration during 1927," *NEA J* 17 (Feb. 1928), 46; Herbert B. Bruner, "The Present Status of Curriculum Construction for the Elementary School in the United States," *North Central Association Quarterly* 6 (March 1932), 403 (paper read at the Conference on Curriculum Organization and Revision, Northwestern Univer., Oct. 30, 1931).

need for vocational, civic, health, recreational, language, parental, religious, and general social activities (p. 43). A "curriculum discoverer" in agriculture, for example, would go to the best farmers to find out what they did as they farmed and the knowledge, attitudes, and skills related to what they did, a technique referred to by Bobbitt as "activity analysis." In this way the curriculum could be planned to increase proficiency from one generation to the next (pp. 48–49).

Whether this was scientific or not, it was accepted as such by many educators in 1918. Two years later, Bobbitt spoke the language of industrial technology more directly and revealed his debt to the model of scientific management. Predetermination, he said, was the secret of success in economic production. "The management," explained Bobbitt with enthusiasm, "predetermines with great exactness the nature of the products to be turned out, and in relation to other factors, the quantity of output." Industrial producers standardize the raw material, the labor, and the conditions of the work. Educators must do likewise. "We, too, must institutionalize foresight, and, so far as the conditions of our work will permit, develop a technique of predetermination of the particularized results to be aimed at." Again, specific and detailed objectives were needed, and Bobbitt prescribed as cure for the vagueness of the seven aims of the Cardinal Principles Report a severe program of analysis, illustrating this with a list of thirty-eight abilities for the aim of health.[33]

During the next several years Bobbitt further developed the itemization of desirable activities observed in adults in various walks and patterns of life. In this technique he was joined by Wesley W. Charters of the Carnegie Institute of Technology, who described it in his book *Curriculum Construction* (New York, 1923), but with some modification to provide for the motivating power and development of ideals. Bobbitt followed this with *How To Make a Curriculum* (Boston, 1924), in which he furnished 160 specific objectives, not including vocational, to illustrate what activity analysis might achieve. He emphasized that these were examples only; it was incumbent on curriculum-makers in each locality to discover their own.

Although the idea of activity analysis brought Bobbitt and Charters much applause, it tended in practice to become burdensome and repetitious, and few school systems followed it literally. Apart from Bobbitt's project in Los Angeles, the most notable application of it was made

33. "The Objectives of Secondary Education," *Sch R* 28 (Dec. 1920), 738, 740–42.

under Charters's direction at Stephens College. Charters and his fellow workers spent three years collecting written statements of weekly activities from 95,000 women and sorted the results into 7,300 activities in 24 groups. Otis Caldwell in science and Carleton Washburne in social studies used a modification of this method, identifying objectives and content from tabulated newspaper, magazine, and book references.[34]

The tedious nature of activity analysis did not, however, diminish the enthusiasm for curriculum-making as a science. If objectives were specific and detailed, they were presumed to be scientific, whether derived from activity analysis or not. There was also a tendency to regard social objectives as inherently scientific; this had shown up before in the prewar influence of scientific management on the curriculum. Sociology was considered by many to be the main source of objectives and content, paralleling psychology as the source of method. David Snedden of Teachers College urged this approach, indicating, however, that while it was widely accepted it was not practiced with competence and skill.[35]

This identification of social with scientific persisted throughout the movement for curriculum revision. The Department of Superintendence in its fourth yearbook, *The Nation at Work on the Public School Curriculum* (Washington, D.C., 1926), characterized the curriculum as "a succession of efforts to change the pupils from self-centered individuals into socially minded cooperative members of the nation" (p .14). Snedden would probably have called this one of the "vague philosophical aspirations" that needed more work from sociologists, but those who set it forth undoubtedly regarded it as a scientific conclusion. To Superintendent H. B. Wilson of Berkeley, California, the scientific curriculum-making of Harold Rugg and his associates was a means of getting rid of material that did not contribute to social efficiency. To a principal in Hudson, Michigan, curriculum-making in the high school meant purging the offerings of "all useless material" to make way for subjects of more value to effective living.[36]

34. "Curriculum for Women," *High School Conference*, 1925, p. 328; "Principles and Types of Curricular Development," *NEA Proc*, 1923, pp. 962–68; "Basic Facts Needed in History and Geography: A Statistical Investigation," *National Society for the Study of Education Twenty-Second Yearbook* (Bloomington, Ill., 1923), part 2, *The Social Studies in the Elementary and Secondary School*, pp. 216–34.

35. *Sociological Determination of Objectives in Education* (Philadelphia, 1921), pp. 17–18.

36. *Ibid.*, p. 26; "Socializing the Social Studies," *J Ed* 98 (Oct. 18, 1923), 382;

Occasionally there were sparks of disagreement, such as the address made by Boyd Bode of Ohio State University to the National Society of College Teachers of Education in 1924. Bode not only criticized but ridiculed the scientific approach, especially with regard to objectives, contending that no scientific analysis known to man could determine the desirability of anything. "Statistical investigation, for example," taunted Bode, "may show that a certain number of burglaries occur annually in a given community, but it does not show whether the community needs a larger police force or more burglars."[37]

Scientific curriculum-making was in any case still far from the promised land of human engineering. When Bobbitt in 1924 referred to the curriculum-maker as an "educational engineer," the technology he had in mind was primitive indeed. By 1927, however, he was also taking the long view. Job analysis could be laid aside. "Let us discover," he challenged, "the science of human behavior as it applies to every field of human conduct; the science of human behavior, so far as we can assemble it, will dictate the curriculum, and that alone."[38]

A second feature of curriculum revision was its organization as a series of steps. The number might vary from five to twenty depending on how they were combined or split. Henry Harap of the Cleveland School of Education hit both ends in recommending twenty steps for general procedure but condensing these to five for small school systems.[39] In 1931, L. Thomas Hopkins of Teachers College presented a ten-step model as a summary incorporating many of the variations from one model to the next. First came organizing curriculum-making machinery in the school system; second, determining objectives; third, selecting content; fourth, defining methods of teaching and learning; fifth, organizing the content for teaching; sixth, selecting outcomes, "the various lines in which the pupils are expected to make growth"; seventh, measuring results; eighth, experimenting with the new course "in a few classrooms" and revising it in the light thereof; ninth, "the installation of the com-

---

Albert Renwick, "The Social Status of the Schools of Calumet and Portage Townships," *Education* 44 (April 1924), 463.

37. "Why Educational Objectives?" *S&S* 19 (May 10, 1924), 535, 539.

38. *How To Make a Curriculum* (Boston, 1924), pp. 1–6; "Some Underlying Principles of Curriculum Construction," *North Central Association Quarterly* 2 (Dec. 1927), 278.

39. "A Critique of the Present Status of Curriculum Making," *S&S* 25 (Feb. 19, 1927), 207–9; "Curriculum Making for Small Towns," *NEA J* 18 (May 1929), 145–46.

pleted product"; and tenth, providing for continuous revision.[40] An interesting variation, and one that would direct attention toward high schools, appeared as step seven on the list made by Douglas Waples of the University of Pittsburgh: classifying students into three groups, those who would probably go to college, those who would probably finish high school only and become managers or proprietors, and those who, not finishing high school, would become skilled or unskilled workmen.[41]

The determination of objectives, of course, appeared in all the lists, usually close to the top. It was taken for granted that no content or "experiences" could be identified until the objectives were stated, and that an inevitable line of science or logic or both extended from the objectives to the selection of means. Another ground rule was that each local system had to write or discover its own objectives rather than cribbing from other school systems. The allegedly widespread practice of so cribbing them, perhaps with minor changes, proceeded surreptitiously and could not be admitted. One might openly start with the seven aims, but even this approach required the discovery of specific local objectives related to the broad categories.

Throughout the 1920s the term *objectives* gradually displaced the older term *aims*. Harap welcomed this as a forward move, since according to him the older term suggested general goals without impact upon actual teaching.[42] Curriculum makers then proceeded to differentiate categories within the general objectives: general and specific, immediate and ultimate, primary and secondary, for example. These refinements helped make the formulation of objectives a subtle process indeed, especially since, as one Sacramento teacher later observed, "to many teachers the term 'objective' carries about the same connotation as a dose of castor oil."[43]

By the 1930s many teachers were hardened veterans of local curriculum campaigns. Cooperative effort was the third tenet of the ideology, particularly the participation of classroom teachers. In part it was an outgrowth of the scientific management principle of involving employees in policy-making. Teachers who helped make the curriculum would have

40. "Curriculum Making: General," *Review of Educational Research* 1 (Jan. 1931), 5–8.

41. "Partial Reconstruction of the High School Course of Study," *S&S* 20 (July 12, 1924), 57–58.

42. *S&S* 25 (Feb. 19, 1927), 210.

43. Verna K. Lawson, "Achieving Objectives in the Social Studies," *Social Studies* 28 (March 1937), 118.

a personal stake in putting it into effect. Furthermore, the experience of the teachers would insure its workability. Curriculum revision came to be identified with in-service education of teachers and as a kind of supervision. In some instances all teachers in a system took part, especially in general discussions of principles and objectives. Some school systems released selected teachers from classroom duties for the time involved to work on curriculum and write materials.

There were roles in this for administrators as well. High schools expected leadership from the principal, who was often criticized for his or her delinquency on this point. Leadership from principals, in fact, was considered crucial, in view of the presumed traditionalism of high school teachers. According to Bobbitt, initiative in the high school could not be left with teachers, for they were "specialists in subject-matter, not specialists in human life." It was up to the principal to supply "genuine educational engineering and generalship." Too often, however, the principal offered alibis and preferred to be a "Director of Routine."[44]

Rounding out the professional cast were those increasingly known as "curriculum experts," consultants from outside the local systems, usually professors. Their expertise was a combination of research in curriculum-making and practical know-how. Itinerant experts, accordingly, helped to standardize the steps in local curriculum revision. A sarcastic editorial in the *Journal of Educational Method* referred to "educators" who offered, "if an abundance of money is kindly provided by some foundation and the humble toilers in the field will give their services, to do the whole job up for us for good and all." The presumed experts, however, did not need to peddle their services; they were in heavy demand. For small school systems, Harap suggested developing local experts by sending the most capable persons "to study the technic of curriculum-making under a competent master" and to bring back a plan that he would direct.[45]

Curriculum revision was an old subject. Like politics it had been discussed since the times of Plato and Aristotle, and in more recent times it had been made a project through the Committee of Ten. In the 1920s it became a self-conscious school enterprise and a field of study only a little newer than other divisions of pedagogy, or indeed, other kinds of

44. "Functions of the High School Principal in Curriculum-Making," *National Association of Secondary School Principals Eighth Yearbook*, 1924, pp. 13–14.
45. 10 (June, 1924), 403; *NEA J* 18 (May, 1929), 145.

social studies. The white heat of local revision gave it a glaring prominence. It developed, therefore, not as an object of inquiry but as a cult
dedicated to a point of view, especially toward the high schools.

IV

The movement scored two major triumphs in local school systems,
those of Los Angeles and Denver, and sustained one major disappointment, in Chicago. Almost every large city and many small ones went
through curriculum revision, but for better or worse, Los Angeles,
Denver, and Chicago drew the national spotlight.

Los Angeles gained its reputation through the leadership of Superintendent Susan Miller Dorsey and the use as a consultant of none other
than Bobbitt himself. Mrs. Dorsey had come to Los Angeles from the
East in 1896 to teach Latin and Greek in the Los Angeles High School.
During her career there as a classroom teacher, vice-principal, assistant
superintendent, and superintendent (1920–29), the system grew from
75 teachers and 4,700 students to nearly 9,000 teachers and 360,000
students. Perhaps she was, as the NEA termed her in 1929, "the greatest
administrative genius in the history of American education";[46] in any
case, she provided Los Angeles with leadership marked by wisdom and
constructive innovation. Like many others she was deeply concerned
about what the great expansion in enrollments would mean for secondary
education, but unlike many she did not indulge in anti-academic pronouncements and did not prejudge the new student bodies.

Shortly after becoming superintendent, Mrs. Dorsey called Bobbitt
to help with curriculum revision, and he spent the first three months of
1922 in the system. Committees of twenty-five teachers each were organized for the various high school departments. As was to be expected,
Bobbitt fostered the use of activity analysis for determining objectives.
He brought with him a list of objectives drawn up by his graduate students at the University of Chicago; these were reprocessed for their
presumably unique application to the Los Angeles city schools. From
this came 500 objectives in seven groups, appropriately parcelled out
to subjects for the production of course-of-study documents. Bobbitt did
not always agree with the teachers, as for instance when they included
writing and speaking objectives in foreign language. "It is doubtful," he

46. "A Tribute to a Great Leader," *NEA J* 18 (April 1929), 136.

observed, "if the taxpayers of the city are justified in investing in a speaking and writing knowledge of French or German. A reading knowledge can be developed inexpensively, if one aims only at that."[47]

According to Bobbitt, most of the 1,200 teachers who took part welcomed the opportunity.[48] Perhaps it had the fascination of being relatively new. Several years later in commenting on the program of curriculum revision in Long Beach, California, the superintendent of schools for that city found the value not in the completed product but in the process: the outstanding benefit was "the rekindling of the intellectual life of all those who have participated in the enterprise."[49] This was probably true of Los Angeles as well, and the program may have stimulated the variety of experimental efforts that later took place there in the high school curriculum.

Denver's program also was initiated by its superintendent, in this instance a newcomer to the system, Jesse H. Newlon, who came to his post there in 1920. Newlon was one of the "new men" in educational leadership, equipped with a doctorate from Teachers College, as well as solid experience in three high school principalships and as superintendent in Lincoln, Nebraska. His doctrines were those of social efficiency and his utterances frequently anti-academic. Later he was to become identified with the movement for social reconstruction through education. Because of his interest in curriculum and in social movements, Newlon has become a modern hero of those who deplore what they see as a tendency of superintendents to confine themselves to managerial roles.[50]

Newlon sounded the call for curriculum revision in Denver in 1921, using Thomas H. Briggs of Teachers College for an opening inspirational address. At first the teachers worked on their own time, but for the year 1923–24 the board provided $31,500, used in part to free the participating teachers from some of their other duties. Newlon judiciously pointed out that under a traditional program at least 10 percent of the time was wasted in the study of dead material, calculating that this cost

47. *Curriculum-Making in Los Angeles* (Chicago, 1922), p. 95.
48. *Ibid.*, p. 2.
49. W. L. Stephens, quoted in "The Curriculum Revision Program in the Long Beach City Schools," *California Quarterly of Secondary Education* 3 (Oct. 1927), 93.
50. For example, William R. Stephens, *An Analysis of the Educational Ideas of Five Leaders in School Administration 1910–1930* (Ph.D. diss., Washington University, St. Louis, 1964).

the taxpayers of Denver $300,000 a year. The use of $31,500 to save $300,000 helped to make curriculum revision attractive.[51]

The Denver program went through the correct steps systematically and with the usual accompaniments, such as the use of outside consultants, among them L. Thomas Hopkins of the University of Colorado. In 1925 Assistant Superintendent A. L. Threlkeld, who had the main responsibility for the program, read to the NEA at Indianapolis an impressive list of courses already printed or in process, ranging over many subjects and including Latin.[52] Newlon, at the Department of Superintendence in that year, enumerated fourteen results of the program, of which number six was "bringing new joys in teaching to the teacher."[53]

Like that of Los Angeles, the Denver program attracted national publicity and approval. To Newlon in 1925 it brought an award by Columbia University of the Butler silver medal "for creative work in the administration of the schools of Denver, Colorado, especially for the leadership in the scientific revision of the curriculum."[54]

Two years later Newlon left Denver to join the faculty at Teachers College, and the work continued under his successor, A. L. Threlkeld, who had been in charge of curriculum work. Teacher participation remained a marked feature of the program. In the 1930s the high schools of Denver were considered to be among the most creative of those in the Eight-Year Study of the Progressive Education Association.

In Chicago the initiative again came from the superintendent. William McAndrew was technically a newcomer in 1924, but he had served many years before as principal of Chicago's Englewood High School. Not only was his arrival a kind of homecoming, but he had other elements in his favor as well. He had been selected in a ten-to-one vote by a reforming board under the auspices of a newly elected reforming mayor, William Dever, after a national canvass to find the best. His reputation and background were impressive indeed. In his sixty years he had enjoyed a distinguished career in New York City, first as principal of the Washington Irving High School for Girls and later as associate superintendent, the position he held when he accepted the Chicago post. Margaret Haley,

51. "Improving the Service through Better Organized Curricula," *Colorado School Journal* 39 (March 1924), 5, 9.

52. "Curriculum Revision," *NEA Proc*, 1925, p. 833.

53. "Outcomes of Our Curriculum Program," *NEA Proc*, 1925, p. 803.

54. "Real Honor for Newlon," *J Ed* 101 (June 25, 1925), 716. For a discussion of Newlon's role see Gary L. Peltier, "Teacher Participation in Curriculum Revision," *History of Education Quarterly* 7 (Summer 1967), 209–19.

the militant leader of the Chicago Teachers Federation, hailed him as one of the three foremost educators in the country.[55] He was a leading figure in the Department of Superintendence, serving as president of that body at its Cincinnati convention in 1924. McAndrew, declared the *Journal of Education*, "returns to Chicago after nearly forty years gloriously triumphant," and at $15,000 a year, $3,000 more than even New York City had ever paid a superintendent.[56]

His fate in Chicago was classical tragedy. Certainly he was a good man trying to do good. To him doing good meant fostering the doctrines of the social efficiency complex, but this was no handicap for an educator in 1924. He at once gave his support to a proposal from a commission of the board of education, made before he assumed office, for the establishment of junior high schools. According to the social efficiency movement, Chicago in this respect was far behind most of the other large city systems. To McAndrew and the board it was time to correct this laggard state of affairs.

What neither McAndrew nor the board took into account were the circumstances of labor history and of vocational education in Illinois dating from a 1913 attempt to set up a dual system. There had also been an earlier national advocacy of junior high schools as a way to begin curricular differentiation along vocational lines in the seventh grade. The Chicago unions therefore reacted strongly against the proposal for junior high schools. In a long address to the board of education, Victor Olander of the Illinois Federation of Labor explained labor's fears that junior high schools would be instruments of class education.[57]

In her attempt to allay Olander's fears about vocationalism, Helen Hefferan, a reform member of the board of education, illustrated the failure of the liberal mentality to grasp the point being made. The policy of the junior high schools, she told Olander, would be carried out by McAndrew and Bogan, "strong advocates of the system of vocational training." Bogan, she went on, was a man who thoroughly understood vocational education in Chicago, "and he would not do one single thing, I believe, to hurt the interests of the children of the industrial class." Olander retorted that there was no industrial class in America.[58]

55. Cited in "Editorial Review and Aspects of Education," *American Educational Digest* 43 (Feb. 1924), 264–65.
56. "McAndrew of Chicago," *J Ed* 99 (Jan. 17, 1924), 59.
57. "Junior High Schools from the Other Side," *ER* 68 (Sept. 1924), 86–94.
58. *Ibid.*, p. 93.

McAndrew and the junior high schools triumphed, but in the process he lost the support of a group on which he might otherwise have relied. Along with this, he antagonized the Chicago Teachers Federation in disputes over the use of school time for the meetings of teachers' councils, institutions that went back to the period of Superintendent Ella Flagg Young. Margaret Haley now saw in McAndrew an example of the influence of Professor Judd, and this in turn she saw as part of a long campaign supposedly initiated by President William Rainey Harper of the University of Chicago to impose regimentation on the Chicago schools from the midway campus.[59]

It was in the midst of this turmoil that McAndrew moved, early in 1926, to initiate the pattern of curriculum revision that had been popularized in Denver and Los Angeles. On January 27, the board authorized a comprehensive program of revision and appropriated $25,000 to pay substitute teachers who would free regular teachers for work on curriculum. In a graphic presentation of aims there appeared a central heading, "Complete Social Efficiency and Good Citizenship," with specific and detailed lists of related objectives. By the end of 1926 the committees had worked out tentative drafts of all courses for elementary schools and half of those that had been projected for the junior and senior high schools, all of them slated for tryouts in September 1927.[60]

Also during 1927, however, former mayor William Hale Thompson, who had prudently stayed out of the 1923 reform campaign that had elected Dever, decided to run again. Incredible though it may seem, Thompson based his campaign largely on the accusation that Mayor Dever and Superintendent McAndrew were agents of British imperialism and servants of King George. This campaign turned McAndrew's tragedy into tragic farce. His previous controversies had lost him the support that might have come from organized labor, in particular from the Chicago Teachers Federation. While these forces did not approve of Thompson's antics, they stood by, and Dever and reform went down to defeat. In the multitude of factors involved, McAndrew's alienation of labor and teachers undoubtedly played some part.

Almost immediately after taking office, Thompson made new appointments to the Chicago board of education and he assumed control. On

59. "From the Masthead by the Lookout," *Margaret Haley's Bulletin* 3 (April 30, 1926), 305.

60. G. C. Phipps, "Curriculum Making in Chicago," *Chicago Schools Journal* 9 (Jan. 1927), 169–71; (Feb. 1927), 213; (May 1927), 325–29.

August 29, 1927, the board accused McAndrew of insubordination and suspended him from his duties. After a ludicrous trial they dismissed him early in 1928. He never took another superintendency, but devoted himself to writing and to editing what became the *Educational Review* section of *School and Society*. Mayor Thompson was not concerned with the basic issues that had divided McAndrew from the teachers and from organized labor. The junior high schools, for example, remained until they were abolished as an economy move in the depression. Superintendent Bogan, McAndrew's successor, shared his social efficiency and anti-academic views, but the program for curriculum revision did not regain the force it had had for nearly two years under McAndrew.

While curriculum revision as such was not directly defeated in Chicago, the elements of defeat already there were too strong for it to overcome. In such a situation it had little or no chance. McAndrew had brought to Chicago the most approved developments in education, including the curriculum revision movement, and in view of this, his fate was a major shock to pedagogical leadership throughout the country. The shock was that a machine politician, through a campaign based on tawdry clowning, could overcome the sincere efforts of a professionally esteemed leader, using the most approved procedures and techniques, to guide a school system along lines which he and other educators were convinced were improvement and progress.

Perhaps the educators had been dreaming alone. Even when pedagogy moves along lines broadly approved by the social order it must do so within social reality. Educators did not always apply their many pronouncements about social realities and forces to themselves. Chicago was not an isolated example of the politics of education. More than other instances, however, and perhaps because it seemed such a contradiction to the serene assumptions of many educators in the 1920s, it tended to shake but not to overthrow the fundamental faith in local control and in local revision of the curriculum.

V

Even apart from the disaster in Chicago, educational leaders in the late 1920s expressed increasing frustration over the rate of change toward their desired goals, especially for high schools. In spite of the Cardinal Principles Report, the work of the Commission on Curriculum, and the vast spread of curriculum revision in local school systems, the high school, according to these spokesmen, remained stuck in its academic traditions and showed little sign of adapting itself to the role proclaimed for it by the NEA in 1919.

Newlon, the very symbol of successful leadership in curriculum revision, told the NEA's National Council of Education in February 1927 that traditional subject matter and methods were so strongly entrenched in the high schools that curriculum revision had made practically no dent on procedures in this institution. An unsigned editorial in the *American Educational Digest* followed, saying that the curriculum of high schools in 1928 differed little from that of the 1880s and deploring the position still occupied by English, history and civics, mathematics, laboratory science, and foreign language, which it referred to as "the college entrance subjects.[61] This lumping together of all five academic fields as college preparatory was becoming increasingly prevalent in the latter 1920s and helps to account for the mistaken notion that the Committee of Ten had imposed a college preparatory curriculum on the schools. Along with this ran the contention that such a curriculum was unsuited to the masses of students in the 1920s, in contrast with those of the 1890s, who according to the folklore had been predominantly college preparatory students.

Much utterance accordingly issued forth on what the "new" high school population would demand. According to David Snedden, these "newcomers" would not long tolerate "the salt-pork and rye-bread of algebra, essay-writing, English classics, dry-as-dust ancient history, Latin, and pre-engineering chemistry." President George W. Frasier of the Colorado State College of Education agreed, and added "that these subjects prepare for nothing in the world but college, and it takes a confirmed optimist to see how it [sic] does that." The survival of the academic subjects symbolized to many the failure of the high schools to live up to the Cardinal Principles Report, especially to the seven aims. Bobbitt in 1929 noted sadly that twelve years after the report the high schools were still aiming at academic subject matter. Either the report was mistaken or misunderstood or its recommendations of the seven aims not seriously considered. Bobbitt thought the latter and urged leaders in high schools everywhere to start considering them seriously.[62]

61. "Chaos or Integration in Educational Thought and Effort," *NEA Proc*, 1927 p. 252; "The High School in Transition," 47 (May 1928), 411–12.
62. "New Aims of Education," *TCR* 29 (Feb. 1928), 401; "Address," *TCR* 30

An interesting variant came from those who argued for changing the high school in response not only to the Cardinal Principles Report but to the doctrines of the founding fathers of the United States. This had long been one of McAndrew's favorite ideas, and in 1929 the Department of Superintendence approved a resolution proposed by a committee of which McAndrew was cochairman. According to this resolution, the state systems of education had been established in accord with proposals made by Washington, Franklin, Jefferson, and others to preserve and improve our political institutions. "Not culture, not scholarship, not self support, nor compliance with the entrance requirements of advanced schools," vowed the department, "shall turn us away from the duty of teaching our youth the needs of our civic life and from inspiring our citizens with a determination to improve it."[63]

In his appraisal of the high schools at the end of the 1920s, Philip W. L. Cox of New York University's School of Education began with a quotation from Dickens's *A Tale of Two Cities* about aristocrats on their way to the guillotine. Cox concluded that "most academic high school people are as unaware of the volcano on which they tread as was the aristocrat of the *ancien régime*."[64]

So it was that the educators began the 1920s with a sense of crisis and ended them with feelings of impending catastrophe and despair.

(Nov. 1928), 113; "The High School Curriculum," *High School Conference*, 1929, p. 37.

63. "Resolutions Adopted February 28, 1929," Superintendence *Report*, 1929, pp. 270–71.

64. Editorial, *Junior-Senior High School Clearing House* 4 (Feb. 1930), 325.

Chapter 3

The anvil

"This old anvil laughs at many broken hammers."
—CARL SANDBURG
IN "THE PEOPLE, YES."

*T*he people of Winston-Salem, North Carolina, were proud of their new high
school in 1923. They had planned ahead and felt that the new building
would not be filled for a quarter of a century, but within six years it was
too small.[1] Their plight was that of the nation at large, where enrollments in the upper four public high school years grew from 2,200,389
students in 1920 to 4,399,422 ten years later. Those in 1920 made up
28 percent of youth fourteen to seventeen years of age; those in 1930
made up 47 percent.[2] The result was an average annual increase in numbers enough to fill some 7,000 classrooms of 30 students each.

Metropolitan schools were bulging. Between 1920 and 1924, Chicago's enrollments went up in all parts of the city. There were increases
from 2,206 to 3,710 students at Englewood High School on the south
side, from 2,599 to 3,517 at Senn on the north side, from 2,711 to 4,154
at Schurz to the northwest, and from 1,348 to 2,238 at Tuley to the
west.[3] Schools could not be built or enlarged fast enough, and new
entrants overflowed into branches, often housed in nearby elementary
schools, and into temporary buildings hastily put up on available vacant
space.

New buildings were objects of pedagogical and civic pride. Especially
in cities, they reflected the ideology of mid-1920s prosperity and power.
Massive and overwhelming on the outside, coldly ostentatious on the

1. "Field Notes," *High School Journal* 12 (Dec. 1929), 336.
2. Kenneth A. Simon and W. Vance Grant, *Digest of Educational Statistics: 1967 Edition*, Off Ed 10024–67, p. 29, table 32.
3. *NC Proc*, 1920, pp. 40a–41a; 1924, p. 42.

inside, they fit well the impersonal dignity of institutions that daily processed several thousand students with efficiency and dispatch. By the
standards of the times they seemed beautiful as well. The new Eastern
High School of Washington, D.C., was glowingly described in 1924 by
one of its English teachers, who wrote, "Within, and you are at the foot
of a marble stairway. One fancies one's self in a palace or some famed
gallery of art. It is a joy to tread those steps, to cross the marble hall
at the top, and to enter the assembly hall with its fourteen hundred
seats."[4]

The new DeWitt Clinton High School in New York City was described
in terms of Versailles, the Walton High School Italian Lombard, and
Richmond Hill the Francois Premier buildings in Toulouse.[5] On the
other hand, a high school principal in Calumet City, Illinois, complained
about expensive buildings that were leaving little money for libraries and
salaries. In some communities, said this dissenter, "so much has gone
into extravagant buildings that it will be fifteen or twenty years before
the high school staff can be paid salaries which will attract and hold well
trained and professionally minded men and women."[6]

As feelings were mixed about the new school buildings, so were they
also about the increase in enrollments that had sprung the new buildings
into existence. Much pedagogical rhetoric hailed the increase as a triumph of democracy and progress. On the other hand, President Henry
S. Pritchett of the Carnegie Foundation for the Advancement of Teaching saw in it a grave threat to the school as an intellectual institution; the
high school would be overrun by students who would not have been
admitted "under reasonable conditions."[7]

Regardless of their attitudes toward the increased enrollments, schoolmen and others sought diligently for reasons that would explain why so
many more youth were in high school. George S. Counts called the
burgeoning high school "the resultant of a whole series of forces and
conditions which we call industrial civilization," and the reflection of

4. Rosemary Arnold, "A Modern City High School, Typical of Approved Ideas
of Today," *School Life* 10 (Dec. 1924), 63.
5. "New High School Buildings in New York City," *Sch R* 34 (Oct. 1926),
571–72.
6. A. V. Lockhart, "Sanity in Building Programs," *American Educational
Digest* 46 (July 1927), 498.
7. "Report of the President," Carnegie Foundation for the Advancement of
Teaching, *Seventeenth Annual Report of the President and Treasurer* (New York,
1922), pp. 102–3.

the social ideals of the United States, the prior growth of elementary education, the integration of society, the complexity of civilization, an increase in wealth, population factors such as decline in both the birth and death rates, and a greater value placed on children and youth.[8]

Although Henry C. Morrison of the University of Chicago doubted that the enrollment increase reflected democracy and social ideals, he agreed with Counts and others about the influence of economics and population growth. He did not, however, interpret the release of children and youth from productive work as the valuing of children and youth more highly, but rather as the result of an increase in primary productive capacity leading to less need for children's labor.[9] In the 1930s some would go farther and see it as deliberate exclusion of youth from the labor market.

Looking at the matter in more personal terms, a professor at Rutgers University, writing in 1934, saw the increase as a reflection of parents' desire for their children's advancement. "The white-collar-job theory that less strenuous work and higher pay are in store for the high school graduate, coupled with general increased income," he concluded, "has probably been the chief cause for rapid growth in high school attendance during the past fifty years."[10]

The possible impact of the campaigns to convince youth and their families of the advantages of going to high school, too, cannot be discounted. Although many educators deplored the motive of getting ahead in the world, those in charge of such campaigns did not spurn the use of it as an appeal. The argument of increased earning power was especially persistent, up to the depression, criticized though it was on factual grounds as well as ideological. According to the dean of the College of Business Administration of Boston University, a high school graduate would earn $33,000 more than an untrained man, presumably one who did not go to high school. Beyond this, the college graduate would earn $72,000 more than the high school graduate.[11] In another popular form

---

8. *Secondary Education and Industrialism* (Cambridge, Massachusetts, 1929), pp. 22–24, 43–45.

9. "The Economics of the New Enrollment," University of Pennsylvania School of Education, *Sixteenth Annual Schoolmen's Week Proceedings*, 1929, pp. 307–8.

10. Albert J. Blackburn, "Recent Changes in the Secondary School Population," University of Pennsylvania School of Education, *Twenty-First Annual Schoolmen's Week Proceedings*, 1934, pp. 139–40.

11. "The Money Value of Education," *Illinois Teacher* 13 (Dec. 1924), 50–51.

of the argument, the money value of schooling was calculated as $9.02 for each day a child stayed in school.[12]

It was true, too, that high school enrollments depended on a supply of youth who had finished the elementary grades. Compulsory-attendance laws, although they required few to continue beyond fourteen, did carry many children to that point, and reduced failure rates produced more students eligible to enter high school. As one writer put it, "the law is carrying more children than formerly through the elementary grades and thus bringing them to the door of the high school with nothing to bar their entrance."[13] Except for rural schools in some states, Pennsylvania, for example, where tests were given for elementary school graduation and admission to high school,[14] completion of the elementary grades served automatically for high school entrance.

In any case, going to high school was increasingly the thing to do. Particularly in cities and suburbs, it was accepted as one of the facts of life. Even the educators who denounced the high school for its presumed evils did not urge youth to stay away.

II

Not only were public high schools growing in size but they were growing in number, from the 14,326 reporting to the Bureau of Education in 1920 (an estimated seven-eighths of those in existence) to the 22,237 reporting in 1930 (an estimated nine-tenths).[15] These were public secondary schools of all types and patterns of organization, including conventional high schools, six-year secondary schools, and separate junior and senior high schools. With the great variations in enrollment from one school to the next, the increase in the number of schools, taken by itself, was neither a meaningful nor an accurate index of the growth of secondary education. Still, the creation of new schools, especially when housed in new buildings, continually reminded local citi-

12. "Taking Stock of the Schools," *Research Bulletin of the National Education Association* 3 (May 1925), 94.

13. William R. Hood, *Legal Provisions for Rural High Schools*, Bur Ed, bull. 1924, no. 40, p. 4.

14. David B. Kraybill, "Admitting Rural Pupils to High School, *Pennsylvania School Journal* 76 (Dec. 1927), 207–8; Q. A. W. Rohrbach, "Appraisal of Rural Eighth-Grade Pupils for High School Entrance," *ibid.* (March 1928), 405.

15. Bur Ed, *Biennial Survey 1918–1920*, bull. 1923, no. 29, p. 497; Off Ed, *Biennial Survey 1928–1930*, bull. 1931, no. 20, 2: 697.

zenries of the thrust being made by secondary education into their lives.

Variations in enrollment were spectacular indeed. In 1929–30 there were 29 high schools with more than 5,000 students each, but there were also 6,000 with fewer than 50 students each, including some with fewer than 10 students. The holding the questionable distinction of being the largest high school in the country was DeWitt Clinton of New York City, with 10,059 students.[16] The overwhelming majority of small high schools were rural, located in places of fewer than 2,500 people. Of 6,189 high schools in 1925–26 with fewer than 50 students each, 6,044 were defined as rural.[17] Consequently the supposed evils of small high schools, such as narrow and restricted programs of study, came to be associated particularly with rural schools. To the critics of small high schools, the answer lay in the consolidation of school districts. Victorious campaigns for consolidation, however, were few enough to be special events, often noted with satisfaction in the educational press, as, for example, the consolidation of fourteen districts with six high schools into the Shawnee-Mission Rural High School District of Johnson County, Kansas, resulting in a single high school of 200 students and 12 teachers.[18] Efforts were doubled and redoubled, and one enthusiastic school board member in Pennsylvania, referring to the consolidation of rural elementary districts, declared that "from now on, our normal schools, colleges, and training schools for teachers will train teachers to be boosters of consolidated rural schools just as we trained the teachers in the past generation to be boosters of hygiene and the evil effects of alcohol."[19]

The main problem of many rural youth, however, was not small high schools but no high schools. One of the anomalies of district organization in many states was the presence of large areas not organized as high school districts. Elementary school districts were universal, but the coverage of high school districts was spotty. According to State Superintendent Charles A. Lee of Missouri, in 1926 one-third of all the children in his state lived in rural areas without provisions for high schools.[20] Superintendent John Callahan of Wisconsin reported that 16,000 of the 34,000 elementary school graduates in the state in 1921 lived in areas not cov-

16. Off Ed, *Biennial Survey 1928–1930*, 2:687–88.

17. Walter H. Gaumnitz, *The Smallness of America's Rural High Schools*, U.S. Office of Education bull. 1930, no. 13, pp. 6–7.

18. F. P. O'Brien, "A Description of the Organization of a Rural Community High School," *High School Quarterly* 10 (April 1922), 155–62.

19. J. Buell Snyder, "Consolidation of Rural Schools," *NEA Proc*, 1922, p. 1225.

20. "A State Program," *School and Community* 12 (Dec. 1926), 521.

ered by high school districts and that such areas comprised 72 percent of the area of the state.[21] Elementary school districts in such areas could send their graduates to high schools by paying tuition for them, but this availed little when the nearest high schools were many miles away, a disadvantage that could be overcome by students only by moving away from home. Some high schools maintained dormitories to house their guests from other districts. "Home ties should not be so early broken," argued a member of the State Department of Public Instruction in Wisconsin, "as must be done when children must leave home to attend high school."[22]

One report of the impact of all this on rural youth came from a girl who grew up in what she referred to as the "backwoods" of central Wisconsin. "When I was graduated from the country school at the age of thirteen," she recalled in an article in the *American Mercury,* "I tried hard to enter high school, but all efforts to find a place where I could work for my room and board, as I would have had to do, failed. Transportation, possible in the early Fall, was out of the question during the Winter and Spring because of the heavy snowfall and poor roads."[23] She did her high school work through a correspondence school in Chicago and later attended Northland College in Ashland, Wisconsin, after being denied admission to the state university for not having come from an approved high school.

So far as rural youth were concerned, then, high schools were poorly and haphazardly distributed. To the critics, many of the rural high schools were too small. The campaigns for greater availability and for fewer and larger schools may have seemed contradictory, but they were not. Clusterings of small high schools in some areas did not help youth in areas with none, and the advocates of consolidation wanted fewer and larger schools better distributed to serve all the youth of their states.

III

It would have been a boon indeed to the users of pedagogical statistics had all institutions classified as high schools covered the same grades. Such was not the case, and the country abounded in "types" of reorgan-

21. "Wisconsin's Educational Program," *Twenty-First Biennial Report, 1922–1924, of the State Department of Public Instruction* (Madison, 1924), p. 13.
22. George S. Dick, *NEA Proc*, 1921, p. 607.
23. Olive Brossow, "Four Years of College," 18 (Oct. 1929), 137.

ized and unreorganized secondary schools, often with differences in the same school system. There were not only the conventional eight-year elementary schools and the newer six-year ones, but in a number of states there were seven-year elementary schools, a few five-year elementary schools, and surviving in Massachusetts and other New England states, the nine-year elementary schools. By 1929 there were at least twenty-eight different plans and arrangements,[24] including some that pushed secondary education, as grades thirteen and fourteen, into the level conventionally occupied by the first two years of college.

To give some appearance of order in this chaos, the Bureau of Education adopted a twofold classification of "regular" and "reorganized" types. A regular type was defined as one in which "the pupil was offered high school work following completion of an elementary school course 7, 8, or 9 years in length."[25] High school programs of the regular type might run one, two, three, or four or more years in length but were usually thought of as the conventional four years. All variations from this definition fell into the heterogeneous category known as reorganized secondary schools, of which the most familiar were those based on the six-year elementary school: either grades seven through twelve were included in a junior-senior high school (the 6-6 plan), or grades seven through nine in a junior high school followed by a senior high school of grades ten through twelve (the 6-3-3 plan).

On the extent of reorganization, the reports of the Bureau of Education for the early 1920s are inconclusive. Probably not more than one-tenth of the public secondary schools in 1920 were of the reorganized type, and probably not more than one-tenth of the students in the upper four high school years were in those schools.[26] In 1920, then, the regular high schools remained in possession of the field. By 1930, however, the proportion of reorganized schools had risen to one-fourth, and the schools enrolled one-third of the students in the upper four high school years.[27] The larger fraction for the students testified to the larger enroll-

---

24. "The Present Chaos in Reorganization," *High School Quarterly* 17 (Jan. 1929), 50.

25. *Biennial Survey 1928–1930*, 2:686.

26. For the difficulties involved see the discussion in the bureau's *Biennial Survey of Education 1924–1926*, bull. 1928, no. 25, pp. 1038–39. The fractions given are my best resolution of some of the difficulties. For a present-day recasting of figures for the early 1920s see Simon and Grant, *Digest of Educational Statistics*, p. 29, table 31, and p. 46, table 60.

27. Off Ed, *Biennial Survey 1928–1930*, 2:686, 689–90.

ments of the reorganized schools and to the urban character of the reorganization movement.

Of all the students in reorganized schools in 1929–30, including those in the seventh and eighth grades, about two-fifths were enrolled in the combined junior-senior high schools, five or six years in length.[28] In the literature of advocacy, however, the 6-3-3 plan was the preferred type. Even in the 1920s the ideology of the preceding decade tended to persist, the idea that the separate junior high school above all provided a new institution free from the traditions of both the elementary school and the high school.[29]

Still another type of school organization emerged in the latter 1920s, the 6-4-4, one including the first two college years. This movement was in part a revival of an older enthusiasm of the late 1890s, associated particularly with the University of Chicago's William Rainey Harper and Harvard's Charles W. Eliot, for bringing the general education of the first two college years into the domain of the secondary school. They saw in this also the means of making added schooling more widely available to youth in their local communities. Taking form in the junior college, the movement had prospered in spots, especially in California, usually resulting in a 6-3-3-2 or 8-4-2 pattern with the college years standing alone. It was this detachment of the junior college from the upper years of the high school that prompted the search for a new and presumably smoother sequence of grades.

Advocacy of the 6-4-4 plan appeared early in the 1920s and continued throughout the decade. Newer voices in its behalf included those of Professor William M. Proctor of Stanford, Professor Leonard V. Koos of the University of Chicago, City Superintendent John F. West of Pasadena, California, and his successor, John A. Sexson. Proctor emphasized its advantages for higher as well as secondary education. "The proposed reorganization," he wrote in 1923, "would bring about a fundamental change in the character of our American universities. Relieved of their present incubus of secondary training, they would become universities in fact as well as in name."[30] According to Sexson, the 6-4-4

28. *Ibid.*, p. 689.
29. See, for example, James M. Glass, "Development of Junior High Schools in Pennsylvania," *Pennsylvania School Journal* 62 (April 1923), 344–46. For a defense of the 6-6 plan see Frank W. Simmonds, "Six Year High School in Lewiston [Idaho]," *EA&S* 7 (May 1921), 291–97.
30. "The Junior College and Educational Reorganization," *ER* 65 (May 1923), 279.

plan demanded "an entirely new conception of the functions, objectives, and theories of administration in the new school."[31]

After having experimented with a separate two-year junior college since 1924, the Pasadena Board of Education established the 6-4-4 plan beginning in September 1928. Grades seven through ten were called the junior high school and grades eleven through fourteen the junior college, adding further confusion to the terminology of reorganized schools. During the 1930s a few other school systems adopted the 6-4-4 plan, but in spite of strenuous efforts by its advocates, it never became a bandwagon movement.

IV

Associated with the movement for reorganization was the "economy of time" movement, an effort to reduce the number of years of schooling from kindergarten through the undergraduate period of college. Back in 1913, a committee of the National Council of Education of the NEA had recommended the use of either a 6-4-4 or a 6-6-2 plan, to carry the student through not only junior college but the entire undergraduate period.[32] The plans were never used and few seemed to care. In 1921, Director George N. Carman of Lewis Institute, Chicago, proposed a resolution to a conference of the North Central Association in which he defined the normal period of secondary and college education as the time between twelve and twenty. The ensuing discussion turned on the question of whether this might imply abandonment of the junior high school, and the resolution was defeated in the ratio of two to one.[33] The preservation of the junior high school had become more important than the saving of two years in the student's program.

Nevertheless a few still did care, and from time to time a gesture was made in the direction of economy of time. Some schools provided for shortening the time spent by individual students. For example, the work of the top sections in the various subjects at Edison Junior High School of Berkeley, California, was arranged to permit covering three semesters' work in two, with ninety students during the school year 1921–22 gaining a full semester. "We sent to the Berkeley High School in August six

31. "Six-Four-Four Plan of School Organization," *American Education Digest* 48 (Oct. 1928), 56–57.
32. *Report of the Committee of the National Council of Education on Economy of Time in Education*, Bur Ed bulletin 1913, no. 38, p. 10.
33. "Report of the Conference on the Junior High School," *NC Proc*, 1922, part 1, pp. 59–60.

pupils out of the high eighth grade who had completed their three years work in two, and will be straight tenth year students," reported the principal.[34] At the other end of the secondary school period, the Joliet Township High School, Illinois, provided what would later be called advanced placement at least into the junior college of the same school system.[35] Such efforts, however, were isolated and did not involve structural reorganization of the units of schooling.

Almost unnoticed, on the other hand, was a long-established practice in certain states and communities that provided a tangible saving of one year. This was the 7-4 plan, under which a seven-year elementary school was followed by four years of a regular high school. Such a program had been running in Kansas City, Missouri, since the late 1860s. It was adopted in Concord, New Hampshire, in 1910 and in Salt Lake City in 1925–26. It was the prevailing organization in various states of the South, including, in 1926, Virginia, North Carolina, South Carolina, Georgia, Louisiana, and Texas.

Research on the 7-4 plan tended to center on the comparative college records of the eleven-year and twelve-year students. Such a study conducted with freshman students from Salt Lake City at the University of Utah showed higher achievement in 1929–30 for those from the first classes graduated under the eleven-year system than for those from the last graduated in Salt Lake City under the twelve-year. Data gathered by the Southern Association throughout the 1920s showed about the same level of college achievement for the two groups, the comparison for 1925 involving some 30,000 freshmen in colleges both North and South. Later studies solely of the University of Georgia seemed to reverse this.[36]

Advocates of the 7-4 plan were ardent in its defense. Sensitive to the accusation that the eleven-year plan deprived youth of an additional year of schooling, the *High School Quarterly* pointed to the example of Augusta, Georgia, in organizing a junior college to cap the eleven-year

34. H. H. Glessner, "Problems of the Junior High School," *Sierra Educatinoal News* 18 (Dec. 1922), 594.

35. W. W. Haggard, "Some Experimentation in the Joliet, Illinois, Township High School and Junior College," *North Central Association Quarterly* 5 (Sept. 1930), 193–94.

36. Arthur E. Arnesen, "Shortening Preparation for College in Salt Lake City," *Sch R* 41 (Sept. 1933), 531–38; "The 7-4 Plan Again," *High School Quarterly* 14 (Jan. 1926), 68–70; A. S. Edwards, "Some Comparisons of Quantitative Studies of Students with 11-Year Preparation vs. Those with 12-Year Preparation before Entering the University of Georgia," *High School Quarterly* 23 (July 1935), 221–27.

system. "Save a year," recommended the *Quarterly*, "and add a year to the present twelve and give the city education through the junior college."[37]

Using a different way of saving time, the Technical High School of Omaha, Nebraska, provided a four-quarter year of forty-eight weeks under which a four-year class was graduated every quarter, some of the students completing the four-year course in three years. This was also possible in cities with conventional summer sessions. The extent to which students used such sessions varied widely. In large-city high schools in the summer of 1923, for example, summer enrollment varied from the 3.4 percent of academic-year enrollment in Boston to the 33.8 percent in Reading, Pennsylvania. Economy of time was not necessarily the motive for offering these sessions. Operating only four summer high schools in 1925, the school authorities of New York City gave first preference to repeaters, who were four-fifths of the enrollment. This was necessary, according to one interpretation in New York City, "because the summer schools were primarily instituted to afford pupils an opportunity to make up deficiencies in prepared subjects."[38]

Economy of time was not universally accepted. Some opposed it on principle as a speedup system and were repelled by the industrial analogy. An editorial in *American Child,* the monthly bulletin of the National Child Labor Committee, in reporting the advocacy of the all-year school by Superintendent McAndrew of Chicago, quoted him as saying that "no industrial concern would voluntarily keep the plant idle for two months each year." The editorial feared that manufacturers would seek to employ children twelve years old on the ground they had finished elementary schooling by that age. "If we, personally," said the editorial, "were a Chicago child faced with the prospect of attending school the whole year round—no matter if it would give us a Ph.D. at the age of sixteen—we would immediately call a strike."[39]

Unfortunately, then, the movement was coming to be associated with the efficiency model. It should be remembered, however, that the early leaders had been schoolmen whose aim was more schooling for the individual, not less. This approach did persist even into the 1920s,

37. "The 7-4 Plan Again," 14 (Jan. 1926), 70.
38. "All-Year Sessions for High Schools," *Sch R* 33 (Dec. 1925), 730; M. David Hoffman, "Status of Summer High Schools in Cities of More Than 100,000 Population," *ibid.* (Feb. 1925), 107–14; "The Summer High Schools of the City of New York," *High Points* 8 (May, 1926), 5.
39. "Efficiency or Deficiency in Schooling," 71 (Sept. 1925), 2.

as reflected in the establishment at Augusta, Georgia, of the junior college as the capstone of a 7-4 system.

V

The 1920s also fell heir to a controversy at least forty years old, one that had been accentuated by the vigorous campaign for vocational education after 1906—the argument over the relative merits of the comprehensive and the special high school. In its 1918 report, *Cardinal Principles of Secondary Education*, the Commission on the Reorganization of Secondary Education recommended the comprehensive high school for both full-time and part-time students. It was argued that such a high school promoted social unity. "In short," said the commission, "the comprehensive school is the prototype of a democracy in which various groups must have a degree of self-consciousness as groups and yet be federated into a larger whole through the recognition of common interests and ideals."[40]

With this ideological force behind it, the comprehensive high school grew in favor and became the preferred form of organization. It was considered distinctively American, while special high schools increasingly labored under the handicap of being thought of as European and as fostering distinctions of social class.

Large cities tended to keep the special high schools they had established before 1920, in some cases adding to them but usually turning to the comprehensive variety for new schools. In Los Angeles, Assistant Superintendent Helen Watson Pierce defended the retention of special schools, pointing to Los Angeles High School's "prestige as the classical high school of Los Angeles" and praising the Polytechnic High School.[41] New York City was to turn particularly to special high schools in the 1930s, but throughout the 1920s maintained those, like the High School of Commerce, that were established. The city system most identified during the 1920s with the advocacy of special high schools was Cleveland, Ohio.[42]

The Arsenal Technical Schools of Indianapolis, Indiana, were a cross-

40. Bur Ed bull. 1918, no. 35, p. 26. See also Commission on the Reorganization of Secondary Education, *Part-Time Education of Various Types*, Bur Ed bull. 1921, no. 5, pp. 16–17.

41. "The Growth of the Los Angeles High Schools," *Los Angeles School Journal* 8 (June 8, 1925), 11–12.

42. "A High School of Music," *Sch R* 33 (Feb. 1925), 91.

breed. Principal Milo H. Stuart defined his school complex as one institution, consisting of a four-year comprehensive high school, with emphasis on the technical, and fourteen all-day vocational schools. Sensitive to the dangers involved in separate technical and vocational schools, Stuart proudly noted that the Arsenal Technical Schools offered "all the academic subjects which modern educational thought sanctions and for which there is sufficient demand," including Latin, French, German, and Spanish.[43] Along similar lines Meta S. Berger of the Milwaukee school board, reported the *Journal of Education,* "did much to maintain academic and cultural emphasis in the technical high schools, urging that they had a higher function than that of turning out expert maids and milliners."[44]

Perhaps the dangers of separatism were greatest in the continuation schools, whose enrollments were largely the result of compulsory laws requiring the part-time attendance till sixteen or eighteen of those permitted to leave full-time school to work. The degree and kind of separation varied from one community to the next. About half of the some three hundred continuation schools reported on by the National Survey of Secondary Education in 1932 were housed in the regular high school buildings, in some instances with the same principals, and often with provisions under which the continuation school students might take work for credit in the high school program.[45]

Continuation schools offered some general education, usually in mathematics and practical English, but their main effort was vocational training. According to one professor at the Northern Illinois Normal School, such part-time education was the public school's second chance with students who had dropped out.[46] One of the most distinctive of part-time schools was the Swift Continuation School of Chicago, maintained for boys employed by Swift and Company. The city board of education paid the teachers and supervised the work, while the company furnished the building and provided the students with books, equipment, and supplies. Although the state law required part-time attendance only until sixteen, Swift and Company extended this for its own employees to eighteen. The students attended two half-days each week for fifty weeks

43. *The Organization of a Comprehensive High School* (New York, 1926), pp. vi–vii, 11–12, 104–7.

44. Albert E. Winship, "Three Famous School Board Members," 103 (May 18, 1931), 528.

45. Monograph no. 1, *Summary,* Off Ed bull. 1932, no. 17, 1934, p. 41

46. S. J. Vaughn, "Part-Time Schools," *NEA Proc,* 1920, pp. 340–42.

of the year. Emphasis was placed on business education, particularly training messenger boys for future office work. "Our greatest turnover," said the director of this school in 1923, "consists of the rougher types of boys from the poorer homes. We make a persistent effort to civilize them, but they almost invariably drift over to the trades when they become old enough to get factory employment." The best students, according to the director, were middle-class boys who had had to go to work to help in family support. Those from foreign homes were found to be good students of mathematics and accounting, but with deficiencies in English and personality making them "uncongenial" members of office forces. He concluded that the "foreign lad" was usually a "misfit" in commercial work and should be directed to the trades.[47]

VI

High schools, taken collectively, had some twelve fields of instruction available to American youth: the academic—English, foreign languages, mathematics, science, and social studies—and the nonacademic—business, manual or industrial arts, agriculture, home economics, art, music, and physical education.[48] Not all high schools offered all twelve, and as the advocates of consolidation pointed out, small schools tended to be the most limited. Most widely offered were English, mathematics, social studies, and science.

The proportions of students in the four high school years who were enrolled in the various fields did not vary greatly between 1922 and 1928, the two points in the decade at which statistics were compiled by the Bureau of Education.[49] Foreign languages went down from 55 percent to 47 percent, a figure still too high for the critics. Most of this decline took place in Latin, which went from 28 percent to 22 percent, but the latter figure still represented 636,592 students who were taking Latin in 1928. The falling off in French and Spanish was slight, as was

47. I. L. Roberts, "The Swift Continuation School," *Chicago Schools Journal* 6 (Oct. 1923), 57, 59–60.

48. As officially defined by the North Central Association. See Charles C. Brown, secretary, "Proceedings of the Commission on Secondary Schools," *North Central Association Quarterly* 4 (June 1929), 80.

49. The figures on relative enrollments in this section are taken from these two surveys. See Bur Ed, *Biennial Survey of Education 1920–1922*, bull. 1924, no. 14, 2:578–79; Off Ed, *Biennial Survey of Education 1926–1928*, bull. 1930, no. 16, pp. 1057–58.

that in Greek, virtually nonexistent in 1928 at .05 of 1 percent. German made a slight increase, from less than 1 percent to nearly 2 percent, a slow comeback from the annihilation of the field between 1915 and 1922. The other major subjects under attack, algebra and geometry, also went down, algebra from 40 percent to 35 percent and plane geometry from 23 percent to 20 percent. Such "traditional" fields as foreign language and mathematics, although giving way, were still hanging on, and this accounted for much of the denunciation of high school programs.

Attitudes of the critics of social studies and science varied, depending on the subject under consideration. Combined enrollments in the various histories went down from 51 percent to 47 percent, while those in the nonhistorical social studies rose only from 26 percent to 29. In the sciences, physics dropped slightly, from 9 to 7 percent, while chemistry, at 7 percent throughout the period, held its own. Favored biology increased from 9 to 14 percent. Separate botany and zoology continued to disappear, their combined figures declining from 5 percent to 2. Physiology joined them, going from 5 percent in 1922 to 3 percent in 1928. General science surprisingly fell off slightly, although remaining at 18 percent in rounded figures for both dates.

Among the "practical" or nonacademic fields, business subjects went from 41 percent to 54 percent, of which typewriting represented 13 and 15 percent respectively. Home economics increased only from 14 to 16 percent, while agriculture fell off slightly, from 5 to 4. Manual training, covering all industrial arts both vocational and general, rose from 10 to 12 percent. Drawing and art, lumped together in the reports, went from 15 to 19 percent, while music went from 25 percent to 26.

These relative enrollments reflected, among other things, the way in which the courses were offered. The policy of offering electives was a central object of controversy. There were some who condemned electives as unmitigated evil. Among these was Princeton's Andrew F. West, who had been fighting for decades what he presumed to be the universal spread of electives in American schools and who was still tilting with this windmill in the early 1920s. The elective system, said West, had "badly damaged the intellectual and moral training of students," and he urged as of "universal value" at least a minimal program for all students in language, social studies, mathematics, and science. West feared loss of the cultural heritage. To the headmaster of the Middlesex School in Concord, Massachusetts, who wrote in the *Atlantic Monthly* that he was sickened by the idea of having secondary school boys decide what to study, electivism connoted flabbiness and effeminacy.[50]

From a quite different point of view, Harold Hand of Columbia's Teachers College, in 1933, found that the elective system conflicted with the interests of the investing state. No investing state in need of an informed citizenry, said Hand, would support a school "which permits and encourages youth to dictate its own educational destinies." Others seemed to dislike electivism because of its association with Charles W. Eliot, who had pursued farther than most the ideal of free election by subjects. As late as 1930 one writer expressed his disapproval of what he called "the almost universally condemned elective system of President Eliot."[51]

Still, it would have been difficult to find someone who believed in a completely uniform program for all students. Even the most sweeping opponents of what they understood to be electivism made some concessions to diversity and choice. Likewise there were few, if any, advocates of electives who believed in unregulated choice of subjects. The practical question became one of the kind of system and the degree of its application. Here it was that controversy arose and divergence in practice appeared.

Among the devices which could regulate student choice were the stipulation of common requirements or "constants," the use of courses of study or curriculums with varying requirements, and the holding of students to some patterns of consistency through majors and minors. These could be and were combined in various ways. A school could require part of the program as constants and leave the rest for free election by subject; this had been recommended by the NEA Committee on College Entrance Requirements back in 1899. It was also possible to offer curriculums with common elements as constants, with or without a limited margin for free election. Schools could also combine constants with election governed by majors and minors.

A 1927–28 survey of public high schools of various sizes in all states showed a practically universal requirement of English and social studies. Foreign language was required in 72 of the 464 high schools, and 23 spe-

---

50. "Free Elective Systems Detrimental," *School Life* 6 (June 1, 1921), 1; Frederick Winsor, "The Unintellectual Boy," 147 (April 1931), 487–96.

51. "Social Reconstruction: Its Implications for Secondary Education," *TCR* 34 (April 1933), 591; George Boas, "What Can Be Done with the Liberal College?" *Prog Ed* 7 (Feb. 1930), 4.

cifically required Latin. Mathematics, another subject of controversy, was required in 319 of the schools, algebra in 242, and plane geometry in 161, while 77 accepted any mathematics, presumably including general or practical. Science was a requirement of 349 of the schools, of which 36 specifically required physics, 9 chemistry, and 31 chemistry or physics. In spite of the strong drive to have physical education universally required, not more than 254 of these schools did so.[52]

On the average, constants were about half the student's program. The rest of the program might include specific requirements in the student's curriculum or some provision for majors and minors or both. Probably not more than one-fourth and often less of the average student's program remained for unrestricted electives.[53]

Slightly more than half the 464 schools in this study administered their constants without the use of curriculums, either combining the requirements with majors and minors or simply leaving the rest of the program open as electives. The remaining schools used constants with curriculums, and some also with majors and minors.[54] Curriculums fell into broad categories, but with much diversity in what they were called. A survey of 65 school systems in 1927 turned up 184 different titles. The main groups were academic and college preparatory, represented by 91 curriculums and 45 titles; commercial, by 119 curriculums and 45 titles; boys' industrial, agricultural, and vocational, by 83 curriculums and 38 titles; and girls' household and vocational, by 41 curriculums and 4 titles. There was a "general" category, usually a modified academic program for non-college-bound students without specific vocational plans, and there were also 14 curriculums in teacher-training, with 9 titles.[55]

There was nothing new about organizing by curriculums. It was in fact the traditional pattern of public secondary education in the United States, going back to the classical and English courses of the early Massachusetts high schools that had combined the statutory requirements for Latin Schools and English Schools. Organization by curriculums (or election by courses in the older terminology) appealed to those who believed in choice of programs but not of subjects. Charles W. Eliot had opposed this

52. Carl A. Jessen, *Requirements for High School Graduation*, Bur Ed bull. 1928, no. 21, pp. 11–14.

53. *Ibid.*, pp. 19, 24.

54. *Ibid.*, pp. 20–21.

55. Carter V. Good and Edward D. Roberts, "Curriculum Titles and Curriculum Constants in Senior High Schools," *Sch R* 36 (Nov. 1928), 680–81.

as the worst kind of choice, since it tended to bind students to decisions affecting their careers through high school. Few shared these apprehensions with Eliot, but in the early 1930s renewed expression of them came from Assistant Superintendent Richard D. Allen of the Providence, Rhode Island, public schools. "Bad, however, as required subjects may be," said Allen, "they exist in their worst form in the grouping of required subjects in specialized high schools or in specialized curriculums within a high school."[56] He, like Eliot, favored free election by subjects accompanied by individual counseling, a program that he inaugurated and carried out in the Providence schools.

Advocates of curriculums in the 1920s agreed on their application to the four high school years, but this agreement did not extend to the seventh and eighth grades. During the preceding decade there had been a strong movement for beginning curricular differentiation in the seventh grade, largely for vocational purposes. In fact, the reluctance of the traditional eight-year elementary school to provide it had furnished one of the motives for creating junior high schools. After 1920, however, opinion ran against such early differentiation. Many junior high schools offered single programs in the seventh grade, usually including English, mathematics, social studies, and varying combinations of general science, art and music, shop for boys, and homemaking for girls. Most of these subjects ran through the eighth grade but often with limited options, for example between foreign language and homemaking or shop.

This approach in the junior high schools of the 1920s was well expressed by James M. Glass, director of junior high schools in the Pennsylvania State Department of Education and one of the main leaders of the junior high school cause. The junior high school, said Glass in 1923, "should continue, with modifications, the single curriculum of the elementary school. Through its general courses of study it should expand the single curriculum into an enriched and varied curriculum." Two years later he said that from the beginning of the movement, "differentiation has been increasingly replaced by the core curriculum. This trend was inevitable as comprehension of the fundamental purposes of the junior high school became clearer and more general."[57]

56. Superintendence *Report*, 1932, p. 201.
57. "Report of Committee on the Reorganization of the Seventh, Eighth, and Ninth Grades," *NEA Proc*, 1923, p. 443; "Recent Developments in the Junior High School Field," *National Association of Secondary School Principals Ninth Yearbook*, 1925, p. 185.

VII

Were the high schools more sinned against than sinning? Those who believed that the high schools were victims had little doubt that the true culprits were the colleges, and the expression "college domination" rolled easily off many an oratorical tongue.

Through most of the nineteenth century, the required subjects in college entrance examinations had been Greek, Latin, and mathematics. Of these, Greek bore the exclusive college preparatory identification; many students not preparing for college took Latin and mathematics. The purpose of the innovators in the 1890s had been to broaden the range of subjects acceptable for college admission by including English, modern languages, science, and history, and to make it possible for students to enter college with neither Latin nor Greek. These were in fact the recommendations made in 1893 by the Committee of Ten.

By the 1920s, whether because of the Committee of Ten or not, the so-called modern academic subjects were included in patterns of college admission, and some of these, foreign languages in particular, modern as well as ancient, came to be spoken of as college preparatory subjects. Critics of the Committee of Ten blamed it for having imposed a college preparatory curriculum on high schools, a strange reverse view of what had been the committee's intent, to gain acceptance of these subjects by the colleges. It became popular accordingly to fix the blame for college domination on the Committee of Ten.

With or without reference to the Committee of Ten, denunciation of the colleges rang on. The elementary school, said Superintendent Thomas W. Gosling of Madison, Wisconsin, had achieved its identity, but the high school was still held down by the university and its emancipation was incomplete. High school principals of California, meeting in convention at Long Beach in 1928, were reportedly "crystallizing . . . the widespread sentiment of secondary school leaders against the despotic control of scholastic standards exercised by the state university." The principal of East High School, Des Moines, Iowa, called on the colleges to center their demands "on the boy or girl rather than the subject matter."[58]

58. "The Relationship between a University and the Public Schools," University of Illinois, *High School Conference*, 1925, p. 19; W. M. Culp, "California High School Principals' Convention," *Western Journal of Education* 34 (April 1928), 9; A. J. Burton, "Articulation between Junior High School and Senior High School," *Proceedings of the National Department of Secondary School Principals*, 1930, p. 160.

There were some who disagreed. The *English Journal,* for example, concluded that colleges had tried to dominate the high school but had failed, and noted that "the colleges must have students and must therefore take the high school graduates as they are." Joseph D. Elliff, professor of high school administration at the University of Missouri, pronounced college domination a myth and said, "We have reached the point where we are virtually compelled to take anything and everything and all of either that is offered." Abraham Flexner of the General Education Board, scornful of "soft pedagogy" and forgetting that he had once, in the *Atlantic,* equated Latin with the making of pumpkin pies, now said that the colleges were too permissive—the University of Chicago, for example, in accepting home economics, agriculture, and business subjects for admission—and he declared that there was no more sense in this than there would have been in accepting "manicuring, hair-bobbing, or toe-dancing." Superintendent Carroll R. Reed of Minneapolis called the conflict between high schools and colleges "a sham battle" and doubted whether the high school "that protests most loudly concerning the domination of the college would have a definite program to follow if all college entrance requirements were suddenly removed."[59]

Surveys of admission requirements were incomplete in coverage and hedged in by qualifications. Part of the problem was that most or all colleges awarded at least several degrees, all with varying requirements for admission. The survey made by Harry C. McKown for the Bureau of Education, covering 314 of the 349 colleges on the accredited list of the American Council on Education, accordingly presented data on over 500 sets of requirements used by these colleges for admission to their various degree programs. Of the controversial subjects, mathematics was required in 94 percent of 501 sets and foreign language in 70 percent of 517 sets. Practically all the required mathematics was in the algebra-geometry sequence. Only 13 percent of the programs required more than one foreign language. Latin was stipulated in 23 percent of the programs and Greek in 2 percent.[60]

In a survey made in 1927 for the Department of Superintendence

59. Editorial, 10 (Sept. 1921), 405; "Presidential Address," *North Central Association Quarterly* 2 (Dec. 1927), 269; "Parents and Schools," *Atlantic Monthly* 118 (July 1916), 30; *Universities: American, English, German* (New York, 1930), p. 59; Carrol R. Reed, "Articulating the School As a Social Agency with the Life of the Community," Superintendence *Report,* 1931, p. 101.

60. *The Trend of College-Entrance Requirements 1913–1922,* U.S. Bureau of Education, bull. 1924, no. 35, pp. 63, 66, 76, 78.

Seventh Yearbook, *The Articulation of the Units of American Education* (Washington, D.C., 1929), each of 331 colleges was asked to state the requirements that it had set in that year and in 1921 for its most commonly conferred degree. There was no shift in the proportions of colleges requiring mathematics and foreign languages over this period: 94 percent for mathematics in both years and 75 percent for foreign language (pp. 341, 344).

So far as 1921, 1922, and 1927 were concerned, then, it could be said that high schools from which students went to college were constrained to offer algebra, geometry, and foreign language. Whether this was bad is another matter. Also unknown is whether high schools would have offered these subjects anyway, regardless of college requirements. What, too, would colleges have done had high schools refused to offer these subjects?

Given their assumptions, the anti-academic educators did have some justification in the 1920s for their complaints about college admission requirements. They could take comfort, however, in some of the regional variations. In the showings of the 1927 study for the Department of Superintendence, 96 percent of the colleges in the territory of the New England Association required foreign languages, and only 60 percent of those in the territory of the North Central Association. Even in North Central territory, however, there was practically no shift in the proportions between 1921 and 1927 (p. 341).

Colleges were criticized also for their reluctance to accept more than small amounts, if any, of such practical electives as homemaking, industrial arts, and business education. "Many institutions," said the 1927 survey of the Department of Superintendence, "do not accept more than three units of the vocational-industrial-commercial group for entrance" (p. 346), thus stopping short of what had been recommended as a free margin of four units by the NEA Committee on the Articulation of High School and College back in 1911. McKown's 1922 survey showed a spreading acceptance of nonacademic subjects: drawing was accepted (not required) in 40 percent of the 542 sets of requirements, shopwork in 30 percent, household arts in 33 percent, agriculture in 27 percent and bookkeeping and stenography in 11 percent each.[61]

Part of the apprehension about college domination involved the program of the ninth grade, because of its place in the three-year junior high school. The junior high school had been designed as a new institution,

61. *Ibid.*, p. 92.

free from tradition, but what would this avail if the ninth grade remained enmeshed in college requirements? Among the first to direct specific attention to this was an assistant superintendent of the Cleveland public schools in his report as chairman of a North Central commission in 1921. His report recommended that colleges base requirements on the upper three high school years only. Along these lines, the entire association voted in 1923 to recommend that colleges base their requirements on only twelve units of work.[62] The issue was taken up in other parts of the country as well.

Some colleges did make the shift. Nine colleges in Pennsylvania responded to such a request from their state department of education and agreed to make the change, among them Bucknell, Lafayette, Pennsylvania State, and the University of Pennsylvania. Three colleges in the state rejected it. In 1926, some nine-tenths of 452 colleges reported to the Bureau of Education that they were not basing their requirements on twelve units or three years, but about three-fourths of them said they would be willing to do so if this were approved by accrediting agencies. Meanwhile the discontent continued, expressed by the *Colorado School Journal* in its editorial comment that the ninth grade had been forced "into the cast iron system under which Senior High Schools must work if their audiences desire to enter college."[63]

VIII

The question of college domination involved not only the subjects required for admission but also the mechanisms used for selecting students to be admitted. Although increasingly supplemented by other means, the two main devices, in a sense mutually opposed, were admission by examination and admission by certificate. Some colleges still gave their own examinations, but most used those of the College Entrance Examination Board, established in 1900. Also, some colleges still handled their own certification, but for the most part accreditation was handled by state departments of education, state universities, and regional associations of colleges and secondary schools.

62. "Report of the Commission on Unit Courses and Curricula," *NC Proc*, 1921, p. 36; "Discussion," *NC Proc*, 1923, pp. 45–49.
63. James N. Rule, "Progress in Pennsylvania in the Adoption of the Twelve-Unit Plan of College Admission," *S&S* 24 (Aug. 14, 1926), 210–12; Arthur J. Klein, "Junior High Schools and College-Entrance Requirements," *School Life* 12 (Sept. 1926), 16–17; "The Junior High School," 42 (April 1927), 17.

By the mid-1920s admission by examination was giving way, and only 5 percent of all entering freshmen in the country were being processed by the College Entrance Examination Board. Only ten institutions were using the College Board for all their students: Harvard, Yale, Princeton, the Massachusetts Institute of Technology, Haverford, Mount Holyoke, Smith, Vassar, Wellesley, and Radcliffe.[64] At the end of the decade, it was estimated that some 90 percent of all college entrants went the certificate route.[65]

Throughout the 1920s, the colleges in regional associations tended to restrict the privilege of admission by certificate to students from accredited high schools, with provisions for reciprocal recognition among the regional bodies. Not all regional associations, of course, carried on such accreditation, and the system was never absolute. Colleges could and did make exceptions, but few high schools that were in the position of gaining accreditation dared to go it alone. Those who sought accreditation had to conform to requirements. Whether these were in themselves good or bad, they were in fact controls over local schools. For example, the rules used by the North Central Association of Colleges and Secondary Schools stipulated fifteen units for graduation, class periods at least forty minutes in length, at least five academic teachers (this serving to exclude most small schools), degrees for academic teachers and from approved colleges, and a school year of thirty-six weeks.[66] Deviation from standards, ascertained either through visits by examining teams or inspection by state committees of written reports, could lead to warnings and suspensions. In 1923, the association accredited 1,534 schools, a net figure arrived at by dropping 28 schools and admitting 193 new ones. Warnings were given to 222 schools.[67] The fates of local school boards and of principals often depended upon such actions. North Central also had a commission for accrediting colleges, a matter affecting transfers and admission to professional schools, and high schools could perhaps take comfort in this.

64. Henry S. Pritchett, "Has the College Entrance Examination Board Justified Its Quarter-Century of Life?" in the College Entrance Examination Board, *The Work of the College Entrance Examination Board 1901–1925* (Boston, 1926), p. 13.

65. "Freshmen in Georgia Colleges," *S&S* 30 (Nov. 23, 1929), 716.

66. Calvin O. Davis, "The North Central Association," *Sch R* 29 (June 1921), 444—50.

67. Calvin O. Davis, secretary, "Report of the Commission on Secondary Schools," *NC Proc*, 1923, pt. 2, p. 110.

The system received an ardent defense from its adherents, usually accompanied by disparagement of entrance by examination and the work of the College Board. North Central stalwarts identified these presumed evils with the East. Referring in 1920 to "the hidebound aristocratic colleges down east," Frank C. Pickell, principal of the high school in Lincoln, Nebraska, expressed the gratitude of people in North Central territory that they were "one thousand physical miles and, at least, ten thousand professional and educational miles removed from their narrow, pedantic, educational philosophy." In 1925 the *School Review* (University of Chicago) congratulated the College Board on its twenty-fifth anniversary, while noting that "to one who lives west of the Alleghany mountains the board is an interesting example of educational history."[68]

Not all the Midwest, however, rejoiced in North Central. As early in the decade as 1922, one professional journal in that territory feared that North Central accreditation was becoming a bed of Procrustes. "Many of the men in the smaller town high schools, where it is not easy to live up to the requirements of the Association in all its details," said *American School* of Milwaukee, "live in mortal terror of being dropped from the North Central list. Especially where a man is not quite sure of his standing in the community or where he has some active and persistent opposition, he is likely to be especially fearful of the 'warning' or of being 'dropped from the list.' "[69]

Even communities on occasion reacted against the pressures. Gallatin, Missouri, High School dropped out of North Central in 1931, allegedly because of the costs of maintaining the standards. According to School Board Secretary F. M. Harrison, school districts could not meet "the demands of 'educational rings.' " Perhaps there were other discontents as well. "The schools of Missouri will be better off," continued Harrison, "and the taxpayers' burden greatly relieved, when demands are lessened, fundamental teaching replaces a lot of theory, over-inspection of schools eliminated, centralization of power done away with, and the school districts of the state permitted to run their districts along the lines of economy and without dictation from some outsider."[70] Fortunately for

68. "Report of the Commission on Unit Courses and Curricula," *NC Proc*, 1920 p. 20; "Anniversary Volume of the College Entrance Examination Board," 34 (Oct. 1926), 569.

69. "North Central Association Discipline," 8 (June 1922), 166–67.

70. Quoted in "The North Central Association," *School Executives Magazine* 51 (May 1932), 406.

the students, the state university and colleges in this case, according to Harrison, would accept them without the blessing of North Central.

Some interpreted accreditation as college domination, although in the case of regional associations, high schools were judged not only by colleges but also by other high schools. Perhaps all domination was a myth. Still, the high school principal must often have felt surrounded by agencies looking over his shoulder or down his throat. Even after satisfying the regional association, a principal might still have a handful of students fearfully contemplating "college boards." Then there were the demands of colleges for recommendations of individual graduates. To recommend some students meant risking his reputation and that of his school, but not to recommend meant risking parental and sometimes community wrath. In the state of New York he had to worry about Regents' examinations, and in New York and other states about the requirements for graduation he was obliged to enforce. Surely he could be excused for rolling all these frustrations together under the single rubric of college domination. For principals and teachers together, the complaint against college domination could also be used to soften the wrath of leaders who denounced them for not meeting the needs of youth.

IX

These were the high schools of the 1920s, the anvil on which were broken or bent so many hammers of curriculum revision. They were indeed a confusing variety of institutions. Their great fault, according to pedagogical leaders, was that they did not boldly seize the opportunity given them to induct youth into the service of society and the state and to equip them for the efficient performance of their other duties in life. Instead, perhaps because of college domination, the principals and the teachers of these schools were allegedly wasting the resources of society and the time of students with outmoded algebra, geometry, foreign languages, and ancient history. Furthermore, communities themselves appeared to be satisfied with this state of affairs, often resolutely defending their schools with outbursts of civic pride. Nor did educational leaders want communities to lose faith in their high schools. They felt obliged, therefore, to both criticize the schools and extol them as institutions of great potential worth.

The apparent hardness of the high school anvil did not necessarily testify to any deep ideological commitment to the academic tradition as such. Two years of mathematics in the algebra-geometry sequence, for example, had become a habit, possibly good, but a habit nonetheless. Foreign language in many instances was merely a ticket for admission to college. True, many colleges accepted students without it, but this was not recognized in the folklore of the times. Two years of foreign language helped provide the middle classes with the security of taking the right thing for college admission, and other children could be directed into a non-college-preparatory curriculum. The survival of some academic subjects in the 1920s was as consistent with the world of George F. Babbitt as were the anti-academic fulminations of leading educators. Perhaps in this lay the strength of the anvil.

Chapter 4

The general subjects in the nineteen-twenties

"What Is 'English'?"

—HENRY SEIDEL CANBY,
NOVEMBER, 1919.

*T*he most visible fields of instruction in the 1920s and the most frequently required for high school graduation were English, social studies, mathematics, and science. Few questioned their right to exist. This, however, guaranteed neither a tranquil life nor immunity from abuse to their teachers. Efficiency educators denounced teachers for clinging to the past. Traditionalists watched them with suspicion for the least sign of soft pedagogy or the lowering of standards.

Teachers in each of these fields, moreover, were at odds among themselves. This was true in other fields as well, but they did not attract as much outside comment. Anti-academic educators worked not to reform but to abolish the teaching of foreign language. Traditionalists scorned the practical subjects but did not enter their internal quarrels. Teachers in foreign languages, the practical subjects, and the fields of art, music, and physical education could and did have their quarrels in private. Those in English, social studies, science, and mathematics held theirs before galleries. Their issues and problems were in fact specific instances of the issues and problems of secondary education as a whole.

II

A tragic virtue shared by nearly all English teachers was the tendency to self-criticism and doubt. They suffered first of all from a continuing crisis of identity. "What Is 'English'?" asked Professor Henry Seidel Canby of Yale in the title of his address to the National Council of the

Teachers of English in November 1919. For his question he had no answer. In his presidential address to the same council in November 1920, James F. Hosic of the Chicago Normal College avoided the question in his title but inserted it in his text: "What is English? Upon a clear and definite answer to that question depend the aims of English teaching, and hence the Council must find the answer." To a columnist for the Indiana Association of Teachers of English, there was little hope that the field would soon be defined. "It has become almost a habit now," he wrote, "for English teachers to write something under the alluring, if almost trite, caption, 'What Is English?'" So far as such things can be discerned, the question was not a flippant one, but uttered in sincerity, possibly in despair.[1]

Aims were a part of identity. Professor E. A. Cross of the Colorado State College of Education reproached his fellow English teachers for aiming too high. "It [the public] will be satisfied," said Cross, "if we turn out pupils free from the common formal errors, and able to speak in correctly constructed sentences and to write simple, straightforward prose without marring errors in spelling or grammar. . . . But the disconcerting fact is that we have not done it, and are not now doing it. Why? Well, for one thing we have scorned the task. We have said that our calling is higher than that."[2]

Whether or not the aims were too cosmic and lofty, they were certainly diverse. There was much head-shaking in 1924 over the announcement by one investigator that he had collected 1,581 objectives for English from various writings on the subject and from several hundred English teachers. Commenting on this report, W. Wilbur Hatfield of the English department of the Chicago Normal College said, "The results are surprising, astounding, disquieting. The outstanding fact is that as a professional group we do not know what we are trying to do." In view of the tendency of respondents in such inquiries to put down as many things as possible, Hatfield perhaps was unduly alarmed by the accumulation of 1,581 aims. Nonetheless, the conclusion reached by an English teacher in New York City that "from rules for the use of the comma to objectives in character-training through literature, there is hardly any proposi-

1. "What Is 'English'?" *EJ* 9 (Sept. 1920), 367–73; "The National Council of Teachers of English," *EJ* 10 (Jan. 1921), 7; William N. Otto, "Once More—'What Is English'?" *Educator-Journal* 21 (Feb. 1921), 337.
2. "Fundamentals for English Teachers," *EJ* 16 (May 1927), 368.

tion that is offered for approval that does not become a subject for sharp debate" was both disquieting and true.[3]

Above the specific objectives that could be variously stated in the thousands were the broader ones involving matters of doctrine. The vogue for American Speech Week that swept the National Council of the Teachers of English reflected enthusiasm not only for oral English but also for English as a vehicle for patriotism and national unity. This was, moreover, only one of the many expressions of social aims for English. Walter Barnes, Professor of English at the Fairmont, West Virginia, State Normal School carried the point farther and into the domain of social efficiency itself. Preparation of each student for "democratic social efficiency" was for Barnes the index of value for every subject and therefore "the test to which the various branches of English must be subjected."[4]

Others held to more individual, personal aims. To some this meant the cultivation of graces through units and even courses of the kind later stereotyped as life adjustment education. The English department at Wadleigh High School, New York City, for example, undertook, at the students' request, to provide an elective course in etiquette. English for enjoyment and leisure was a popular concept with many teachers, at times linked to such social objectives as the decrease in working hours for wage earners.[5]

Personal and social aims could, of course, be combined, and a teacher in Cobleskill, New York, did so in a manner reminiscent of the Cardinal Principles Report. The teaching of English, she said, "should make the home life of our people better; help to meet the problems of social service; cultivate a higher standard of citizenship and prepare the men and women of the future for a more wholesome use of leisure time." Further sustaining this dual effort, she called on the teaching of literature to "promote attitudes that make for social efficiency and happiness."[6]

There were inevitable protests from those who rejected the drift to

---

3. Charles S. Pendleton, *The Social Objectives of School English* (Nashville, Tennessee, 1924); Book review, *EJ* 13 (Dec. 1924), 753–54; "The Council and the Classroom Teacher," *EJ* 17 (Jan. 1928), 1.
4. "English—Its Relation to the 'Ten Essentials,' " *NEA Proc*, 1922, p. 448.
5. Elizabeth S. Rogers, "A School Paper's Contribution to Courtesy," *High Points* 10 (May 1928), 62–64; see for example Althea Payne, "Education for Leisure As Well As for Vocation," *EJ* 10 (April 1921), 209.
6. Ada Young Franklin, "Why Teach English in a New York State High School?" *New York State Education* 16 (Jan. 1929), 350.

aims which they considered external to the field of English. Perhaps the protesters had fewer doubts than their colleagues about what English was. One teacher called for a declaration of independence from service functions. "I would have them [English teachers] vigorously assert," he declared "that English is English, that it is an art subject and should so be taught. Just what place current events have in an English class I have never clearly seen; except in so far as it contributes to the income of the proprietors of the *Literary Digest* and other similarly well-advertised periodicals." He further scored the use of literature to promote good citizenship and to build Americanism. Such uses, he felt, had "something almost if not quite wicked" about them.[7]

Beyond their own self-doubts, English teachers in high schools faced continuing criticism from their colleagues in universities and colleges. This had been a chronic state of affairs, but the criticism became more strident in the 1920s. "The writer has personally observed," said a professor at the University of Wisconsin in 1922, "that the Freshmen of Texas, Georgia, Indiana, and Wisconsin are all suffering from the same ailment," defectiveness in the mechanics of English. Similarly, in 1926, an official of the University of California noted that 38 percent of the preceding year's entrants had failed the placement examination in English, although he acknowledged the improvement from a corresponding figure of 61 percent in 1921. The failing papers, he said, averaged 49.5 errors each, or 1 for every 10 words in a 500-word composition. A professor at Western Illinois State Teachers College, in a survey of conditions in his state, reported that an average of one-fifth of the entering freshmen in its colleges and universities were unprepared for college English.[8]

Not all the critics blamed the high schools. A professor at the University of Toledo in 1927 complained that prosperity was flooding the colleges with "hordes of students who have little genuine interest in *anything purely intellectual*." In attributing the demoralization of college English teachers to the presence of "students entirely uninterested in literature and other liberal arts subjects," he seemed to be calling for the

7. Earl Daniels, "English That Works," *ER* 68 (Dec. 1924), 235.

8. George P. Wilson, "What Is Wrong with High School English?" *EJ* 11 (June 1922), 355; Roscoe E. Parker, "The English of High School Students," *California Quarterly of Secondary Education* 1 (Jan. 1926), 196–97; Irving Garwood, "Some Lessons from the College Freshman Classes in English," *High School Conference*, 1927, p. 160.

abandonment of required college English. Some found the fault in the colleges themselves. Literary critic Bernard De Voto, formerly a college teacher of English, wrote in the *American Mercury* of the horrors and futilities of freshman composition. A professor of English at the University of Iowa castigated the colleges for their ignorance of what was being done in high school English and for damaging their own cause by pointless repetition of much of the high school work.[9]

Teachers of English in high schools were themselves concerned about the transition to college and the subsequent successes or failures of their graduates. The chairman of the English Department at Bay Ridge High School, Brooklyn, for instance, solicited comments from graduates of her school who had gone to college. The criticisms that came to her did not dwell on the shortcomings in mechanics of which the professors complained, but on such matters as note-taking, length of assignments, and planning of reports. "We were not taught," said one of these student critics, "how to make proper use of libraries and reference books and didn't have enough practice in digging out information for ourselves. Daily assignments, I believe, are largely responsible for the dependence of the pupils on the teacher." Another asked, "Have you ever tried giving long-range assignments at school?"[10]

Such observations, however, were lost in the volume of complaints about mechanics, grammar, and usage, aspects of English that offered the security of concrete tasks, and the emphasis on grammar swelled to outsize proportions indeed. What was usually meant by grammar was a conglomerate of rules and definitions governing forms of words, construction of sentences, and details of punctuation. The enterprise of grammar, so understood, involved not only high school teachers of English but the nonspecialist teachers in elementary schools as well.

By the 1920s, American elementary and secondary schools had already embraced and rejected the direct teaching of grammar several times. The issue was whether to inculcate the art through forms and terms or to depend on its incidental acquisition through other study. During the decade 1910–20 the direct teaching of grammar had been out; in

9. Carl Holliday, "Hamstringing the Liberal Arts College," *S&S* 25 (Feb. 5, 1927), 153–54; "English A," 13 (Feb. 1928), 204–12; Hardin Craig, "The Correlation of English in College and High School," *EJ* 10 (March 1921), 165–67.

10. Quoted in Mabel A. Bessey, "What Is the High School Doing in English in Preparation for College?" *New York State Education* 13 (March 1926), 455–56.

the 1920s it reappeared, although this was not always apparent to its more ardent exponents.

The swing to so-called formal grammar was pronounced enough, however, to evoke alarmed editorials about it in the *English Journal.* "Hardly a week passes," complained an editorial in 1926, "without bringing to our reviewing desk another drill book on grammar or the mechanics of written English or both. . . . *Must* education constantly veer from no grammar at all to a mind-numbing grind on useless details of the subject?" (15 [Dec. 1926], 779). Four years later another editorial in the same journal lamented the ready market for practice pads (workbooks) in grammar and mechanics. "One pad," said this editorial, "published in 1926, with only limited magazine and mail publicity, has had a constantly growing patronage in the face of rapidly increasing competition, and has sold 75,000 copies. And it is only a straw in the wind, for there are now at least a score of such publications" (19 [Dec. 1930], 829).

Direct teaching of grammar, however, did not necessarily involve unpleasant drills or mere memorization of rules. Howard R. Driggs, professor of English education at New York University, for example, attacked what he called the recurring grammar grind, but protested that what he wanted was not less but better grammar. One advocate of what he called formal or technical grammar was concerned nonetheless that it not be isolated from other aspects of language. "English is an art," he wrote, "and is indivisible. We cannot break it up into reading, spelling, writing, grammar, composition and rhetoric, treating them all as independent subjects."[11]

A far more serious challenge, however, came from linguists who questioned the very ideal of grammatical correctness. The challenge had been repeatedly hurled for at least half a century, but it was in the 1920s that it came to the fore in discussions of the teaching of English. The linguists' idea of grammar as a description of language did not make the study of grammar easier, and in some ways it made it more difficult. It involved, among other things, the historical patterns of language and for English specifically the history of the English tongue. It also involved surveys of usage in various regions and among various groups in society. Communicating the results of this enterprise to students was a more demanding task than teaching rules.

11. "The Grammatical Merry-Go-Round," *Junior-Senior High School Clearing House* 4 (May 1930), 557–59; E. E. Cates, "More Technical Grammar," *Education* 41 (Dec. 1920), 261–62.

Among the major figures in this challenge were Professors Charles C. Fries of the University of Michigan and Sterling Andrus Leonard of the University of Wisconsin. Fries was primarily a scholar of linguistics, Leonard a teacher of English, but both combined qualities of scholarship with talents of concrete application. The National Council of the Teachers of English, for the most part, took up the cause of usage against correctness, at least in its convention programs, although this choice was by no means that of the whole membership.

The ensuing debate aroused bitterness and recrimination. Advocates of the usage point of view pushed hard and, what was especially irritating, tended to imply deficient scholarship on the part of their opponents. In his favorable review of Fries's *The Teaching of the English Language* (New York, 1927), Professor Allan Abbott of Columbia Teachers College called for more linguistic training of teachers, for "only on a basis of sound linguistic scholarship can we hope to effect a change from the petty pedantry of school English." A reviewer of Leonard's *The Doctrine of Correctness in English Usage 1700–1800* (Madison, Wisconsin, 1929) recommended it as "a trip-hammer that will bring conviction to anyone whose mind is not made of granite." Professor Kemp Malone of Johns Hopkins University prescribed more study of "historical English grammar" for prospective English teachers. Lacking such study, teachers went forth, according to Malone, with "a naive rather than a scientific attitude toward the linguistic questions that come up every day, and their fight for good standards of English speech, however valiant, is ill-directed and often wrong-headed."[12]

In spite of these admonitions and attacks, the school enterprise in English continued for the most part to pursue correctness and to stamp out mistakes. Even the National Council of the Teachers of English admitted to its 1927 summer meeting in Seattle a representative of an agency known as Correct English Service. She presented what she called the "key method" for "teaching correctness," and apparently took her hearers convincingly through the paces of her method.[13] Believers in correctness were also undoubtedly encouraged by the existence of the

12. "Four Good Books on English," *Journal of Educational Method* 7 (May 1928), 382; C. H. Ward, *EJ* 19 (March 1930), 253; quoted in "Conference on English Problems," *EJ* 18 (Jan. 1929), 81–82.
13. "News and Notes," *EJ* 16 (Sept. 1927), 558–59.

journal *Correct English: How To Use It*, published by the Correct English Publishing Company of Evanston, Illinois.[14]

Symbolic of the chasm between the linguists and the right-thinking, hard-headed schoolman was a protest made by Superintendent S. B. Tobey of Wausau, Wisconsin, against Leonard's approval of such expressions as "It is me," "Who are you looking for?" and "There was a bed, a dresser, and two chairs in the room." These, according to Tobey, clearly violated established rules, and their widespread use was no more reason for their adoption than would be "the use of profanity or vulgarity by those who live in an atmosphere constantly charged by them" Leonard blandly retorted that Tobey's rules were invented in the eighteenth century and were not ancient landmarks but merely "recent purist rubbish."[15]

There was little hope then of an amicable resolution to the conflict. At the end of the decade, the linguists clearly held the commanding heights of scholarship, but the purists remained in firm possession of the plain. The life of the English teacher on these matters was insecure at best. Rules and terminology varied widely from one textbook to the next, from one purist to the next, and among school systems. What constituted errors to the examining committee at one university were not necessarily such to committees at others. Little wonder then if the English teacher sought and clung not only to rules, but to the rules of a given textbook or of the college or university most frequently attended by graduates of the local school.

In addition to inculcating the rules, English teachers were expected to see that students applied them "correctly" in oral and written composition, and to promote creativity, forcefulness, clarity, and interest in speech and writing. Written composition, especially, served to bring out the noble impulses of English teachers, as well as to lead them into the darker nights of the soul. The sheer logistics of the matter was enough to produce frustration. English teachers were castigated for not having students write enough papers and themes. Surveys, however, repeatedly showed that teachers were overloaded with such work.[16] They were willing to settle for a load of one hundred students, and frequently passed resolutions to that effect. Of course there were experts who assured them

14. Advertisement, *School Science and Mathematics* 22 (Feb. 1922), 185.
15. Letter to the editor, *Wisconsin Journal of Education* 60 (Sept. 1927), 26–27; letter to the editor, *ibid.* (Oct. 1927), 87–88.
16. "English Instruction in Large Cities," *Sch R* 30 (Oct. 1922), 571–73.

that not all the themes had to be read by the teacher and who proposed devices such as mutual reading by students, reading themes before assemblies, and posting themes on bulletin boards. It would have taken rare courage for teachers to expose their students' products on bulletin boards without scanning them for "errors" and "correcting" them.

On the other hand, some critics argued that written composition was overemphasized at the expense of speech. "Nearly all business and professional work, with the exception of advertising and literary writing," said one critic in 1924, "is carried on through spoken language." Moreover, she added, the shift to spoken language would involve "the acquisition of a social viewpoint and the reorganization and renewal of subject matter based on social needs." Even this alluring possibility did not offer the English teachers escape from criticism. Their presumed shortcomings would be exposed by the way they taught speech. According to Walter Barnes, they were guilty of fostering "a pure-bred and a blue-blooded language . . . a high-brow and 'hifalutin' speech, patrician English, nasty-nice, top-lofty, schoolroom English." He challenged them to produce "a robust, vigorous American speech, full of snap and sparkle, of warmth and color, close to the life rooted in the soil."[17]

Still, while suppressing errors, inspiring creative themes, and motivating the use of sparkling speech, the English teacher could find refuge in the teaching of literature. It was probably literature that had seduced him as an undergraduate English major into teaching English, and some critics found in this a cause of students' defects in mechanics and grammar. One university professor voiced the suspicion that English teachers slighted composition and mechanics for what he called the "easier and more pleasant" task of teaching literature. A stern junior high school teacher went so far as to recommend putting literature into elective courses so that more of required English time could be spent on "drill in correct forms and in the recognition of incorrect forms."[18]

Very likely the teaching of literature was more pleasant, but it had its problems too, and closest to the heart of many teachers was that of elevating the taste of their students. The Tarzan books, said an English professor of Iowa State College in 1921, were "mere bosh"; students must

17. Elizabeth W. Baker, "Causes for the Demand for Spoken English," *EJ* 13 (Oct. 1924), 596; *NEA Proc*, 1922, p. 450.

18. Wilson, *EJ* 11 (June, 1922), 359; Cornell Atkinson, "The Need of Radical Revision in Our Junior High School English Courses of Study," *EA&S* 16 (April 1930), 301.

be brought to appreciate Hawthorne, Shakespeare, and George Eliot. "And the trinity of truth, imagination, and beauty," he said, "will conduct them to the goal of correct taste, even though they started at Tarzanville."[19] Not just grammar, apparently, but taste also could be correct.

In this task, English teachers felt confronted by students who came from a culture presumably indifferent, perhaps even hostile, to elevated taste. The chief enemy, some felt, was not Tarzan but the *Saturday Evening Post* and what was called the Saturday Evening Post mind. Surveys did show student preference for the *Saturday Evening Post, American Magazine,* and the like, and the prevalence of such magazines in homes. Favorite authors of books, according to a 1922 survey of high school students, were Zane Grey, Harold Bell Wright, and Arthur Conan Doyle. The call therefore seemed clear, to convert the children of George F. Babbitt to higher things. As one teacher expressed it, "We must meet them upon their own grounds or, to use their own expression, we must 'sell' them the idea of literature."[20]

The question was what to sell. Much of the merchandise for elevating taste, according to the critics, was too old to have market value. It consisted of the so-called classics inherited from the National Conference on Uniform Entrance Requirements in English. Many high schools were no longer preparing students to take examinations for college admission based on these selections, but the selections persisted nonetheless. Among them were various Shakespeare plays, essays by Macaulay and Carlyle, portions of *Paradise Lost*, novels by Dickens, and above all, the archsymbol of the classics to those who decried them, George Eliot's *Silas Marner.*

Survival of this list was indicated by various surveys in the 1920s. Conscientious teachers worked hard to interest their students in these and other standard works of literature and happily reported their successes in motivating their students to wide reading beyond the assigned tasks. One was rewarded for her work on *The Talisman* by having the students ask for more works by Scott. "Is not five weeks spent in the opening of such a vista to the immature mind," she asked, "of as much,

19. A. B. Noble, "Stepping-Stones to Correct Taste," *NEA Proc*, 1921, pp. 497, 501.
20. Dorrice A. Richards, "The Average Student," *EJ* 13 (Jan. 1924), 73; H. T. Eaton, "What High School Students Like To Read," *Education* 43 (Dec. 1922), 204–9; John J. Parry, " 'Selling' English Literature to Non-Literary Students," *EJ* 13 (Jan. 1924), 10–11.

if not more worth, than the same number of weeks spent on repeated drill of verbs, adverbs, and adjectives?"[21]

Critics might have agreed with her judgment about the value of literature over grammar, but not with her enthusiasm for the established classics. Scorn for these as materials for high schools came not only from professors of education: Howard Mumford Jones, then a professor of English at the University of North Carolina, in addressing the Northeastern Teachers Association of that state, called raising the level of their enjoyment "bologny." This, he said, was teaching literature, but not teaching Willie and Susie. In an age of jazz, radio, and airplanes, said Jones, knowledge of the English classics was no longer central, as it had been in the age of Byron. He proposed the substitution of Kipling and the Sherlock Holmes stories, and even these should be stripped of long descriptions. Apparently he thought *Ivanhoe* might be kept, for he prescribed cutting this classic to one-fourth its length.[22]

Educational sociologist David Snedden matched this by observing that the "rank and file of Americans" would "wisely prefer the *Saturday Evening Post* to Homer or Chaucer, or even Scott or Dickens." Sociologist and historian Harry Elmer Barnes agreed with Snedden and denounced "the bunk and snobbery which are the sole supports of the old-time classical education." Literary critic Louis Untermeyer, more gentle and possibly more devastating, observed that English teachers were no longer sticking to the old Bryant-Whittier line. "The golden day in American education may not yet have dawned," wrote Untermeyer, "but the teachers of Hannibal (Mo.) and Bloomington (Ill.) are no longer living in the dark ages."[23]

Only brief glimpses appear of what the students may have thought. One, purportedly at Los Angeles High School, characterized as "idiotic" the spending of weeks and weeks on *Idylls of the King* when there was

---

21. See Clara Hawks, "High School Classics—Surveys and Suggestions," *High School Conference*, 1921, p. 194, and Erna B. Conrad and Katherine Hickok, "Placement of Literary Selections for Junior and Senior High Schools," *EJ* 19 (May 1930), 381–82; Rosalie W. Ullman, "The Dalton Plan Awakens Desired Interest in the Study of Literature," *Education* 47 (June 1927), 606–11; Jennie Allensworth, "Teaching *The Talisman* in Ninth-Grade English," *EJ* 18 (Dec. 1929), 839–42.

22. "The Fetish of the Classics," *EJ* 18 (March 1929), 225, 227, 238–39.

23. Quoted in "Professor Snedden Attacks the Classics; Professor Abbott Defends Them," *TCR* 32 (Jan. 1931), 387; "Dr. Barnes Approves Professor Snedden's Attack on 'Bunk and Snobbery,'" *ibid.* (May 1931), 752; "Pegasus in High School," *American Mercury* 17 (June 1929), 64.

literature worth studying. Moreover, continued this "Disgusted Student," as he signed himself, 90 percent of the students did no creative thinking but were merely " 'Yes-yessing' everything the teacher says." One must, however, take on faith the authenticity of this letter as coming from a student. In another glimpse, a teacher recorded her delight when a senior girl in "a commercial division" said, "I wish we could read 'L'Allegro'; I'm sick of business letters."[24]

As Untermeyer had noted, however, some teachers were using contemporary literature along with or in place of the classics, moving students from Zane Grey and the Tom Swift series to Willa Cather, Joseph Conrad, Sinclair Lewis, and George Bernard Shaw, along with Hawthorne and George Eliot; or to Amy Lowell, with readings in Robert Frost, Carl Sandburg, and Edwin Arlington Robinson. In one of the most positive of the observations recorded in this period, a visitor to an English class at the DeWitt Clinton High School of New York City enthusiastically described a discussion on Thoreau to which the students related the writings of Sinclair Lewis, Sherwood Anderson, and Zona Gale. "The teacher," said this visitor, "was splendid in his ability to get the boys to talk. He was one with them, stimulating free discussion and offering suggestions without imposing his opinions on them."[25]

Inevitably there was much concern in this period about adapting the grammar and literature of English to those variously known as slow learners, the retarded, or low ability students. "Children of weak intellects," observed one teacher, "will rarely learn to distinguish a full sentence from a part of one." For such students, she recommended doing away with formal grammar, requiring little written work apart from letters, and using simple content material in place of classical literature. Contrariwise, the English subcommittee in the Department of Superintendence fifth yearbook, *The Junior High School Curriculum* (Washington, D.C., 1927, pp. 111–12), recommended more time on systematic grammar for slow students. One study proposed that the goal in reading and literature for slow groups be getting them to read *American Magazine* and *Liberty* with some understanding and discrimination, to which

24. Quoted in "Too Strong on 'Idylls'!" *California Quarterly of Secondary Education* 4 (June 1926), 449; Doris P. Merrill, "The Fascinating Game of Teaching," *EJ* 18 (Sept. 1929), 573.

25. Carie Belle Parks, "Literary Escalators: Literature for Everybody," *EJ* 19 (Sept. 1930), 526–43; Edith R. Glaser, "A Project in Modern Poetry," *EJ* 18 (June 1929), 477–82; J. U., "Report of a Visit to the English Department of the De Witt [Clinton] High School," *High Points* 9 (May 1927), 57–58.

the writer who reported this added, "I hope you will not think me face-
tious if I set up the *Saturday Evening Post* as a higher activity for the
more enterprising and able of the group."[26]

Teachers of English in the 1920s contended as mightily as they could
with the realities of the times. They tried to promote good writing and
speech; to please the professors who demanded graduates free from
errors and other professors who scoffed at the idea of errors as purist
nonsense; to raise the level of reading tastes, perhaps in concession to
what some call the genteel tradition, both by enlivening the classics and
by introducing more recent works; and to adapt all these efforts to students of widely varying ability and background. These things they sought
in an age characterized by Howard Mumford Jones as one of radio,
airplanes, and jazz.

Some teachers went beyond this. A group in Cleveland in 1928–29
stimulated the writing of more than four hundred plays, and students in
an unnamed high school in California "acted more than a hundred
comedies long and short." Wadleigh High School in New York City
allowed some of its seniors to elect English courses in comparative literature, modern drama and stagecraft, or modern drama and playwriting.[27]
Perhaps no one could really tell just what English was, but there were
those who showed by example what it could be.

III

Except when taken to mean an integrated and seamless entity, the
term *social studies* referred generically to a collection of separate subjects
including history. Some doubted the credentials of history, but what was
known as the "new history" proudly displayed its expansion beyond the
chronology of wars and kings.

By the 1920s the new history was beginning to show signs of age,
although Harry Elmer Barnes as late as 1927 was still attacking the
"desperate" historians of the old school, who driven from their "previous
havens of refuge" in the "political framework of history and the national-

26. Louise Anderson Macdonald, "English for the Inferior Section of the Ninth
Grade," *EJ* 12 (Nov. 1923), 613; G. Derwood Baker, "Curricular Adjustments To
Meet the Needs of Individual Pupils in the Junior High School," *California
Quarterly of Secondary Education* 4 (June 1929), 359.

27. Kenneth Macgowan, "Drama's New Domain—The High School," *Harper's
Magazine* 159 (Nov. 1929), 774; "Elective Courses in Senior English," *High Points*
10 (May 1928), 16–22.

istic mode of compartmentalization" were trying to set up a last line of defense in such categories as ancient, medieval, and modern history. The new historian, said Barnes, sought his insights through biology, anthropogeography, psychology, and sociology.[28]

This shift undoubtedly gave history more respectability among educators and helped guarantee its survival in the high school curriculum. At the same time it exposed history even more to extrinsic demands. As a high school teacher of Eureka, California, drawing inspiration from the Cardinal Principles Report, expressed it, only as history presented "a complete and reliable picture of the past" would it arrive at understanding of how present civilization came to be, and only then would it "contribute its fullest measure towards the end of social efficiency . . . and justify its demands for a place in the high school curriculum."[29]

For another teacher, at Westport High School, Kansas City, Missouri, history could be regarded as a social science only if regarded as training for citizenship. "Social welfare," he concluded, "should be the aim of all courses in social sciences such as History, Civics, Sociology, etc. History may be written for the sake of history only for adults. *There is no place in the elementary school nor in the high school for pure history.*" He was backed up in this by a professor at the University of Iowa who declared that "whatever is for social efficiency should occupy the paramount place in the curriculum" and that the primary aim of teaching history was to make good citizens.[30]

Such observations were by no means new. History and other subjects had long since been claimed as vehicles for broad external aims such as character-building and citizenship. More specifically, selected materials from history had been used by partisans for political and religious ends. Now in 1924 David Snedden, who had earlier been skeptical of the value of history, conceded that it could be used "to produce certain kinds and degrees of civic qualities"; The problem was one of selection. For civic purposes, explained Snedden, history "must be drawn upon when and where needs are indicated by a . . . plan of civic education in much the

28. "The Essentials of the New History," *Historical Outlook* 18 (May 1927), 202–6.
29. Frances N. Ahl, "Objectives and Methods in History," *Historical Outlook* 13 (June 1922), 215.
30. H. V. Harmon, "History and Social Sciences in the Secondary Schools," *School and Community* 9 (June 1923), 265; Horace T. C. Tu, "The Chief Social Objectives of Social Studies in the High School," *Educator-Journal* 23 (Jan. 1923), 163–64.

same way that navigation or bridge-building draws upon mathematics or mechanics for materials needed at the moment."[31]

There were protests of course. Professor Elmer Ellis of the University of Missouri objected to what he called job analysis for citizenship. He agreed with the civic aim, but felt it would be better promoted by "making modern life comprehensible to the individual so that he can act intelligently in relation to it."[32] Few, however, had the temerity to defend history for its own sake. History in the 1920s was meant to be good for something other than itself.

The question became what kind of history would do the most such good. American history was taken for granted, not only because of its closeness to the student's environment but also because of its relationship to citizenship and patriotism. Widespread public commitment to American history, however, proved to be a source of discomfort and even danger, since it evoked outbursts against the supposedly un-American character of the teaching of the subject, especially of the textbooks used in it.

Although agitation about American history textbooks flared up in all parts of the country, books used in New York City (1920–22) and in Chicago (1927–28) attracted the most widespread attention. In New York, the report of a special committee of principals and teachers, chaired by the district superintendent for Queens, distinguished between the functions of historians and those of textbook writers. Historians, said the report, wrote for open markets, but the job of textbook writers was "to furnish the teacher with the material the latter needs to carry out the aims and purposes set by the course of study." Textbooks should avoid controversial topics. The committee absolved the authors of intentional lack of patriotism, but found the usefulness of some of the books impaired because they were "written from the point of view of a critical historian rather than from the point of view of a teacher." Among other faults of textbook writers charged in this report was failure to realize that many facts of history should be taught not as ends, but as means to ends.[33]

The conflict in Chicago was a part of William Hale Thompson's suc-

31. "History Studies in Schools: For What Purpose?" *TCR* 25 (Jan. 1924), 7–9.
32. "A Basis for the Selection of Materials in Social Studies Teaching," *Historical Outlook* 22 (April 1931), 157.
33. Quoted in "Report on History Textbooks Used in the Public Schools of New York City," *Historical Outlook* 13 (Oct. 1922), 251, 255.

cessful campaign for mayor and its accompanying denunciation of Superintendent William McAndrew. As in New York, the Chicago episode hung on allegedly pro-British influence and the supposed disparagement of the American revolution and its leaders. An article published over Thompson's name in *Current History* argued that just as the spiritual life of the Christian church rested on belief in the divinity of Christ, so did American patriotism rest on an acceptance of George Washington and the righteousness of his cause. Take that away, said this article, and "the patriotic structure falls."[34]

Some educators were shocked by, others acquiesced in, the ideas represented by these attacks.[35] Those who acquiesced did so not necessarily from fear but from conviction. The following, for example, appeared in an editorial note in *American Educational Digest:* "The exposures relating to history text-books in New York City and State, Washington, D.C., Wisconsin, and Oregon led to considerable public indignation throughout the country. . . . What has been called a purification movement should be continued until text-books are freed from foreign influence and cease to be a vehicle for exploiting the personal opinions of authors on international or domestic politics."[36]

Agreement came also from some of the publishers. "Radical writing in newspapers and weeklies," said an April 1920 Macmillan Company advertisement in *Historical Outlook,* "radical talking from platforms and street corners sow seeds of dreadful potentiality. Sound teaching from sound textbooks in every school in the land is the nation's surest defense against the reversion to barbarism toward which loose thinking and ignorance tends" (11:132). In the same magazine the American Book Company advertised its commitment to the right kind of instruction in history needed to implant "an intelligent and enduring patriotism" to counteract tendencies to "lack of high ideals, unbridled criticism of our government, and the idea that liberty means license" (p. 130). Doubleday, Page & Company in a February 1924 issue claimed that its textbook was "so permeated by a healthy Americanism as to leave an enduring impression for good on the mind of the student" (15:95). On the other

34. "Shall We Shatter the Nation's Idols in School Histories?" *Current History* 27 (Feb. 1928), 625.
35. For example, Albert Bushnell Hart, " 'Treasonable' Textbooks and True Patriotism," *Current History* 27 (Feb. 1928), 630–32; editorial, *ER* 66 (Oct. 1923), 168–70.
36. "The Purification Movement," 43 (Oct. 2, 1923), 72.

hand, in the September 1923 issue of the *Illinois Teacher* the Public School Publishing Company proudly advertised its *Story of Our English Grandfathers,* by George P. Brown (Bloomington, Illinois, 1903), in explicit defiance of the attacks in New York City (12:18).

Only rarely were attacks made against textbooks in any but American history.[37] There were problems, however, of course organization and the program of studies. In the 1920s these centered on a seemingly new course called world history. No national group explicitly recommended this course, although two committees made proposals tending in that direction, both of them in the period immediately following the war. The Committee on History and Education for Citizenship in the Schools (American Historical Association) suggested a course in modern world history from the mid-seventeenth century to the present.[38] The Committee on the Teaching of Sociology in Elementary and High Schools (American Sociological Society) did not confine itself to sociology, but recommended a course in European history taught as social evolution.[39] This recommendation was interpreted by the chairman, Ross L. Finney, as one for a survey of general history;[40] the term *general history* was an older one that had been used to describe courses in universal history or the history of mankind from earliest times. Such courses had flourished spasmodically, usually under the stern disapproval of historians,[41] and the title still appeared in some schools in the 1920s.

The new world history, for many teachers, promised to be a vehicle for teaching the meaning of progress; in the words of a teacher at the William Penn High School in Philadelphia, "the best preparation for an acceptance of growth and change in contemporary society." Noting the embarrassing resemblance of world history to the older general history, she found in the themes of evolution and progress clarity and unity that made world history a better course. Some of the enthusiasm for the evolutionary view of world history came from the appearance in 1920 of

37. See "Educational Notes and News," *S&S* 31 (May 10, 1930), 643, for a controversy in New York City.
38. American Historical Association, *Annual Report for the Year 1920* (Washington, D.C., 1925), pp. 91–93.
39. American Sociological Society, *Papers and Proceedings of the Fourteenth Annual Meeting* (Chicago, 1919), pp. 243–46.
40. "Course in General History from the Sociologists' Standpoint," *Historical Outlook* 11 (June 1920), 221.
41. For example, Committee of Seven of the American Historical Association, *The Study of History in Schools* (New York, 1899), pp. 44–52.

H. G. Wells' *The Outline of History*. A classroom teacher in Palestine, Illinois, for example, used Wells' book and its "evolutionary idea" in advancing what he called general European history. Professor J. Montgomery Gambrill of Teachers College also saw the influence of H. G. Wells in the world history course.[42]

In a survey made for the American Historical Association in 1923, world history appeared in the offerings of 14 percent of the 2,404 schools in the responding group. This survey also showed the persistence of older courses, with ancient history in 44 percent of the schools, mediaeval and modern in 35 percent, and English history in 14 percent,[43] courses that had been recommended by the Committee of Seven of the American Historical Association in 1899.[44] A survey at the end of the decade showed that world history was offered in slightly more than half of some 2,000 schools in the North Central Association.[45] The 1928 survey of subject enrollments by the Bureau of Education showed a relative enrollment for world history of 7 percent, still behind ancient history at 10 percent and mediaeval and modern at 11.[46] Ancient history was stereotyped as a college preparatory subject, and its survival was taken as evidence of college domination. The high school at Morris, Illinois, for example, in 1923 provided ancient history for those in the groups called general and college preparatory, but world history for the commercial group.[47]

To the efficiency educators of this period all history was academic but in varying degrees: ancient hopelessly so, world history less, and American almost not at all. The subjects really favored by them and promoted in programs of curriculum revision were the other social studies: community civics, civil government, sociology, economics, and a course in problems of democracy that had been recommended by the social studies

42. Jessie C. Evans, "The Teaching of International Relations through the Social Studies,"*Historical Outlook* 14 (Oct. 1923), 253, 251; O. L. Bockstahler, "European History in High Schools," *J Ed* 95 (Jan. 12, 1922), 39; "The New World History," *Historical Outlook* 18 (Oct. 1927), 265–66.

43. Edgar Dawson, "The History Inquiry," *Historical Outlook* 15 (June 1924), 252–60.

44. *Study of History in Schools*, pp. 34–43.

45. Arthur D. Gray, "The One-Year Course in World History," *Historical Outlook* 23 (Dec. 1932), 408.

46. *Off Ed bull* 1930, no. 16, *Biennial Survey of Education 1926–1928*, p. 1057. Subsequent enrollment figures for 1922 and 1928 in this chapter are from this reference.

47. L. B. Maxwell, "Social Science Curriculum in the Morris High School," *High School Conference*, 1923, p. 375.

report of the Commission on the Reorganization of Secondary Education of 1916.[48] Geography had a marginal existence as a kind of poor relation that could be forgotten or ignored. The various subjects in this category of other social studies competed vigorously with one another, especially in the twelfth grade, where the course in problems of democracy helped resolve the claims of civil government, sociology, and economics on the school's time by incorporating all three.

Government appeared twice in the sequence, first in the eighth or ninth grade as part of community civics, later in eleventh or twelfth as civil government (in the terminology of the Bureau of Education), or simply as either government or civics. The study of government received massive support from groups, such as the National Security League, that identified patriotism with knowledge of the constitution. The league, originating in the period of the World War, during which it had fought the teaching of German, dedicated itself in the early 1920s to promoting state laws on the teaching of the constitution, and was successful in twenty-two states by the summer of 1923. The model bill offered by the league did not specify a particular course, but called for continuous instruction beginning not later than the eighth grade and extending through high school and college. The league's Committee on Constitutional Instruction set aside the summer of 1923 for the follow-up of "the state and local superintendents where the law has been passed to see that it is carried into effect."[49]

Economics was promoted by the American Bankers' Association as protection against radicalism. According to Lewis E. Pierson, chairman of the fiftieth-anniversary committee of the association in 1925, there was nothing to fear from radicalism if the people understood "the unchangeable laws" underlying business and government.[50] Individual bankers also supported economics, for example Orrin C. Lester, vice-president of the Bowery Savings Bank in New York City, who in his address to the metropolitan district of the New York State Congress of Parents and

48. Committee on Social Studies of the Commission on the Reorganization of Secondary Education, *The Social Studies in Secondary Education,* Bur Ed bull 1916, no. 28, pp. 52–53.

49. "Teaching Children United States Constitution Now Required in Twenty-Two States," *Educator-Journal* 23 (July 1923), 529–30.

50. Quoted in "The Proposed Scholarships of the American Bankers' Association," *S&S* 22 (Oct. 10, 1925), 458.

Teachers said the subject would help youth gain "a clearer realization of their economic responsibilities."[51]

Advocacy of economics was not confined to bankers. Teaching economics was teaching prosperity, said a writer in *American Review of Reviews* in 1925. Within a generation or two, "generally accepted economic truths" would be taught to all students in junior and senior high schools, and he wanted to hasten the day. Economics obviously involved a variety of social aims, and these were invoked by those who supported the cause. Identifying economic life with social life, E. L. Bogart of the University of Illinois branded those who disobeyed economic law as dangerous members of society. On a loftier plane, Walter C. Pankratz of the University of Chicago claimed that economics promoted ethical values, such as seeking the good of humanity and the development of public spirit.[52]

Sociology had less colorful sponsorship and a more obscure image in the public mind. According to a group of school administrators who were asked their opinions in a survey, the use of a problems approach in sociology emphasized abnormalities and led to a distorted view of society. The professor at the University of Washington who reported this survey recommended taking their advice, so that people would not confuse sociology with socialism, bolshevism, altruism, reform, and social work. Ross L. Finney feared that the course in problems of democracy also emphasized social pathology. Social studies, thought Finney, should emphasize the normality of everyday relationships rather than problems.[53]

Although problems of democracy combined sociology, government, and economics, it did not present the completely integrated or unified social studies which flourished in this period in elementary schools and to some extent in secondary education, particularly the junior high school grades. Identified with Harold Rugg and his associates at Lincoln School of Teachers College, it was not merely "progressive" but avant-garde. Rugg made his approach to unification through "the insistent and permanent problems and issues of contemporary economic, social, and politi-

51. Quoted in "Practical Economics," *Sch R* 36 (June 1928), 406–7.
52. Alvan T. Simonds, "Teaching Prosperity," 71 (Feb. 1925), 186–88; "How and Why Economics Should Be Taught in the High Schools," *ER* 61 (May 1921), 427–28; "Economics As a High-School Subject," *Historical Outlook* 17 (Dec. 1926), 378.
53. Bain Read, "Sociology in Washington High Schools," *Sch R* 34 (Sept. 1926), 537–38; "What Do We Mean by 'Community Civics' and 'Problems of Democracy'?" *Sch R* 32 (Sept. 1924), 521–28.

cal life," drawing these from the writings of "frontier thinkers," such as Beard, Lippmann, Laski, and Bryce.[54]

In 1923 Rugg, his brother Earle, and Emma Schweppe, all of Lincoln School, recommended a unified social studies curriculum for junior high schools. The program was presented for students in six pamphlets based on Rugg's research and destined to form the basis for his later controversial textbooks. The unifying subjects appeared in the pamphlet titles: *America and Her Immigrants, The City and Key Industries in Modern Nations, The Westward Movement and the Growth of Transportation, The Mechanical Conquest of America, Americanizing Our Foreign-Born,* and *Resources and Industries in a Machine World.* "Current modes of living, contemporary problems and their historical backgrounds," explained Rugg and his associates, "can be learned more effectively through one unified social science curriculum than through the separate school subjects, history, geography, civics, and economics." Furthermore, they said, this unification was not based on the merger of established subjects, but rather was one that "completely disregards current courses."[55]

Rugg's efforts were by no means the only experiments in social studies, nor even the only ones aimed at unification. A survey made in 1923–24 uncovered a number of others, including the Pennsylvania program under the direction of J. Lynn Barnard in the state department of public instruction, the program of the University High School of the University of Missouri, and the proposals of Leon C. Marshall of the University of Chicago. Marshall worked out his ideas in a series of pamphlets for junior high schools organized around the story of human progress, the individual's place in society, and the principles of social organization.[56]

This ferment attracted widespread attention and evoked both applause and criticism from the toilers in the social studies field. To some, even, the term *social studies* came to mean exclusively the attempts at unification. In defending the name of the newly formed National Council for the Social Studies in 1922, Edgar Dawson felt compelled to offset this

54. "Problems of Contemporary Life As the Bases for Curriculum-Making in the Social Studies," National Society for the Study of Education twenty-second yearbook, part 2, *The Social Studies in the Elementary and Secondary School* (Bloomington, Ill., 1923), pp. 262, 266–68.

55. "A Proposed Social Science Course for the Junior High School," National Society for the Study of Education twenty-second yearbook, part 2, pp. 186–87.

56. J. Montgomery Gambrill, "Experimental Curriculum-Making in the Social Studies," *Historical Outlook* 15 (Jan. 1924), 37–55; (Feb. 1924), 384–406.

impression by pointing out that the council's use of the term did not mean endorsement "of a hash of all kinds of subject matter thrown together either at random or under the stimulus of the temporary and fleeting inclination of children." Culinary imagery appealed to the critics, and some referred to unified social studies as social stew. By 1926, however, Rugg's experimental pamphlets were being used in more than one hundred school systems, and according to one teacher in Chicago Heights, Illinois, were being used with enthusiasm. The only criticism was that some of the material was too technical or difficult for the junior high school grades.[57]

Some critics of Rugg's materials favored unification but disagreed with his approach. Robert S. Lynd, a social scientist, feared that Rugg stressed large public questions at the expense of the face-to-face skills needed in everyday social life. Perhaps, thought Lynd, the idea of social studies was already beginning to harden into fixed forms. As important as learning about the tariff and international affairs, in his view, was "the learning of the elaborate switchboard of keys by which one comes to terms with the person and property of others with the minimum of social friction." Finally, said Lynd, there probably was no reason for unification to stop at the boundaries of the social studies, and the future might well see "the obliteration of the line between 'social' and 'natural' sciences and the organization of the activity of training the young around man's life-activities."[58] Such flights would begin to engage the attention of curriculum workers, including Rugg himself, in the following decade. In the 1920s, Rugg's proposals for unified social studies caused consternation enough.

IV

Mathematics, too, had a movement for unification. "What we propose to do," declared William David Reeve of the University of Minnesota High School to his audience of principals and superintendents in April, 1920, "what we are already doing in the University High School . . . is to arrange all these courses so that we shall not have courses in algebra, geometry, or trigonometry as such, but a definitely arranged and psycho-

---

57. "The National Council Again," *Historical Outlook* 13 (Feb. 1922), 49; Floyd T. Goodier, "The Rugg Plan of Teaching History," *High School Conference,* 1926, pp. 323–27.
58. "What Are 'Social Studies'?" *S&S* 25 (Feb. 19, 1927), 216–19.

logically ordered course in mathematics." Such reorganization, Reeve promised, would include analytic geometry and some of the calculus, thereby making possible a four-year course in mathematics for high schools that would cover the materials of the conventional program plus those of the first two or three semesters of college work.[59]

Reeve spoke in the context of an international movement among mathematicians that had been in progress since the turn of the century. He was expressing also what was to be a major theme in the discussions of mathematics education throughout the 1920s. Support for this movement, variously called general, correlated, or unified mathematics, came from various quarters, but especially from the National Committee on Mathematical Requirements, a group that had been formed under the auspices of the Mathematical Association of America in 1916. Among the members of this committee were academic mathematicians from universities and colleges, representatives of state departments, and secondary school teachers of mathematics.

In its complete report, *The Reorganization of Mathematics in Secondary Education,* published in 1923, the committee recommended three years of required mathematics for grades seven through nine and electives for grades ten through twelve. For the three junior high school years it offered five plans for courses incorporating combinations of arithmetic, algebra, geometry, and parts of trigonometry. The elective work of grades ten through twelve was to continue work in algebra, geometry, and trigonometry and add materials in statistics and calculus. As the committee saw the state of affairs in the early 1920s, the materials for grades ten to twelve could probably be given "most advantageously" as separate units. It added its opinion, however, that "methods of organization are being experimentally perfected whereby teachers will be enabled to present much of this material more effectively in combined courses unified by one or more of such central ideas as functionality and graphic representation."[60]

Possibly the 1923 report was not "one that stood unparalleled in the annals of all nations," as one enthusiastic teacher in Quincy, Illinois, described it,[61] but it was widely distributed, applauded, and discussed.

59. "General Mathematics for the High School," *EA&S* 6 (May-June 1920), 263.

60. National Committee on Mathematical Requirements, *The Reorganization of Mathematics in Secondary Education* (Hanover, N.H., 1923), pp. 39–40.

61. Marie E. Nelson, "Ideals in the Teaching of Mathematics As Presented in the National Committee Report," *High School Conference,* 1924, p. 192.

Even Harold Rugg praised it as one approach to curriculum planning, although he criticized it for not involving experts in curriculum construction and for not basing its recommendations on social and psychological needs.[62] Some textbook companies were proud to set forth their wares as in line with the committee's recommendations. It enjoyed then what might be called a good pedagogical press.

The term *general mathematics,* however, evoked a variety of images. Some thought of it as a way of organizing mathematics for non-college-preparatory students. One principal who advocated this, however, expressed the hope that the colleges would come to accept general mathematics too.[63] To others, general mathematics was meant for students of low ability in mathematics or with little interest in the subject. A teacher at New Trier Township High School, Illinois, was willing to permit general mathematics for those who probably would never take more than a year or two of mathematics in high school, but he regarded this clearly as second best. "Never have we received a student transferred from a school where they are using this system," he said, "who seemed to know very much about either algebra or geometry."[64]

Not only direct attacks, but friendly misunderstandings, therefore, plagued true believers in general mathematics like Assistant Superintendent Marie Gugle of Columbus, Ohio. A better name for general mathematics, she felt, would be real mathematics. She objected to its identification with categories of the school population, and implied that it had originated from dissatisfaction with the traditional college-preparatory mathematics. General mathematics, she argued, was the best possible foundation for further work in either college or shop.[65]

By the end of the decade, the advocates of general mathematics were discouraged. In 1928 William Betz, vice-principal of East High School in Rochester, New York, was expressing the fear that the recommendations of the 1923 report were still in large measure visions.[66] John A. Swenson of Teachers College was even more pessimistic: "Two things

62. "Curriculum-Making: What Shall Constitute the Procedure of National Committees?" *Journal of Educational Psychology* 15 (Jan. 1924), 23–39.

63. R. D. Shouse, "Required Mathematics in the Four Year High School," *School Science and Mathematics* 22 (Jan. 1922), 15–19.

64. W. A. Snyder, "The Middle of the Road," *High School Conference,* 1926, p. 251.

65. "Mathematics in the Junior and Senior High Schools," *School Science and Mathematics* 25 (Jan. 1925), 31-35.

66. "The Reorganization of Secondary School Mathematics," *Prog. Ed.* 5 (Oct. 1928), 376.

dominate the high school field in mathematics today," said Swenson in 1931, "the puzzle problem and the old-type Euclidean geometry. The National Committee recommended something more than this for us, but we do not seem able to agree to accept their recommendation."[67] Actually these expressions of defeat were more poignant than accurate. The movement had made some headway in grades seven through nine of junior high schools. Above ninth grade there was little change, possibly because the recommendations of the 1923 report had been less explicit for that level.

Another movement for curriculum revision in mathematics was directed toward practical application. The issue, said Henry Harap of the Cleveland School of Education, was whether to prepare for enjoyment of intellectual pleasures or for change in modes of living. Much of what went on in the name of education, explained Harap, was a heritage of the "privileged few" which the proletariat too often aspired to regardless of its worth. The American people, he said, "are the factory workers and farm hands who live simple lives on a low intellectual and economic level." He proceeded accordingly to outline the mathematics that could be used for family budgeting and recommended its study in relation to taxes, rent, home decoration, nutrition, and fuel. Such mathematics might be the equal of "pure mathematics" even in preparation for college.[68]

Along similar lines, Theodore Lindquist of the Emporia, Kansas, State Normal School proposed business applications for the work of the ninth grade, not as specialized business mathematics in the business course but for all students. With the consumer emphasis in mind, Lindquist declared that business applications should be taught for "the person outside of the counter" rather than for "the one inside of the counter." He suggested the study of interest, bank accounts, investments, and insurance. "Civic and economic questions," said Lindquist, "must be studied from the quantitative standpoint in order to produce real results in the development of good citizenship. This is merely the application of business mathematics to the social group in place of the individual."[69] After the 1920s the term *general mathematics* was increasingly used for courses with such practical applications, and it gradually became identified with such

67. "The Newer Type of Secondary Mathematics," University of Pennsylvania School of Education, *Eighteenth Annual Schoolmen's Week Proceedings*, 1931, p. 565.
68. "Mathematics for the Consumer," *ER* 74 (Oct. 3, 1927), 162–67.
69. "Application of Business Principles in Junior High School Mathematics," *S&S* 12 (Oct. 9, 1920), 306–7.

courses. Much of the material recommended by Lindquist had been an accepted part of the old grammar school arithmetic for the upper grades.

Demands for the practical did not evoke approval in all quarters. Headmaster Eugene Randolph Smith of the Beaver Country Day School, Chestnut Hill, Massachusetts, for one, was willing to make some concessions to practical aims, but he argued eloquently for broader values, especially what he called an attitude of "happily and confidently undertaking problems of whatever sort, attained only through having been led by past experience to appreciate the joy of accomplishment," a statement reminiscent of what Charles W. Eliot had called joy and gladness in achievement.[70] Charles H. Judd of the University of Chicago saw mathematics as one of the "intellectual methods of arrangement by which the complexities of the world may be unraveled and a new pattern made of experience,"[71] a sophisticated version of the functional aims, perhaps.

Although long condemned by the efficiency educators, mental discipline was still invoked as a goal in the 1920s by those who defended academic mathematics. According to the superintendent of schools of Baldwin, New York, mathematics developed accuracy, thoroughness, perseverance, and clear thinking. The principal of the Port Leyden, New York, high school said that there was no subject like first-year algebra for developing the powers of abstraction and generalization.[72]

Another who was deeply committed to mental discipline was George S. Painter of the Albany, New York, State College for Teachers, for whom education was "far less valuable in the knowledge we acquire than in the mental power and discriminative judgment developed by the process." Sharp-tongued in his advocacy of this point of view, Painter denounced what he called the vulgar utility of the parvenu educational iconoclast who was "abroad in the land" in the 1920s and who with "opprobrious assurance" did not hesitate "to lay unholy hands upon our most sacred educational traditions and institutions."[73]

Painter was reacting not only to the more soberly couched demands for practical aims but to a general pattern of hostility often voiced against

---

70. "Mathematics in the School of the Future," *TCR* 30 (May 1929), 803; "Status of Education at Close of Century," *NEA Proc*, 1900, p. 198.
71. "The Fallacy of Treating School Subjects As 'Tool Subjects,' " *NEA Proc*, 1927, p. 251.
72. Arthur E. Newton and Edward W. Glasby, quoted in "Why Teach Mathematics in the New York State High Schools?" *New York State Education* 16 (March 1929), 536 and 538.
73. "Mathematics As a Study," *ER* 59 (Jan. 1920), 36, 19.

mathematics or its academic aspects. Even the most acrimonious critics rarely suggested that mathematics teaching be abolished, but their pronouncements inevitably gave offense to those who loved the subject and had given their careers to it. Algebra and geometry as traditionally taught, said a caustic editorial in the *School Review* in November 1921, were intolerable failures and out of keeping with the legitimate demands of the times. Teachers of algebra and geometry, continued this editorial, had remained static while "civilization has marched on" (29:641).

One textbook company, The American Book Company, sought to promote its own series in mathematics by ridiculing teachers afflicted with what it called "mathematical passion," an expression attributed in the text of the advertisement to an unidentified "doctor in education." Such mathematical passion, according to both the doctor and the copywriter, was a bad thing indeed. "The presence of this disease," the advertisement pointed out, "is indicated by an obsession that mathematics is mainly significant for itself—that mathematical power is the main objective." Those afflicted with the disease wanted "book problems to furnish exercises for the development of mathematical power, instead of real, environmental problems that need solving for efficient living here and now." Its own three-book series, promised the company, was free of such passion and instead presented mathematics "for the control of socioeconomic factors in the actual lives of young people." Those who suffered from mathematical passion were advised to read John Dewey for the cure.[74]

Some of the critics were concerned with abolishing algebra and geometry, not as offerings but as requirements for graduation. Their zeal often led to hostile rhetoric. "For surely," said Philip W. L. Cox of the New York University School of Education, "the slaughter of the innocents is not justified in the vain effort to teach youths knowledges and skills for which they have no use and which even the few who succeed in passing the subjects do not retain." If the advocates of mathematics studied the failure rates, said Cox, they "might be aghast at the death and destruction that prescribed and even recommended mathematics courses scatter in their trains." Cox did favor elective mathematics for "intellectual play such as characterizes true mathematicians," but with this concession he could not resist a final barb on how elective mathematics "would proba-

74. *California Quarterly of Secondary Education* 5 (June 1930), inside front cover.

bly mean that those of us who are peddling bogus wares will have to seek new jobs."[75]

Perhaps Cox and his fellow critics had a point in that algebra and geometry were still widely required. Was it fair to ask all students to contend with algebra and geometry? Were some incapable of learning these subjects? Teacher response was mixed on these questions, but teachers struggled with them often and long. "Either we had to change our curriculum so that little or no algebra was required for graduation," said a teacher at the Bloomington, Illinois, high school, "or we had to adjust the courses we had been requiring so that better results could be accomplished. After much thought and deliberation, we decided to attempt the latter policy." She felt that adjusting the work had reduced failures, but whether this was worth the effort she did not know. "As I look at the report cards of the pupils who are enrolled in our slow sections in algebra," she added, "I wonder what we could attempt to teach them in order to have the results justify the time spent, for their slowness is not confined to algebra."[76]

Some teachers looked for an index of ability that would identify in advance those students capable of pursuing mathematics in the algebra-geometry sequence. The answer for Stephen Emery of the Erasmus Hall High School in Brooklyn was an intelligence quotient of 110 on the Terman Group Test. He found to his dismay that 1,462 students, or 41 percent of a group of 3,534 students taking mathematics at his school, were below this level. The failure rate in mathematics, however, was only 24 percent, but Emery explained the disparity as "representing the pressure of various kinds to pass students." Either the Terman test was not valid, he said, "or the programming of so many students into mathematics is a blunder, if not a crime, and should be discontinued." He concluded that it was the programming and not the test that was at fault. Even greater faith was expressed by a teacher at the Mount Hermon School in Massachusetts, who said that not all boys were able to learn algebra but that one with an intelligence quotient of 110 could do so if he wished.[77]

---

75. Editorial, *Junior-Senior High School Clearing House* 5 (Feb. 1931), 320–21.

76. Jessie M. Cline, "Adjusting Algebra to Ability Levels thru the Time Limits," *High School Conference*, 1928, pp. 214, 216.

77. "Intelligence Quotients and Mathematics at Erasmus Hall High School," *High Points* 11 (March, 1929), 35–38; Nelson A. Jackson, "Learning in First-Year Algebra," *School Science and Mathematics* 31 (Nov. 1931), 986.

It was a teacher of the so-called slow learners in geometry at the Proviso Township High School, Illinois, who came in 1924 to the disillusioned conclusion that some would not and others could not learn mathematics. "I wonder," she asked, "how many teachers really look forward to teaching a class of pupils, made up of those who are usually conceded to be slow to grasp a subject—especially when that subject is geometry?" Not very many, she thought, "if the comments of the average teacher of Mathematics may be used as a basis for forming this opinion." There were, she said, various kinds of students in such classes. Some were slow, some lazy, some afraid, and "the very fewest are really so utterly stupid that they are unable to grasp anything." Moreover, some of the students to whom she gave extra help thought she was doing it for overtime pay. "These people of limited ability," she asked, "do they ever amount to anything? Is it worth while?"[78]

For some, mathematics was going down in the ruins of all scholarship, for others who shared the booster spirit of the times, it was triumphant over all. Among the first was a teacher at Quincy, Illinois, who felt like one of a beleaguered host whose only chance for rescue came from the universities. "We are told by those who inspire us at our educational gatherings," she complained, "to 'teach boys and girls, not subjects.'" It was from "servility to the system" that she hoped universities could free the teachers, and she called on these last champions of scholarship to outline "concisely and specifically" what they wanted the high schools to do in mathematics. "Today she [the teacher] is bound by stupid demands and ethical sophistries," she observed. In her concluding outburst against what would later be called the establishment, she declared that silence was "the great dictum," but that if teachers were to tell what they knew—"well—."[79]

The booster spirit, on the other hand, appeared in a 1928 article by a journalist extolling the jazzing-up of mathematics. To her, all was being taken care of by modern content and methods. She directed her attention especially to geometry and arithmetic. The latter, she noted, was not what it used to be. "The hooped-skirt, puffed-hair age in this formerly regarded 'exact science,'" she said, "has changed to the bobbed-hair, short-skirt style." Modern students were figuring baseball records, the

78. Martha Hildebrandt, "Adapting Plane Geometry to Pupils of Limited Ability," *High School Conference*, 1924, pp. 185–88.

79. Jessie Brakensiek, "How the University May Help the High School Teachers." *High School Conference*, 1927, pp. 234–35.

increase in the number of aviators on long-distance flights, and the number of calories in a plate of corned beef and cabbage. By emphasizing the practical and cutting out nonessentials, high school students were learning not only algebra and geometry but trigonometry as well.[80] Thus were the critics confounded and the difficulties resolved. This was the Indian summer of the great age of American optimism. To some of its children, all questions were easy, including those in the curriculum of mathematics.

V

Some called it an age of science. Others saw in it antiscience, "with an active emotional hostility to science; to its conclusions, and especially to the process of reaching them."[81] What made it an age of science for many was the miracle technology of telephones, airplanes, and radios. What alarmed others was the wave of laws and proposed laws against the teaching of evolution, a phenomenon in the science curriculum that paralleled attacks against history textbooks.[82] The Dayton, Tennessee, trial of John Scopes was no unique episode but rather an instance of the times.

In this context of contradictions the science teachers of the 1920s, like the English teachers, grappled with the identity of their field. They rarely asked outright what science was, but they did discuss their own and the public's perceptions of it. Many were quite sure what science was not, particularly that science was not technology, a distinction seemingly rediscovered three decades later. As one teacher at the Eastern High School of Washington, D.C., put it, it was this distinction that made it necessary to reject the 1920s as an age of science. "Rather," he said, "it is an Age of Button Pushers."[83]

Purists deplored not only the view of science as technology but also that of science as a body of settled doctrines and facts. Benjamin C. Gruenberg, managing director of the American Association for Medical Progress and a former high school science teacher, for example, expressed the fear that the American mind was possessed by the idea of sound doctrine in science as well as in other fields. "This view of truth

80. Arretta L. Watts, "Jazzing Up Our Mathematics, *ER* 76 (Sept. 1928), 120–22.

81. Chester H. Rowell, "The Spread of Anti-Science in an American Commonwealth," *The Survey* 55 (Nov. 1, 1925), 159.

82. Maynard Shipley, *The War on Modern Science* (New York, 1927).

83. Henry Flury, "Is This an Age of Science?" *School Science and Mathematics* 28 (Jan. 1928), 76.

and of teaching," said Gruenberg, "is so ancient, so well established, and so widely accepted, that even teachers of science succumb to it, even while we are engaged in the teaching of science. In fact, we often take so much delight in exposing the errors of our predecessors that we help to fix more firmly than ever the notion that we have at last attained to true beliefs."[84]

As an example, perhaps, of what Gruenberg feared, a science teacher at the John Marshall High School, Rochester, New York, invoked science as a substitute for religion, possibly as religion itself. Convinced by Walter Lippmann that modernity had dissolved religion and other bases of authority, she declared "that if we wish to inculcate principles of right living and respect for law into our race, we must find an inner authority for so doing. This can come best through science and scientific thinking." Herbert Spencer had based both ethics and religion on science, "and for many of us in the world today, it is the only way we can accept them."[85] From this point of view the function of science was to deliver correct conclusions. The evil of the anti-evolution laws then lay in the obstacles they provided to the communication of truth.

If science was rejected as technology or as a body of settled conclusions, what then was the nature of the scientific enterprise? The answer of the critics and skeptics was one that would seem naive to a later generation: science was a universalized method for inquiry. Dedicated practice of this "scientific method" would, it was hoped, produce scientific-mindedness and reflective thought. "Science as a method of thinking," said a teacher at Hollywood High School, California, "is more valuable than science as a collection of facts." Furthermore, he declared, this would be the almost unanimous verdict of science teachers. What he feared was that it was not practiced, that among science teachers one could "easily find those who distribute facts for their pupils to hoard up, as old gentlemen in the park distribute nuts to squirrels." He did concede, however, that for many science teachers such behavior could be interpreted as "lapses."[86]

Other science teachers added their testimony of faith in scientific

84. "Scientific Education as a Defense against Propaganda and Dogma," *NEA Proc*, 1925, p. 600.
85. Edith Bradshaw, "What Do We Desire As Outcomes of Our Science Teaching Today?" *School Science and Mathematics* 31 (June 1931), 693.
86. Lowell C. Frost, "Teaching Science vs. Teaching Facts," *General Science Quarterly* 10 (Jan. 1926), 412.

method, along with expressions of uneasy conscience as to whether the faith was being kept. It was much more important, said the head of the department of science of the Washington, D.C., public schools, for students to be shown how conclusions are reached than to memorize the conclusions. Unfortunately, he said, "too many students acquire the idea that the scientific laws, theories, and hypotheses spring full-armed from the brains of geniuses as the result of some occult phenomenon which the average man never experiences."[87]

Comfort undoubtedly came to these self-doubting science teachers from the words of Joel H. Hildebrand, professor of chemistry at the University of California. "The students whom I like to have you send into my class," said Hildebrand to the NEA Department of Science Instruction in 1923, "and whom, I am glad to say, many of you do send in considerable numbers, are interested in science, are able to think and speak accurately, and are able to make some use of the scientific method." The primary aim, he said, was to teach science, not a science, "for science is a method, a point of view, a way of ascertaining truth."[88]

For some, both method and substance were important. Edwin E. Slosson, the director of Science Service, Washington, D.C., and the author of popular books on science, made an appeal for the "esthetic, intellectual, and moral benefit of scientific training." The science teacher had a double duty, first toward scientific method, but second to acquaint the student "with the mass of facts and laws that science has acquired, to see that he gets his share of the accumulated wisdom of the ages." Slosson was defending science as a cultural subject against the counter-claims of the humanities, "meaning mostly by that," he observed sarcastically, "the atrocities of the Trojan, Gallic, and Peloponnesian wars."[89]

This was the science not of technology but of wonderment, a survival in the twentieth century of the popular romanticism about science that had prevailed in the nineteenth. Fifty years before, said Ernest Von Nardroff, principal of Stuyvesant High School in New York City, natural philosophy had been one of the most popular subjects in school. "Then," he declared, "physics meant fascinating phenomena reproduced by the

87. Ellis Haworth, "What Shall Be the Science Program for the Junior and Senior High Schools?" NEA Proc, 1932, p. 470.

88. "Relation between College and Secondary School Science," NEA Proc, 1923, pp. 856, 860.

89. "Science-Teaching in a Democracy," National Association of Secondary School Principals Eighth Yearbook, 1924, 139–40.

teacher in superb and effective demonstrations. It meant animated discussion of these phenomena with the pupils. It provoked a deep admiration of the rich wonders of nature." By way of contrast, he feared, physics in 1928 meant "a stupid lot of quantitative exercises in the laboratory, followed by the preparation of elaborate notebooks, and often by a tiresome number of uninteresting problems—the whole thing largely a bore." According to Von Nardroff, demonstrations had disappeared first from the colleges, and the younger teachers had no model before them "of the opportunity for thrills that Physics affords."[90]

Some of the university academicians also favored this more "cultural" science, perhaps for more sophisticated reasons. Professor Alfred C. Kinsey of Indiana University did not hesitate to defend "a scientifically established nature study" for the biology courses in the schools. "The green of the hills and of the fields, the flash of the bird's wing," he rhapsodized, "the depth of the flower, the vibrant hum of the midsummer noon, the breath of the evening garden, the crashing forms of the midwinter storm—these are but chapters in the drama we call life." The task of the biology teacher was that "of introducing youth to the glory of this living world that is about us." He underscored his enthusiasm by bringing out a high school textbook in biology himself (*Introduction to Biology*, Philadelphia, 1926), one that was advertised as "human and enjoyable, enlivened by an unusual narrative gift and a practical sympathetic understanding of youth."[91]

There were those, also, who sought to bend science to the life-activities uses of the Cardinal Principles Report. In this they followed the tradition made explicit by Herbert Spencer in his 1859 essay "What Knowledge Is of Most Worth?" Arguing that all subjects should make their contribution to citizenship, J. Lynn Barnard, director of social studies in the Pennsylvania State Department of Public Instruction, observed that "problems of race assimilation, of public health and sanitation, can be solved only in the light of biological laws, which are as inescapable and universal in their nature and operation as are the laws of gravity."[92]

90. "Some Suggestions for Improving the Present Status of Physics in Our Schools," *High Points* 10 (March 1928), 3–4.

91. "Vitalizing the Biology Course," *High School Conference*, 1930, p. 69; "The Content of the Biology Course," *School Science and Mathematics* 30 (April 1930), 376; *TCR* 28 (Feb. 1927), inside front cover.

92. "Training in Citizenship in the Public School," *Pennsylvania School Journal* 71 (May 1923), 405.

The reference to race assimilation indicated the appeal such external aims for science had to those with leanings toward eugenics. A teacher at the Austin High School, Chicago, for example, felt that many of our social problems could be solved only by application of biological heredity and that this was threatened by the movement against evolution. "Since heredity and eugenics," he said, "are intimately related to the study of evolution, they are often omitted. It is a difficult matter to enlighten the public in regard to these subjects without the use of schools."[93]

In science as in all fields, there was the question of the relationship between university academicians and high school teachers. Chemistry provided an example of what such a relationship might be. The American Chemical Society created a National Committee on Chemical Education, with Neil C. Gordon, professor of chemistry at the University of Maryland, as chairman. The committee was made up of four college and university professors, two secondary school teachers, and three representatives from the chemical industry, and it held its first session in April 1923.[94] To the committee, the major problem was poor correlation between chemistry in high school and college, a fault attributed to both levels, and calling for radical reform.[95] Early in 1924 the society, through its division of chemical education, began publishing the *Journal of Chemical Education*, and in the same year the society's national committee proposed its "standard minimum high school course in chemistry."[96]

The work of the academicians in chemistry aroused the admiration and possibly the envy of those in physics, although the American Physical Society also had a committee on education. A college physics teacher, but one severely critical of physics teaching in college and university, praised the chemists for their interest in matters pedagogical. He called the *Journal of Chemical Education* a veritable "mine of information to the teacher" and said that one could see many effects of this work.[97]

Teachers in all the sciences were beset by the problem of keeping up

93. Amer M. Ballew, "Evolution, Heredity and Eugenics in High School Biology," *School Science and Mathematics* 29 (April 1929), 353.

94. Neil E. Gordon, "Preliminary Report of Committee on Chemical Education Relative to the Correlation of High School and College Chemistry," *School Science and Mathematics* 23 (Nov. 1923), 777–85.

95. "News Notes," *ER* 66 (Nov. 1923), 236.

96. "Correlation of High School and College Chemistry," *Journal of Chemical Education* 1 (May 1924), 87–99.

97. John A. Frayne, "The Plight of College Physics," *School Science and Mathematics* 28 (April 1928), 350.

with developments in their fields. It was one of the objects of the American Chemical Society to help chemistry teachers in this, a task of no mean proportions, since, according to Professor H. A. Webb of the George Peabody College for Teachers, the journal of abstracts of the Society published 22,800 items of research in chemistry for the year 1921 alone. "How difficult," he said, "to teach literally up-to-date chemistry, to present the latest, to even be sure of the best."[98]

Physics teachers were bombarded by mysterious references to something known as the new physics with which they were not keeping up. If ordinary physics was hard for the student, the new physics would presumably be harder, even for the teacher. One observer, C. F. Hagenow of Colgate University, dated what he called "modern physics" from 1895, or the discovery of the X ray. The importance of X rays, he said, lay in their ability to ionize gases, which led to the idea that the atom had constituents.[99]

According to two professors, one at the University of Iowa, the other at the University of Michigan, the physics student in 1930 was studying the physics of two generations before, and they set out to survey the opinions of 966 high school and 77 college teachers of physics on this matter. Some 80 percent of the high school teachers agreed that "the basic ideas of physics" had changed greatly over the preceding forty years, and almost all said that the new ideas should be in the high school course. In 1931, Professor Edwin C. Kemble of Harvard addressed the Eastern Association of Physics Teachers on the topic "The New Physics and the Secondary School," doubting, however, that much of what he called the new physics could be taught either in high school or in the undergraduate program of the college. What he recommended for high school students was an occasional glimpse of it for stimulation.[100]

Even the identity of physics itself, old or new, was not always clear. Professor A. A. Bless of Cornell University complained in 1928 that he could find little or no perception among his students of what physics was. He added that the high school and college textbooks themselves presented little or no idea of the meaning of the subject. The attempts at

98. "What College Men Think of High School Chemistry," *School Science and Mathematics* 23 (Feb. 1923), 156.

99. "Modern Physics," *School Science and Mathematics* 28 (Oct. 1928), 717.

100. Gerald W. Fox and D. L. Rich, "An Investigation of the Attitude of Physics Teachers toward the Content of the High School Physics Course," *Science Education* 15 (Nov. 1930), 9–13; reported in *School Science and Mathematics* 31 (Oct. 1931), 871–72.

definition which he extracted from such books were characterized by him as "plainly ridiculous," for example, one that defined physics as the study of how to measure things. "I am sorry for these people: Physics must be very dull for them," said Bless about this definition. Another defined physics as sense perception, and Bless sarcastically observed that smell and taste should be included. From his own struggle with the question, Bless proposed a definition of physics as a study of energy, one that he felt would eliminate some of the topics from overloaded courses.[101]

Beyond the question of what physics was was the question of whether physics was different from chemistry, whether there was really a valid dividing line from one natural science to another. There had been similar questions in social studies and in mathematics which had evoked unified social studies and general mathematics. In the natural sciences they called forth the movement known as general science.

General science came into the 1920s with some two decades of advocacy and scattered instances of practice behind it. Although potentially applicable to all levels of secondary education (at least partly so in combined physical science in the upper high school years),[102] general science, like general mathematics, had its main impact in the junior high school grades. The South Philadelphia High School for Girls, however, carried general or unified science through a four-year program.[103]

In the eighth- or ninth-grade course, general science usually included materials from fields not otherwise widely offered, such as astronomy, geology, and physical geography, as well as from biology, physics, and chemistry. The course varied from book to book and school to school in the materials included and in the degree of unification achieved. On the whole, it tended to be practical and to use such topics as water supply, food, heating and ventilation, and health and sanitation, to approach unification.[104]

Like other impulses toward unified studies, general science was, at least briefly, a crusading movement. It had its journal, *General Science*

101. "The Teaching of Physics," *School Science and Mathematics* 28 (May 1928), 485–87.
102. Recommended, for example, by W. J. A. Bliss of Johns Hopkins University, "Suggestions As to Changes in Entrance Requirements in Science," *School Science and Mathematics* 22 (Dec. 1922), 825.
103. M. Louise Nichols, "Making the Study of Science a Social Factor at the South Philadelphia High School," *Prog Ed* 3 (Oct. 1926), 366–70.
104. W. S. Kellogg, "General Science Teaching in California," *Sierra Educational News* 18 (March 1922), 118–20.

Quarterly, founded in 1915 and published by enthusiast Walter G. Whitman of the State Normal School at Salem, Massachusetts, with an editorial board, going into the 1920s, that included Otis Caldwell of Lincoln School, Teachers College, and David Snedden. Whitman's views in the 1920s anticipated in an oblique way the strictures with which C. P. Snow three decades later would spread consternation among those in the humanities. "The time has passed," he said, "when one is considered well educated if he can read a page of Latin, but cannot tell how the electric bell works. Science information upon common things is now considered essential to every member of society." Moving to a higher plane he added, "Many questions of public importance involving knowledge of science must be settled by the public."[105]

The *Quarterly* published articles on all aspects of science-teaching, but its special dedication was to the advancement of general science. By the end of the decade, however, it had been absorbed by the larger field. In 1928 it became identified with the newly formed National Association for Research in Science Teaching and in the year following changed its name to *Science Education.*

During its prime years, general science aroused strong emotions both ways. For J. Richard Lunt, a teacher at Boston's English High School in 1921, it was playing "the part of the emancipator in the new education," and he predicted that it would "free our schools from the bondage of books." On the other hand, Professor Robert A. Millikan of the California Institute, Pasadena, admitted having been an early advocate of the movement "for which," he said, "I hope God may some time forgive me."[106]

VI

English, social studies, mathematics, and science in the 1920s gave no clear victories to any of the contending pedagogical factions. To the educators of social efficiency, much of what was taught was wasteful and in the parlance of a later age irrelevant. Some of it, particularly algebra, was considered harmful, for driving students away from school. Idealistic

---

105. "Civic Science: General Science for the Junior High School," *General Science Quarterly* 6 (Jan. 1921), 87.
106. "Methods for Vitalizing the Study and Teaching of General Science," *ibid.* 5 (May 1921), 206; "The Problem of Science Teaching in the Secondary Schools," *S&S* 22 (Nov. 21, 1925), 634.

teachers who loved their subjects, on the other hand, felt that far too much had been conceded to the spirit of the times and to the presumed inadequacy of students.

On the surface, the main concessions were those made to the practical side of life, such as technology in relation to science. These represented the dominant mood of the times. The cliché of "learning by doing" was really attributable less to progressive education than to values identified with Lindbergh, Edison, and Ford. There was above all the popular conviction that the country club prosperity exalted by the *Saturday Evening Post* flowed naturally from American know-how in the technology of production, in business, and in economics.

Yet with all this there was something more, an undercurrent in which Lindbergh, Edison, and Ford were also involved. What made their reputations as heroes was not their practical work alone but their charismatic qualities as mystics and seers. Strangely, the same strain in American life showed itself in the outbursts against evolution and for patriotic history. These movements were romantic, sentimental, at times irrational, but practical and hard-headed they most emphatically were not.

In this romantic undercurrent of the 1920s flowed also the nineteenth-century impulse for popular culture. The colorful side of scholarship had a ready market even when it contributed nothing to practical aims, a fact that was well understood by those who put out Sunday supplements and wrote popular books on science. The same appeal may have served to maintain in the English curriculum the so-called outmoded classics scorned alike by efficiency educators and by academicians such as Howard Mumford Jones.

In one sense this was a quest for scholarship made easy, and it was the idea of physics-made-easy as well as that of physics-made-colorful that moved those who castigated mathematical and laboratory physics. It was perhaps anti-intellectual without being anti-academic. After all, if prosperity was easy to come by, why should not physics be easy too? The real motive, however, was probably the adding of color and enrichment to the non-working hours of the day and week, the "worthy use of leisure time" of the Cardinal Principles Report, symbolized not only by baseball and golf but by the latest volume, possibly unread, from the Book of the Month Club. Even the efficiency educators succumbed to the lure and found room for it in their desire to use the high school as an instrument for channeling youth into American society. At least part of life could be allocated (on a time budget) to the pursuit of culture.

Provided that he did not make his material too hard, the academic teacher could and did survive by recognizing this romantic appeal. The most immediate possibilities, of course, were in English literature, history, and two fields not common to all students, music and the fine arts. Mathematics, especially algebra, was more of a problem. The possibilities in the sciences were diverse. Within them biology seemed to have the best chance and physics the least, although there were those who stoutly contended that physics, too, could furnish thrills.

Chapter 5

The students of the nineteen-twenties

> "The high school is no longer the selective institution it was in another generation."
> —JESSE H. NEWLON,
> 1929.

*F*rom the high school population of the twenties we now have men and women between fifty and seventy years of age. It may be difficult to visualize in these generations now grown old the flaming youth, the restless, the bored, the eager, the alienated, and the student strikers of that remote age, but such indeed they were. These departing generations have lived as adults through social change at least as cataclysmic as that of the decade when they were in high school, have contributed their strengths and shortcomings to the achievements and the follies of the past four decades, and have viewed new generations of high school students on whom they have passed successive judgments. Who were these high school students of the 1920s? What were they like?

Numerically, they were a select minority, and the selection worked progressively through the four high school years. Of those who were freshmen in public high schools in 1920, only some 46 percent remained to be seniors in 1923, with a corresponding rate of 44 percent for those who were freshmen in 1925 and seniors in 1928. And there were those who never started high school. The freshmen or high school starters of 1925 made up only 54 percent of those with whom they had been in the second grade back in 1918.[1]

This process of numerical selection, however, did not necessarily produce a high school population of academic excellence, and it was not so regarded at the time. Today's older people would not be flattered by what was said about them then. According to the pedagogical rhetoric of the 1920s, the academic quality of the students then in high

1. Off Ed, *Biennial Survey of Education 1926–1928*, bull. 1930, no. 16, p. 454.

107

school represented a calamitous decline from the heights of excellence that had been occupied by their predecessors before the war.

Even though the students of the twenties were only a fraction of all youth, there were large numbers of them, many more than before. It was assumed that when large numbers were involved many of them had to be stupid. "We are now attempting," said State Superintendent Will C. Wood of California in 1920, "to educate all the children of all the people, and a considerable proportion of human beings have not been endowed with minds capable of development along the lines of academic scholarship. The schools may develop brains; they cannot supply them."[2]

Dramatic comparisons were invoked to describe the state of affairs. Referring to the increase in numbers since 1900, A. C. Olney, commissioner of secondary schools in California, called it the invasion of "an ancient institution" by a great army, adding that "the invasion of Rome by the barbarians was small in comparison." Another who dwelt in colorful figures of speech was William McAndrew, who compared the high school of the past to "a silk mill, built and equipped to weave the most delicate threads into ornamental patterns," but into which was "dumped . . . wool and flax, sisal, hemp, and wood pulp."[3]

Negative opinion was not confined to such lofty pronouncements from on high. Eight applicants for principalships in New York City were asked for their views on the matter. Of these, five unqualifiedly endorsed the assertion that more students of lower quality were coming to high school. A lone dissenter doubted that the students were of lower quality and attributed their difficulties to poor training in English. The other two were not sure, but felt that the availability of tests made it easier to identify such students.[4]

This reference to tests was an interesting one indeed. Intelligence testing, so-called, was relatively new and owed part of its vogue to the publicity given the army tests and their wartime use. The Stanford-Binet individual examination had appeared in 1916, only one year

2. "The Recognition of the Relation of Education to Our National Life," *NEA Proc*, 1920, p. 51.

3. "Equal Opportunity vs. Same Opportunity," *California Quarterly of Secondary Education* 1 (Oct. 1925), 42; "Supervision from the Viewpoint of the Superintendent," Superintendence *Report*, 1928, p. 70.

4. "The Evaluation of Candidates for the Principalship of a High School," *High Points* 9 (Feb. 1927), 3–8.

before our entry into the war. By 1923 those who remained uncon-
vinced faced questions sharply put to them by the World Book Company in its advertisement for the Otis group tests: "Have you measured
the minds of your pupils? Do you know that it is now almost as easy
to measure the mental ability of a child as it is to weigh him or to
measure his height?"[5]

Unfortunately, since school populations had never before taken such
tests, the movement contributed nothing to comparisons with the past.
Edward L. Thorndike in 1922 attempted to construct a comparison by
using correlations between intelligence levels and grades reached in
school, finding in these "excellent reasons for believing" that the one
student in ten who entered high school in 1890 had greater capacities
for algebra and other intellectual tasks than the one in three entering
in 1918.[6] Since he had to assume that motives and opportunities in 1890
were the same as those in 1918, the conclusion was worth little more
than the nostalgic reminiscences of old-timers in a faculty lounge.

In any case, the new technology of intelligence-testing was available
to provide data on those who were in the high school of the 1920s. A
summary of studies made on high school student populations of the
years from 1916 to 1942 indicated that there was no decline in the
average (reported) IQ throughout that period, a period of marked
expansion in enrollments.[7] It should be noted, in view of what was
later said about the 1930s, that this summary did include the period of
expanding enrollments in the depression.

A breakdown of the statistics indicated the proportions of people in
various IQ categories. Professor Lewis M. Terman of Stanford, who
had developed the Stanford-Binet test, showed that 33.9 percent of a
group of 905 children five to fourteen years old had IQs of 96 to 105.
Slightly less than one-third of the children were below this figure and
slightly more than one-third above. Only five had IQs of 136 or higher.
Terms from everyday speech were used to label the various categories,
contributing further to some of the popular impressions involved. Those
above 140 were called genius or near genius. At the other end, those

5. *S&S* 9 (Jan. 1923), 47.

6. "Changes in the Quality of Pupils Entering High School," *Sch R* 30 (May
1922), 355–59.

7. F. H. Finch, *Enrollment Increases and Changes in the Mental Level of the
High School Population*, American Psychological Association Applied Psychology
Monograph no. 10 (Stanford, Cal., 1946), p. 70.

from 80 to 90 were labeled "dull," from 70 to 80 of "border-line deficiency," and below 70 of "definite feeble-mindedness." Terman's comment on the group labeled of border-line deficiency ran as follows: "Children of this group should be segregated in special classes and be given instruction which is concrete and practical. They cannot master abstractions, but they can often be made efficient workers, able to look out for themselves. There is no possibility at present of convincing society that they should not be allowed to reproduce, although from a eugenic point of view they constitute a grave problem because of their unusually prolific breeding."[8]

Little wonder that educators made proclamations about the fractions of the high school population judged by them as incapable of doing the work. Since 22 percent of the entering high school students of Pittsburgh in 1920 had IQs under 90, the director of research concluded they would have difficulty with foreign languages and mathematics. In New York City, a teacher of Flushing High School found 17 percent of the entrants below 90 and concluded that these would fail in their school work. Strangely enough, the figures from the Terman distribution served as a restraint. Those who drew inspiration from other sources had even more dramatic conclusions. Using data from the army tests, a professor at the University of Pennsylvania proclaimed to the American Sociological Society that 70 percent of the children were "incapable of acquiring a high school education."[9]

Skeptics about intelligence testing, including such strange bedfellows as William C. Bagley and John Dewey, were quick to raise the cry of educational determinism. Often they suspected the determinists of wanting to keep so-called inferior children out of high school. What most of the determinists asked for, however, were differentiated programs. Even Terman hastened to protest that psychologists were merely demanding new kinds of secondary education better suited to "inferior intellects."[10] Only rarely did someone suggest, as did a professor at

8. *The Measurement of Intelligence* (Boston, 1916), pp. 66, 79, 92.

9. J. Freeman Guy, "The Intelligence of the High School Pupil," *Pennsylvania School Journal* 70 (Nov. 1921), 84–86; Samuel Goldman, "Results of the Terman Group Intelligence Tests in Flushing High School," *High Points* 11 (Sept. 1929), 29; J. P. Lichtenberger, "Social Significance of Mental Levels," American Sociological Society, *Papers and Proceedings of the Fifteenth Annual Meeting* (Chicago, 1921), p. 110.

10. "The Psychological Determinist, or Democracy and the IQ," *Journal of Educational Research* 6 (June 1922), 57–62.

Lawrence College in 1923, that "we should seriously begin the work of eliminating the inferior pupils from our high schools."[11]

In defending their position, determinists invoked the presumed interests of the individual and society to argue for a nonexclusion policy. Assistant Superintendent E. L. Miller of Detroit, in his 1925 presidential address to the North Central Association, declared one-third of the students "congenitally incapable of doing high school work as it is now organized," but did not feel that "these stupid children should be excluded from high school." After all, he thought, they needed "further training in citizenship, in morals, in health, and in the social arts." Thomas H. Briggs of Columbia's Teachers College supported this generous impulse from the point of view of social efficiency. "Without question," he said, increased enrollments had lowered the ability level of the students, but education as "an investment of the state" must provide for all. "Just as truly as a manufacturing plant," concluded Briggs, "it [the investing state] must work up all its raw material so as to make it maximally useful."[12]

The issues were indeed complex, especially as brought out in the controversy in New York City between those who favored tests and those who favored ratings from elementary schools in the making of predictions and in the organizing of ability groups. The chairman of the French department at De Witt Clinton High School was startled in 1923 by the disparities between the two measures. Moreover, he said, the ratings did a better job than the tests in predicting success in high school work. He concluded, therefore, that the intelligence tests might better be omitted and the ratings used alone.[13]

No indeed, countered a teacher at the Girls' Commercial High School in the same year. "The school's marks," he asserted, "tell us what the child has done in his school work. The intelligence tests, on the other hand, tell us of the native capacity of the child—what he is able to do." A psychologist at the Washington Irving High School also found marked

---

11. G. C. Cast, "Elimination of the Unfit: A Problem of Waste in Public Education," *S&S* 18 (July 21, 1923), 86.

12. "A Good Word for the High School," *NC Proc*, 1925, p. 110; "What's Next in Secondary Education," *Sch R* 30 (Sept. 1922), 523, 528.

13. Colman D. Frank, "A Ray of Light Let In by a Study of First-Term Failures," *High Points* 5 (May 1923), 6–7.

differences between tests and ratings, but supported the conclusion that it would be "unsafe" to accept the elementary school classifications.[14]

Both sides apparently overlooked some of the realities involved and both were partly correct. Test results could be wrong. On the other hand, elementary school records were affected by other factors than academic ability. With the use of ratings only, students with high capacity and poor records could be shunted into programs more than likely to alienate them. The contribution of the intelligence test, imperfect as it was, consisted in sometimes rescuing students from such a fate.

After presumably inferior students were identified, appropriate programs had to be developed. What were these new programs that Terman had called for, and who had the magic answers? Many fell back on the alleged distinction between hand work and mind work. Assistant Superintendent J. A. Starkweather of the Duluth, Minnesota, public schools reported in 1921 the creation of a separate department for such students, with basket-weaving and rug- and carpet-making as the main activities. Charles A. Bennett, a veteran of the earlier manual-training movement, found "one of the great opportunities for manual arts education" in the proposition that 70 percent of the population could not do high school work.[15]

Vocational shopwork was another matter, but this was also proposed for "inferior" students, reviving some of the rhetoric from the vocational thrust of 1906–17. The question persisted, nonetheless, whether students presumably incapable of academic work made good prospects for the skilled trades. Two investigators studied the performance of a group of twenty-five boys with IQs from 71 to 111, averaging 90, in learning fundamental operations on the engine lathe. They found a coefficient of correlation between performance and IQ of only .14, with the best shop score made by a boy with an IQ of seventy-six. Their conclusion was "that such fairly simple mechanical work can be done successfully by a boy with a rather low IQ and that, in general, the boys of low-grade intelligence turn out a better grade of work than the brighter boys." They warned against the idea, however, that the machine

14. Meyer E. Zinman, "The Value of Intelligence Tests," *High Points* 5 (Oct. 1923), 17; F. Edith Carothers, "Elementary School Group Classification of Pupils versus Intelligence Test Classification," *ibid.* 6 (Sept. 1924), 9–12.

15. "Selling a City Its School System," *Journal of Educational Method* 4 (Dec. 1921), 159; "Seventy Per Cent of the Children Should Never Go to High School," *Industrial Education Magazine* 24 (July 1922), 1.

trades offered little to those of high intelligence. "The finer grades of work in tool-and-gauge and model making," they pointed out, "call for abilities which are not in demand in this study."[16]

Such studies were infrequent, but the debates were not. "If your vocational department," scolded Superintendent W. L. Bachrodt of San Jose, California, at the Department of Superintendence in 1927, "is merely the catch-all for all the fractious, stupid boys in the school, you certainly have not caught the vision of vocational education. The boy with an IQ of seventy is not material for a skilled trade." The director of the Vocation Bureau, Cincinnati Public Schools, took issue with Bachrodt not so much on the facts of the case as from a missionary impulse. Vocational educators should bear their share of the responsibility for students with low IQ's. "It is just as much the duty and responsibility of a vocational teacher paid from federal funds to care for a dull child," she argued, "as it is the responsibility of the already overburdened principal."

Another vocational educator, however, at the University of Toledo, vehemently expressed a point of view similar to Bachrodt's. "Principal after principal," he complained, "is absolutely sure that if Johnny fails in everything in High School, he must be mechanically minded. Therefore, the vocational course at once! Guidance? Would you dignify the process by such a name? No!" If a vocational coordinator can get the idea across to his superiors, he continued, "that an incorrigible or one of low IQ is not necessarily material for a vocational course (from whence there is no return) without getting himself fired, he has done a splendid piece of work."[17]

Some school systems developed more comprehensive provisions for students of presumed low ability. "As far as the child is concerned," reported a teacher of such work in the Los Angeles City Schools in 1926, "he is not stamped as 'misfit,' but is given opportunity to work in a smaller group (usually twenty-two in number) where he can mingle with children of his own abilities and capacities, and where he can work

16. Verne A. Bird and L. A. Pechstein, "General Intelligence, Machine Shop Work, and Educational Guidance in the Junior High," *Sch R* 29 (Dec. 1921); 783, 785–86.

17. "The Administration of the Industrial and Vocational Work of the Schools," Superintendence *Report*, 1927, p. 278; M. Edith Campbell, "The Lowest Fourth: Their Educational, Social, Civic, and Vocational Welfare," *ibid.*, p. 184; H. W. Paine, "Guidance Problems and Responsibilities of Coordinators in Our Smaller Vocational Centers," *Vocational Guidance Magazine* 7 (March 1929), 252.

at his own rate of speed." She herself had charge of a girls' opportunity room for ages fourteen to sixteen in which all the work was individualized. Most of these students, she said, were then doing fifth or sixth grade academic work, presumably in the conventional subjects.[18] Her report, which showed sensitivity and imagination, was nonetheless unfortunately entitled "What To Do with Misfits"—but writers do not always get to choose their own titles.

Such programs did not necessarily exclude manual or vocational work. The special rooms at the Roosevelt Junior High School in Fond du Lac, Wisconsin, were organized around English, mathematics, and social studies, plus some manual training and work in the slow sections of household arts.[19] In the Central High School of Fort Wayne, Indiana, the program of the special rooms included English, vocational information and guidance, commercial arithmetic, and shopwork for boys and sewing for girls, and it gave much attention to the capacities and needs of the students as individuals.[20] In such opportunity or adjustment rooms, as they were often called, one teacher would have either the entire responsibility for a small group of students or would have most of it, with some special work outside. William McAndrew in 1924 paid tribute to those teachers who would "rather help the mentally lame and halt and blind than doctor those who need no physician."[21]

From the Julia Richman High School of New York City in 1928, two teachers reported the development, not of special rooms, but of a fairly large-scale program consisting of modified academic and vocational subjects. The girls in this program were those who had low IQs and had failed two or more major subjects. It included English, social studies, general science, and some academic electives, plus office machines, selling, and merchandising (rather than the bookkeeping and stenography of the commercial course), with provision for on-the-job experience through cooperative part-time work. Even more institutionally ambitious was the creation in Okmulgee, Oklahoma, of a special unit, the Lee High School, for students thirteen or over who had not reached sixth-grade attainment. "The academic subjects and practical

18. Anna Adelson, "What To Do with Misfits," *California Quarterly of Secondary Education* 1 (Jan. 1926), 251.

19. S. P. Unzicker, "The Junior High School and the Mentally Handicapped Adolescent," *Sch R* 36 (Jan. 1928), 57.

20. "A Special Class for Dull Pupils," *Sch R* 37 (June 1929), 408.

21. Editor's note, *ER* 68 (Nov. 1924), 178.

arts," reported the superintendent, "are offered to all but in varied proportions based on abilities, aptitudes, and futures."[22]

Whether such programs were good or bad, they did avoid the conventional distinctions between hand work and mind work and between academic and vocational training. Other efforts to avoid such dualisms included the use of "low ability" sections in academic subjects, including algebra and geometry, where timing and content might be adjusted. Ability-sectioning or grouping often included sections for middle and high groups as well. The 1920s, according to recorded expression, favored ability-sectioning, and significant opposition did not appear until the decade's end.[23]

It is not true, as has often since been assumed, that the educators of the twenties and thirties overlooked the high-ability students. One positive result of the intelligence-testing movement, in fact, was that it created more precise awareness of such students and of the need to learn more about them. Terman dedicated his major research efforts to the identification of gifted students and the study of their characteristics, dispelling in the process much of the folklore that had grown up about their neurotic tendencies and personality maladjustments.[24]

Even those who did not share the conventional assumptions about genius tended in their approach to the gifted to take a social point of view. In one of his expressions of concern about the self-interest motive in education, George S. Counts declared that every time a person without a sense of social obligation was graduated from high school or college "a dangerous man is turned loose to prey upon the community."

22. Ellen Osgood and Cornelia M. Beall, "Experimenting with the High School Misfit," *Sch R* 12 (Dec. 1928), 779–86; Eugene S. Briggs, "What About the 'Sub-Merged One-Tenth?' " *Proceedings of the National Association of Secondary School Principals,* 1927, pp. 184–85.

23. For examples of statements favoring ability sectioning, see Ray H. Bracewell, "Segregation in Ability Groups As a Means of Taking into Account Individual Differences," *NEA Proc,* 1921, pp. 674–75, and Frances R. North, chairman, "Report of Committee on Improving Scholarship," *Proceedings of the National Association of Secondary School Principals,* 1927, pp. 246–49. For counter-argument, see Alice V. Keliher, *A Critical Study of Homogeneous Grouping* (New York, 1931). For a summary of practice at the end of the decade, see Austin H. Turney, "The Status of Ability Grouping," *EA&S* 17 (Jan. 1931), 21–42, (Feb. 1931), 110–27.

24. "The Physical and Mental Traits of Gifted Children," National Society for the Study of Education twenty-third yearbook, part 1, *Report of the Society's Committee on the Education of Gifted Children* (Bloomington, Ill., 1924), pp. 155–67.

The more talented the person, added Counts, "the more mischief he will do." Others feared the loss to society if the gifted were not cultivated. "The national welfare," said Vernon Kellogg, secretary of the National Research Council and a former science professor at Stanford, "depends in large measure on the use made by the nation of its superior brains. The extent of this use depends on the discovery and encouragement of these superior brains and the provision of opportunity for them to render their highest service to the nation." The National Society for the Study of Education devoted a yearbook to the gifted, and in it Harold Rugg called for the discovery of such children, their organization into working groups, and the provision for them of "the most far-reaching course of training our intelligence can organize." He included not only those of high "abstract intelligence" but also "the prospective painters, musicians, humanitarian leaders, research investigators in the special scientific fields, inventors and leaders in the mechanical professions, etc."[25]

Both advocacy and practice ran heavily toward placing the gifted in separate classes or sections. There was associated controversy about the relative merits of advancing gifted students more rapidly through school, under a banner marked "acceleration," or keeping them with their age groups while providing more work and more advanced work in their sections, under a banner marked "enrichment." The program in 1920 in the junior high schools of Detroit was aimed at getting gifted students through the three years in two years and a half.[26] There were, of course, individual students who accelerated themselves by taking extra subjects and going to summer schools, but these were outside formalized programs.

On the whole, educators were reluctant to endorse chronological acceleration, perhaps for the same reason they disapproved of eleven-year programs. Enrichment, on the other hand, enjoyed widespread advocacy. "Is it not more just to the gifted children," asked a child psychologist in 1923, "to allow them their full quota of school years

25. "Education As an Individual Right," *S&S* 15 (April 22, 1922), 435; "The National Research Council," *ER* 62 (Dec. 1921), 373; "The Curriculum for Gifted Children," National Society for the Study of Education twenty-third yearbook, part 1, *Report of the Society's Committee on the Education of Gifted Children* (Bloomington, Ill., 1924), p. 110.

26. Elizabeth Cleveland, "Detroit's Experiment with Gifted Children," *S&S* 12 (Sept. 11, 1920), 179–83.

and with them a broader culture and perhaps the development of some special talent? Would not such an opportunity be more valuable to them than the shifting of a few years from the school period of life to the adult period?" Principal M. R. McDaniel of the Oak Park and River Forest Township High School, Illinois, also spoke against promoting students beyond their age groups, but favored more advanced work in the high ability sections. "For the sake of the pupils as well as the teacher," he said, "let us put the brighter ones together and then let the teacher turn on the gas, put her in high, and with the pupils experience the joy of intellectual speeding."[27]

II

Firmly fixed in the idea that students of the past had universally possessed good manners and high IQs was the conviction that the overwhelming majority of them had been college preparatory students. This golden age was usually assumed to have existed sometime about 1900. Yet the commissioner of education in his report for 1900 had identified only 31 percent of the graduates of public high schools as prepared for college, and although he did not give the actual college-going rate, supplementary evidence from that period indicates that it ran no higher than one-third.[28] In the 1920s, reports from the Bureau of Education did give the rates not only for college-going but also for attendance beyond high school in what were called "other institutions."

A college-going rate of 31 percent was reported for public high schools for the class of 1921, and for other institutions one of 14 percent. For the class of 1927 the college rate was the same, with 13 percent for the others.[29] The public high school population of the 1920s, then, was probably no less college-preparatory or college-going than that of 1900, but school people and others did believe that a great reduction had taken place. To them, the college preparatory students of

27. Clara Harrison Town, "The Superior Child in Our Schools," *ER* 65 (Jan. 1923), 21; "A Square Deal for the Brilliant Pupil," *NEA Proc*, 1921, p. 677.
28. U.S. Commissioner of Education, *Report for the Year 1899–1900* (Washington, D.C., 1901), pp. 2122, 2125; Edward A. Krug, "High School Graduates in and around 1900: Did Most of Them Go to College?" *Sch R* 70 (Autumn 1962), 262–70.
29. Bur Ed, *Biennial Survey of Education 1920–1922*, bull. 1924, no. 14, 2: 559–60; Off Ed, *Biennial Survey 1926–1928*, pp. 1042–43.

the 1920s were a saving remnant symbolic of glory fled, now over-whelmed by the non-college-preparatory mass.

Surveys of the students enrolled in the various differentiated curricula did show higher medians or averages in academic ability for the college-preparatory groups, but usually with overlap. One of the most compre-hensive of these was made in May, 1919, by Professor William F. Book of Indiana University, involving over 5,000 seniors in 320 commissioned high schools (those with the highest ratings) in the state. Classifying the students A through E on their scores on the Indiana University Intelli-gence Scale, he found 29 percent of the students in classical curricula falling into the top two categories of A and B, 25 percent of those in the academic, and at the lower end, 16 percent of those in commercial and vocational. These were differences, but they were hardly over-whelming. Moreover, while 3 percent of the students in academic cur-ricula and 2 percent of those in classical were A-plus (the top 1 percent of the distribution), this classification was achieved by 2 percent of those in vocational and 1 percent of those in commercial curricula.[30]

Similar patterns appeared in reports from individual schools. In a survey of girls planning to enter Washington Irving High School, New York City, in the fall of 1923, F. Edith Carothers found an average IQ of 103 on the Terman Group Test for those choosing the academic curriculum, with corresponding figures for the other curricula varying from 100 in commercial to 90 in trade cookery. The academic group, however, had a range from 78 to 144, while commercial varied from 74 to 133 and trade cookery from 76 to 111. A survey reported in 1931 from the Isaac C. Elston Senior High School of Michigan City, Indiana, showed median Otis IQs of 103 for those in the academic curriculum, with 97 for commercial and 94 for vocational. While 12 percent of the academic students had IQs below 90, 8 percent of those in commercial and 5 percent of those in vocational were 110 and above.[31]

Comparative studies of those intending and not intending to go to college also showed overlap. Nearly one-fourth of the seniors rated A-plus and A in the Indiana survey were not planning on college. A

30. William F. Book, *The Intelligence of High School Seniors* (New York, 1922), p. 144.
31. "Results of the Terman Group Test Given to Entering Students in Wash-ington Irving High School," *High Points* 6 (June 1924), 25; T. L. Engle, "A Com-parative Study of Pupils in Academic, Commercial, and Vocational Curriculums," *Sch R* 39 (Nov. 1931), 667, 669.

report from Illinois in 1925 showed that one-fourth of the seniors with IQs of 110 and above did not have college plans. In a survey reported in 1929 of almost all the seniors in Wisconsin, about one-third of those in the upper fourth of a distribution on the state psychological testing program did not intend to go to college, while nearly one-third of those in the lowest fourth did have such intentions.[32]

Some feared that too many students were going or planning to go to college. In his 1925 survey of the Sequoia Union High School, Redwood City, California, Professor John C. Almack of Stanford University concluded that the 45 percent of the students planning on college represented twice the number that had even a fair chance of success. He feared also that too many were planning to enter the professions. "Thus the need arises," said Almack, "for a strong guidance program and for the development of many courses that lead to other than college entrance." The school took his advice, and perhaps as a result, the college-intending rate by 1930 was down to 31 percent. Others worried about the presence in college preparatory curricula of students not really planning on college. The Bureau of Education, in its survey of the public schools of Wilmington, Delaware, reported in 1922, warned against this on the grounds that it would deprive students of subjects needed "for the vocations which they will follow after leaving high school."[33]

On the other hand, there were those who realized the difficulties faced by many high school students in deciding whether or not to go to college. In an investigation sponsored by the National Committee on Mathematical Requirements, some 2,000 college freshmen were asked what their plans had been at the time of entering high school. Of these, only 31 percent had been certain of going to college and only 30 percent fairly sure, while 14 percent had thought it probable, 12 percent possible, and 11 percent had been sure they were not going at all. A teacher in the high school at New Rochelle, New York, urged all students of high intelligence to get at least "the minimum essentials" for college admission. Some of those with financial handicaps, she feared, were not aware of the

32. Book, *Intelligence*, p. 36; "Vocational Problems in the High School," *Sch R* 33 (Oct. 1925), 570; "Expectation of College Attendance among High School Seniors in Wisconsin," *Sch R* 37 (Nov. 1929), 642.

33. A. C. Argo and S. S. Mayo, "Some Values of a School Survey," *California Quarterly of Secondary Education* 3 (April 1930), 249–50; *Survey of the Schools of Wilmington, Delaware*, bull. 1921, no. 2, 2:80.

possibilities for scholarships and other aids.[34] The important thing was not to close the doors.

III

The public high school population of the 1920s did not uniformly represent the various groups in American life. Among the underrepresented were boys, rural youth, those from lower socio-economic groups, and black youth. Boys made up only 44 percent of the enrollment in 1920 and only 46 percent in 1930, and they survived less well, comprising in 1930 only 39 percent of the graduates.[35] Rural youth fourteen to seventeen years old, although in 1930 making up nearly half the youth of this age, furnished only one-third of the total high school enrollment. Furthermore, only 30 percent of all rural youth were in the rural high schools, as contrasted with 60 percent of all urban youth in the urban high schools. Some rural youth, however, did go to urban high schools, and with this taken into account the estimate was made that 39 percent of rural youth, as contrasted with 58 percent of urban youth, were in high school somewhere.[36] The absence of high schools in many rural areas was directly related to this state of affairs.

Everpresent in the discussions of the student population of the 1920s, directly or by implication, was the matter of social class. While not precisely defined in most instances, the term was taken for granted in a rough-and-ready way as having something to do with income, occupation, level of schooling, and inevitably in the context of the times with immigration, especially the so-called new immigration. This was not a new question, and at least as far back as 1890 there had been much concern about the "masses" who were invading the high school. With some two million students enrolled in 1920, many felt that the masses had taken it over.

Still, these two million students were less than one-third of all youth fourteen to seventeen years of age. Did this selection really represent the

34. A. R. Crathorne, "Change of Mind between High School and College As To Life Work," *EA&S* 5 (May–June 1920), 282; Elsie M. Flint, "Freshman Fatalities," *ER* 70 (Sept. 1925), 82.

35. Bur Ed, *Biennial Survey of Education 1918–1920*, bull. 1923, no. 29, p. 497; Off Ed, *Biennial Survey of Education 1928–1930*, bull. 1931, no. 20, 2:697.

36. Grayson N. Kefauver, Victor Noll, and C. Ellwood Drake, *The Secondary School Population*, Off Ed, bull. 1932, no. 17, National Survey of Secondary Education monograph no. 4, pp. 6–7.

so-called masses? Among those who questioned this assumption was George S. Counts, who directed his attention toward the nearly eighteen thousand youth who were in the high schools of St. Louis, Seattle, and Bridgeport, Connecticut, and showed the numbers of students with fathers in various occupational groups in relation to every one thousand men in those groups. The figures ranged from 400 in managerial occupations and 360 in professional, to 50 in personal service and 17 in what was called common labor. Among others between these extremes were clerical service at 219, machine trades at 159, building trades at 145, and miners, lumber workers, and fishermen at 58 (*The Selective Character of American Secondary Education,* Chicago, 1922, p. 33).

Counts drew the conclusion that high school education was "a privilege being extended at public expense to those very classes that already occupy the privileged positions in modern society. The poor are contributing to provide secondary education for the children of the rich, but are either too poor or too ignorant to avail themselves of the opportunities which they help to provide" (p. 152). This dramatic conclusion was perhaps overdrawn. Disparities in representation among children of occupational groups were clearly there, but they appeared in progression or series rather than as the dualism Counts set forth between poor and rich, unless those terms were meant to apply only to the extremes. Counts did not present income figures, and while managers were obviously rich in comparison with men in common labor, it was by no means evident that the other categories of declining representation progressively matched the income levels.

Competing rhetoric was becoming confusing indeed. According to the dominant, the high school population was of lower quality than that of the past because the children of the masses were now in it. On the other hand, interpretations of Counts's study had it that such children were really not there at all. The idea of the high school as a class institution was in any case a disturbing one to those who cherished the ideal of equal opportunity. A writer for the Bureau of Education in 1927 thought that some modification of its class character was taking place. Conceding that the selective principle as shown by Counts was still working, he added that "significant percentages of all occupational and social groups are finding their way into the high schools at the present time."[37] Perhaps he was right, but the question was still not whether there were more

37. Eustace E. Windes, *Trends in the Development of Secondary Education,* Bur Ed, bull. 1927, no. 26, p. 12.

children of the poor in high school, but whether they were adequately represented in proportion to their numbers in the population.

In Counts's study, moreover, there was no clear evidence of academic inferiority in the children of the masses, at least those who were in high school (p. 129). Counts concluded that the children of manual laborers who got into high school were highly selected, adding that the testing of an unselected group of children from that category showed a level of academic ability appreciably lower than that of the children from the professional or more prosperous classes" (p. 130). Some other investigations seemed to support the stereotype of lower academic ability in the lower socio-economic groups. In their survey of high school seniors in Massachusetts in 1922–23, for example, two investigators showed scores on the Brown University Psychological Test that declined progressively as levels of parental income declined. For those with a family income over $4,500 the median score was 51, for those below $1,000 it had declined to 45.[38] These were not great differences, and there was evidently much overlap, although this was not noted.

One study conducted with fewer cases, but perhaps more insight, attempted to relate several possible indices of class status. In this, a teacher of the James Madison High School in New York City examined students in the school's three ability tracks, and found a median IQ on the Stanford-Binet Test of 113 for those in the top track and of 90 for those in the bottom. She found the backgrounds of the students in the top and bottom tracks quite similar with regard to income and such matters as home ownership and telephones. On the other hand, the students in the top track had parents with higher levels of formal education. She concluded that the poorer cultural and educational backgrounds led children in the bottom track to come to school bewildered and without feeling that schoolwork was their job.[39]

This reflected another line of argument, that the children of the masses were not inherently inferior but were in fact so because of what a later age would call cultural deprivation. In some utterances, however, cultural deprivation seemed to shade into inherent inferiority as perceived by those who so wrote and spoke. "The child of foreign parents who have always been hand workers, hardly able to read and write," declared an

38. Stephen S. Colvin and Andrew H. MacPhail, *Intelligence of Seniors in the High Schools of Massachusetts*, Bur Ed, bull. 1924, no. 9, p. 35.
39. Adeline D. Englert, "A Survey of Thirty Students in the James Madison High School," *High Points* 11 (Sept. 1929), 3–15.

editorial in one pedagogical journal, "can seldom assimilate the amount of book learning which the child of mind-working people can absorb without difficulty. The former can take, and should be given, more than his parents had, but there comes a point beyond which he cannot go to much advantage." This apparent blending of the two was, on the other hand, avoided by a professor at the University of Wisconsin, who granted that the native endowments of such children might be equal to those of others but stressed the importance of what he called "differences which are sociologically significant."[40]

Enrollments in the academic or college preparatory curricula did reflect social class backgrounds. Children of proprietors, professionals, and managers made up only 43 percent of the students at the Bridgeport High School at the time of Counts's study, but 56 percent of those in the college curriculum (p. 56). In Seattle, such children were 44 percent of the total enrollment but 54 percent of those in the academic course (p. 70). These tendencies were more pronounced among girls than boys. In Bridgeport, girls from the three "upper" groups comprised only 42 percent of all the girls in the school but 67 percent of those in the college curriculum. The corresponding figures for boys in Bridgeport were 44 percent and 48 percent (p. 56).

What the parents and the children of the lower socio-economic groups thought about education does not appear on the record, but schoolmen and sociologists were willing to debate the matter for them. In one version of the cultural deprivation idea, the children of the masses suffered from the standoffish or even hostile attitudes of their parents toward education. Robert S. and Helen Merrell Lynd, however, in their Middletown study, did ask what they called working class parents for their views and reported that "if education is sometimes taken for granted by the business class, it is no exaggeration to say that it evokes the fervor of a religion, a means of salvation, among a large section of the working class." A teacher at the South Philadelphia High School for Girls reported similar enthusiasm among the people in the lower socio-economic areas from which the students came. According to this teacher, the opinion of the neighbors in these areas was "a mighty force . . . the neighbors believe

40. "Too Much Education?" *Sierra Educational News* 19 (Jan. 1923), 36; Willis L. Uhl, "Trends in Research in Secondary Education," University of Pennsylvania School of Education, *Fifteenth Annual Schoolmen's Week Proceedings,* 1928, p. 496.

that a high school education is the door which opens the way to that Elysian field, the modern office."[41]

Educators who recognized the ambition of the masses and their children, or of some of them, were not sure that they approved, for it smacked of individual rather than social goals. Counts himself was fearful of this among the gifted children of the lower classes. There was need, he felt, "in each calling, however humble, for a limited number of individuals of high intellectual and moral gifts who may aspire to and occupy positions of leadership within their own class and thus lead that class into a richer and fuller life." Otherwise, there was danger that schools might "drain out of the less fortunate classes all the superior talent born to them," thus closing the door "to the general improvement of the condition of these classes." William McAndrew expressed his disapproval of an open class society as well as of a caste society, contrasting both of these with what he called cultural democracy. Open class society implied opportunity to rise or fall. "We are hypnotized by it. The conception of it paralyzes the proper motives of public education." Pure American democracy, felt McAndrew, should reject classes altogether and not strive to lift "overalls boys into white-collars jobs."[42]

The open class society deplored by McAndrew was not nearly so open as he imagined. Neither, however, was the high school as presented in Counts's own evidence as closed to the lower economic classes as Counts interpreted it to be. The high school as a channel of mobility, such as it was, remained partly open, and the children of the poor had a gambler's chance, although with the odds high against them.

Whatever defects the high school population of the 1920s had may be charged to the middle classes as well as to the lower. Heavily underrepresented as they were, the lower socio-economic groups were unlikely by themselves to have created the prevailing images. The low cultural level complained of by English teachers appears, from their own descriptions, not just in the children from the other side of the tracks but from those of George F. Babbitt as well.

Although he did not use the terminology of social class, Philip W. L. Cox in his discussion of new culture groups in the high school made

41. *Middletown: A Study in Contemporary American Culture* (New York, 1929), p. 187; Anna W. Nock, "Low IQ's in the High School," *Sch R* 38 (Nov. 1930), 674.

42. "The Social Purpose of the Education of the Gifted Child," *ER* 64 (Oct. 1922), 243; "Books for the Profession," *S&S* 30 (July 6, 1929), 31.

references which could apply to either the middle and the lower classes or to the middle classes alone. "Such a youth [one from new culture groups]," said Cox, "has perhaps never met an adult who speaks or reads or writes an ancient or modern language—except immigrants for whom he may have little respect. Of adults whom he knows personally, few discuss historical causes and effects, scientific procedures, mathematical manipulations, or English classics." One may ask where youth would have found many such adults in any class. "Is it reasonable to assume," continued Cox, "that he will sacrifice parties, shows, dresses [sic], gossip, magazines, athletics, and the rest of the alluring activities which seem so important to his mothers and sisters and neighbors? These are the life!"[43] Here Cox could not have been talking about the poor, for the only activity in his list freely available to them was gossip.

The middle classes not only contributed to the problems of the schools, but in turn, at least according to some of them, suffered from problems of their own. One middle class mother writing in the *Atlantic Monthly* castigated middle class parents, especially the upper middles, for imposing too strenuous and regimented a program of education on their children. Just as there was a need to forbid child labor for the poor, so, thought this mother, there was need to protect the children of the well-to-do from laborious education. The existing system, she felt, "may thwart the real mental and spiritual growth of these privileged children just as surely as long days in mines, factories, and sweatshops once thwarted the physical growth of the children of the poor." Thousands were being conscripted into "the standardized schooling which we ignorantly call education."[44] Such views as these help account for the passion in some middle class circles for experimental private schools.

Not all the upper-middle-class desire for private schooling, however, arose from a rejection of standardized or regimented public schools. In the metropolitan centers of the 1920s there was already sentiment toward a flight from the public schools. "In the big city," one mother complained in *Harper's Magazine*, "people of the upper middle class find it impossible to entrust their children to public schools. The group there is so polyglot and so undisciplined that the child's standard of

43. "The Junior High School and the Secondary School Curriculum," *Proceedings of the National Association of Secondary School Principals*, 1930, p. 139.
44. Maude Dutton Lynch, "Conscripted Children," 148 (Aug. 1931), 232, 237.

conduct is bound to deteriorate."[45] In any case, the decade did witness an upsurge in private secondary education, the number of students increasing from 184,153 to 309,052 between 1920 and 1930 and the number of graduates per year from 46,189 to 51,447. There was an increase in private secondary schools, in this period, from 2,093 to 2,760.[46]

IV

Black children were strikingly underrepresented in the high school population of the 1920s. Where blacks comprised slightly less than 10 percent of the total population in 1920 and 1930, black students in 1920 made up only 1.5 percent of the students in public high schools and in 1930 only 3 percent.[47] It was sometimes assumed that these figures were offset by the large numbers of black students in private secondary schools, but in 1920 there were only 9,526 such students compared with 27,631 in public high schools, and in 1930 only 9,868 compared with 118,897.[48]

The underrepresentation of blacks was a result partly of *de jure* segregation in the South. Segregation, of course, existed both North and South, but under *de jure* segregation black youth went to the segregated high school, if there was one, or to none. High schools for blacks in such states were largely developed after 1920 and in cities. As late as 1929 there were 282 counties in these states with one-eighth or more of their population black that provided no such high schools. In these 282 counties lived 1,600,000 black people, between one-fourth and one-third of the total black population in the fourteen states involved.[49] Thousands of black youth in these states, especially rural youth, had no public high schools to attend.

When they had the opportunity, did the black youth want to go to

45. Anonymous, "A Social Background for Our Children," 163 (Sept. 1931), 483–84.

46. Bur Ed, *Biennial Survey of Education 1928–1930*, 2:784.

47. Bur Ed, *Biennial Survey 1918–1920*, p. 497; Off Ed, *Biennial Survey 1928–1930*, p. 697.

48. Bur Ed, *Biennial Survey 1918–1920*, pp. 497, 537; Off Ed, *Biennial Survey 1928–1930*, pp. 697, 784.

49. Leo M. Favrot, "Some Facts about Negro Schools and Their Distribution and Development in Fourteen Southern States," *High School Quarterly* 17 (April 1929), 143.

high school? A report from the Chicago public schools clearly indicated that some did. In 1921 Letitia Fyffe Merrill of the Department of Vocational Guidance surveyed the post-grade-school plans of 596 eighth-grade graduates in one of the poverty afflicted districts of the city. Included were 63 black youth, of whom 59, or 90 percent, expressed plans for going to high school. Referring to these children she said, "Parents are ready to make real sacrifices in order to give their children a chance. In one school where the graduating class was 100 percent colored, each child was interviewed. As a group, their plans for the future showed more thought and originality than did those of any of the other children." Of the 596 children, 72 percent planned on high school.[50]

One by-product of the testing movement was the discussion of comparative intelligence levels of blacks and whites. The tone of this discussion for the 1920s had been set by Terman in his 1916 book. After commenting on two students with IQs of 77 and 78, Terman said that these represented "the level of intelligence which is very, very common among Spanish-Indian and Mexican families of the Southwest and also among negroes." He predicted that with the use of "experimental methods" there would be discovered "enormously significant racial differences in general intelligence, differences which cannot be wiped out by any scheme of mental culture" (*Measurement of Intelligence*, pp. 91–92). Others, like Cornelia James Cannon, drew on the always controversial army tests from the World War to proclaim the mental inferiority of blacks.[51] There were many aspects to the army tests, however, and in one of them literate blacks from some northern states had higher medians on Army Alpha than did literate whites from some states in the South.[52]

Psychologist Thorndike directed his attention specifically to the comparative intelligence levels of white and black students in high schools. With a grant from the Commonwealth Fund, he administered tests of selective and rational thinking, generalizing, and organizing to white and black students in the high schools of an unidentified city in the north central region. Fewer than 4 percent of the black students, he

50. "A Report Concerning the Plans of 596 Children on Leaving the Eighth Grade," *Chicago Schools Journal* 5 (Dec. 1922), 156.
51. "American Misgivings," *Atlantic Monthly* 129 (Feb. 1922), 145–57.
52. See William C. Bagley, "The Army Tests and the Pro-Nordic Propaganda," *ER* 67 (April 1924), 184, 186.

reported, passed the median white scores for the corresponding grades.[53] Such reports reinforced the conventional wisdom and for the most part throughout the 1920s were accepted without question. The raising of such questions was to wait until the following decade.

In the 1920s, acceptance of the conventional findings seemed even to preclude awareness of the overlap in the distributions, and only rarely was such awareness indicated. One who did show it was Professor A. S. Edwards of the University of Georgia. Calling attention to the variations concealed by averages, Edwards said "that a few negroes may be as capable as a larger number of white children is as important from the scientific point of view as it is to know that the central tendency is lower than that of whites."[54] This was not a long step forward, but it showed unusual insight for the times.

Another educator who showed some insight and was in a position to act on it was guidance director Albert Fertsch of the Gary, Indiana, public schools, who in his work with the "colored trade school" of that city found individual black students of high intelligence subsumed in a group presumably retarded. These were transferred to the high school. Although open to criticism for his apparent assumption about the nature of trade education, Fertsch did regard black students as individuals rather than as members of a category. He also attributed the academic retardation he found in some of these students not to inferiority, but to their lack of "adequate educational advantages" before coming to Gary.[55]

In any case, the black student who went to high school, whether segregated or not, did so in a context of attitudes held by white educators. These were expressed through a confusing assortment of awkward, embarrassed, and self-conscious utterances and actions. The NEA outdid itself to establish formalized relationships with the National Association of Teachers in Colored Schools, even having an official committee to cooperate with that organization. In 1928 this committee made various recommendations, such as including at each NEA convention an address by a leader in Negro education at a general session, inviting Negro musical groups to furnish music for at least one program of the general sessions, and making a motion picture to describe on a factual

53. "Intelligence Scores of Colored Pupils in High Schools," S&S 18 (Nov. 10, 1923), 569–70.
54. Book review, EA&S 11 (Sept. 1925), 431.
55. "Colored Trade School at Gary, Indiana," School Life 7 (Nov. 1921), 65.

basis the history of Negroes in America, "their struggles, their accomplishments in education, literature, art, music, and in the accumulation of wealth, their contributions to America in industry, agriculture, and in the arts and sciences, and in peace and war."[56] The Department of Superintendence had already anticipated one suggestion by having at their Dallas convention in 1927 a chorus of 600 voices from the Booker T. Washington High School in a program of spirituals. "No convention in the South," noted the secretary of the department, "is complete without Negro spirituals."[57]

The expressions of white educators also included a theme of praise for what blacks had accomplished. "There is no more amazing picture in the history of education," said Ray Lyman Wilbur, Secretary of the Interior (on leave from his Stanford presidency), "than that presented by the American citizen of the Negro race. His advance forward with our civilization has been phenomenal." In 1927, the *Journal of Education* pointed happily to the fact that 102 students had been graduated from the "colored high school" of Louisville, Kentucky, the previous year and that this high school had a college-going rate among its graduates of 60 percent. The *Journal* noted further that Louisville had ten colored lawyers, three hospitals, seventy-five churches, and five newspapers and that "they have their own swimming pool, parks, and playgrounds, each carefully elaborated for best uses." In contrast with some other expressions on the matter, the *Journal* testified to the "readiness" with which Negro youth in the South went to high school when they had one available.[58]

V

"Pupils are permitted to enter all gates regularly assigned to them," wrote the administrative assistant of the James Monroe High School of New York City, "but no pupil is permitted to enter his section room after the late gong has sounded. He must report to the attendance

56. N. C. Newbold, "Report of the Committee To Cooperate with the National Association of Teachers in Colored Schools," *NEA Proc*, 1928, p. 218.

57. S. D. Shankland, "A Review for Superintendents," *ER* 63 (May 1927), 259.

58. "Negro Education Rise Traced by Secretary Wilbur," *School Life* 16 (Dec. 1930), 70; "Education of Negroes," *J Ed* 105 (May 30, 1927), 588.

adviser for a late slip, for recording, for investigation, and, if necessary, for punishment."[59]

The foregoing illustrates the assumptions made about students, individually and collectively, by teachers and administrators, as well as the institutional environment of the high schools. There were, of course, many variations in school rules and policies, but student populations lived under tight regulation and control, some of it contributed by themselves. The period of the 1920s, of course, was not unique in this, but every age contributes its own concerns. The teachers and administrators of the twenties were interacting not only with the idea of confronting a student group much less highly selected than that of the past, but also with the stereotype of "flaming youth" engaged in flouting prewar norms and conventions. Although student misconduct (especially in colleges) was part of the American tradition, the school staffs of the 1920s sighed with nostalgia over the presumably easier tasks of their predecessors and deplored what they felt to be the especially unfair and troublesome nature of their own.

Many of the rules, of course, like those of the James Monroe High School, dealt with administrative routines such as attendance checking. That even such matters were not emotionally neutral, however, appears in the administrative assistant's use of such charged words as investigation and punishment. Even so, the routines were not always inhumanely applied. Authorities at the Wadleigh High School in New York City sought to take into account the "weighty" problems of a student "who must pit her arrival at school on schedule against the overwhelming odds of crowded subways, slow trolleys, and dilatory trains," and they gave teachers discretionary power to excuse the tardiness or to assign the culprit to extra time in school. Wadleigh High also experimented with a 9:30 starting time for girls who lived great distances from the school.[60] These, of course, were schools of the metropolis. Rural students brought by bus had the advantage of a situation in which only the bus or its driver could be blamed. Many rural high school students, however, still walked long distances to school, as did many students in cities. Perhaps these problems were simplest for the rural students in western states who lived too far from school to commute and who stayed throughout the school week in campus dormitories maintained

59. Israel Appell, "Absence and Lateness in the James Monroe High School," *High Points* 13 (June 1931), 69.

60. A. Noll, "Curing Lateness," *High Points* 11 (Jan. 1929), 44–45.

by the districts. (In the mid-1920s, for instance, Montana maintained nineteen, housing some 500 students.)[61]

Tardiness and attendance, in any case, constituted only one domain of control, perhaps the least emotionally charged and the most directly traceable to a passion for administrative efficiency as an end in itself. Another domain, not clearly identifiable as administrative routine but considered of overwhelming importance, was that of student dress, both as general policy and as enforced with individual students. One of the "problem cases" at Tilden Technical High School, Chicago, was a boy who refused to close his shirt collar and pull up his tie. The boy said that the buttoned-up collar and pulled-up tie gave him headaches, whereupon the authorities took the trouble to refute this by giving him a physical examination supposedly showing no such connection. "He was questioned," said the report, "and finally confessed that he had been used to doing as he pleased at home and intended to do as he pleased at school as well." The danger in this situation, explained the report, was that this boy, considered a room leader, might lead other boys to think "they should have such rights."[62]

In other such episodes larger numbers were involved. By order of the principal, girls at the Hackensack, New Jersey, high school in 1929 were forbidden to attend school without wearing stockings. The principal of the Elwood, Indiana, high school dismissed twenty-four boys wearing bib overalls, instructing them not to return unless dressed otherwise. According to the principal, the bib overalls were worn to "cause a disturbance," and he was probably right, indicating that to both students and faculty the issue was not the overalls but the challenge to authority. Whether students would have regarded it so had not the authority been claimed is another question. Other reports sounded the notes of proprietorship and fear. "If the parents of the Southbridge [Massachusetts] High girls," said its principal, who had sent twenty-five girls home for alleged improprieties in dress, "do not make their daughters dress properly I will, or they will not be students in my school." Some schools required girls to wear uniforms; in the Knoxville, Tennessee, high school in 1920 the uniform consisted of a blue wool serge middy suit with brown or black low-heeled shoes, modified in fall and spring by an

61. Edith A. Lathrop, "Dormitories from Montana Public High School Pupils," *School Life* 13 (Jan. 1928), 92–93.

62. Ray A. Bixler, "High School Problem Cases," *Chicago Schools Journal* 13 (Nov. 1930), 142.

optional white or khaki middy blouse, all this worked up "by a committee of the local parent-teachers' association from specifications adopted by the board."[63]

Dress codes also came from students, or at least were voted into effect by them. The girls of West High School, Denver, for example, passed resolutions in 1921 against eyebrow pencils, lipstick, rouge, heavy face powder, extreme low necks and formal evening gowns, and fancy hose, and added a comment that silk hose were unnecessary for school wear. Also in 1921, the girls of East High School, Columbus, Ohio, by a vote of 261 to 54 condemned rouge, lipsticks, eyebrow pencils, high heels, thin georgette waists, and elaborate silks. In May 1922 the girls of the Madison, Wisconsin, high school voted against skirts too short and scant, the use of powder puffs in public, loud and boisterous talking, and undue familiarity with boys. Most of the reported actions of this kind came from and affected girls, but at the Stevens Point, Wisconsin, high school the boys in 1923 reportedly formed a secret organization to abolish "sheiks," who they claimed were bringing the school into disrepute. The *Wisconsin Journal of Education* complacently reflected that "disapproval of classmates will do more than hours of lengthy speeches by principals and teachers to rid a school of silly fads."[64]

The main issue in the academic life of the school was homework. Forty-five minutes of outside preparation a day for each major subject was usually expected, and the principal of Morris High School in New York City urged his teachers not to require more than that. A four-subject schedule required three hours of preparation, the amount of time at home varying with what was done in study halls. At the High School of Commerce in New York City, the authorities stipulated time allotments in a manual for parents. "Even though a pupil may have a study period each day in school," said this manual, "his outside preparation should extend from one and a half to two and a half hours, depending upon the number of lessons prepared and the aptitude of

63. "Sun-Tan Backs and Bare Legs Hit," *J Ed* 110 (July 8, 1929), 41; "High School Boys Must Dress Properly," *J Ed* 109 (June 3, 1929), 618; quoted in "News Note," *J Ed* 110:41; "Notes and Comment," *Sierra Educational News* 16 (Dec. 1920), 613.

64. "High School High Spots for Journal Readers," *J Ed* 94 (Sept. 8, 1921), 204; "Educational News," *Ohio Educational Monthly* 70 (Feb. 1921), 66; "Wisconsin Section," *American School* 8 (June 1922), 176bw; "Wisconsin Educational News," 55 (Feb. 1923), 36.

the boy for the subject." In the end, of course, students responded to homework as they saw fit. A survey made in the high schools of Lincoln, Nebraska, showed that the amount of time their students spent on it varied from none to twenty hours a week.[65] Meanwhile some of the educators began to react against homework with the idea that more of the preparation should be done in school, not just in conventional study halls but in extended class periods and longer school days.[66] According to Superintendent Frank D. Boynton of Ithaca, New York, homework served only as a "bone of family contention," and its abolition would relieve parents of having to drive children from their family circles, and restore the home as a center of leisure-time activities.[67]

Others argued that the competition with homework came not from home activities but from the outside social life of high school youth. Printed matter on a report card from Ohio in 1917–18 officially expressed the conviction "that three-fourths of all our low grades and failures are due to the 'social party craze.'" Things apparently got no better in Ohio, for another report card in 1926–27 declared "that social functions leading to 'late hours,' frequent theatre-going or any other enterprise consuming much of the pupil's time or enlisting his interests are highly detrimental to good schoolwork."[68] Apparently Iowa was also much affected, and Superintendent M. G. Clark of Sioux City attributed school failure to "abnormal night hours" and night after night "of social intoxication." Youth of 1922, said Clark, felt that a social function should not begin before nine o'clock or break up before one.[69]

There were high schools in Indiana, reported the *Educator-Journal,* where students were "jazzed to death," with "dances till two A.M.," plus parties, receptions, matinees, movies, in fact everything but work. "It is a wonder," said this editorial, "that some of them learn anything!" In

65. Reported by John M. Conway, "Suggestions Given to First-Term Pupils at the Morris High School," *High Points* 9 (May 1927), 71; quoted in "Informing the Parents," *High Points* 10 (April 1928), 34; Inez M. Cook and T. V. Goodrich, "How High School Pupils Spend Their Time," *Sch R* 10 (Dec. 1928), 774.

66. See for example Frank B. Cooper, "The Ideals and Accomplishments of the Seattle School System," *NEA Proc,* 1921, p. 717. For such schedules in rural high schools see "State News," *Colorado School Journal* 41 (Sept. 1925), 48; 41 (May 1926), 42.

67. "Education for Leisure," Superintendence *Report,* 1930, pp. 175–76.

68. Findlay, Ohio, report card, 1917–18; Jefferson County, Ohio, schools, report card, 1926–27. In the report card collection, Educational Archives, College of Education, Ohio State Univ., Columbus.

69. "Making High School a Success," *J Ed* 96 (Oct. 5, 1922), 323–25.

Dallas, Texas, reported the *Journal of Education*, the students even owned up to all this. When 240 students who had failed examinations in that city were asked on a questionnaire to explain it, a "large percent" of the boys blamed dating, while a similar but also unstated "large percent" of the girls blamed it on the Charleston. Just how bad things could get was shown in Madison, Wisconsin, where, according to one professor at the university, the parents themselves encouraged youth to join the social whirl.[70]

Although school authorities could not directly control the out-of-school lives of their charges, some provided parties and dances in the school program, hoping to offset the students' desire for an unsponsored social life. Not all schoolmen, however, agreed. Of fifty-three large high schools in Indiana surveyed in 1929, eighteen reported that they prohibited dancing, twelve that they permitted it only as part of another school function, and twenty-two that they permitted regular dances. Social control invaded the dances in some schools, such as the Central High School of Tulsa, Oklahoma, where the music had to be approved by a committee. Even controls did not suffice at Meriden, Connecticut, where the superintendent resigned in 1926 over the decision of the school board to resume the high school dances that had been suspended three years before. According to him, the dances had been immodest, and the school had lost control over the students when they left the building after the dance.[71]

In some cases the reputedly excessive social life of high school students was blamed on fraternities, and presumably sororities, too, although these were usually not mentioned. Many school authorities took a stern view of these matters, and Jesse H. Newlon in 1921 proudly reported how he had driven the fraternities out of the Lincoln, Nebraska, high school three years before.[72] A questionnaire study of 171 school systems in 1931 indicated that fraternities were forbidden

70. 33 (February 1923), 244; "Failures Laid to Dance and Dating," *J Ed* 103 (Feb. 18, 1926), 190; Michael Vincent O'Shea to Mrs. Starbuck Smith, Sept. 30, 1925, Michael Vincent O'Shea Papers, State Historical Society of Wisconsin, Madison, Wisconsin.

71. D. S. Weller, "The Status of Dancing in the Larger Indiana High Schools," *Sch R* 37 (March 1929), 215; Merle Prunty, "Sane and Systematic Direction of Extra-Curricular Activities," *National Association of Secondary School Principals Sixth Yearbook*, 1922, p. 7; "Resigns As Protest against Dances," *J Ed* 103 (Feb. 4, 1926), 134.

72. "High School Fraternities," *EA&S* 7 (Oct. 1921), 378.

by state or local rules in 101 of them. In 22 of these cities the penalty was expulsion and in 15 others suspension. Among penalties listed for the remaining cities were the withholding of credits, denial of right to take part in school activities, fines, and withholding of class standings and honors.[73]

On the whole, penalties for misconduct were applied by principals and teachers, but the practice of using student courts, operated with varying degrees of formality and faculty control, was increasing. The student court at the North Side Junior High School in Colorado Springs was described as simple, but it aped the procedures of regular courts with a full apparatus of judges, clerks, bailiffs, prosecuting attorneys, and defense attorneys.[74] A teacher at the William Penn High School for Girls in Philadelphia glowingly extolled its organization of student government, including courts. "That an association of such students," said she, "*properly guided and led* can be not only an 'agency in control'— but can be *the* controlling factor in school government, has been frequently demonstrated!"[75]

On occasion during the 1920s, student bodies rose up in demonstrations and strikes, not always for purposes that would be considered laudable by later generations. White students at Emerson High School, Gary, Indiana, for example, struck against the presence of nineteen black students. Under the settlement of this strike, negotiated finally in the mayor's office, three of the blacks who were seniors were allowed to remain until graduation, three were to be transferred to another high school, and the remaining thirteen were assigned to a temporary school for Negroes, with a new million-dollar segregated high school planned for the future.[76]

Students at the junior and senior high schools of Watertown, Massachusetts, supported by their parents, carried through a partially successful strike against a change in the daily schedule. The schools had been running from 8:20 to 1:30, a relic of the short daily schedules that had prevailed at the turn of the century, but the authorities in 1930 changed the closing hour to 2:45. Interestingly enough, the change was made to

---

73. "High School Fraternities Widely Banned," *J Ed* 113 (Feb. 23, 1931), 236.
74. R. J. Wasson, "The Student Court As an Adjunct in School Control," *Colorado State Journal* 43 (March 1928), 5.
75. Lillian K. Wyman, "The Student Association As an Agency for the Development of Control in the Secondary School," University of Pennsylvania School of Education, *Fifteenth Annual Schoolmen's Week Proceedings*, 1928, p. 460.
76. "Negro Students in a Gary High School," *S&S* 26 (Oct. 8, 1927), 453.

provide more time for supervised study. In January 1931 the school committee compromised by setting 2:15 as the closing time.[77] The issues raised by this strike greatly disturbed the *Harvard Educational Review*, which asked editorially how far schools should be run by students. "And if the parents," further queried the editorial, "are allowed to determine curricula or methods, is not the way laid open toward a reign of ignorance, with consequences everywhere like those which followed public interference with the schools in Tennessee?"[78]

VI

It was in the program of nonacademic activities as a whole, not just parties and dances, that some teachers and administrators saw the greatest possibility for resolving issues in student life. This did not mean an attempt to divert student impulses into fun and games, although such might sometimes have been the case. Rather it was a conviction that activities were important to the process of socialization, to the growth of students toward adult responsibilities, and, in the minds of many, to the fostering of social efficiency. Activities, of course, were nothing new, and the handbooks of nineteenth-century academies indicate the esteem in which they were then held. From about 1910, however, they came to be regarded as more than desirable adjuncts to the academic program, as of equal, possibly even greater, importance. As a teacher in the Lincoln, Nebraska, high school characterized them in 1921, they were of special significance in developing the school as "a miniature community which can furnish boys and girls with actual laboratory training, as it were, in many of the most important experiences they will have through life."[79]

In spite of such commitment, there was still worry that activities would impinge on academic work. Ideally students could do both successfully. Since this was not always the reality, some schools worked up systems of control based on the allocation of points. "No pupil," wrote the principal of the Painesville, Ohio, high school in 1928, "may hold a position rated at five or more points, if he failed any subject during the immediately preceding semester. . . . Any pupil may be removed from

77. "Watertown Lops Off Part of Increased Hours," *J Ed* 113 (Jan. 26, 1931), 103.
78. "School Strikes," 1 (Feb. 1931), 5.
79. Olivia Pound, "Social Reconstruction in the High School," *S&S* 14 (Dec. 3, 1921), 509–10.

an activity by the faculty sponsor if the pupil's school work is suffering because of extra-class work." Those who failed no subjects at Painesville High were allowed to carry up to sixteen points. In the high school at Kearney, Nebraska, on the other hand, students were required to get at least five points each semester as freshmen, eight a semester as sophomores, and ten a semester as juniors and seniors. "Some form of club activity, not including athletics and music," wrote the principal of the Sedgwick County high school, Julesburg, Colorado, in 1927, "is required of all high school students."[80]

Inevitably, activities generated other administrative arrangements, such as their place in the schedule. To get more students into them, some principals incorporated activities into the regular school day with special periods, these sometimes being merged with periods for home rooms. The Richmond, Indiana, high school used a fifty-minute activities advisory period each day in which 70 percent of the students took part, although they did have the option of remaining in the advisory room or going to study hall. Activities even invaded the school records. "The record cards in use at the Alexander Graham Junior High School [Charlotte, North Carolina]," reported one investigator, "provide several spaces for data regarding the extra-curriculum activities of the pupil. On the teacher's annual record card and in the permanent report card, space is provided for listing the organizations with which the student has been identified."[81]

Large high schools in this period, and some small ones as well, displayed a truly amazing range and variety of clubs, perhaps in imitation of and preparation for the complex club life of adults. This also reflected the desire of school authorities to have clubs enough for every student to find one to suit his capacities and interests. Among the clubs listed in a survey of high schools in Massachusetts were chess, stamp, ski, camera, travel, radio, service, sewing, salesmanship, story-telling, junior aircraft, prose, etiquette, poetry, gun, mandolin, banjo, ethics,

80. R. O. Billett, "The High School Extra-Class Program," *American Educational Digest* 47 (April 1928), 355; Cloy S. Hobson, "An Experiment in Organization and Administration of High School Extra-Curricular Activities," *Sch R* 31 (Feb. 1923), 121; F. H. Rost, "The Julesburg Plan of Extra-Curricular Activities," *Colorado School Journal* 42 (May 1927), 18.

81. E. C. Cline, "Extra-Curricular Activities in a Senior High School," *Educator-Journal* 24 (Feb. 1924), 339; Paul W. Terry, "The Social Experiences of Junior High School Pupils," *Sch R* 35 (April 1927), 280.

press, rifle, current events, prohibition, poultry, cartooning, folk song and dance, Izaak Walton, violin, ukelele, book, Audubon, and hikers', plus the more conventional ones organized around school subjects.[82] One Massachusetts principal, however, drew the line at bridge clubs and turned down a petition of seventy-five students at Lynn English High School for such an organization. "Bridge is responsible for wrecking homes," he declared, "and I will not allow it to interfere with school work."[83]

Much of the work on manners, social graces, and the like was conducted in home rooms, known in some schools as advisory, division, or section rooms. In its least cosmic aspects, the home room, usually a group of about thirty students, served as a device for checking attendance and making announcements. Home room teachers could and did advise students on course selection and class schedules. The doctrine of the home room in the 1920s, however, went far beyond this, and the ideal became that of a time and place for teaching personal-social matters, and other topics such as school spirit and citizenship. Accordingly, there was generated in many schools an elaborate array of home room lessons. "The home room period then," said the principal of Collinswood Junior High School, Cleveland, "becomes of vital significance as a period for the treatment of various important phases of the social and moral life of pupils that are not directly dealt with in our ordinary class work." The home room, said a teacher at the Central Junior High School of Greensboro, North Carolina, was the best way for pupils and teachers "to catch the spirit of a creative program of really living together."[84]

The principal of Foreman Junior High School, Chicago, was even more enthusiastic. "So the home room," she wrote, "becomes a family. It acquires family characteristics, family loyalties, and family unity. . . . A poor record in conduct for an individual pupil or group of pupils becomes a matter of group consideration, group diagnosis, and group insistence upon reform as an essential to the maintenance of high standards for the home room. Phyllis likes to dawdle along to school, but her

82. M. Barbara Dee, "Extra-Curriculum Activities in Massachusetts High Schools," *Sch R* 36 (Jan. 1928), 44–47.
83. Quoted in "News Digest," *J Ed* 115 (Nov 7, 1932), 613.
84. Emerson T. Cockrell, "The Home-Room Period," *Junior High School Clearing House* 2 (Oct. 1923), 12; Nell Almon, "Personal Experience with the Home Room Period," *High School Journal* 13 (May 1930), 228.

tardiness is a disgrace to the home room, so public opinion requires her to get to school on time." Home rooms, however, were not always small enough to be families. In the widely publicized "house plan" of Detroit's Central High School, they expanded into units of several hundred students each, partly to simulate the conditions of a small high school. This plan was also adopted at Evanston Township High School, Illinois, where each of the large home rooms was known as a school within a school.[85]

The assembly was even more favored than the home room by some administrators, partly because of its expression of school unity, although in large schools only part of the student body could occupy the auditorium at any one time. The assembly, too, was a bequest from the nineteenth century, from the opening exercises that had been used for attendance checking, group singing, and announcements and exhortations by the principal, functioning then in the tradition of the headmaster or principal teacher. In the 1920s the assembly was drawn into the doctrine of social aims. "No other phase of school life," wrote the vice-principal of the Stamford, Connecticut, high school "reveals quite so completely the morale of a school as does the assembly. The singing, the salute, the attention, the filing, and the applause are ragged and perfunctory or united and spirited. The individual, the numerator, is submerged; the common denominator, the group, is what matters. Wisely conceived and efficiently directed, the assembly, in its larger aspects, has a homogeneous tendency, a unity and power that carries over into every classroom and every home."[86]

Assemblies were not without their critics. "Jazz hatcheries and spooning factories" was one adverse comment reported from a survey of opinion made among schoolmen in 1923, but also reported were such expressions as "centers of social efficiency" and "socializers of the best in school life."[87] Throughout the 1920s, the believers in assemblies, if not more numerous than the skeptics, were certainly far more articulate and energetic in publishing their views. The auditorium was extolled as

85. Sophie A. Theilgaard, "Socializing Activities in Junior High School," *Chicago Schools Journal* 12 (Jan. 1930), 186; W. R. Stocking, Jr., "The Detroit House Plan," *National Association of Secondary School Principals Tenth Yearbook*, 1926, pp. 83–90.

86. Perley W. Lane, "The Assembly," *American Educational Digest* 47 (Aug. 1928), 564.

87. "Improving High School Assemblies," *American Educational Digest* 43 (Oct. 1923), 51.

the center of the building, and a high school without one was considered mutilated and incomplete.

Opening exercises of public high schools in the past had often included Bible readings and prayers. Assemblies of the twenties for the most part avoided such explicit religious reference, but in some ways followed a moral or even quasi-religious pattern. The principal of the Lewistown, Pennsylvania, high school feared that released time provisions for religious teaching were not gaining approval and that school courses in morality were ineffective. He concluded, however, that the assembly could be a major resource in character development, especially when conducted by the students.[88]

At Central High School, Tulsa, assembly programs were like church services, with the recitation of the student's creed, the singing of the school hymn, and the saying of the student's prayer, the usual pledge of allegiance and singing of "The Star-Spangled Banner," and an amen chant on the organ to conclude the entire proceedings. "The benefit to 2500 students assembled each week," wrote the principal, "is enormous." Much of the symbolism was built around the Great Spirit, and the statue, The Appeal to the Great Spirit, stood just inside the main entrance to the school. "The Appeal to the Great Spirit," further noted the principal, "has become a great integrating force in inspiring the student's life to higher ideals."[89]

Even more explicitly religious were the assembly programs at the high school in Findlay, Ohio, as reported by its principal in 1927. Two years before it had been decided to give one hour a week to "a purely religious service" in what was called the chapel. "A group of boys who were leaders in the school," said the principal, "formed the nucleus for the first service. This was carefully planned and supervised with a definite religious purpose in mind. A type of program was patterned after a Protestant church service. Athletic heroes prayed, editors of the school newspaper read the scripture, club presidents offered sermonettes on Christian life, and twenty or more boys offered sentence prayers from the assembly." By 1927 the school was running on a definite schedule of such services, with responsibilities "allotted to home rooms, club

---

88. F. Thomas Beck, "Major Objectives of Secondary Education," *Pennsylvania School Journal* 76 (Jan. 1928), 282.

89. Eli C. Foster, "Integrating Guidance Agencies in the Reorganized Secondary Schools," *Proceedings of the National Association of Secondary School Principals*, 1930, pp. 11, 15–16.

organizations, and classes of the school." Obviously such practices were not widespread, and one principal sternly declared that religion was "absolutely taboo from the school platform," although he reported with approval the holding in his school of a Christmas pageant "with Mary seated in the shadow, holding the Child."[90]

Another feature of many an assembly program was the inspirational orator from outside. Foremost among these in the 1920s was Cameron Beck, personnel director of the New York Stock Exchange, who was reputed in 1929 to have addressed more than one hundred thousand youth in California alone.[91] Beck stressed the importance of what some might call middle class virtues: honesty, courtesy, ability and character in work, and the mutual responsibilities of employers and employees. His views were characteristic of the 1920s and as such contributed to his popularity.

VII

With parties and dances arranged by the school, with a dazzling variety of school clubs to engage his interest, and with the inspiration offered by assemblies, the high school student of the 1920s, even with dress codes, homework, and punishments for coming late, might be thought of as fortunate indeed. If nothing else, there were the football and basketball games to lift him out of himself and into the exaltation of school spirit. Back of all this, however, were grades (to a purist, marks). Students passed or flunked, and thereby hung many a tale of crisis and achievement. Grades were the one truly common factor in the lives of high school students, low and high IQs alike, rich and poor, native stock and immigrant, those of all races, colors, and creeds, urban and rural, college bound and not.

Flunking was more than a remote possibility. In a survey of some three hundred high schools reported in 1927, it was found that 30 percent of first-year students failed at least one subject, with corresponding figures of 29 percent, 24 percent and 11 percent for the second, third, and fourth years. "On an average," said this report, "one pupil in four gets a record of failure which amounts to 1.6 credits per year for pupil

90. F. L. Kinley, "Experiment in Religious Education," *American Educational Digest* 46 (July 1927), 510–11; Lane, *ibid.* 47 (Aug. 1928), 563.

91. Ruth Brennan, "A Heart-to-Heart Talk," *Los Angeles School Journal* 12 (Jan. 7, 1929), 20.

failing." The chances varied from one subject to the next. First-year Latin led in Pennsylvania high schools, as reported in 1921, with a failure rate of 16.9 percent, followed closely by beginning algebra at 16.1 percent, and somewhat less closely by ancient history at 11.5 percent and first-year English at 10.3 percent. In Cleveland in 1922 the failure rate for all mathematics was 18.1 percent, for all Latin 16.7 percent, and for all English 10.5 percent.[92]

Some school systems took a stern attitude toward failure. In 1920–21 Seattle placed students who did not pass at least three subjects on probation, and excluded students on probation who failed three subjects, illness counting as exemption. Those excluded could not be reinstated until two semesters had elapsed.[93] Others suggested fees for repeaters, an idea adopted by at least one system, Grand Junction, Colorado, where a fee of twenty-five dollars for a repeated course was charged students who were judged to have failed through inattention or laziness.[94]

Students were marked in various ways, but most commonly with either a system based on percentages or with a group system, usually a five-point scale with the conventional symbols of A, B, C, D, and E or F. In 1922 the group system was already ahead and in use in 60 percent of 259 school systems.[95] Professional opinion favored the group system, but percentages managed to hang on in some states well through the decade.[96] About three-fourths of the high schools surveyed at mid-decade in Illinois used percentages, as did slightly more than half those in Wisconsin in 1929.[97]

There was more fundamental disagreement over the use of the grading curve, a practice that had become fairly prevalent by the beginning of the 1920s, perhaps in imitation of some of the colleges. It evoked

92. Eustace E. Windes, *Trends in the Development of Secondary Education*, Bur Ed bull. 1927, no. 26, p. 11; G. C. L. Riemer, "High School Failures," *High School Quarterly* 9 (July 1921), 225; "Failures in High School," *Sch R* 30 (Sept. 1922), 487.

93. "Educational News and Editorial Comment," *Sch R* 29 (May 1921), 321–22.

94. "Personalities and Events," *School Executives Magazine* 49 (April 1930), 398.

95. C. W. Whitten, chairman, "Report of Committee on Standardizing and Making Uniform Teachers' Marks," *National Association of Secondary School Principals Sixth Yearbook*, 1922, p. 185.

96. C. W. Odell, "High School Marking Systems," *Sch R* 33 (May 1925), 346–54.

97. C. C. Bishop, "What Didya Get?" *Wisconsin Journal of Education* 61 (Jan. 1929), 234–35.

alarmed protest in 1921 from Principal William A. Wetzel of the Trenton, New Jersey, high school, who objected to its relativism. "Pupils' ratings," said Wetzel, "should be stated in terms of achievement, measured by objective standards, and not in terms of relative standing in a group."[98] By 1928 one survey had reported that 84 of 262 high schools made use of some kind of distribution and that 67 explicitly recommended the normal frequency curve.[99] A committee appointed by the Wisconsin state superintendent of public instruction also endorsed the use of the normal curve and reported that it was used in 301 of the 388 high schools surveyed in the state.[100]

Students were the recipients of whatever blessings or evils the grading system may have conferred, but the giving of grades lay heavily on the professional consciences of teachers. Many teachers and administrators questioned either the system or some aspects of it. Consequently, the 1920s witnessed a variety of modifications, not always consistent with one another or forming any unified pattern of change. When ability sections were used, for example, with or without curve grading, attempts were sometimes made to adjust the grades to the abilities of the students at the various levels. This happened in the junior high school grades of Kansas City, Kansas, where three main levels of ability were recognized, with further refinements within each of these. "A rank of 1 in English, for example," said Professor R. L. Lyman of the University of Chicago in describing this system, "given to a child in a VII-X-1 group may represent achievement intrinsically far in advance of that represented by a rank of 1 given to a child in a VII-Z-3 group, but both are 1 and carry the same connotation of achievement with reference to the pupils's individual potentialities."[101]

In favor with some was the idea of making it possible for all students who expended creditable effort to get a passing grade, especially in required subjects. Such was the recommendation made in 1922 by a committee of the National Association of Secondary School Principals dealing with standard requirements for high school graduation. The committee said "that the passing grade in all prescribed subjects should

98. "The Use of the Normal Curve of Distribution in Estimating Students' Marks," *SR* 29 (May 1921), 377.

99. Whitten, *National Association of Secondary School Principals Sixth Yearbook*, 1922, pp. 185–86.

100. Bishop, *Wisconsin Journal of Education* 61 (Jan. 1929), 234–35.

101. "The Junior High Schools of Kansas City, Kansas," *Sch R* 36 (March 1928), 185–86.

not be so high but that every mentally normal child who tries shall be able to pass. Electives may be pitched to a higher key . . . but for the core curriculum to be eliminative, to foredoom to failure any earnest boy or girl admitted to the high school, is thoroughly undemocratic, unjustifiable, and indeed, vicious in its effects."[102] The NEA representative assembly in 1927 unanimously passed a resolution declaring that "failure and repetition be considered abnormal."[103] Cutting loose even from these assumptions, the Thomas Starr King Junior High School of Los Angeles abandoned grades and report cards altogether, substituting letters to parents.[104]

Consistent with the aim of socialization, separate grades for nonacademic qualities were developed. The Oakland, California, high school in 1920–21 introduced a report card providing grades on open-mindedness, seriousness of purpose, assumption of responsibility, willingness to cooperate, thoroughness, initiative, systematic method of working, behavior, physical fitness, and prompt and regular attendance. The reverse side of the card addressed the student in justification of this move, observing that every course should be a course in citizenship and that in a democracy symmetrical training was all important. Through this card, according to the writer describing it, "pupils are made aware of the fact that they are under constant observation by proper officials, who are each term recording a careful estimate of their progress in civic moral habits." The vice-principal of the McKinley Avenue Junior High School in Los Angeles recommended grades for attendance and promptness, general attitude, initiative and work habits, and cooperation and group consciousness. "If social efficiency is our aim in modern education," she argued, "then it would seem logical that the outstanding elements that contribute to its realization should be recognized in a modern system of marking."[105]

102. Philip W. L. Cox, chairman, "Standard Requirements for High School Graduation," *National Association of Secondary School Principals Sixth Yearbook*, 1922, pp. 89–90.

103. "Report of Resolutions Committee," *NEA Proc*, 1927, pp. 1095, 1157.

104. Reported in Roy O. Billett, *Provisions for Individual Differences, Marking, and Promotion*, Off Ed bull. 1932, no. 17, National Survey of Secondary Education monograph no. 13, pp. 452–53.

105. Roy T. Granger, "Record Card in Qualities of Citizenship," *Sch R* 29 (March 1921), 173; Alice Struthers, "An Examination of Present Marking Systems, with Suggestions for Their Improvement," *Los Angeles School Journal* 7 (March 17, 1924), 12–13.

Such grades could be, but were not always, mere window-dressing. Under a plan adopted by the faculty of the Morris High School in New York City, students were required to have ratings of A or B in citizenship to be eligible for class or school offices or interscholastic athletics. "We are hoping, too," added the teacher who reported this, "that our educational superiors will soon insist that promotion from class to class and graduation from the high school will be contingent upon a satisfactory mark in school citizenship."[106]

Modifications made in the grading system, then, did not always imply greater permissiveness or softer pedagogy. For students they could mean a change from demands they knew to those they did not know. At the Washington Junior High School of Mount Vernon, New York, grading on the basis of ability could be punitive as well as humane. "That is," explained Principal Jasper T. Palmer in 1931, "a student doing the traditional 80 percent work might be marked U (unsatisfactory) if he had an IQ of 120, and was not using it to full capacity. Likewise, it would be possible for a pupil of 90 IQ to get the traditional mark of 65 percent and yet be marked S (satisfactory) on his report card."[107]

Probably the ultimate in socialization of grading was carried out at the Owensboro, Kentucky, junior high school, where the report cards, instead of being distributed individually to students, were published quarterly in the school paper. Under this system, according to the enthusiastic reporter, "the rating system in use is no longer a private matter between pupil and teacher." It constituted "a socialization of the rating system into a public forum of recognitions of merit or demerit" and served as "a source of inspiration to the children."[108]

This was an extreme, perhaps isolated, example, but it symbolized the use of many aspects of school life as pressures for conformity. Whether through voting of rules or through planned disapproval of wayward individuals, as in the home rooms at Chicago's Foreman Junior High, students were thoroughly involved in socializing one another according to the expectations of the times. Advocates of social efficiency need not have despaired about the outcome of their cause. Failing perhaps to

106. James E. Peabody, "The Morris Service League—A Training School in Citizenship," *S&S* 16 (July 22, 1922), 98.
107. "Marking and Home Reports," *Junior-Senior High School Clearing House* 6 (December 1931), 218.
108. K. C. Waggoner, "The School a Community Center," *J Ed* 113 (May 25, 1931), 552.

break the academic pattern, they triumphed in other ways. After all, the displeasure of one's home room colleagues must have been more fearful than official punishment from teachers. Students, moreover, could be ingenious enough about such matters on their own and needed very little teaching to refine the process.

Chapter 6

The teachers of the nineteen-twenties

> "Teachers must be chosen from a proper background."
>
> —NEA JOURNAL,
> DECEMBER 1925.

Writing in 1923, a visiting educator from Sweden praised much of the work being done by teachers in the United States, but found them to be tired and nervous, a condition he attributed to their lack of independence. "They seem to be," he said, "three-fold dependent—dependent with regard to the school authorities, to the parents, and, mirabile dictu, to the pupils. What an untroubled and secure position we Swedish teachers have in comparison with them."[1]

This perhaps explains the note of discontent among American teachers indicated by a 1920 report that one-fifth of the teaching force had dropped out the year before. In a survey reported in 1921, only 25 of 272 former teachers working for the War Risk Insurance Board said they would return to teaching, while 139 definitely said they would not. Among reasons given by those who would not were low salaries, the nerve-racking nature of the work, methods of school administration, and objectionable supervision. Consistent with these expressions was the charge made by the *Ohio Educational Monthly* in 1922 that the public school system throughout the country was "becoming more and more involved in a mesh of red tape which both discourages the teachers and militates against the efficacy of school work."[2] According

---

1. Per Skantz, "Educational Matters, Swedish and American," *School Life* 9 (Nov. 1923), 54.
2. "Questionnaire of the National Education Association," *S&S* 11 (Feb. 21, 1920), 221–22; Edith A. Lathrop, "Former Teachers as Government Employees," *School Life* 6 (April 15, 1921), 5–6; "This Way Out," 61 (Jan. 1922), 14–15.

to a teacher at the West High School, Minneapolis, the trouble in high schools came from administrative policies aimed at controlling masses of students, apparently some 2,000 at his school. Teachers, he concluded, were really police, a traffic squad "hired by society at a beggarly wage."[3]

The beggarly wage undoubtedly contributed much to the low morale. Especially painful was the contrast between this wage and the optimistic rhetoric that proclaimed cosmic missions for schools. In 1918 the national average salary for teachers was $635, and $1,099 was the average for high school teachers.[4] In 1922 the Bureau of Education reported an average salary of $1,769 for teachers in accredited high schools, a group in which 71 percent of the members were college graduates. True, salaries were increasing, but according to the bureau's report it had taken until 1921 to catch up with the cost-of-living index and to provide real wages equal to those of teachers before 1913.[5]

Averages, of course, concealed the more favorable and unfavorable schedules. Philadelphia, for example, adopted a new schedule in 1921 providing a maximum of $3,200 to regular high school teachers and of $3,600 to those in a "superior" class attainable through credits, ratings, and examinations. High school teachers in Newark, New Jersey, with a maximum of $4,400, were reputedly the highest paid in the United States in 1924. Toward the lower end of the same distribution for city systems was the $450 maximum figure for black elementary school teachers in Rome, Georgia.[6] Some indication of the comparative value of these dollars is provided by consumer price indices of 69.8 and 61.1 respectively for 1920 and 1925 in relation to a base of 100 for 1957–59, and an index of 127.7 for 1969.[7]

Fears and tremblings about impending revolt by teachers proved nevertheless to be unfounded. No such revolt took place. Neither was there widespread formal action by teachers for better salaries

---

3. E. Dudley Parsons, "Fallacious Economy in Education," *S&S* 11 (Jan. 3, 1920), 11–13.

4. Philander P. Claxton, "What We Pay Teachers in Our Public Schools," *School Life* 6 (May 15, 1921), 5–6.

5. H. R. Bonner, "The Salaries and Equipment of Teachers in Accredited High Schools," *ER* 64 (June 1922), 26–27, 31, 33.

6. "New Salary Schedule in Philadelphia," *Pennsylvania School Journal* 62 (Nov. 1921), 105; Bur Ed City School Leaflet no. 15, cited in *School Science and Mathematics* 24 (May 1924), 525n.

7. U.S. Bureau of the Census, *Statistical Abstract of the United States*, 91st annual ed. (Washington, D.C., 1970), p. 344.

and greater control of school policies. The American Federation of Teachers, organized in 1916, provided one mechanism for such action, but relatively few teachers cared or dared to join it. Some militancy appeared in the movement for teachers' councils,[8] but those in Chicago, reputed to be among the strongest in the nation, went down to defeat in a trial of strength with the efficiency administration of Superintendent William McAndrew.[9] The failure of teachers to rise in organized protest, however, did not mean that they had learned to be content with their lot. Teacher discontent remained throughout the twenties, but as a chaotic and unorganized force.

Chances for effective militancy, moreover, were hampered by the repeated and massive influx of new teachers. Youth fresh from college apparently were not deterred by the rumbles of discontent. A survey of the graduating classes of 1922 in 101 colleges and universities indicated that 18 percent of the men and 50 percent of the women planned to teach that fall, most of them undoubtedly in high schools.[10] Although the increase in enrollments kept on creating new jobs, the number of teachers in the upper four years of high school went from 98,000 to 213,000 during the decade and the situation by 1929 was being referred to as one of dangerous oversupply.[11] School boards gained in bargaining power, and the teachers lost.

II

The lives of teachers were defined in part by what was expected of them in attitude and style. Some of these expectations—particularly in personal habits and ideological conformity—have been much worked over in American educational history. They were epitomized for the 1920s by a superintendent at Rice Lake, Wisconsin, in his conclusion that "no superintendent can afford to burden the system with a teacher

8. Cornelia S. Adair, "Report of the Committee on Participation of Teachers in School Management," *NEA Proc*, 1922, pp. 546–47.

9. George S. Counts, *School and Society in Chicago* (New York, 1928), pp. 107–30.

10. Julius H. Barnes, "Professional Sunshine and Shadow," *J Ed* 95 (June 29, 1922), 722.

11. Off Ed, *Biennial Survey of Education* 1928–1930, bull. 1931, no. 20, 2:697; Clyde R. Miller, "Too Many Teachers," *Proceedings of the Department of Secondary School Principals*, 1929, p. 175.

who disregards the prejudices or requirements of the community concerning its teachers."[12]

Conformity to local codes of dress, conduct, and thought did not suffice. Educators expected much besides from those who did the daily work of keeping school. Above all, they expected unselfish and lofty dedication to a cause. They loved the story about the workman who when asked what he was doing replied that he was building a cathedral, while the others said they were merely laying bricks or cutting stone.[13]

There were, of course, various kinds of cathedrals, but in the 1920s it was mainly the cathedral of social efficiency that teachers were exhorted to build. Since school activities loomed large in the achievement of this ideal, teachers were expected to seize with enthusiasm their responsibilities for homerooms, assemblies, and clubs. "If education or schooling is to result in right development," said an assistant superintendent in Newark, New Jersey, "the school must provide a social regime and opportunities for pupils to participate in social activities. . . . So fully is this recognized by secondary and collegiate institutes that teachers everywhere are expected to make contributions to one or more phases of such school work."[14]

According to the official rules of the LaSalle-Peru Township High School, Illinois, in 1931, all teachers were expected to "take the same interest in the general programs, social and class work of the school as they take in their own special departments," and it was further noted that "the value of their services will be estimated from this point of view as well as from that of their purely instructional work."[15] The principal of the North Dallas High School, Dallas, Texas, was more realistic. After pointing out that the coach of the senior play got $80 to $100 extra pay twice each year and that teaching loads were reduced for athletic coaches and sponsors of publications, he admitted that other teachers served without adjustments and for the satisfaction of the service given. Nevertheless, he observed, "it is a fact that promotion to a

---

12. "Open Forum," *Wisconsin Journal of Education* 62 (March 1930), 328. For a detailed inventory of such restrictions see Howard K. Beale, *Are American Teachers Free?* (New York, 1936).

13. See for example, "High School High Spots from Journal Readers," *J Ed* 93 (Feb. 24, 1921), 205.

14. Lambert L. Jackson, "What Modern School Administration Expects of High School Teachers of Mathematics," *Mathematics Teacher* 25 (Jan. 1932), 69.

15. Quoted by John Rufi, "The High School Teacher Does More Than Teach," *School Life* 16 (May 1931), 176.

more lucrative position is often given to one who is seen to give freely of time and energy for the good of our youth."[16]

Service to the community was a logical extension of such service to the school. Community leaders who didn't have to earn their living teaching led the way in voicing this demand. "A teacher," said a staff member of Rotary International, Chicago, "is a servant of the community paying her salary." From this, he felt, flowed the consequence that teachers should devote their evenings to furthering education "by means of direct social contacts." A board member in Claremont, New Hampshire, pursuing the same theme, said that "a teacher to be successful needs to cooperate with the community in all its worthwhile activities," for example, church work, girl or boy scouts, the grange, and community clubs. She warned communities, however, not to expect so much evening work that teachers would become sleepy in class. Educators inevitably tied community service to social aims. According to a professor of education at Baylor College, Texas, it was mandatory for teachers as agents in training individual students for social participation. "Teachers should concern themselves," he explained, "with definite preparation to teach boys and girls group solidarity, the cultivation of social attitudes, ideals, adaptability, and team work."[17]

As for the more general virtues, teachers were expected to be obedient and loyal. In a letter to the *Educational Review*, Milton Fairchild of the Character Education Institution of Washington, D.C., argued the case for obedience on the grounds that correct methods were based on controlled experimental research (68 [Sept. 1924], 107). Loyalty covered many things, among them belonging to the NEA and other approved organizations. It included accepting the efficient administration many teachers tended to resist. Professor Calvin O. Davis of the University of Michigan deplored the way teachers clung to their preference for small or medium-sized classes in the teeth of his evidence that class size did not affect instructional results.[18] The preference of high school teachers for all-day possession of their own classrooms also came under

16. E. B. Comstock, "How I Control Student Organizations," *National Association of Secondary School Principals Tenth Yearbook*, 1926, p. 193.

17. Philip Lovejoy, "The Teacher's Part in the Public Relations Program," *Education* 53 (Oct. 1932), 75; Elsie P. Johnson, "What a Community May Reasonably Expect of Its Teachers," *School Life* 14 (Oct. 1928), 29; Joseph McElhannon, "The Social Failure of Teachers," *Journal of Educational Sociology* 2 (May 1929), 539, 544.

18. "The Size of Classes and the Teaching Load," *NC Proc*, 1923, part 1, p. 56.

scrutiny. This, felt Professor Nicholas L. Engelhardt of Columbia's Teachers College in 1929, was an outmoded concept, a holdover from the old academic program, with younger teachers picking it up "from the attitudes of older teachers on the staff." Although he granted it the merit of permitting teachers to keep in close touch with their materials, he found it "an expensive policy when considered from the standpoint of total cost to public education."[19]

One thing not expected of teachers, at least in some quarters, was high intelligence. The director of training at the Lewiston, Idaho, State Normal School concluded from local data that intelligence and success in student teaching were not highly related. If a student had enough intelligence to be graduated from high school, "further intelligence" seemed to have "little effect upon student teaching success."[20] While his conclusions did not escape criticism, they did fit popular folklore. Another who arrived at the same conclusions was Joseph K. Van Denburg, chairman of the board of examiners of the New York City public schools. "Tests of ability recently administered to a large number of teachers of a varying degree of intelligence," said Van Denburg, "have revealed that there exists a higher correlation between moderate intelligence and a high degree of success in teaching than between the latter and a high degree of intelligence. Quick people make poor teachers. They cannot slow down their mental processes to a speed compatible with the childish mind."[21] High intelligence, then, not only was no asset to a teacher, but might even be a handicap!

III

The teachers of the 1920s, as well as the students, were weighed in the balance and found wanting. Criticism involved not only their failure to live up to routine expectations such as serving the community and joining the NEA, but their presumed deficiencies in "background" and in their ability to teach. "Teachers," said the *NEA Journal* in 1925, "must be chosen from a proper background. The racial and family back-

---

19. "The Effective Utilization of the High School Plant," *Proceedings of the National Association of Secondary School Principals*, 1929, p. 162.

20. Clark M. Frasier, "Intelligence As a Factor in Determining Student Teaching Success," *EA&S* 29 (Nov. 1929), 629.

21. Quoted in "Teachers Who Achieve Success," *American Educational Digest* 44 (Jan. 1925), 211.

grounds of many teachers is such that they are not prepared to transmit the best American political and social ideals to the children under their care. In some States a high percentage of normal school students comes from homes which, although in America, are entirely foreign in language, customs, and ideals."[22]

One-fourth of the students in forty-two normal schools throughout the country were of foreign-born parentage, according to a survey by E. V. Hollis of the Morehead, Kentucky, State Teachers College. Hollis took great satisfaction, accordingly, from his finding that all the students at his Kentucky school had native-born parents and that almost all were of pure Anglo-Saxon stock. Moreover, only 2 percent of the students at his school had parents engaged in unskilled labor. He was pleased that some half of the students came from farm families.[23]

The same note of approval for rural backgrounds was struck by Superintendent R. G. Jones of Cleveland. "Hard work and constancy in service," he told his supervisory staff in 1921, "are more commonly to be found in rural trained persons." He found Michigan to be an exceptionally good source of teachers, since it tended to provide many "of pure American stock, reared on farms, accustomed to work and frugal living and enjoying the best educational advantages."[24] Perhaps the rural leanings of educators reflected satisfaction with their own backgrounds, for some two-fifths of the students who took masters' degrees in education at the University of Chicago in the period 1924–27 gave farming as their parents' occupation.[25]

There were some, however, who worried that so many teachers were children of farmers, mechanics, and small trades people. Professor E. A. Cross of the Greeley, Colorado, State Teachers College, for one, feared that they lacked "the social refinements that come from familiar association with cultured people, with the best in art, in music, in literature," and that they lacked a social heritage with "a discriminating caution-free use of conventionally good English." Too many teachers, in his opinion, had to make their speech over after sixteen, and he concluded that no one "who does not regularly and without conscious effort

22. "How To Strengthen the Schools," 14 (Jan. 1925), 3.
23. "A Personnel Study of Teachers College Students," *Journal of Educational Sociology* 4 (Dec. 1929), 205–6.
24. "How He Picks Good Teachers," *Ohio Educational Monthly* 62 (April 1921), 104.
25. "Education in Action," *J Ed* 106 (Sept. 1927), 197.

speak good English should be employed to teach anything to high school children."[26]

Another critic was especially concerned about teachers from the middle or lower middle classes. On the basis of his survey of students at the Kearney, Nebraska, State Teachers College, he concluded that they were like "the folk" of Main Street in their ideals of amusement, recreation, religion, and literature. He was distressed by their preferences for *McCall's, Literary Digest, American Magazine, Good Housekeeping,* and the *Ladies' Home Journal.* Their favorite authors were Harold Bell Wright, Zane Grey, Gene Stratton Porter, Kathleen Norris, Oliver Wendell Holmes, and, perhaps strangely out of place, Edgar Allen Poe. On religion, he found their ideals "rather dogmatic, traditional and sterile," but "in keeping with the thinking of the masses." Similar notes were sounded in a survey of more than a thousand students in fifteen teachers' colleges throughout the country. "Her contacts with art, music, and literature," wrote this investigator about the so-called typical future teacher, "are limited. Within these fields of culture her standards reflect those of the mass of people with whom she associates in her home or community rather than those generally held best in her high school or college education."[27]

The alleged lack of interest of teachers in reading and their presumed bad choices of books to read drew the scorn of many a critic, some of them, naturally, librarians. "One of the disappointments of life," said the librarian of Central High School, Binghamton, New York, "is the apparent apathy and lack of interest in a library of the average teacher. The average high school teacher does not read."[28] No one explained how a teacher could be both an avid reader and a dedicated nightly participant in community activities.

IV

What of the teacher in the classroom? Was he not there the monarch of all he surveyed? Perhaps so, but there also he was under indictment

---

26. "The English Language Equipment of High School Teachers," *Colorado School Journal* 41 (Feb. 1926), 5–6.

27. I. D. Weeks, "Ideas and Ideals of Teachers," *Education* 49 (March 1929), 427–29; Mary Ledger Moffett, *The Social Backgrounds and Activities of Teachers College Students* (New York, 1929), p. 63.

28. Ellen F. Chamberlayne, "The Relation of the High School Library to the Other Departments of the School," *NEA Proc,* 1921, p. 493.

from his superior officers, derided by them in print as a routine-follow-ing, unimaginative slave of tradition, running his classes as question-and-answer recitations based on assigned lessons presumably gotten up by students the night before. The recitation was inherited from the nine-teenth-century college and high school, to a lesser degree from the academy. Lecturing was tolerated in universities, but for the high school teacher it was taboo and for the most part remained so until the coming of team teaching. Recitation was the most immediately available means of getting from one bell to the next. To the critics of the 1920s it became the all-embracing symbol of whatever they felt was wrong with teaching, so much so that V. T. Thayer entitled his book on method *The Passing of the Recitation* (Boston, 1928), using the term to repre-sent a multitude of evils.

Commenting on the field of English, Professor Allan Abbott of Teachers College reported a total impression of teaching bound by traditional routines, particularly "the use of valuable recitation time in finding out whether pupils have learned their lessons." Another pro-fessor, John C. Almack of Stanford University, sadly concluded from classroom visits and reading of stenographic reports that the teachers who used "what experts call modern methods" were in the minority. "Nearly all," he reported, "make oral assignments of the 'take from page 80 to page 87' type. The forms of motivation include the tradi-tional ones of examinations, grades, and discipline. The examinations are of the essay type, and are given frequently. Teachers do not use objective tests. Few of them supervise study. Still fewer employ visual aids, such as charts, pictures, and objects." Even their questioning, he thought, was inept. "Almost all the class exercises consist of drill. The stimuli addressed to the pupils are the familiar 'tell,' 'state,' 'who,' 'when,' 'explain'; the responses consist of a single word 'yes,' and 'no,' single sentences and very infrequently a topical discussion."[29]

Practical teachers were concerned about good ways of doing the job, however, and the recitation method generated its own body of tech-niques. One experienced teacher set forth her style in a how-to-do-it address to "new and inexperienced comrades" in Mason County, Mis-souri. "The necessary books, paper, and material," she said, "are laid ready on the desk. Do not wait until the class is there before you get

29. Book review, *EJ* 16 (June 1927), 480–81; "High School Supervision," Superintendence *Report*, 1928, p. 179.

your material ready. At once: 'Tomorrow's lesson will be—' and I devote ten or fifteen or more minutes to the assignment. Occasionally the assignment is better at the close of the recitation; but it is difficult to leave just the proper amount of time and there must be no time left over." She advised her audience to let the students talk in class if they were helping one another with their work (implying that there was some time for classroom study), only on no account should they be left "to sit and talk, powder their noses, comb their bobbed locks, or sleek up their pompadours." Also, she confided, "don't 'bawl' them out too often." The principal of the Rockford, Illinois, high school in 1925 included the following questions in a list he discussed with his teachers: "Should the teacher stand or sit? What is the art of questioning? Should the teacher call a pupil's name before asking a question? What is the danger of questioning in a uniform order? Should pupils be prompted in recitations?"[30]

V

Neither the teachers nor their critics could undo the past, but school authorities, true to the energetic optimism of the times, refused to accept its presumed consequences as inevitable. They stood ready to apply remedial measures. For deficiencies in home background, culture, and professional preparation, they prescribed institutes, reading circles, and summer schools; for incompetence in the classroom, they prescribed supervision.

The institute or convention was by the 1920s a relatively ancient institution in American pedagogy, going back to the times and influence of Henry Barnard and Horace Mann. Its speakers covered both professional and general topics. The Missouri state convention in 1927 offered Harold Rugg presumably for the one and Bertrand Russell and Will Durant for the other.[31] Wisconsin invited Walter Lippmann in 1926 and Bertrand Russell the following year.[32] County and local institutes

---

30. Iva Z. Butler, "Classroom Technique," *School and Community* 9 (Nov. 1923), 401; "Questions for Discussions at Teachers' Meetings," *Sch R* 33 (May 1925), 332.

31. Genevieve Turk, "Our State MSTA Program 1927," *School and Community* 13 (Sept. 1927), 352–53.

32. Note, *Wisconsin Journal of Education* 59 (Oct. 1926), 87–89; 60 (Oct. 1927), 120.

usually had to be content with speakers of less than national fame, although some large metropolitan school systems were able to draw impressive national talent as well. Music was an inevitable feature of institutes, large and small, as it was of NEA and Department of Superintendence conventions, and it served to supplement the culture brought by the general speakers.

An enthusiastic report of the Los Angeles City Schools Institute of 1922 stated that it had "come and gone in a blaze of glory." It had been "a colossal program," said this reporter, one requiring six days and nights. Each annual institute, he explained, reflected "the dominant educational thought of the hour": Americanization one year, vocational training the next, junior high schools in a third, and in 1922, the spiritual values of life. There had been twelve banquets, with "eminent speakers," and "the elegance and distinction of these occasions" tended "to lift teachers out of their ruts and create a wholesome class-consciousness and pride in their profession."[33]

There were frequent complaints about badly prepared schedules and mismanaged arrangements. Perhaps such complaints offered teachers one way to retaliate, as did also the traditional practice of gossiping and talking while sessions were in progress. "I have heard," said William McAndrew in 1928, "the chairman of teachers' meetings in Boston stop the speaker until whisperers could be quieted." He reported, not entirely with approval, a stern warning issued by a county superintendent at the beginning of a session. "I want you to understand," said this disciplinarian, "that the state is paying good money to hire these expensive speakers to address you. I don't want that money wasted by your gossiping during the speeches. If I see any teacher communicating to her neighbor I will stop the speaker and reprimand the offender." He got perfect order, said McAndrew, but it was that "of the jail and whipping post." However he added, "you can't rely on the unaided honor and good manners of us teachers in meetings of this kind."[34]

Like the institutes, reading circles too had originated in the nineteenth century, and more than half the states had them in 1922. In its mechanical arrangement, a reading circle was a kind of cooperative formed, usually under the auspices of the state teachers' association or the state department of public instruction, to buy books on an approved

33. Charles T. Conger, "A Resume of the Institute of 1922," *Los Angeles School Journal* 6 (Jan. 2, 1923), 11–12.
34. "Matters of Moment," *S&S* 28 (Nov. 3, 1928), 554–55.

list inexpensively. Participating teachers in Ohio in 1920–21 could buy five books for seven dollars, four of these on professional topics.[35] Participation was semivoluntary, and there were various inducements. In some states the circles were involved in certificate renewal: questions might be taken from the adopted books or provision made that papers written for the reading course could be substituted for the examinations in whole or part. The numbers of teachers enrolled ran into the thousands in some states: four to five thousand in Missouri and seven thousand in Indiana in 1922,[36] for example, and eight thousand in Wisconsin in 1925.[37] It was obviously no small plum for a writer to get his book on one of the approved lists.

Of the many testimonials to the circles, one of the most moving came from Lewis M. Terman of Stanford, father of the Stanford-Binet intelligence examination. Seeking to explain the large number of national educational leaders who had come from Indiana, where he had started his career, he found the answer in the reading circles. His own career, he felt, had been greatly influenced "by studying, when I was a poorly prepared rural teacher of that state, Plato's *Republic*, James's *Talks to Teachers*, and other reading circle books of those years."[38]

Standing highest in the estimation of pedagogical leaders was summer school, an institution grown to staggering proportions and in 1927 enrolling some 45 percent of the entire force of 845,000 teachers, administrators, and supervisors throughout the nation. Contrary to folklore, not all of them took courses in education, although about two-thirds did.[39] Presumably some in education courses took other courses as well. A substantial portion of the summer school enterprise, accordingly, was used by teachers either for more work in their teaching fields or for general study.

Summer school, said the positive-thinking *Journal of Education* in 1921, was "the one great summer luxury" for teachers. "It is a great combination of pleasure and professional profit, of recreation and inspi-

35. Advertisement, *Ohio Educational Monthly* 70 (April 1921), inside front cover.

36. Richard G. Boone, "State Teachers' Reading Circles," *Sierra Educational News* 18 (May 1922), 278.

37. John Callahan, "State Department of Public Instruction," *Wisconsin Journal of Education* 57 (Jan. 1925), 147.

38. "Growth through Professional Reading," *NEA J* 17 (May 1928), 137.

39. "Teachers Everywhere Seek Professional Improvement," *School Science and Mathematics* 25 (April 1928), 375.

ration, of comradeship and scholastic credit," said this editorial, adding, however, that teachers should not make it too strenuous and should regard it as "primarily recreational." Moreover, teachers could get better jobs by getting to know people from other school systems. The *New York World-Telegram* took a positive although somewhat amused view of summer school at Teachers College, Columbia. "The knowledge-hunger, growing during the winter," said this metropolitan paper, "takes the wings of adventure, and the provincial comes for a time to sip peda-gogical wine in the metropolis. So does the liberalizing, humanizing influence not only of Columbia University but of New York City also penetrate into the remotest and obscurest localities of the country."[40]

Some teachers felt they were in summer school under duress and hated it. One wrote anonymously in 1929, "Having received the com-mand from our superintendent, as usual, that we must attend summer school . . . thousands of us flocked to the State Universities this year, as usual, and enrolled in the school of education. . . . 'Scholarship is no longer the primary purpose of the public school,' the lecturer informs us; and recalling our year's duties of supervising vaudeville shows and other 'extracurricular activities,' we understand." Perhaps it was danger-ous, wrote a tongue-in-cheek observer, to bring such teachers together in summer school where discontent could spread. "Rebels find one another in the crowd," she pointed out, "and the tiny flame of revolt is fanned. The summer school, with its intermingling of people from all parts of the country, contains within it a perilous germ. Slave looks at slave and wonders what will make them free."[41]

According to Professor Edgar W. Knight of the University of North Carolina, however, the overwhelming majority of teachers in summer schools, or at least those at which he had taught, found something more than even the pleasant luxury described by the *Journal of Education*. Many of them, he said, "take their course with apostolic fervor, as if they were going to prayers" and consult the professor in his office "until his tongue hangs out for sheer exhaustion." The ancestry of the summer school, he concluded, could be found in Chautauqua, the Sun-day School, and the camp meeting; the sessions of the 1920s were still

40. "Summer Schools Supreme," 93 (April 7, 1921), 380; "On Morningside Heights," July 6, 1931.

41. A Schoolma'am, "Summer School Is Over," *The Nation* 129 (Aug. 28, 1929), 220; Lorinne Pruette, "Summer School," *ibid.* 127 (July 25, 1928), 87.

marked by the emotional characteristics of those ancestral institutions.[42]

Regardless of what teachers may have thought about summer school, it is clear that they did not respond with apostolic fervor to supervision in their own local systems. Criticism of supervision, wrote a teacher at the Technical High School, Omaha, in 1925, "has blossomed perennially, for the last seven years, in many state or national conventions of public school teachers."[43] Supervision in the formal sense was newer in high schools than in elementary schools, and much of the dissent came from high school teachers. Those in Chicago in 1925 voted 1,038 to 76 against the proposal to inaugurate supervision in the high schools of that city.[44]

As an aspect of scientific management, supervision was aimed at the efficient realization of school aims through coordinating "the work of all teachers . . . with the philosophy on which the school is built." Assistant Superintendent William J. Bogan of Chicago was anxious to push a "philosophy" of reducing failures, thereby also cutting costs. The failures in Chicago were said to cost $3,000,000 a year, and it was believed, said Bogan, that "adequate supervision" could "reduce this amount to a marked degree." Sustaining the note of scientific management, the superintendent of schools in Detroit defined a supervisor as one who had behind him "so large a body of scientific knowledge, so large a fund of technical skill and approved practice" that he was "more an engineer than a teacher." Charles H. Judd of the University of Chicago saw "true scientific supervision" as those practices that would "convert the school into a laboratory of human engineering." A high school principal in Oakland, California, endorsed the view that a supervised school system was "a factory flooded with light and teeming with activity under the skilled hand of the electrical engineer." More prosaically supervision was considered a way of correcting defects in classroom teaching.[45]

42. "It's the People We Meet," *Outlook and Independent* 152 (July 3, 1929), 373.

43. Fannie B. Hayes, "Supervision from the Point of View of the Teacher," *Sch R* 33 (March 1925), 221.

44. William J. Bogan, letter to William McAndrew, *Margaret Haley's Bulletin* 3 (October 31, 1925), 74.

45. Thomas H. Briggs, "The Responsibility of Supervision," *Proceedings of the National Association of Secondary School Principals,* 1929, p. 7; Bogan, *Margaret Haley's Bulletin* 3 (Oct. 31, 1925), 74; "Why Is a Supervisor?" *EA&S* 6 (Feb. 1920), 104; "Examples of Scientific Procedure in Supervision," *Proceedings of the National Association of Secondary School Principals,* 1929, p. 39; Howard O. Welty, "Administration of Supervision in Larger High Schools," *California Quarterly of Secondary Education* 5 (Jan. 1930), 181; Almack, Superintendence *Report,* 1928, p. 179.

Supervision from the central office was directed especially at elementary schools. In Detroit, the superintendent regarded the central office supervisors as his eyes and ears, but with discretionary power to permit irregularities when these seemed to be justified by local conditions. One report, for example, pointed out that where the schedule called for 75 minutes a week to be spent on writing, the time from building to building varied from 30 to 100 minutes. While some of this may have been legitimate, more of it, thought the writer, resulted from the failures of principals and teachers to see themselves as part of a system. "It is a part of a supervisor's duty," he observed, "to detect and report all such obstacles to the working out of the superintendent's plans." In the past five months the supervisors had made 3,328 visits to schools and had turned in 5,683 ratings of teachers, but no teacher, he said, had been "disturbed by supervisory visits more than twice a week."[46]

Supervision in high schools was usually regarded as the peculiar responsibility of the principal, delegated when feasible to department heads, usually part-time teachers. Having department heads did not necessarily give the teachers more freedom, and tight departmental organization could be restrictive. Sometimes there were both school rules and departmental rules. The Bucyrus, Ohio, high school, for example, in 1923 stipulated that teachers use the first 27 minutes of a 62-minute period for recitation or discussion and the remaining 35 for study or investigation. Recitations, furthermore, were to be socialized. The policy of the social science department called for the use of notebooks, outside reading, local data, and textbooks, which the department head justified by referring to the chaotic conditions that had existed before when each teacher had "followed very largely the method that seemed best to him." The necessary changes achieved since then, he felt, had been brought about "by that detailed supervision which departmental organization alone could give."[47]

Although much of this could be accomplished through meetings and discussions, classroom visits (known appropriately enough in some quarters as visitations) were needed to check performance. Technology, moreover, was emerging as an aid to this process. By 1928, some principals already had public address systems leading from their offices to

46. Frank Cody, *EA&S* 6 (Feb. 1920), 105.

47. Edward S. Dowell, "Developing a Departmental Policy of Instruction in the Social Sciences," *Historical Outlook* 14 (May 1923), 176–79, and "Coordinating the Courses in Social Science in Bucyrus High School by Means of Departmental Meetings," *ibid.* (March 1923), 107.

classrooms, and one prophetic writer saw further possibilities. "Some genius with an eye to capturing the school market," he wrote, "is going to contrive a mechanism which will permit the principal or other authority to observe, with both ear and eye, what is going on in any given classroom, without either teacher or pupils being aware that their acts are being noted." This might not, he hurried to add, be quite fair. "Least of all am I saying," he went on, "that all teachers would be delighted. Only watch out. It will come."[48]

Perhaps this threat was mitigated somewhat by a shift in the doctrine of supervision toward the end of the decade. It was becoming popular to disparage supervision as enforcement of rules and to emphasize its more creative aspects. Supervision was no longer inspection, but inspiration, declared NEA president Cornelia S. Adair, herself a classroom teacher, in 1928. The aim of supervision, she said, was "not to enslave the teacher to a fixed way of doing things, but to free the teacher by bringing out the facts and the principles so that they may be applied in the readaptation of our secondary schools." A year later Jesse H. Newlon, who had moved to Teachers College, called for new and creative approaches to the supervisory process. He and others were beginning to urge curriculum planning as such a new and creative approach. All teachers should take part, said Prudence Cutright, director of research in Minneapolis, for then "the teachers' acceptance and the use of a course of study is a foregone conclusion. The course of study is in use before it appears in print."[49]

Teachers, then, were called upon to be free, though supervised, but ways of bringing this about were sometimes passing strange. One supervisor asked the conductor of a question-and-answer column in a journal when a teacher could be permitted to deviate from the prescribed course of study. "When her methods as shown by tests of a scientific nature are as good or better than the ones the course of study prescribe," came the answer. This would be only temporary, the expert pointed out, for the supervisor would then incorporate such a teacher's scientifically verified methods "into a revised course of study or bulletin

---

48. Anson W. Belding, "Aids to the Principal," *J Ed* 107 (May 28, 1928), 634.
49. "What Teachers Want in Supervision," Superintendence *Report*, 1928, p. 71; "Creative Supervision in High School," *Proceedings of the Department of Secondary School Principals*, 1929, p. 20; "Teacher Participation in Curriculum Construction," *Journal of Educational Method* 8 (April 1929), 405.

of instruction to your teachers which will take the place of the older methods."[50]

In spite of the awesome connotations of the term to timid classroom teachers and its plausible though superficial resemblance to industrial organization, supervision remained a nebulous idea in the high schools. The people who did it had other and more clearly identifiable roles. Department heads were teachers and principals were administrators (although in many schools, especially small ones, principals also did their classroom stint). True, some of the things done by department heads were clearly supervisory, such as visiting classes, but in the new doctrines of the late 1920s these no longer constituted respectable supervision. Even the National Conference of Supervisors and Directors of Instruction was not sure of its identity and it had only in 1928 changed from its earlier name as the National Conference on Educational Method. Although curriculum-planning was being advocated as the new supervision, some felt uneasy and even threatened by this development.

VI

The question-and-answer recitation may have been the norm of the 1920s, but it did not account for everything that went on in all classrooms. Many teachers avidly sought devices that would palliate dullness and give time a shove, while others enrolled themselves in mass movements dedicated to presumably new and modern methods. Among the stop-gap devices offered to teachers were lessons arranged like football and baseball games.[51] Handwork was also highly favored, especially in English and social studies. Students made puppets, costumes, and models, the latter often in wax or soap. There were those who sternly disapproved. "Latin has ably withstood the attacks of its enemies; it remains to be seen," said one Latin teacher, "whether it will survive the coddling of its friends. . . . The carving of the colosseum in ivory soap has no place in the study of the Latin language."[52]

Slides and other visual aids were already flourishing at the beginning

50. Roy Woods, "Your Schools and Mine," *Education* 53 (Nov. 1932), 186–87.
51. For example, O. W. Stephenson and Lucile [C]opass, "Review Work As a Game," *Historical Outlook* 21 (April 1930), 172–74; C. C. B., "Football for History Review," *Social Studies* 25 (Jan. 1934), 34–35.
52. Ellen A. Ford, "The Service Bureau—A Caution to Young Teachers," *High School Conference*, 1929, p. 84.

of the decade, and the NEA created its Department of Visual Education in 1923. Happy superintendents wrote to the journals about their acquisitions. The superintendent at Chillicothe, Ohio, in 1921, for example, reported the purchase of six hundred sets of Keystone View slides and stereographs for the teachers of his system. From Wisconsin came a report in 1922 that the public school systems of Beloit, Racine, Watertown, and Oshkosh had been completely equipped with slides and stereographs. By 1926 interest in teaching films had developed to the point where a major research project in ten cities was undertaken through the Eastman Kodak Company. There was less fanfare about audio devices, but reports were coming in on these as well. A teacher at the Wadleigh High School, New York City, enthusiastically reported great success in arousing and sustaining interest in history through use of "the victrola" for such selections as Tschaikowsky's "1812 Overture," "The Ride of the Valkyrie," "The Marseillaise," and "The Two Grenadiers."[53]

One device of the mid-twenties was designed not so much to interest the students as to take some of the work from the backs of teachers. It was a teaching machine, or what Professor S. L. Pressey of Ohio State University, its inventor, called "a simple apparatus which gives tests and scores—and teaches." To those who might cry out against education by machines, Pressey said that he was freeing the teacher from routine work and paper drill "so that she may be a real teacher, not largely a clerical worker."[54]

Such exotic devices as football games, soap models, slides and films, and teaching machines, however, were only on the outer fringes of what was known as the methods craze. What claimed the attention, if not necessarily the following, of the pedagogical world was a body of approaches often referred to generically as new or modern methods. "Wherever teachers meet today," wrote one of them in 1921, "one of the topics of discussion is the 'new' method of teaching."[55] The use of

53. F. J. Prout, "Visual Education Equipment Is Practical," *Ohio Educational Monthly* 70 (April 1921), 113–14; "Visual Education Making Headway in Wisconsin," *Wisconsin Journal of Education* 53 (Sept. 1921), 194; "Classroom Films and the Eastman Kodak Company," *S&S* 24 (Sept. 25, 1926), 386–87; Mazzini S. Lapolla, "The Use of Music in the Teaching of History," *High Points* 6 (Dec. 1924), 10–12.

54. "A Simple Apparatus Which Gives Tests and Scores—and Teaches," *S&S* 23 (March 20, 1926), 373–76.

55. George W. Gammon, "Contributions of the Social Reformers in Education," *Education* 41 (March 1921), 449.

the singular perhaps testified to the fierce and exclusive loyalty exhibited by the followers of each method, although later in the decade some ecumenical tendencies began to appear. Among the most widely known were the Dalton Plan, the contract plan, supervised study, the project method, socialized recitation, and Morrison's method. Under these various banners numerous adherents were enrolled.

In all this, there was probably more dialogue than practice. At least, the dialogue was pervasive enough to evoke sarcastic reactions from those who tired of it and regarded all of the new methods as fads. "Last year," wrote a teacher at New York City's Wadleigh High School in 1923, "it was the socialized recitation, or the Gary Plan, or dramatization or correlation; this year it is motivation, silent reading, or the Dalton plan. Each is taken up in turn, indiscriminately adopted, presently elbowed out to make room for the next new comer, and yet we are not saved. The same old problems remain."[56] Her description, while dramatic, was not quite accurate. Most of the new methods had originated before 1920 and continued to run side-by-side as competitors throughout the decade, although there were rapid shifts in local and regional enthusiasms. The shifts were of course extremely confusing, especially since the various plans resembled one another and it became necessary for the ardent cultists to insist on hair-splitting definitions to exclude contamination and heresy. The definitions, even so, tended to remain vague, and while it was one thing to show, for example, what the project method was not, particularly how it was not like the Dalton Plan, it was not easy to state or to understand what the project method was.

The Dalton Plan was reasonably identifiable as something that had originated in the high school of Dalton, Massachusetts, presumably in 1918–19, under the practical leadership of Ernest Jackman and the inspirational ideology of Helen Parkhurst, who had worked earlier with the idea of a laboratory plan in a private school.[57] The key idea, in fact, was that of a laboratory in which students worked on their assignments, usually individualized ones. The assignments or "contracts" were not daily lessons, but fairly long-term enterprises occupying a week or more of the student's time, involving the use of a variety of reference materials, and concluding in a comprehensive written report, possibly with some oral reporting to and discussion with the group.

56. Helen E. Bacon, "Ruts and Others," *High Points* 5 (Nov. 1923), 5.
57. Ernest Jackman, "The Dalton Plan," *Sch R* 28 (Nov. 1920), 688–96; Helen Parkhurst, *Education on the Dalton Plan* (New York, 1922).

This deceptively simple idea soon roared its way into national and international fame. The plan became the institutional trademark of the South Philadelphia High School for Girls, whose principal, Lucy L. W. Wilson, was prominently identified as an American proponent.[58] It received a phenomenal welcome in England where, according to varying reports, some two to three thousand schools were using it by 1924. Beatrice Ensor, editor of the *New Education* magazine of London, thought the plan was received more enthusiastically in England than in the United States because "we are far more individualistic as a nation." Two years later, Lucy L. W. Wilson reported on the basis of a visit that over one thousand schools in the Soviet Union were working with the plan and that a bibliography of one hundred Russian titles had been developed.[59]

Use of the Dalton Plan in the Soviet Union provided N. Ognyov with material for his novel *The Diary of a Communist Schoolboy*. As described by its fictitious narrator, the boys in one school, disliking the Dalton Plan, chose to view it as a plot to make serfs of them by transferring the work from the teachers to the students. Frustrated in their efforts to get rid of the plan, they took out their wrath by inventing a Lord Dalton who had started it and burning him in effigy.[60]

Even with the alluring possibility of getting rid of all work except making assignments, holding conferences, and reading reports, American teachers did not overwhelmingly take to the idea in practice, and by the late 1920s its tones were subdued; perhaps the teachers missed question-and-answer recitations. The plan did live on in the name of a private school, the Dalton School of New York City, which did not, however, exclusively follow the plan itself.

Part of the Dalton Plan was reborn, with some modification, as the contract plan, a plan identified with the leadership given to it by Principal Henry L. Miller of the Wisconsin High School, the campus school of the University of Wisconsin, and set forth in his book *Creative Teaching and Learning* (New York, 1927). In the Dalton Plan the contract had meant an individualized assignment agreed upon by student and teacher. In the contract plan it became a scheme for grading, under which students agreed in advance to a contract calling for a spe-

58. See Lucy L. W. Wilson, "A New Road to Freedom in Education," *National Association of Secondary School Principals Tenth Yearbook*, 1926, pp. 90–100.
59. "Progressive Education in England," Superintendence *Report*, 1928, p. 143; "The New Schools in the New Russia," *S&S* 23 (March 12, 1926), 318–19.
60. Tr. Alexander Werth (New York, 1928), pp. 14, 75–77, 80–82, 101–4.

cific grade, a means of providing for differing levels of ability without using ability sections. The chosen grade was then given to the student on completion of the stipulated tasks.

In the study of *Julius Caesar* in English at the New Utrecht High School, New York City, for example, the student who signed up for a B contract was held to the following: "With other members of the class form a group to produce for the class one of the important scenes in the play. All parts must be memorized. Costumes may be used."[61] At the Missoula County High School, Montana, differentiation in a class in problems of democracy was represented by supplementary readings in various kinds of magazines. The C contract called for reading in such magazines as *Literary Digest, Collier's*, the *Nation*, and *World's Work;* the B contract for the *Outlook*; and the A for the *Annals, Foreign Affairs*, and *Congressional Digest.* [62] Some contracts were cumulative, requiring that students signing up for A's also work their way through the requirements, or some of them, for the lower grades. The contract plan could also incorporate features that were pure Dalton, such as laboratory time, or a combination of these with conventional recitations.

As late as 1932, the *English Journal* reported editorially that it was receiving many requests for help in organizing contracts. The editor advised against using the contract plan in English, largely on the grounds of its individualized or "asocial" character, a criticism that could have been applied also to the Dalton model (21 [Dec. 1932], 842–43). A defender of contracts, in a letter to the editor, denied that the plan was asocial (Blanford Jennings, 22 [March 1933], 222–24). Whether it was or not, it apparently suffered from overuse in some quarters. Fictional students had attacked the Dalton Plan in Russia, but real ones attacked the contract plan in the United States. A former high school student in 1931 wrote retrospectively of having been subjected to the plan in high school for three years. "What is the ogre in our high schools," she asked, "that frightens the students, keeps their heads bent, sucks their enthusiasm, and kills their energy? It's the contract system. It's like a poison unwittingly administered by the teachers."[63] In the 1930s it gave way, but a derivative survived for years afterward, the

61. William M. Sternberg, " 'Contracts' in Literature," *High Points* 11 (Dec. 1929), 53–54.

62. Ruth Porter Barrows, "Problems of American Democracy," *Sch R* 34 (June 1926), 422–23.

63. Alison Comish, "The Contract Plan in Retrospect," *S&S* 34 (July 18, 1931), 95.

practice of not giving A's (or even B's) to students unless they did something for extra credit.

It is possible to interpret the Dalton Plan, and in some of its settings the contract plan as well, as one phase of a widespread desire to achieve what was known as individualization. Another expression of this was the far-famed system of Winnetka, Illinois, under superintendent Carleton Washburne. Underlying all of these was the idea of using time in school, or part of the time, not for recitations or other activities involving the entire class, but for the individual work of students. In the Dalton Plan this meant working through a comprehensive body of material organized around a topic and the production of reports. The Winnetka program, very likely because of its application in an elementary school district, focussed on skills in language and arithmetic, with materials much like those of programmed instruction, although there were provisions for other kinds of activities as well.

One may well ask how the drive for individualization gained such vogue in a period otherwise dedicated to social aims. Possibly it was a recoil against such doctrines. Then too, individualization did not necessarily mean individuality. Teaching one student at a time could be aimed at social control fully as much as teaching fifty students at a time. This may not have been the intent of most advocates of individualization, but the possibility was there nonetheless.

The use of individualized methods for social ends appeared explicitly in the movement for supervised study, which in itself was perhaps an offshoot of the Dalton Plan. Rather than herding students into large study halls, provision was made for them to study in class under the direction of the subject teacher. Here teachers could check with students individually on their skills in reading, taking notes, answering questions, and making summaries. "Habit formation," wrote Professor Alfred L. Hall-Quest of the University of Cincinnati in 1921, "requires close supervision. . . . The school is a training camp, where habits of living and working are established. Supervised study is the organization that promotes such training."[64]

Administrators seemed to like this supervised study and were eager to help bring it about, especially through schedules with lengthened class periods. The pattern often became one like that of Bucyrus, Ohio,

64. Alfred L. Hall-Quest, "Supervised Study As a Preparation for Citizenship," *J Ed* 51 (Jan. 1, 1920), 3, 6.

with a long period, sometimes an hour or more, split into two parts, one for recitation and one for study. Soon the movement acquired a literature, typified by Joseph S. Butterweck's *The Problem of Teaching High School Pupils How To Study* (New York, 1926), and a mystique of how to teach how to study. It presented teachers the most tangible route of escape from the grind of lesson-hearing, with less complex ideological involvement than the Dalton Plan and with definite things to teach, such as how to make outlines and take notes. If it tended to degenerate into what was called the workbook craze, of students merely filling in blanks, it perhaps suffered no more than did the other sovereign alchemies of method designed to transmute the base metal of teaching into gold.

Parallel to the Dalton plan ran what was known as project method. Projects could be both individual and group, although much of the early discussion and practice tended to be individual. On the face of it, a project was a piece of work, and when done individually, difficult to distinguish from an assignment or contract under the Dalton Plan. But while many of the assignments under Dalton were "academic," such as learning about feudalism or *Hamlet*, the early projects, such as making furniture or taking care of livestock, seemed more closely related to "life," although proponents of the method by no means sought to limit it to practical or construction projects.

More obscure in its origins than the Dalton Plan, the history of project method became a matter of dispute. Some claimed that it had started with home projects in agriculture, others with the case method of law schools. What brought it into national prominence was a paper devoted to it in 1918 by Professor William H. Kilpatrick of Teachers College and an address given by him that year to the Department of Superintendence.[65] Kilpatrick was less evangelistic then than in some of his later utterances, and was seeking not so much to advocate the project method as to examine it, particularly its meaning and significance. Most distinctive in his approach was the idea of the "purposeful act," the direction of the student's activity, whether practical or academic, toward purposes of his own.

In the massive body of literature that followed, discussions of project method accordingly tended to center on its spirit. One anonymous writer

65. "The Project Method," *TCR* 19 (Sept. 1918), 319–35; "The Problem-Project Attack in Organization, Subject-Matter, and Teaching," *NEA Proc*, 1918, pp. 528–31.

concluded that projects could be used in mathematics, English, and history by a teacher "who is filled with the project spirit, and who is willing to exercise his ingenuity to work out clever approaches."[66] The *English Journal* feared as early as October 1920 that there was too much loose talk about projects and urged the fixing of one's sights on pupil-purposing. "If we can hold to this point of view," said a *Journal* editorial, "we shall save the project from becoming a narrow, dangerous device and establish it as a broad, useful principle" (9:476).

Principles could be broad indeed, and the project tended to expand in the thinking of many of its advocates from a method of teaching to a doctrine of curriculum.[67] Gertrude Hartman, known as a progressive, saw it as a unit of experience within a view of the curriculum itself as a series of guided experiences. Kilpatrick in 1921 defined a project as "any unit of experience dominated by such a purpose as sets an aim for the experience, guides its process, and furnishes the drive for its vigorous prosecution." He had earlier identified purposing with a worthy life, characteristic of free men. The project accordingly was a comprehensive view of the world, with admiration for "the man who is master of his fate."[68]

The examples of projects sent by enthusiastic teachers to the educational press were varied indeed. A chemistry teacher from the Shortridge High School, Indianapolis, reported that in a majority of projects students chose to make soap or glass. "Most of the recitation time," she said, "is used for the pupils' reports. The rest of the class takes notes on the reports as given, and answers a list of questions which the pupil conducting the class has made to cover the subject as he has presented it." From a teacher at the James Monroe High School in New York City came the description of a project in German in which the students selected such topics as German history, art, geography, and industries and gave their reports in class, some with projected lantern slides. A project in modern European history at Horace Mann School for Girls

66. "The Project Method in High School," *Journal of Educational Method* 1 (April 1922), 325, 328.

67. This development is traced by Milton Bleeke, "The Project: From a Device for Teaching to a Principle of Curriculum" (Ph.D. diss., University of Wisconsin, 1968).

68. "The Changing Conception of the Curriculum," *Prog Ed* 1 (July 1924), 62; introductory statement, symposium, "Dangers and Difficulties of the Project Method and How To Overcome Them," *TCR* 22 (Sept. 1921), 288; *TCR* 19 (Sept. 1918), 322.

of Columbia's Teachers College worked on the question of how Switzerland had been able to maintain neutrality during the war.[69]

Just how fast a project could happen to a class was shown by a seventh-grade teacher in Chicago, one of whose students concluded a recitation on the products of the Central Plain by saying it supplied everything that was needed. "There," exclaimed this teacher in triumph, "was a project." She asked the class to think of items not supplied and from this came a group project entitled "How does it happen that nearly all the plant products needed by man can be raised in the Great Central Plain?" In her appraisal of project method she wrote that the day was no longer "an endurance test" for the children, that they were living and growing as never before, and "oh, the joy to their teacher!" Not all students reacted with such enthusiasm. An anonymous teacher in 1924 said that "sometimes the more sophisticated pupils recognize our bait and groan, 'Another project!' "[70]

Publishing companies geared their materials to the project approach. "Teachers of history," said an advertisement of the McKinley Publishing Company, "in applying the project-problem method find difficulty in getting the necessary teaching materials for their classes. . . . These Topics [their *Illustrated Topics for History Classes*] contain references to outside reading, they furnish a specimen outline, and afford opportunity to embody the study of pictures, the use of maps, and the critical study of source-material. They are absolutely unique in their adaptability to the project-problem method."[71] The publishers of the *World Book* encyclopedia asked the readers of one of its advertisements whether they were taking advantage of the opportunities in the *World Book* for doing projects. "If you are attempting," said the publishers, "to do project work without the help which the publishers of the *World Book* can give you, or if you haven't been making a 'go' of projects for any reasons; or if you spend hours searching, digging out and organ-

69. Elinor Garber, "The Project Method in Teaching Chemistry," *School Science and Mathematics* 22 (Jan. 1922), 69; Alma J. Greenwald, "An Application of the Project Method to Visual Work in German," *High Points* 11 (March 1929), 45–47; R. W. Hatch, "Teaching History by the Project Method," *TCR* 21 (Nov. 1920), 458.

70. Corinne G. Wilson, "The Joy of the Problem Project," *Chicago Schools Journal* 5 (Sept. 1922), 2, 4; "A Bit on the Project Method," *EJ* 13 (March 1924), 211.

71. *Historical Outlook* 12 (Dec. 1921), 335.

izing project material, here is good news indeed. The *World Book* has been built with the teacher's needs in project-work in mind."[72]

Inevitably, so much fanfare attracted criticism. Professor Ernest Horn of Iowa commented that the project method had departed from its origins in agriculture, manual training, and domestic science, where the emphasis had been placed on "efficiency in performance." Viewing projects as purposeful acts, said Horn, had shifted the whole approach to what he called "the subjective" and away from social utility. "Cakes are now baked," he said, "because the pupils propose to bake them. In the former plan cakes were baked because that is the way to learn to bake cakes." Professor William C. Ruediger of George Washington University also deplored what he called Kilpatrick's subjectivism and said that the project method originally had not been applied to academic subjects. He apparently identified true projects with handwork and material objects, such as "something of objective significance" in agriculture. Whether he felt that projects were too good for the academic subjects or not good enough was not clear.[73]

From the progressive side, Superintendent Carleton Washburne of Winnetka, Illinois, suggested that projects, when carried too far, tended "to give children a random, unscientific training and to ignore the wide differences which exist among individuals." Margaret Naumburg criticized Kilpatrick for dwelling on "his own pet 'project method'" and on another occasion criticized projects as worked out by American educators under Dewey's leadership. She feared that "an entire generation" had become "obsessed with the urge to socialize the world by compulsion" rather than dwelling on the inner life of the child.[74] Yet the project method in fact tended to support the drive for individualization, even if less exclusively than the Dalton Plan. Perhaps it was tribute to the method that it could invite such diverse attacks.

The socialized recitation, as implied by its name, was more explicitly a device for socialization. Appearing in the title of a book by Superintendent William T. Whitney of Port Chester, New York (*The Socialized Recitation*, New York, 1915), the term and its movement proved

72. *New York State Education* 16 (Nov. 1928), 181.
73. "Criteria for Judging the Project Method," *ER* 63 (Feb. 1922), 93–95; "Project Tangentials," *ER* 65 (April 1923), 243.
74. "The Limitations of the Project Method," Superintendence *Report*, 1928, pp. 187–88; "Progressive Education," *Nation* 126 (March 28, 1928), 345; "A Challenge to John Dewey," *Survey* 60 (Sept. 15, 1928), 598–99.

able competitors of the various devices for individualization. In its simplest dimensions, a socialized recitation was discussion carried on by students without formal leadership by the teacher (in the stereotype the teacher sat at the back of the room). Some socialized recitations ran without formal conducting at all, others with the students taking turns "up front" with the baton.[75]

The significant element in this method was that the student was taken out of a one-to-one relationship with the teacher and thrown into relationship with the group. "The children," said Whitney, "become members of a working community which adopts the principles of character and of good citizenship as the standard of living and working" (p. x). "Responsibility to the group rather than to the teacher" constituted the foundation of all socialized recitations, confirmed teacher Mabel Wilson of Duluth.[76]

Some of the students who lived through socialized recitations were willing to record themselves enthusiastically in favor of the plan, among them two at Queen Anne High School, Seattle, in 1920. "The teacher stands in the background," they said, "stimulating and encouraging the students"; the method eliminated dullness, made the class one of mental activity, and promoted expression rather than repression. But they also caught the ideological note. "Instead of each pupil working solely for his own benefit," they explained, "each works for the benefit of the whole class."[77]

Three students from San Francisco's Girls High School also gave an enthusiastic account of their experience with socialized recitations. They found in them "a personal fellowship" that enabled all the students in a class to know one another. "We work as a group," they pointed out, "and exchange views. Self-consciousness is lost when the girls recite to their friends. Sometimes it is easier to tell the girls what one thinks than it is to tell the teacher. Often it is not a teacher whom the girls fear as much as the girls themselves. In this type of class, we have real friends. Mistakes are corrected in a friendly manner, so that the fear of reciting is banished." Could fear and friendliness exist together? Perhaps this

75. Transcripts of socialized recitations appear in Whitney's book; also in Bessie L. Pierce, "The Socialized Recitation," *Historical Outlook* 11 (May 1920), 189–93.

76. "The Socialized Recitation in High School History," *Historical Outlook* 17 (Oct. 1926), 279.

77. Lois Colborn and Signe Mauren, "The Socialized Recitation from the Students' Standpoint," *Education* 41 (Nov. 1920), 172–74.

was the essence of group living. In any case, these students found that "sociability leads to understanding, and understanding between the teacher and the class, and between the members of the class." This, they said, was possible, "because we know what we are all thinking."[78]

From within the ranks of pedagogy came the inevitable sour notes. The consultant in English for the Indiana *Educator-Journal* in 1922 feared that socialized recitation, "however much might be said in its favor," had contributed to chaos in English, leading "many a class far afield in eager pursuit of the butter-flies of alluring topics for interesting discussion that can only be connected with the study of English by the farthest stretch of the imagination." Some who were sympathetic to the idea felt nonetheless that it had become formalized and rigid. The essence of socialization, according to the master of the John Winthrop Intermediate District, Dorchester, Massachusetts, in 1924, was helping students to act naturally and to feel free to express themselves before the group. He rejected the ceremonial of using pupils as chairmen, and called for what he called a forum.[79] His utterance was prophetic, and the idea behind the socialized recitation later gained partial fulfillment through forums, round tables, and panels.

Somewhat apart from the mainstream of the methods movement was Morrison's method, based on ideas developed by Professor Henry C. Morrison of the University of Chicago and summarized by him in *The Practice of Teaching in the Secondary School* (Chicago, 1926). It was known to some as the unit plan. Morrison in his early career had been a stern state superintendent in New Hampshire who favored social control (although he had been capable of sympathetically and perceptively supervising the classroom teaching done by Robert Frost[80]). He showed that a strong social point of view did not necessarily imply anti-intellectualism or at least anti-intelligence, and he was drawn increasingly toward intellectual or academic aims.

His book presented a system for teaching in what he called units, in a sequence of exploration, presentation, assimilation, organization, and

78. Alta McShane, Margaret Hammond, and Elizabeth Travis, "Student Thoughts on the Project Method," *California Quarterly of Secondary Education* 2 (June 1927), 318.

79. William N. Otto, "Minimum Essentials in the English Course," 22 (Feb. 1922), 341; James A. Crowley, "The Socialization of the School Program: I. The Socialized Recitation," *Journal of Education Method* 3 (May 1924), 386.

80. Robert S. Newdick, "Robert Frost As Teacher of Literature and Composition," *EJ* 25 (Oct. 1936), 632–37.

recitation, and he explained in detail how to apply this process to various subjects. To some this seemed a 1920s version of the Herbartian five formal steps. Morrison, however, found his teaching sequence in what he called the mastery formula, namely, "pre-test, teach, test the result, adapt procedure, teach and test again to the point of actual learning" (p. 79).

Morrison's method aroused particular interest among state and county leaders in Wisconsin. Before Morrison's book appeared, wrote a state high school supervisor, there had been some interest in the Dalton and contract plans, but it was the book that had a "marked effect" on teaching practices. "I can testify," he wrote in 1927, "that last year Wisconsin high school teachers devoted more time and energy to professional study for the modification of their teaching procedures than they ever did before." A year later he reported that the reform in method was then "in full swing," presumably everywhere, and that the "traditional routine of question-and-answer recitation and daily textbook assignment" was rapidly passing. He ascribed this to Morrison and also to Henry L. Miller, the advocate of contracts.[81]

Special enthusiasm for the unit plan was reported in 1927 by a supervising teacher of Washington County, Wisconsin. It had been used there for three years in seventh- and eighth-grade civics and history, with definite materials for it worked out in detail in the county superintendent's office. "The plan used," he said, "follows very closely the technique of Professor Morrison," and he used Morrison's terms for the various phases of the unit. Someone from Washington County presumably had become acquainted with the plan before the appearance of Morrison's book. More than one hundred teachers in the county were applying the plan, "and getting much better results than they did with other plans."[82]

Other parts of the country also responded to Morrison's method, although probably not to the degree of saturation achieved in Washington County. Teachers who tried it usually expressed satisfaction. A history teacher in the Highland Park, Michigan, high school said he and his fellow teachers there had experimented with Dalton Plan, projects,

81. J. T. Giles, "A Review of High School Progress," *Wisconsin Journal of Education* 60 (Dec. 1927), 210-11; "Secondary Education in 1928," *NEA J* 18 (March 1929), 91.

82. Harvey M. Genskow, "Washington County's Experience with the Unit Plan," *Wisconsin Journal of Education* 60 (Sept. 1927), 38–40.

and socialized recitations, but now found that Morrison's method combined all these. In Oakland, California, use of "the Morrison, or contract, or unit plan of teaching" by five high schools meant adjustments in the procedures of school libraries. In another instance, a teacher found students unfamiliar with the method. The seniors in the class where he tried it out "felt that they were deprived of their rights because they could not spend the whole hour reciting."[83]

VI

The widespread dialogue on methods and the reports in the journals seem to contradict the impression of critics in the 1920s that the norm was still the question-and-answer recitation. Unfortunately no one polled high school teachers on this matter. An interesting survey, however, was reported in 1931 involving 1,417 history teachers in thirty-eight states, mostly in the South and Midwest. Among these teachers question-and-answer recitation was clearly the favorite, with socialized recitation and the project method lagging far behind.[84]

A list issued by one publisher indicates what they considered interesting to the teachers of the time. Two hundred leaflets at five cents each were offered under the title *Helpful Hints for Teachers*. A 1924 advertisement of this company, the Harter School Supply Company of Cleveland, listed *Supervised Study, Technical Grammar in the Grades, A History Bulletin Board, Teaching History in the Grades and High School, Making History Real, Socializing the Recitation Period, Sugar Coating The Drill Pill, How To Encourage Self-Activity in the Study of Geography, Some Phenomena of Adolescence, History and Geography Games*, and possibly closest of all to the teachers' hearts, *Whispering, Its Causes and Its Remedy*. Some of these were for elementary schools, but others clearly for high schools as well. Each leaflet contained four pages and from 1,500 to 2,500 words. All were promised to be both inspirational and practical.[85]

83. Ross H. Smith, "The Unit Plan in Operation," *J Ed* 112 (Dec. 29, 1930), 548–49; Elizabeth Madison, "Adjustment of a School Library To Meet the Morrison Plan of Teaching," *California Quarterly of Secondary Education* 5 (Jan. 1930), 131; A. K. King, "Teaching History by Units," *High School Journal* 12 (March 1929), 127.

84. Fremont P. Wirth, "Classroom Difficulties in the Teaching of History," *Historical Outlook* 29 (March 1931), 116–17.

85. *Pennsylvania School Journal* 73 (Oct. 1924), 126.

When all this is viewed as a whole—the fads and devices as well as the broader ideologies of Dalton Plan and projects—it looms as an impressive phenomenon indeed. In part it was a continuation of a long-standing preoccupation with the technology of teaching that in the United States went back at least as far as Horace Mann. One can also speculate that the methods craze of the 1920s represented a peculiarly American obsession with gadgetry and how-to-do-it in a culture whose heroes were Edison and Ford. Some, in fact, advocated and discussed project method as a reflection of industrial processes and the alleged drive in American industry toward practical innovation.[86] This would not explain the avid reception of the Dalton Plan and project method in many other countries, especially England, although it might in the Soviet Union. Still another possibility is that methods became the peculiar preoccupation of all nations moving toward the popularization of secondary schools, with the United States leading the way.

There may be a clue also in the implied doctrines of the various methods cults (or perhaps negatively the absence of doctrines) that gave academic teachers a chance to innovate without subscribing to an anti-academic view of content. One could teach Latin and perhaps escape the taunt of traditionalism by having students make soap models of public buildings in classical Rome. The Dalton Plan was excitingly new, but it could be used to teach mediaeval history. As one perceptive observer noted, "The Dalton plan is revolutionary as to method alone, not as to the content or aims of instruction."[87]

86. William Bishop Owen, "The Problem Method," *Journal of Educational Method* 1 (Jan. 1922), 178–82; Stuart Grayson Noble, "The Progressive Teacher's Attitude toward New Theory and Practice," *E R* 65 (May 1923), 290–94.
87. Agnes De Lima, "The Dalton Plan," *New Republic* 37 (Feb. 13, 1924), 308–9.

Chapter 7

The culture of protest

"Let us not permit our great secondary stage of education . . . to develop Main Street minds, Middletown minds, mediocre minds. . . . How I yearn to see America develop on the contrary, *patrician minds!*"

—STANWOOD COBB,
APRIL 1930.

*A*lthough the 1920s allowed head-shaking about crime, corrupt politics, and the waywardness of youth, toward other aspects of American life the decade demanded boosterism and uncritical trust. Right-thinking Americans were expected to assert the presence of business prosperity, the righteousness of the business ethos, the superiority of the United States above all other nations and within it the superiority of old American stock, the evils of radicalism, the virtues of public as contrasted with private schools, the desirability of strict control of the individual by the group, and their support of schools that increasingly sloughed off academic tradition in favor of producing good workers and efficient citizens, with some provision for "refinement" on the side. These were the accepted values; they were attacked by those who in one way or another considered themselves part of a minority culture.

It is all too easy in this, however, to be led astray by some of the colorful stereotypes of the period, especially as Frederick Lewis Allen has presented them under the heading of "the revolution in manners and in morals" in *Only Yesterday* (New York, 1931). Few decades in our history have had so many expressive and at the same time misleading symbols. The culture of protest, whether genteel or raucous, was not identical with Greenwich Village or with the behavior rightly or wrongly attributed to flaming youth. In fact some of this behavior, by no means confined to the young, seems more characteristic of the coun-

178

try club culture against which the protest was in part directed. There may have been a revolution in sexual conduct, but if so it was not uniquely characteristic of the culture of protest, although the latter favored a more open discussion of such matters, and more open discussion undoubtedly there was, especially in print. What the protest was against was the repression of dialogue, not only about sex but other matters as well, especially social and economic.

There were in fact three main streams in the out-culture, intermingling much and at some points joined. One of them was directed against the prevailing ideology of business. A second was in recoil against cultural uniformity reinforced by a militant chauvinism in international affairs, expressed in this period, strangely enough, as hostile isolationism. A third was concerned with life styles and the idea of a good life. The objects of distaste were, inevitably, the *Saturday Evening Post*, popular movies, commercialized sport, and mass radio.

All three involved some revulsion toward practice and ideology in the schools, with intellectuals especially active in the third phase and with particular reference to higher education. When abstracted from their economic, social, and cultural contexts, these minority expressions about schools served to define not a fourth domain of protest but one of the common themes that cut across the other three. The phenomenon known as progressive education helped pull together the various elements of pedagogical protest, and if nothing else, the Progressive Education Association provided a platform from which to proclaim the recommendations for a better America and a better world.

II

Prosperity was proclaimed not only by the business leaders who took the credit for it but also by government, radio, and press. Yet, according to criticism of this point of view, the prosperity of the 1920s was poorly distributed. The idea of prosperity was partly maintained by the rapid development of new industries which combined with installment buying to effect wide distribution of automobiles, radios, refrigerators, and other products of a technology for which businessmen and industrial leaders took the credit. To challenge these claims was not only to attack the image of business omniscience in economic affairs, but also the idea that businessmen had superior insight on other matters as well, particularly the management of schools.[1]

Advice on matters pedagogical from business leaders tended to support the anti-academic, no-nonsense, hard-hitting, practical schooling extolled by social efficiency. This is not to say that the private tastes of business leaders were of necessity anti-academic and anti-intellectual. Certainly in the case of Charles F. Kettering of General Motors, one of the founders of the Moraine Park School in Dayton, Ohio, they were not. Nonetheless these characteristics did become earmarks of a businessman's cult, or of its stereotype. Young Ted Babbitt, for example, derided the study of Latin and Shakespeare in his high school program and with the cruelty of youth pointed out that the local Latin teacher of Zenith High, "Shimmy" Peters, worked for $1,800 a year, a sum no traveling salesman would accept. Senior George Babbitt realistically ordered his son Ted to cope with these academic subjects as tickets to a career, although confessing himself unable to see why Shakespeare was kept in a modern system of high schools.[2]

There were, of course, diverse aspects of what James Truslow Adams referred to in the title of his book *Our Business Civilization* (New York, 1929); undoubtedly few if any businessmen fit the prevailing stereotypes either of virtue or disreputability. Critic Duncan Aikman concentrated on a reasonably identifiable subgroup of the business order, the supersalesmen, the branch managers, and the agency promoters—what he termed the new Babbitry, which flourished largely in the consumer world of appliances, automobiles, and radios. He found its members energetic, intelligent, expert, and vulgar. This new class believed that the way to enjoy life was "to belong to the biggest clubs, play at the most popular games, stop at the best-known hotels, travel to the most-advertised places, read (according to the year's fashions) the most talked of risqué or detective fiction, see the most applauded plays and movies, keep the latest jazz going on the radio, dress . . . in the styles recommended by the latest fashion magazines . . . and hold, when the discussion of anything beyond golf, business, and the latest night club attractions becomes obligatory, the most orthodox and least contentious opinions."[3] This was written toward the end of the decade

1. For example, editorial, *Nation* 128 (April 10, 1929), 412; Daisy L. W. Worcester, "This Amazing Prosperity," *Survey* 61 (Nov. 1, 1928), 120–24).
2. Sinclair Lewis, *Babbitt* (New York, 1922; Harbrace Modern Classics, 1950), pp. 75–77.
3. "Our New Sub-Plutocracy," *Harper's Magazine* 158 (April 1929), 578.

and testified, perhaps, to the death dance of the false and glittering prosperity so soon to be repudiated and destroyed.

In any case, John Dewey sadly concluded in 1929 that "anthropologically speaking, we are living in a money culture. Its cults and rites dominate." Few shared his apprehensions even at this point, or at the turn of the decade when he reflected that "if our public school system merely turns out efficient industrial fodder and citizenship in a state controlled by pecuniary industry, as other schools in other nations have turned out efficient cannon fodder, it is not helping to solve the problem of building a distinctive American culture."[4]

Labor challenged the doctrine of business success; both national and state conventions of the American Federation of Labor were prolific in offering recommendations pertaining to schools. In 1923 the New York State Federation of Labor, for example, called for reductions in class size and teaching loads (opposing the "research" of efficiency educators and their business allies), provisions for teacher tenure, elimination of supervisory ratings, and the limiting of vocational training to children over sixteen. It supported the NEA plank for compulsory schooling until the eighteenth year. Also in 1923, the American Federation of Labor's committee on education condemned censorship of teachers and all practices undermining the teacher's dignity and independence, putting the blame for these on chambers of commerce and service clubs.[5]

The Illinois and Chicago federations identified themselves as explicitly against such efficiency devices as the platoon organization, and resisted the junior high school as an entering wedge for class education. President John H. Walker of the Illinois federation in 1924 called for a coalition of labor, farmers, and educators on behalf of social and educational reform. Even on matters not involving economic problems, labor often defended the freedom of teaching; the Georgia federation in 1925, for example, came out against state laws prohibiting the teaching of evolution. These expressions were perhaps all the more important for the culture of protest in view of the tendency of labor to move not in radical, but in conservative directions, as expressed in the alarm felt by the New Orleans convention of the American Federation of Labor in 1928

---

4. "The House Divided against Itself," *New Republic* 58 (April 24, 1929), 271; "The Crisis in Culture," *ibid.* 62 (March 19, 1930), 124.

5. "Education Program of the New York State Federation of Labor," *S&S* 18 (Sept. 29, 1923), 385–386; "Committee on Education of the American Federation of Labor," *ibid.* (Dec. 29, 1923), 764.

over allegedly favorable expressions made about Russian education by John Dewey.[6]

The economic and social values of the pro-business ideology undoubtedly alienated many who might otherwise have remained adherents of the dominant culture. After the election of 1928, the *Saturday Evening Post* found it difficult to explain the defection of Protestant "liberals" from the Hoover cause. One such group of Protestants, 142 in number, according to the *Post*, declared they could not reconcile Hoover's economic policies with the values taught in their churches. The *Post* wanted to be shown which policies and which churches, but its insistence was futile; the defection probably represented broad-scale rejection of the standards of business and industrial success. John Dewey, in testifying why he was for Smith, acknowledged his personal recoil from what he called Hoover's "hard efficiency." If Hoover had human insight, said Dewey, "I have never seen the signs of it," and Dewey found Hoover's creed to be that "hypocritical religion of 'prosperity' responsible for the unrealities of our social tone and temper."[7]

III

Just as wisdom was conceived as peculiarly characteristic of business leadership, so goodness was viewed in the dominant culture as a monopoly of white old-American stock. Immigrants and children of immigrants were low on a scale that assigned the highest values to the so-called old immigrants. The new were primarily Italians, Poles, Russian Jews, and other Southern and Eastern Europeans. Religion obviously was involved as well; Protestantism was identified with old immigration and Catholicism with new, although Irish Catholics, long in the United States, did not fit this pattern.

From all this came a division between a conservative and traditional America and an emerging America of the less favored groups. Dominant America was white, Protestant, Anglo-Saxon, and rural or small-town in character; the challenging culture was mixed in color and creed, diverse in ethnic background, and urban and metropolitan in context.

6. "The Interest of Labor in Education," *Illinois Teacher* 13 (Oct. 1924), 20–22; "Educational Notes and News," *S&S* 21 (June 27, 1925), 783; "The American Federation of Labor Disapproves Dr. Dewey's Views on Russia," *TCR* 30 (March 1929), 628.

7. 31 (Feb. 2, 1929), 22; "Why I Am for Smith," *New Republic* 56 (Nov. 7, 1928), 321.

Obviously there were many exceptions, for example, rural Americans of new immigrant stock and metropolitan families with approved Anglo-Saxon heritage, or Protestants who joined the culture of protest and Catholics who sought feverishly to identify themselves with the establishment. Still, the prevailing pattern created the stereotype and largely governed the thinking and feeling of those who involved themselves in the political, economic, and ideological struggles of the times.

On the other hand, there were educators and others who began to question the more general assumptions of white, Anglo-Saxon, and Protestant superiority. Jane Addams struck the note of this protest late in 1919 when she characterized American nationalism as as blind and burning as the nationalism of Europe. The American people, she feared, were repudiating their own best traditions and showing the same "exaltation of blind patriotism above intelligent citizenship, as that evidenced elsewhere." In his refusal to endorse a proposed abolition of parochial schools in Massachusetts, Charles W. Eliot objected to the term *melting pot* because it implied the wiping out of the unique identities of various groups in American life.[8]

A feeling was developing among many Americans for retaining and emphasizing the characteristics of the new-immigrant culture. The term *cultural pluralism* had been used as early as 1924 by Joseph K. Hart, who expressed the hope that some day humanity would be "our group." To many others, however, like one Vanderbilt University professor of economics, diversity, far from being a virtue, was a dangerous idea which fostered a heterogeneous population and even called into question the idea of immigration exclusion itself.[9]

In the beginnings of what would later be called intercultural or intergroup education, an effort was made to show the distinctive contributions of immigrant groups to the arts, especially music and dance. As an indication that terms do not always mean what they seem to mean, the "melting pot" Christmas celebration held in December 1919 at New York's Crystal Palace, instead of obliterating differences, sought to accentuate them through music and entertainments in Bohemian, Swed-

8. "Americanization," *Papers and Proceedings of the American Sociological Society* 14 (March 1920), 210–12; Eliot to Mrs. William Tilton, Feb. 7, 1921, Charles W. Eliot Papers, Harvard University Archives, Cambridge, Mass.

9. "Our Group and Our Culture," *Survey* 52 (May 15, 1924), 260; R. L. Garis, "We Must Be On Our Guard," *Saturday Evening Post* 201 (Jan. 5, 1929), 29, 197.

ish, Swiss, Lithuanian, Ukrainian, and other settings.[10] This approach was endorsed in 1921 by Cecilia Razovski of the New York City Council of Jewish Women, who reported with approval the encouragement given to children in the primary grades for bringing "interesting pictures or pieces of embroidery or quaint costumes from their homes."[11] At the high school level, a teacher at the Woodbury, New Jersey, high school reported a series of assembly programs based on contributions of racial and ethnic groups. "When you realize," said this teacher, "that South Jersey has been a center of activities of the Ku Klux Klan you can appreciate what an eye-opener it was to hear a cultured Italian woman lawyer give a short address; or a young Jewish Rabbi speak on ideals such as one would hear from any YMCA leader. Then such terms as 'Dago' or the idea of long whiskers being a necessary adjunct for a rabbi vanished into thin air."[12]

There was an ever-present danger of condescension in such an approach, and a commonly accepted exploitation of ethnic groups by politicians. William Hale Thompson, in his campaign for mayor of Chicago, openly appealed to the self-conscious militancy of a number of nationalities. After his election in 1927, the schools obligingly produced a new syllabus in American history stressing the contributions of these groups and their members, highlighting such immigrants and outlanders as Carnegie, Caruso, De Kalb, Kosciuszko, Pulaski, Riis, Schurz, and Von Steuben;[13] a worthy effort indeed, but in this context serving neither the groups involved nor the study of American history.

Monolithic Americanism was as suspicious of internationalism as an attitude in foreign affairs as it was of cultural pluralism at home. The term *isolationism* that has been used to characterize American sentiments in this period refers to complex phenomena indeed: not an indifference toward other countries, but rather a bristling hostility overlaid by presumably neutral sentiments. Protest against this aggressive isolationism in foreign affairs tended to be more popular among educators than protest against super-Americanism at home. The attitudes of teachers were expressed in various movements for international peace

10. News note, *J Ed* 41 (Feb. 5, 1920), 153.
11. "Approved Methods in Americanization Work," *NEA Proc*, 1921, 655–61.
12. "Expanding Democracy in Our Schools through the Assembly Program," University of Pennsylvania School of Education, *Fifteenth Annual Schoolmen's Week Proceedings*, 1928, pp. 466–67.
13. "U.S. History De Luxe," *American Education Digest* 46 (July 1927), 497.

and understanding among nations, symbolized in 1923 by the NEA sponsorship of the World Conference on Education held in connection with the San Francisco NEA convention. The sessions rang with expressions of international brotherhood, not only on matters pedagogical but in other domains. American doctrines of social efficiency and control were not inconsistent with some aspects of internationalism, and NEA president (and president of Chicago's Normal College) William B. Owen in his official address to the world conference spelled out a doctrine of education as "the control of individual life, of national life, of international life." Education as a form of social control, he warned, would not come about by itself, for the world still did not believe that it was as effective as control through armies, navies, diplomacy, and statecraft.[14]

There were international activities in the schools, too, for example a demonstration Assembly of the League of Nations at Morris High School, New York City, in December 1927, using materials from the League of Nations Nonpartisan Association and attended by six hundred people. Schools also had international clubs; they were found in more than fifty high schools in California, affiliated mainly with the California State Federation of World Friendship Clubs or the World League of International Education Associations, of which the president was Stanford's Ray Lyman Wilbur. In the fall semester of 1928–29, some twenty-seven hundred high school students in California enrolled. The clubs studied foreign cultures, discussed the Kellogg-Briand Pact and the League of Nations, and carried on correspondence with students in other countries. The American Junior Red Cross was also involved in promoting international understanding, even to the extent of discussing world citizenship. Its director in the late 1920s was old-time efficiency educator H. B. Wilson, formerly superintendent of schools in Berkeley, California.[15]

In spite of the defections of some Republicans on such matters as international affairs, and the commitment to the dominant culture of many southern Democrats, the election of 1928 became a contest

14. "Education for World Conduct," *NEA J* 12 (Sept. 1923), 259.
15. Harriet F. Hale, "Model Assembly of the League of Nations," *High Points* 10 (Feb. 1928), 24–26; Hattie H. Jacobs, "International Education through Club Activities," *California Quarterly of Secondary Education* 5 (April 1930), 295–99; H. B. Wilson, "Training for Efficient American Citizenship through the Junior Red Cross," *NEA Proc*, 1928, pp. 91–103.

between the dominant and older America, represented by the Republicans and Hoover, and the America of protest, represented by the Democrats and Smith. It was Hoover, the efficient businessman and engineer of traditional American stock and rural background and of a definite although nonparticularized Protestantism, against Smith, the symbol of big city politics, Irish in ancestry, Catholic in religion. Even the issue of prohibition was stereotyped by the dry image of fundamentalist, rural, old-stock America against sabbath-breaking new immigrants among the wets.

Schoolmen, of course, took no official sides in the election, but the adherence of the NEA and other educational groups to the cause of prohibition showed the way educators leaned. Nicholas Murray Butler was about the only prominent educator to oppose prohibition, a defection that horrified his old associates in the NEA. When Superintendent Daniel S. Kealey of Hoboken, New Jersey, spoke against the pro-prohibition resolution in the Department of Superintendence in 1931, nearly one hundred of his fellow New Jersey superintendents, evidently fearing that someone might think they agreed with Kealey's sentiments, assured the convention that he did not have their support. Kealey got in the last jibe by threatening never again to offer any of his New Jersey colleagues a drink, but needless to say, the convention overwhelmingly affirmed the resolution in favor of prohibition.[16]

Schoolmen for the most part were in fact still representative of the majority culture, and there were not many by the end of the 1920s who followed Eliot and Dewey in estranging themselves from it. According to a survey in the early thirties, the superintendent "in norm" at that time was "a native, of long-established American ancestry and tradition, 44 years old, reared in a large family on a farm by parents with a common school education who were church members and regular attendants. . . . a member, active worker, and regular attendant of the church" who belonged to five professional societies and half a dozen community organizations, "let us say the Masons, the Rotary Club, the Chamber of Commerce, a men's discussion group, and the Young Men's Christian Association—which he serves as a member of boards and committees." Only 32 of the some 1,700 parents of the respondents

16. "Discussion of the Report of the Committee on Resolutions," *Superintendence Report*, 1931, pp. 116–20; "Newspaper Comments," *ibid.*, pp. 307–8; William McAndrew, "The Detroit Dud," *S&S* 33 (April 4, 1931), 469–70. See also H. S. Bucholz, editorial, *EA&S* 18 (Feb. 1932), 86.

had been Roman Catholics, and only 6 of the superintendents were Roman Catholics at the time of the survey. Methodism led the field with 442 of the parents and 264 of the superintendents themselves.[17]

IV

Finally, after the out-culture's rejection of Babbitt's occupation (real estate promoter) and ethnic membership (old American stock), there was a rejection of his patterns of likes and dislikes, satisfactions and joys. As portrayed in the novel, poor Babbitt was an empty creature, more deserving of compassion than blame; the stereotype evolved from him was that of an aggressive and virulent bore. Some of the minor characters in Lewis's *Main Street* might have served better, but perhaps because his name was the title of the book, it was Babbitt who came to symbolize the dominant culture and its presumed shortcomings.

Abuse of Babbitt was mingled with criticism of other aspects of American life, and in the realm of pedagogy with criticism of the university and college. This ran directly counter to the tendency of educators to blame the high school's problems on the academic traditionalism of higher education. Yet according to the critics of Babbittry it was the college that had sold out to materialism, bigotry, dullness, and bad taste.

Even professors, according to H. L. Mencken, were incapable of learning anything. Writing just before the twenties in the short-lived *Seven Arts* magazine (and before the unveiling of Babbitt), Mencken was answering a professorial attack on Theodore Dreiser. What had gotten Dreiser into trouble, according to him, was Dreiser's hostility "to the mellowed Methodism that has become the national ethic."[18] Babbitt, then, need not have been a real estate promoter at all; he could have been presented by Lewis as a professor. Joined by many others, Mencken continued his derision of American higher education throughout the 1920s, pausing only occasionally for a glancing attack on the lower schools.

To some (especially professors) it was not the college that was to blame, but the students who crowded its sacred halls, representing as they allegedly did the *Saturday Evening Post* minds of their home backgrounds. One professor (anonymous) who had been to dinner with the

17. Frederick H. Bair, *The Social Understandings of the Superintendent of Schools* (New York, 1934), pp. 80–81, 161.
18. "The Dreiser Bugaboo," *Seven Arts* 1 (Aug. 1917), 512.

parents of one of his students and turned out to be both an ungracious and an ungrateful guest described his experience in the following words: "In the bookcases . . . the sets on the top shelves were dummies. On the walls were brightly-colored prints in heavy gilt frames. Mrs. Walker smiled as she knitted and listened to Andy (with Amos on the radio). Mr. Walker laughed out loud and occasionally slapped his leg to emphasize his enjoyment. . . . And suddenly I understood. Betty's high school was not to blame. Her college was not to blame. Nor was she. How could she love Shakespeare, Rembrandt, and Beethoven, when she had been reared with sets of dummy books, cheap prints, and radio comedians?"[19]

This anonymous professor belonged to the genteel culture of protest, just as Mencken led what could be called the raucous tradition. To the genteel protesters, the American college had become vulgar and banal; to the raucous, it had become (or remained) stupid. There were others in neither group who concluded sadly, but as they saw it objectively, that American higher education had shortcomings indeed. According to Headmaster Wilford M. Aikin of the John Burroughs School, St. Louis, Missouri, the efforts of the faculty at that school to kindle intellectual enthusiasm and love of learning were nullified by the first year that their graduates spent in the average college, with its obsession with fraternities and athletics.[20]

V

Criticism of colleges and universities was more than a pedagogical footnote to the denunciation of Babbittry; it was a major feature of the out-culture's response to American education as a whole, and came from many directions. At the end of the preceding decade, Thorstein Veblen had published his essays entitled *The Higher Learning in America* (New York, 1918) with the significant subtitle *A Memorandum on the Conduct of Universities by Business Men*. Upton Sinclair sustained this two-pronged attack on higher education and the cult of business in *The Goose Step* (Pasadena, California, 1923), following this with criticism of control of the lower schools in *The Goslings* (Pasadena, California, 1924), somewhat as an afterthought to what he obviously regarded as the main villain of the American pedagogical scene.

The colleges were also a target for the more radical left, and the

19. "Confessions of a College Teacher," *Scribner's* 94 (Oct. 1933), 224.
20. "Steps toward Liberal Education," *Prog Ed* 4 (July 1927), 207–9.

New Masses devoted an entire issue to this in 1929, with one writer referring to the American college as a "vast tomb which capitalistic imperialism in its declining years is erecting as the Pharaohs of Egypt built the imposing burial chambers in which their mummified bodies were laid to rest." A student critic writing in the same issue said that American colleges existed for Babbitt, for the church, and for the faculties, for everybody, that is, except the students. He noted with approval that the *Harvard Crimson* published a critique of courses and that a student paper at Indiana University distributed stenographic reports of lectures to expose the drivel in some courses.[21]

This was the extreme left, but a Boston businessman, formerly an assistant dean at Harvard, used the conservative columns of the *Atlantic Monthly* for equally bitter remarks, concluding that since colleges were made for middle-of-the-roaders it was essential for society to keep out of them the creative individuals who could be ruined by attending. "I appeal for them," he said, "because it is more important to our civilization that one potential artist like Shelley, one scholar like Gibbon, one artisan like Edison, one adventurer like Lindbergh, be kept out of college than that a thousand incipient junior executives, Ph.D. candidates, and museum curators be let in."[22]

Whether Babbittry made its greatest inroads through perpetuating the traditional admission requirements or through partially dismantling them was far from clear. On the higher levels of social sophistication (if not intellectual), the snobbery of the traditional eastern men's and women's colleges was sustained by combining traditional requirements with competition for too-few places. Had this been directed toward academic goals all might have been well, but according to many, including Principal Herbert W. Smith of Fieldston School in 1929, the process was directed instead toward social snobbery. "At present," he said, "there is no social equivalent for the competitive Eastern college. It is useless to recommend intellectual equivalents. Leland Stanford or Michigan or Wisconsin may offer quite as good training, but they mean defeat and humiliation to the parent who intended sending his child

21. Scott Nearing, "Academic Mortuaries," *New Masses* 4 (April 1929), 7; Norman Studer, "Revolt in the American College," *New Masses* 1 (May 1926), 16–23.

22. William I. Nichols, "The Convention of Going to College," *Atlantic Monthly* 144 (Oct. 1929), 456.

to Princeton or Bryn Mawr." This, he felt, was what terrified secondary school masters into conservatism and submission.[23]

H. L. Mencken, of course in agreement, explained that many went to college for the same reason that many joined Rotary or Kiwanis, to feel part of a privileged group. Graduates of colleges with low social status, however, found that in escaping from the scullery they hadn't made it to the first table in the hall. If he had a son, continued Mencken, he would send him to Harvard, not to learn more than he would at Siwash but to get more help for later life, and if necessary he would even vote for Hoover and prohibition to get him in.[24]

Babbitt, it should be recalled, was a college graduate himself (from a state university). His college reminiscences, as reported in the novel, were consistent with the anti-intellectual pattern. One critic blamed it all on electivism and said that Babbitt had passed through the arts college at "the turn of the century when the elective system had attained its deadliest powers." What this critic understood by electivism, however, was the multiplication of trivial courses like his imaginary "Kodaking in Cairo." Electivism in this sense could have been consistent with sales campaigns as known and practiced by Babbitt, the real estate promoter of metropolitan Zenith, but it may have existed more in the imaginations of the critics than in the realities of the colleges, although Stanford reportedly distinguished itself with a credit course in yell-leading in 1924.[25]

What most evoked the culture of protest was the pattern of campus life, its mechanical operation, the superorganization of activities, and the apparatus of credit-counting, all of which seemed to make the college a replica of big industry and business. In the modern American university, declared a graduating student orator at the University of California in 1928, there was "too much teaching, and not enough learning; too much information, and not enough thought; too much thinking about things, and not enough thinking through them; too much organization and not enough individuality . . . too much mechanism and not enough soul."[26]

---

23. "The College Entrance Bugaboo," *Junior-Senior High School Clearing House* 4 (Sept. 1929), 33, 37.

24. Editorial, *American Mercury* 24 (Sept. 1931), 36–38.

25. L. E. Crossman, "On Reviving the Arts College," *ER* 66 (Dec. 1923), 272–75; "Americana," *American Mercury* 1 (March 1924), 429.

26. Louis Henry Heilbron, "Is Our Educational Advance an Illusion?" *California Quarterly of Secondary Education* 3 (June 1928), 339.

The aggressive competition among professors, who promoted their enterprises much as Babbitt did his real estate plats, was also reminiscent of business and Babbittry. According to Harold J. Laski, writing in 1928, "trustees look to university presidents to pick the professors most likely to attract endowments from the foundation; university presidents look for professors who can produce the kind of research in which the foundations are interested. . . . There are endless committees to coordinate or correlate or integrate. There are new executive positions for men who do not themselves do research but judge whether other people are suitable for the task of their research." One professor of English complained of the activity-ridden life imposed upon professors or which they had imposed upon themselves through endless rounds of committees. "Perhaps the worst feature of this activity-ridden life is that we come to like it. . . . When we are rushing from one meeting to another, consulting the memorandum pad to see where we are due next, we have a comfortable sense that our existence is justified."[27]

From such environments, then, went forth the minority of American youth who managed to enter college and to stay long enough to pick up their bachelor's degrees. Obviously they were too few to make up the whole of the dominant culture. As a college graduate, Babbitt was in the minority, but it was his minority of business-oriented, old-stock American leaders, whether college graduates or not, who put their stamp on American life. When they went to college, or sent their children, or served on boards of governance, they put their stamp on higher education as well. They were the ones who imparted Babbittry and its life-style to the American college dream that had once lured farm youth like Horace Mann to the joys and treasures of the classical tongues.

Those college graduates who chose high school teaching rather than real estate promotion may have loved learning more than Babbitt, but they were pulled, on a lower level of affluence, into the Babbitt life-style nonetheless. To many of the men, not the least of the rewards of becoming a principal or superintendent was election to local Kiwanis or Rotary, Kiwanis if principal, Rotary if superintendent. English teachers were most likely to identify with the culture of protest; many expressed themselves in the columns of the *English Journal*, nor were their pro-

27. "Foundations, Universities, and Research," *Harper's Magazine* 157 (Aug. 1928), 296; Clara F. McIntyre, "The Professor and the Side-Shows," *S&S* 32 (Oct. 4, 1930), 446.

tests confined to aesthetics. Another journal which published more than an occasional protest was *High Points*, a periodical of the New York public schools.

Much of what passed for Babbittry in high schools was derivative and frankly imitative of the colleges, notably interscholastic athletics and such features of social life as the senior prom; on the other hand, high school authorities did resist social fraternities and sororities. Other aspects of high school life suggestive of the dominant culture were explicitly promoted by school leadership, namely, proliferation of activities and the social controls set forth and exercised through home rooms and assemblies.

In the end, although college attracted most of the criticism from the out-culture, it was the high school that categorically received and absorbed most of the general public criticism of education. Colleges were derided for their concessions to the life-style of Babbittry. High schools were attacked for not having adapted themselves sufficiently to the anti-academic demands of social efficiency and social control of the peculiar form taken by a businessman's civilization in the United States of the 1920s.

VI

The main vehicle for the culture of protest in the domain of pedagogy was the Progressive Education Association, organized in the spring of 1919 largely through the efforts of an English teacher named Stanwood Cobb. In choosing their assertive title, the founders of the association provoked challenges to both their implied exclusive claims and their right to the term *progressive*, but these challenges did not become explicit until later in the decade.

That the association did not consider itself committed to any particular doctrine of progressive education is borne out by the casual way in which the name was chosen. The small group that met in the winter of 1918–19 discussed several other names such as *experimental education* or *new education*, a term that was in vogue in Europe. They finally settled on *progressive education* because of its emphasis on the idea of progress. Cobb felt the term had justified itself by gaining the acceptance of the public and press. According to him it had not been used before 1919.[28] The modifier *progressive* can be found before 1919, but usually not applied to *education;* rather to such substantives as *schools, practices, ideas,* and *methods.*

One approach to understanding the association is to take at face value what it said about itself. This is by no means simple, since it said many things, some of them irritatingly contradictory, but the main lines are clear. They put the organization definitely in the mainstream of protest. Freedom, individuality, interest, diversity, creativeness, and independence of thought—these are the values claimed by the association and those who adhered to it, at least in the early period. Obviously they are also the values that can be and have been distorted into the less-than-flattering stereotypes a la *Auntie Mame.* The specific headings used in the association platform were as follows: "Freedom to develop naturally"; "Interest, the motive of all work"; "The teacher a guide, not a taskmaster"; "Scientific study of pupil development"; "Greater attention to all that affects the child's physical development"; "Cooperation between home and school"; and "The progressive school a leader in educational movements."[29]

The association felt free to develop its role of criticism and protest as it saw fit. When it was less than two years old, Cobb addressed himself directly to the question, What is progressive education? To answer it he looked for the characteristics of experimental schools, including Marietta Johnson's Organic School of Fairhope, Alabama. "They all seek," he said, "to afford more freedom and more responsibility to the pupils. It is a daring experiment. The freedom and responsibility heretofore reserved for the maturity of college years is now given to all children, no matter what their age." Here then was the underscoring of the first point in the platform of the association, the freedom (of the child) to develop naturally. Most cultured and intelligent parents, said Cobb in another statement at this time, were in rebellion against "the long hours of physical, mental, and emotional suppression of their children within the public schools." He was apparently inviting support from an audience of upper-middle-class parents, in this case readers of

28. Stanwood Cobb, "The Founding and Early Organization of the Progressive Education Association," undated manuscript, Teachers College Library, Columbia University; "The Romance of Beginnings," *Prog Ed* 6 (Jan. 1929), 67; "A New Movement in Education," *Atlantic Monthly* 77 (Feb. 1921), 227.

29. As printed in *Progressive Education* until April 1929, after which they were replaced by a revised version.

the *Atlantic Monthly*, even seeking to involve them as partners. "It is a movement still open to change," he pointed out, "ready and eager for your intelligent criticism and aid. It is a movement for you and for me; and its ultimate will be what you and I conspire to make it."[30]

Using the international term *the new education*, Evelyn Dewey, John Dewey's daughter, also found her model in various experimental schools and in their values of freedom and individuality. Democracy, she argued in 1921 for her liberal lay audience in the *Nation,* could "succeed only to the extent that each man's or woman's individuality finds expression."[31] This she found exemplified in such schools as Lincoln School of Columbia's Teachers College, Francis Parker School of Chicago, and the Moraine Park School of Dayton, Ohio (the special pride of Arthur E. Morgan and Charles F. Kettering, a General Motors automotive engineer).

Although these schools varied widely in their practices, she observed, they had one fundamental point of agreement, that "without freedom interest is impossible and without interest real work is impossible."[32] She and her father had reviewed a number of experimental schools in their book *Schools of Tomorrow* (New York, 1915). They had included one group subject to varying interpretations, the platoon system schools of Gary, Indiana, but they had also included Marietta Johnson's Organic School at Fairhope, Alabama, and others clearly identifiable with individuality and freedom. The identification of the new or progressive education with the pre-1919 experimental schools remained a characteristic of the discussion throughout the 1920s. As late as 1929, Professor Frederick G. Bonser of Teachers College found the background of the movement in such schools.[33]

The views of Charles W. Eliot as honorary president of the association as well as a long-term leader in educational thought and practice were of peculiar interest in the identification of progressive or new education. He had spoken of new education as early as 1869. Freedom and interest had served as his guidelines for many decades before they appeared as key planks in the 1919 platform of the association. The platform might almost have been his personal creed. Beyond this, Eliot

30. "The Essence of Progressive Education," *Ed R* 61 (Jan. 1921), 1; *Atlantic Monthly* 77 (Feb. 1921), 228, 234.

31. "The New Education," 112 (May 4, 1921), 655.

32. *Nation* 112 (May 11, 1921), 684.

33. "Ten Years of Progress in Elementary Education," *Prog Ed* 6 (Jan. 1929), 11.

contributed much to the culture of protest, including his reaction against standardization and uniformity in business and industrial America, especially time-motion studies and other devices beloved by scientific management.

"A new blight," he wrote in an article for the *New York Times* of August 17, 1923, "is afflicting education and industries in the United States. . . . Its name is standardization, and there is a very general movement to give it application in a great variety of American activities. The blight seems to have started in the industrial domain. . . . Soon standardization began to affect the school and college programmes, the conditions of admission to college, and the qualifications for degrees. It limited injuriously freedom of election of studies in both school and college." Eliot's article aroused controversy with some defenders of scientific management. In one of his letters in this controversy, Eliot granted that scientific management could increase production and wealth, but feared its effects on people.[34]

Other expressions sustained this note of protest. Professor Joseph K. Hart asked where the "new school" could find its community, concluding that it was not yet in existence but was in process of being formed by the rebellions in American life against industrial, political, religious, moralistic, and educational machines turning out the standardized product "which is the boast of all our Babbitts." It was difficult, he believed, for the educational rebel to join the other rebellions, for the educator "would still rather be a doorkeeper for the National Education Association than to dwell in the tents of wickedness." Nevertheless, felt Hart, "the real community of the educational rebel, that is, of the New School" was in "these fragments of rebellion against all other institutionalisms." Henry Neumann of the Ethical Culture Society wrote a tongue-in-cheek characterization of the dangers involved in the new education and warned that its accents were "Investigate. Protest. Rebuild." These he found strongly in contrast with the slogan of "adjustment to environment" of school people a generation before, which he attributed to Herbert Spencer. There were many parents, however, sending their children to the new schools "merely because so many other 'nice' people do the same."[35]

34. Eliot to George K. Burgess, Aug. 30, 1923, Charles W. Eliot Papers, Harvard University Archives, Cambridge, Mass.
35. "Where Is the New School's Community?" *Survey* 52 (May 15, 1924), 237; "The Social Portent of the New Education," *ibid.* 61 (March 15, 1929), 785–86.

Babbittry was a specific target of many besides Hart. Robert S. Lynd of Middletown fame assumed this in his address to the 1930 convention of the Progressive Education Association and asked, "Why Is a Babbitt?" Cobb, the founder of the association, feared in 1930 that American education was developing "Main Street minds, Middletown minds, mediocre minds." What then did he seek? "How I yearn," he cried out in his presidential address of that year, "to see America develop on the contrary, *patrician minds!* By that I mean honest minds, keen and fearless in the discovery of truth, and dedicated to apply this discovered truth to the onward progress of mankind."[36]

At no point in the 1920s did the association become a mass movement, although its membership grew rapidly after 1925. From only 1,844 members on January 1 of that year it rose to 5,172 by June of 1927.[37] This was obviously only a pinpoint minority of teachers, parents, and other interested citizens. Perhaps the lack of clear defintion held back its growth; for those who wanted to know exactly what progressive education was, there was still no satisfactory answer. Examples of schools could be given, but they varied widely in their practices. Commitment to individuality and freedom involved methodology of teaching, and the progressives were heavily involved in the methods craze of the 1920s, especially with Dalton plans and project method. Yet even here diversity was the rule. South Philadelphia High School for Girls and the Winnetka, Illinois, public schools were both "progressive," as were also the reputations of their administrative leaders, Lucy L. W. Wilson and Carleton Washburne. Both were dedicated to method, but the South Philadelphia High School for Girls religiously followed Dalton Plan, while Winnetka had its workbook-type plan of individualized instruction in the skills.

Yet in spite of low membership and wavering identity, the association made itself heard and felt. It stayed with its early ideology throughout the 1920s, revising the 1919 platform for the April 1929 issue of the magazine *Progressive Education* and substituting turgidity for directness, but not changing the ideas set forth. It was still at the decade's end an aspect of the protest culture. Its clientele of parents was still drawn from a middle class intelligentsia that could not adjust with comfort to the model of business America, Anglo-Saxon Protestant dominance, and

36. "Education and Some Realities of American Life," *Prog Ed* 7 (May 1930), 171, 176; Stanwood Cobb, "Retiring President's Message," *ibid.*, p. 158.
37. "Report of the Annual Business Meeting," *Prog Ed* 4 (July 1927), 229.

the life style of Babbitt, even though many of them, including John
Dewey and Charles W. Eliot, were Anglo-Saxon Protestants of the
deepest dye.

The protest character of the association was further delineated by
the criticism hurled against it. It invariably drew the scorn of "sensible"
right-thinkers and proponents of social efficiency. One of the early critics
was O. T. Corson, formerly state commissioner of common schools in
Ohio, who objected to Cobb's 1921 articles on behalf of more freedom
for the child. Corson argued that children in 1921 were too pampered
as it was and needed not more freedom but the regulation of the freedom they already had. He ridiculed Cobb's suggestions for abandoning
compulsory studies, formal recitations, and drill, saying that if this were
done the next logical step would be to abandon the school.[38]

A year later, efficiency educator A. Duncan Yocum of the University
of Pennsylvania praised progressive education for its virtues but chided
it for its faults, one of which, as he saw it, was that it strengthened a
tendency toward too much personal liberty. "When progressive schools,"
said Yocum, "are as impressive a model for willing submission to superior knowledge and justly constituted authority, and for the cheerful
sacrificing of individual rights for the common welfare, as they are
for 'free activities' and 'self-expression'—they will be truer and safer
pioneers of tomorrow."[39]

Jesse H. Newlon, former superintendent of schools in Denver but
now of Columbia's Teachers College, was another who found progressive education deficient in social aims, although he was in sympathy
with much of the work of the association. "It is apparently often forgotten," he complained in 1931, "that an important objective of the
school is to make the individual a social being : . . Both the conventional school and the new have sinned in exalting individual success as
the most important achievement in life." The term *progressive school*,
he feared, suggested concern only with methods of teaching, not with
the "great social, moral, economic, and political problems of modern
life." A similar expression came from the superintendent of schools at
North Adams, Massachusetts, who at the 1932 convention of the
Department of Superintendence expressed fears of "the destructive

38. "More Freedom for the Child," *Ohio Educational Monthly* 70 (March
1921), 93–95.
39. "The Virtues and Limitations of the Progressive Movement," *S&S* 15 (Jan.
21, 1922), 75.

instability and incoherence which the individualism desired by the progressives is sure to bring." Any philosophy "that denies the social control of the educative process," he concluded, is destructive of society itself.[40]

The criticisms attracted by the association clearly marked it, then, as part of the minority culture. Whether the progressives were right or wrong about such matters as freedom or individuality, they were nonetheless regarded with suspicion for their commitment to these values and for going too far in seeking to put them into practice. There was, it appeared, something solidly sensible and "American" about group welfare and the need for subordinating the individual to group effort and concern. Conversely, there was a kind of un-American taint in too feverish an advocacy of freedom.

This identification was reinforced by the many and varied international connections of the association. Groups for the new education in Europe were getting under way about the same time as the association in the United States. *New Era* magazine, sponsored by the New Education Fellowship, began its English edition in 1920 and its French and German editions in 1922. Offices of the fellowship were established in London, Geneva, and Berlin, with international conferences taking place every two years. Principles set forth in the magazine resembled the association platform in their endorsement of respect for the individuality of the child, children's innate and spontaneous interests, and freedom for the child's spiritual faculties.[41]

According to American observers, the European new schools were more spectacular than the American experimental schools in efforts to practice individuality and freedom. A specialist in foreign education of the United States Bureau of Education in 1923 found some of the German schools to be "adventures rather than experiments." He specifically identified the Hamburg community schools as characterized by much pupil freedom and choice with self-conscious avoidance of repression and restraint. Winnetka's Carleton Washburne visited new schools in England, Belgium, Holland, France, Switzerland, Austria, Czechoslovakia, and Germany and in his 1923 report emphasized their common

40. "The Status of the New School," *TCR* 32 (April 1931), 612, 615; Grover C. Bowman, "Resolved That the Idea of the Child-Centered School Has Been More Detrimental Than Beneficial to Public School Systems," Superintendence *Report*, 1932, p. 203.

41. Beatrice Ensor, "The New Education Fellowship," *Prog Ed* 1 (Oct. 1924), 137–38.

dedication to freedom. He had regarded Marietta Johnson as an extremist, but found her conservative in comparison with the innovators in Germany and England.[42]

Increasingly the American and European movements drew together. Beatrice Ensor, editor of *New Era*, visited and wrote most sympathetically about experimental schools in the United States in the spring of 1926. It was she who identified another feature of new or progressive education, one so much an aspect of American tradition as to have escaped specific notice here. "We have faith," she had said in the opening address of the third international conference of the New Education Fellowship at Heidelberg the year before, "in the good that is in every child and we trust him." At the fourth conference, held in Locarno, Switzerland, in 1927, there were eleven hundred delegates from fifty-one countries, including several hundred from the United States. Among Americans who gave speeches were Winnetka's Washburne, Harold Rugg, Marietta Johnson, and Lucy L. W. Wilson. Significantly, the entire first day's discussion was given over to the topic of freedom. "Progressive education," said an editorial in the association's magazine three years later, "is a world movement." In that year a formal arrangement was made for joint membership in the association and in the New Education Fellowship.[43]

VII

The culture of protest waxed strong after the midpoint of the decade, but it could not catch up with the culture of good business. In the election of 1928, protest was beaten off; the dominant culture remained dominant. With Hoover, the very symbol of efficiency, as President, greater and still greater triumphs were expected for and from our business civilization. Few realized at the time that the dominant culture in its very moment of victory was already doomed. Neither the boosters nor the critics of our business civilization foresaw the depression that

42. Peter H. Pearson, "Recent German Experiments in Folk Schools," *School Life* 9 (Nov. 1923), 49, 66–67; *Progressive Tendencies in European Education*, Bur Ed bull. 1923, no. 37, p. 22.

43. "An English View of Newer Efforts in American Education," *S&S* 24 (Aug. 14, 1926), 198–99; quoted by W. Carson Ryan, Jr., "The Third International Pedagogical Conference at Heidelberg," *S&S* 22 (Sept. 19, 1925), 357; "New Freedom in Education," *American Educational Digest* 47 (Oct. 1927), 75–76; *Prog Ed* 7 (Dec. 1930), 412; "Notes and News," *ibid.* (May 1930), 201–2.

would strip from business and industrial leaders their reputations as the guarantors of American social and economic welfare. This collapse of the industrial facade brought no great comfort to the culture of protest. So far as its constituency was concerned, what they sought was not a victory based on economic disaster, but rather the incorporation of their values into a normal and growing America. This was a greater and perhaps impossible task. Depression meant tragedy for all Americans, not victory for the protesting culture.

What was left of the academic tradition survived precariously in the high schools at the decade's end, but survive it did. Since 1900 it had been warding off the solid blows directed against it by the proponents of social efficiency and social control. These did not diminish after 1920, and to their effect was added the erosion of the academic tradition by the culture of Babbitt and his children. The culture of protest may have been ineffectual in many aspects of American life. It undoubtedly helped to account for such survival of the academic tradition as in fact took place.

The devastation wrought in the high schools by the majority culture was probably more spiritual and inward than material and external, just as the real symbol of the 1920s as a whole may not have been the crashing success of monolithic Americanism as much as the almost total unawareness in 1926 of the death of former president Charles W. Eliot of Harvard. It did happen that movie actor Rudolph Valentino's death on the day after Eliot's received the overwhelming newspaper, radio, and magazine publicity. The tragedy, however, lay not in the great tribute paid to Valentino; there were perhaps good reasons for the publicity and the tribute. It lay in the apparent irrelevance of Eliot's social and educational values for the kind of society the United States had become by 1926. Back at the turn of the century Eliot, in an address to the Department of Superintendence, had declared "the new and happy aim in modern education" to be that of "joy and gladness in achievement," adding immediately that freedom was "necessary to this joy."[44] It was perhaps the mission of the culture of protest to keep these sentiments alive in an age that, so far as education was concerned, valued neither joy nor achievement.

44. "Status of Education at Close of Century," *NEA Proc*, 1900, p. 198.

Chapter 8

Depression

"Let us talk no more of education as a business."
—SCHOOL LIFE,
DECEMBER 1932.

*P*rosperity had been the trademark of the 1920s. The decade survived its trademark only a few weeks. In retrospect the period just before the market crash seemed like the last days of Pompeii, and looking back to it in 1933 Frederick Lewis Allen, chronicler of the twenties, recalled, "One evening during the summer of 1929 I spent several hours with a group of men and women who were discussing what the nineteen-thirties might be like in America. . . . Not one of us foresaw the depression. . . . The truth is that in those gaudy days of 1929 almost nobody saw it."[1]

Among other dwellers in those last days was the commentator Mark Sullivan, who late in 1929 celebrated "thirty years of progress" using a check list of what he considered to be important reforms, such as women's suffrage, the income tax, direct election of senators, immigration restriction, and prohibition. He found also a new philosophy of business. "Since 1900," he wrote, "it has been learned that the surer path to wealth is diffusion." Not only was depression not predicted, but in this formulation the possibility of it did not even arise.[2]

Even those who questioned the reality of prosperity expected what passed for prosperity to continue. Newsman Laurence Todd noticed that Hoover, the first millionaire in the White House, had chosen six other millionaires for his cabinet. Although this might have been expected to alienate the lower-income groups, Todd expected Hoover's efficiency to carry his regime beyond major protest. It would be free of petty graft and corruption and would create "a new feudalism in which

1. "Since Yesterday," *American Magazine* 115 (Jan. 1933), 11–12.
2. "Thirty Years of Progress," *World's Work* 58 (Nov. 1929), 47.

201

no man shall consider himself poor," a feudal allegiance the American people would readily accept. Another journalist and commentator, Elmer Davis, agreed. Faith in Hoover and old-time Americanism, Davis felt in March 1929, would fail only if prosperity failed; Hoover was "as well equipped as any man in the country" to keep up the appearance of prosperity. "While prosperity exists, or seems to exist," said Davis, "they [Hoover and old-time Americanism] are safe enough."[3]

Some few had seen portents of depression as far back as the winter of 1928–29. Lillian Wald of the Henry Street Settlement in New York City pointed out that hard times hit the poor first and said that "months before the stock market crash, we were made aware of the forebodings among our neighbors." Political writer and analyst George Soule was likewise pessimistic. "Building construction," he wrote in February 1929, "is already falling off. Indeed, there is a possibility that, even if credit to the speculative builders becomes as easy as before, the long-predicted slump will occur."[4]

Educators who feared hard times ahead based their fears on the growing surplus of teachers, as well as on rumblings from taxpayers. "This year," wrote Deputy Superintendent Charles L. Spain of the Detroit public schools in 1928, "most school systems are in a state of unrest. . . . On the surface the trouble appears to be financial. The great wave of prosperity has passed; there is much unemployment." Below the surface, Spain feared, superintendents had failed to convince communities of the value of education. In 1928 the *American Education Digest* was discussing with concern the growing number of reports of joblessness among teachers.[5]

Still, educators with this much perception were in a minority indeed. To many schoolmen of the late 1920s a depression seemed about as likely as an invasion from Mars. Bigger and better budgets were the order of the day. A Chicago principal who visited eighteen school systems in the spring of 1929 came home bubbling with optimism about the many new schools, "dozens of them," in every city, the efficiency with which schools were being conducted, and a greatly expanded curricu-

3. "Government by Millionaires," *Nation* 128 (March 27, 1929), 367–68; "If Hoover Fails," *Harper's Magazine* 158 (March 1929), 411–12.
4. "The Lean Years," *Atlantic Monthly* 152 (Dec. 1933), 650; "Hoover's Task At Home," *New Republic* 58 (Feb. 27, 1929), 35.
5. "Major Problems in Administration," *American Educational Digest* 47 (June 1928), 460; "Editorial Review," *ibid.* (May 1928), 408.

lum with many special services, all of this without the least expressed anticipation of the coming tragedy that would wipe out many such services and programs.[6]

II

Optimism survived even after the October crash, for nothing immediate seemed to happen. To many Americans, Wall Street was far away. The market crash was like a dam breaking far upstream with a flood crest remote from local waterfronts. Visiting the Midwest in 1930, New York writer Bruce Bliven found that signs of hard times were below the surface. "The unemployed," he reported, "are herded away out of sight."[7] Ideology triumphed, and the poor were regarded as traitors to the American ideal of success.

Gradually the truth began to sink in. Times were really getting hard. Optimists no longer dismissed the crash as insignificant, but shifted to predictions of early recovery and readjustment. No longer was it treason to acknowledge that America could have a depression, but it remained so to believe that it would not be shortly over and done with. This also fit the explanation of the depression based on popular morality, that it had been caused by get-rich-quick speculators and by the abandonment of true American qualities of sobriety and thrift.

School children in America had been bombarded at least since 1920 by thrift campaigns and school savings projects sponsored and promoted by the Savings Bank Division of the American Bankers Association with the blessing of the NEA. For the school year 1929–30 14,000 schools were involved, 4,500,000 children, and $29,000,000 in deposits, with net savings over withdrawals of $7,690,530 and $52,000,000 in total bank balances.[8] One of the tragedies of the depression was the failure of some of the banks in which children had made these deposits. An unsung hero in this period was Superintendent Henry J. Gerling of St. Louis, who in 1935 pledged $25,000 of his own money in opening a campaign to reimburse children in that city for their losses.[9]

To blame the depression on extravagance put the burden on the

6. Edward H. Stullken, "Impressions of Modern School Systems," *Chicago Schools Journal* 12 (Dec. 1929), 150–51.
7. "Twenty Hours to New York," *New Republic* 64 (Oct. 8, 1930), 201.
8. "Unemployment and Withdrawal of School Savings," *S&S* 32 (Oct. 18, 1930), 520–21.
9. Reported in "Among the Schools," *J Ed* 118 (Oct. 21, 1935), 461.

individual citizen and his shortcomings, and the picture was filled out by itemizing additional and related character defects. "Various factors," pronounced State Superintendent Vierling Kersey of California in 1931, "brought about the present result: over-stimulation, unwise investment, unwarranted extension, overproduction, careless speculation, resistances to denial and easy work attitudes." Fortunately, thought Kersey, "we seem to be returning to a normal state. . . . a safe, sane, constructive level of production, earning, spending, and living," and with this return to normalcy the depression would soon be overcome.[10]

Some went further and argued that the depression was a good thing in that it brought us back to the good, old values and taught some badly needed lessons. "We are broadening our interests," said author Bruce Barton; "we are re-laying the foundations of faith." The *Literary Digest*, universal conveyor of culture to thousands of captive English classes, found that "many of us" were more sensible and "not a few" were happier because of the depression, and it was by no means to be regarded as an unmitigated calamity. Also, went on the *Digest*, "a lot of us have found new pleasures" conveyed through libraries, museums, art, and music, plus such extra dividends as better health and many deeds of kindness. More of this self-castigating, it's-good-for-us thinking appeared in the *American Magazine* from a contributor who signed only her initials. The family income of $5,000 had been reduced by two cuts of 10 percent each. Learning from this experience how to make and use a budget, they decided to cut out the maid and Jack's membership in the golf club.[11]

To others it was not the entire culture but one segment of it that had been guilty of incompetence and defective character, the businessmen and bankers. This reversal of the businessman's reputation was sharp indeed. The wizards had lost their magic touch and with it their leadership roles in American life. At their annual institute in 1933, the teachers of Sonoma County, California, denounced "selfish industrial leadership" that had combined with "wrong standards" to bring about the industrial collapse of America. Before the depression, educators had joined their fellow citizens in admiring business, and now they too were turning to

10. "Education and These Times," *California Schools* 2 (July 1931), 291.
11. "Are We Getting a New Idea about 'Values?'" *American Magazine* 114 (July 1932), 128; "The Beneficent Depression," 114 (August 20, 1932), 36; H. M. S., "Two Salary Cuts Have Taught Us What a Budget's For," 114 (Sept. 1932), 120–21.

moods of disillusionment and reproach. Perhaps all public leadership had failed, thought Principal Olive Ely Hart of the Philadelphia High School for Girls, for example, that of business and industry as well as of religion and government. She suggested the possibility that new and better leadership might now come from the schools.[12]

Many did not forget the fact that they had been urged to emulate business and industrial leaders. "How well we remember," observed Charles H. Judd of the University of Chicago in 1932, "the arrogance with which business vaunted itself before October, 1929. How often we were exhorted to learn from business management how to conduct schools." "During the days of prosperity," wrote George S. Counts, "we were told through every agency of propaganda that authentic giants ruled the economic order."[13] Now these giants seemed giants no more. Educators could seek new models or create their own.

It was open season on bankers especially. People have been taught to fear burglars, said Robert C. Moore, secretary of the Illinois State Teachers Association, "but now it seems that the real danger to society has been the bankers who have been speculating with other people's money." Judd pronounced acid judgment on the role of bankers in thrift education. "The banker," he said, "who was teaching thrift to children a few years ago in a pompous and abstract way was not efficient. He did not himself understand how to deal with the savings that he lured into his vaults. . . . He was a propagandist, not an educator."[14]

Under these circumstances, the notion that education itself was a business and should be conducted in a businesslike way was open to attack. Some educators confessed their past misdeeds and promised to sin no more. "By borrowing the terms of the market place," said an editorial in *School Life* called "Bad Business," "we tried to borrow from the temporary glory of the market place. We tried to improve education's estate by clothing her in scraps of royal purple snipped from the hem of the new king of America. Business was the undisputed

12. "Resolutions of Teachers of Sonoma County," *California Schools* 5 (Jan. 1934), 30; "The Teacher of English and a Changing Social Order," University of Pennsylvania School of Education, *Nineteenth Annual Schoolmen's Week Proceedings*, 1932, pp. 470–71.
13. "Education, the Nation's Safeguard," Superintendence *Report*, 1932, p. 37; "Secondary Education and the Social Problem," *School Executives Magazine* 51 (Aug. 1932), 500.
14. "Applying Ethics to Economics," *NEA Proc*, 1933, p. 161; "Teaching Government in Public Schools," *S&S* 35 (Jan. 23, 1932), 104.

monarch of America during the last decade. Let us talk no more of education as a business. Let us divest education of its unseemly costume, not merely because the king is deposed but because education should never be false to its high purpose" (18 [Dec. 1932], 70).

Among those from other walks of life who joined the educators in their denunciations of business was businessman Edward A. Filene. "Great financiers," declared Filene in 1934 to the Department of Superintendence, "wrecked our finances. Power kings turned out to be weaklings. Captains of industry fled from the battle at the first smell of danger and, by cutting wages and curtailing the public buying power, led the grand stampede away from industry and toward unemployment." They were good men, not immoral. "Some of them," he added, "did not even break the law; but they broke the country."[15]

The quest for scapegoats accounted also for the sudden reversal of the dominant culture with respect to prohibition and Hoover. As late as 1932 educators had still been passing resolutions on behalf of the Eighteenth Amendment.[16] Prohibition, once the darling of reformers, including progressives, and the symbol in 1928 of the Protestant ascendancy, was equated by 1933 with crime, immorality, and corruption and in some vague way held accountable for the depression itself. In H. L. Mencken's judgment, the public reversal on prohibition was the deciding factor in Hoover's defeat in 1932. Had Hoover seized the leadership of "the wet uprising," said Mencken in January 1933, he would have been re-elected, "depression or no depression."[17] This was ascribing too much to prohibition as a cause of Hoover's defeat, perhaps, but it indicated the extent to which the question intruded itself into the discussion of other public issues.

According to pedagogical publisher H. E. Buchholz (*Educational Administration and Supervision, Journal of Educational Psychology*), the NEA alliance between prohibitionists and the advocates of a federal department of education disintegrated with the federal department group throwing the prohibitionists overboard. Buchholz liked neither group. He identified the prohibitionists with Methodists and Baptists of the uplift school. Although scarcely a neutral commentator on NEA matters, Buchholz was right that it too had given up on the good ship

15. "Education in the New Age," Superintendence *Report*, 1934, pp. 71, 73.
16. "Report of the Committee on Resolutions," *NEA Proc*, 1932, p. 219; "Report of the Committee on Resolutions," Superintendence *Report*, 1932, p. 277.
17. "What Is Going On in the World," *American Mercury* 28 (Jan. 1933), 2.

prohibition. In the end it was Nicholas Murray Butler, an enemy of prohibition from the beginning, who triumphed and turned up ironically enough as a culture hero with "liberals," even to the extent of being named by the *Nation* to its honor roll for 1932 and for 1933, largely for his valiant struggle against prohibition![18]

Most remarkable of all was the reversal of judgment on Herbert Hoover himself. Hoover's landslide victory in 1928 symbolized the triumph of the older monolithic America and of the newer doctrines of efficiency and mechanization. "What brought out the vote," wrote Elmer Davis of the election of 1928, "was the conviction that the faith of the fathers had been challenged." Old values through new technology might well have served as the rallying cry of the Hoover cult. The NEA announced its judgment early in 1929 through Lyle W. Ashby of its Division of Publications. Ashby found Hoover eminent as an engineer of physical technology, but more. "In the field of human engineering," Ashby concluded, "his achievements are yet greater."[19]

Adulation of Hoover had come easy in those golden days of 1929. "There is a power house in the White House," concluded writer Isaac F. Marcosson. In its issue of May 1, 1929, *Outlook and Independent* ran a photograph of Hoover with the caption, "The Engineer, the Efficiency Expert, the Field Marshal of American Business." The American Philosophical Society for the Promotion of Useful Knowledge paid tribute to Hoover in an effusive testimonial, crediting him with "that happy combination of the natural and moral philosophies which this society has cherished these two centuries since the day of its founding by Benjamin Franklin."[20] On February 23, 1929, the *Saturday Evening Post* (201, p. 24) editorially paid tribute to the magnificent quality of Hoover's preparation for his role. "He combines," said the *Post*, "the idealistic and the practical as have few men in our history."

Perhaps not so carefully cultivated, but important to some sectors of pedagogical thought in this period, was Hoover's reputation as intelli-

18. "The Pedagogues at Armageddon," *American Mercury* 29 (June 1933), 129–31; "The Nation's Honor Roll for 1932," *Nation* 136 (Jan. 4, 1933), 7; "The Nation's Honor Roll for 1933," *ibid.* 138 (Jan. 3, 1934), 4–5.

19. *Harper's Magazine* 158 (March 1929), 410; "Herbert Hoover and Education," *Wisconsin Journal of Education* 61 (March 1929), 332.

20. "The President Gets Down to Business," *Saturday Evening Post* 202 (Dec. 21, 1929), 82; Henry Kittredge Norton, "Back Stage in Washington," 152 (May 1, 1929), 5; quoted in "Washington Correspondence," *School Executives Magazine* 48 (March 1929), 318.

gent but not intellectual. "I never thought Herbert was bright," said one of his teachers from his West Branch, Iowa, school days, "but he was a good boy always, studious and obedient." The educator who reported this drew the moral that "recitations and tests fail to tell the whole story about any child" and said that there was for all teachers "a lesson in the career of this lad who gave no impression of brilliance."[21]

The subsequent collapse of Hoover's reputation, like that of businessmen in general, did not portend a new set of American values. Even the outcome of the 1932 election did not mean the complete abandonment of Hoover or what he was taken to represent. Nearly sixteen million Americans voted for him in 1932, about the same number that had voted for Smith in defeat back in 1928. Those supporters who turned against him may have felt, not that the faith of the fathers had failed them, but that Hoover had failed the faith of the fathers. Educators, at any rate, showed little or no disposition to abandon their faith in the efficiency aim.

III

Just as the economic aftermath of the market crash developed slowly enough to leave its prospective victims with a false sense of assurance, so did the financial impact of the depression upon the schools creep up relentlessly but without haste. The effect on the schools was even more delayed than on the culture as a whole, since budgets for 1930–31 had been made early in 1930 when optimism still reigned. With respect to national per-pupil cost, the high point had been reached with $90.22 in 1929–30, but the decline was only a slight one to $88.89 for the following year. The first major reduction came in 1931–32 with a figure of $83.22 per pupil. After 1932 the decline became a collapse, with $73.96 for 1932–33 and $66.53 for 1933–34.[22]

Nevertheless, the decline did not greatly outrun that of the consumer price index: school spending between 1930 and 1934 declined 23 percent and the price index 18 percent (58.2 to 47.8, with 1957–59 as the base of 100, and 1969 showing 127.7, using the same base).[23]

21. "Belding's Page [Anson W. Belding]," *J Ed* 109 (March 18, 1929), 306.
22. "Meeting the Emergency in Education," *Bulletin of the National Department of Secondary School Principals*, no. 46, April 1933, p. 5; Beulah Amidon, "Schools in the Red," *Survey Graphic* 23 (June 1934), 296.
23. U.S. Bureau of the Census, *Statistical Abstract of the United States 1970*, 91st Annual Ed. (Washington, D.C., 1970), p. 344.

From the outcries of educators in this period, however, it is evident that the cuts really hurt. So much cutting, when it did come, came quickly, and the high point from which school budgets declined had not itself been very high. Moreover, with great variations among regions, clientele, and school systems, cuts in certain localities could be catastrophic indeed. Chicago, for example, riddled its budget 20 percent in a single year between 1931–32 and 1932–33,[24] and this turned out to be only a prelude to further financial mayhem. The separate black schools in the segregated (*de jure*) South turned out to be special victims of the financial debacle that was taking place.[25]

The worst period psychologically was that of budget-planning in 1932 for the school year 1932–33. *School Executives Magazine*, in an editorial called "Budget-Cutting Gone Mad," referred to 1932 as "the year when we completely lost our reason and our intelligence in the mad hysteria of budget-cutting" (51 [June 1932], 448). This mood of apprehension persisted into the following winter, accompanied, of course, by the paralysis that afflicted the entire economy at that time. The meeting of the Department of Superintendence at Minneapolis in the winter of 1933, with only five thousand in attendance, was dominated by fear of nameless catastrophes ahead. "Dread of what might happen," said one observer, "gripped most of those in attendance." Some educators castigated themselves and surrendered to a mood of defeat, foreseeing depression as a permanent condition in American life. "The cornucopia," wrote one of them, "may have shed its plenty; our golden and careless years may come no more."[26]

On the other hand, the traditional sense of battle among schoolmen was intensified. Superintendents came to feel like a beleaguered host, a mood that spread to teachers and to public groups that believed in schools. The NEA and the Department of Superintendence created a Joint Commission on the Emergency in Education to keep close watch on reductions in school budgets and those who brought them about. "A continuing survey has been begun," wrote chairman John K. Norton in 1933, "of organizations which are critical of or antagonistic toward

---

24. Fred W. Sargent, "The Taxpayer Takes Charge," *Saturday Evening Post* 205 (Jan. 14, 1933), 74.

25. N. C. Newbold, "The Public Education of Negroes and the Current Depression," *Journal of Negro Education* 2 (Jan. 1933), 5–15.

26. "Superintendents Militant," *School Executives Magazine* 52 (April 1933), 273; Adolph Gillis, "Schools for the Lean Days," *High Points* 14 (April 1932), 18.

public education."[27] He hinted at "motives" behind the attacks and hoped these might emerge from the survey.

Rhetoric and emotion flowed freely in those days. A Chicago teacher at the NEA Department of Classroom Teachers declared in 1933 that "we in Chicago believe there is a nationwide plot to cripple public education, to take it out of the reach of the common man's children and restrict it to those who can pay for it." Dean Henry Lester Smith of the School of Education, Indiana University, warned his NEA audience in 1932 against "the enemies of general educational opportunities for the masses" operating under "the guise of economic necessity." Helen Hefferan, a dissenting liberal on Chicago's budget-cutting board of education, saw a sinister program to wrest from America's children what had been gained over a hundred years. The struggle for free public schools, she feared, had to be fought again in the twentieth century "against foes more powerful, united, and sinister than those Horace Mann met and conquered."[28]

Helping to sustain the mood of battle, the New York State delegation brought to the Chicago NEA of 1933 a rallying song written by Superintendent W. H. Holmes of Mount Vernon, New York, and performed it for the second business section. The concluding stanza ran as follows:

> Stand by the Schools! Make it a sacred pledge.
> Stand by the Schools! Our children's heritage.
> Stand by the Schools! The millions in them cry.
> Stand by the Schools! America stand by![29]

Still, the psychology of battle was not exclusive to the school people, in fact much of it was a response to the verbal onslaught of the budget-cutters and their allies. One of the attackers, castigating all government spending in the *Saturday Evening Post*, included sharp digs at the schools, such as the story of a teacher who complained of being unable to go to Bermuda for Christmas because of salary cuts. The writer blamed some of the school spending on the communities themselves.

27. "Report of the Joint Commission on the Emergency in Education," *NEA Proc*, 1933, p. 185.

28. Robert C. Keenan, "Critical Present Day Issues in Education," *NEA Proc*, 1933, p. 333; "A Forward Look in Education," *NEA Proc*, 1932, p. 27; "The Chicago Schools Situation," *Prog Ed* 10 (Oct. 1933), 320.

29. "Minutes of the Thirteenth Representative Assembly, Chicago, Illinois, July 1–7, 1933," *NEA Proc*, 1933, p. 874.

"Hickville," he asserted, "must have a better high school than Rube-town."[30]

Mencken, too, was by now turning away from his earlier role in the culture of protest and attacking school spending. He charged that the public schools had fallen into the hands of "a well-organized and pretentious bureaucracy" that "made off" in 1932 with one-fourth of the fourteen billion dollars spent for all governments in the country. The "pedagogues," charged Mencken, had repudiated old-time teaching, and the child, who had formerly played the role in school of a prisoner, was now "a guinea pig in a low-comedy laboratory." Who would not feel embattled after being accused of all that? The antischool rhetoric of battle could flow as freely as the proschool. A Kansas journalist applauded the school cuts in his state, declaring that the people of Kansas had suffered "mental, moral and financial distress" from public education. Some critics wrote in tones of loftier objectivity, but the hostile notes came through nonetheless, as in the case of Fred W. Sargent, president of the Chicago & Northwestern Railroad, who in his capacity as chairman of the Committee on Public Expenditures, an extralegal body in Chicago, declared polite but unmistakeable war on school spending in an article entitled "The Taxpayer Takes Charge."[31]

One consequence of the drive for lower costs was the rescuing of the ideal of efficiency, somewhat tarnished by the decline and fall of efficiency expert Herbert Hoover. The cuts of 1932–35 stimulated schoolmen to a wave of cost-saving devices. Among these were larger classes, increased teacher-student ratios, shorter school terms, fewer programs, use of teaching assistants and aides, the charging of high school tuition, and (although this was not usually paraded as an efficiency device) the cutting of salaries, particularly those of classroom teachers.

It was in relation to some of these devices that the United States Chamber of Commerce found itself cast among the enemies of public education. The charge was made by none other than John Dewey himself, at the Minneapolis meeting of the Department of Supervisors and Directors of Instruction on March 1, 1933. According to Dewey, the

30. Edwin Lefèvre, "Tax Blindness," 205 (Jan. 28, 1933), 3–5, 57–58; "They Spend and We Pay," 206 (Nov. 25, 1933), 36.
31. "What Is Going On in the World," *American Mercury* 28 (Feb. 1933), 134; W. G. Clugston, "Kansas Begins To Doubt the Public School," *ibid.* 28 (April 1933), 454–56; *Saturday Evening Post* 205 (Jan. 14, 1933), 21, 74, 78, 80–82.

national chamber had suggested reduction of the school day and year, larger classes, abolition of programs, and imposing of high school tuition fees. The chamber denied all this, contending that the items had appeared as questions from a conference in which it had taken part, the Citizens Conference on the Crisis in Education called by Hoover while he was still President in January 1933.[32]

Most or all of the items on which Dewey castigated the chamber were at one time or another proposed or seriously discussed by educators themselves. It was Superintendent Ben Graham of the Pittsburgh public schools who in an address at Pennsylvania Schoolmen's Week in 1932 recommended forty students a class in elementary school and thirty-five in junior and senior high schools. Graham enthusiastically reported that excellent results had been obtained at Hamtramck, Michigan, with forty to forty-five students a class, and in an experimental class of seventy students where the teacher had the services of an assistant clerk.[33]

The comprehensive program of economy in the Des Moines, Iowa, school system attracted a great deal of attention. One of its devices was the collection of tuition fees from students who insisted on taking more than the twelve units required for graduation from the senior high school, thus saving teaching costs for extra credits, according to one principal who described the program. Three teachers in his school were eliminated by cutting out double-period work in science. Class sizes were increased to thirty-five as compared with an average figure of twenty-three that had prevailed in 1920.[34] Two of the high schools in the system were experimenting with double-sized classes in English and social studies with the use of assistants to grade papers and help with clerical work. "The salary of such assistants was about half that of a regular teacher," reported this principal, "thus saving about one-half a regular teacher's salary in each experiment. On the pay of one and one-

32. John Dewey, "Education and Our Present Social Problems," *Educational Method* 12 (April 1933), 385–90; "Attitude of the U.S. Chamber of Commerce," *School Executives Magazine* 53 (March 1934), 201; "The Attitudes of Two Service Organizations toward Retrenchment in Education," *Sch R* 42 (Jan. 1934), 2–8.

33. "Balancing the Budget through Professional Adjustments," University of Pennsylvania School of Education, *Nineteenth Annual Schoolmen's Week Proceedings*, 1932, pp. 9–10.

34. H. T. Steeper, "Legitimate Economies in the High School Program," *Proceedings of the Department of Secondary School Principals*, 1934, pp. 216–18.

half teachers we have handled the work of two teachers or 300 to 325 students."

Through these various devices, Des Moines eliminated sixty-two teachers, twelve in elementary, the others in junior and senior highs.[35] Some classwork was also eliminated, increasing the need for study hall space, a need met by using cafeterias. In protest against this, the March 1937 *Progressive Education* ran photographs of the crowded cafeterias as they appeared in study periods. " 'Discipline,' " said the magazine, "is maintained by an adult supervisor with the assistance of student 'monitors' " (14:168).

Discussion of tuition for high school was especially agitated. Although resorted to in part by the Des Moines school system, tuition was usually identified with the enemies in their battles against schools. In Connecticut, a proposal to require tuition of so-called maladjusted pupils was ruled out by order of the state commissioner of education.[36] A general proposal for tuition was raised in the Citizens Conference on the Crisis in Education with the suggestion that it had not been fully explored.[37] By November 1933, the NEA was reporting through its journal that "a definite movement" was under way throughout the country "to place the support of the high school on the shoulders of the poor by putting it on a tuition basis" (22:225).

The quarrels over cuts in subjects and programs were heavily freighted with ideology, and accompanied by use of the term *fads and frills*, one that went back at least as far as Dewey's use of it in his lectures *The School and Society* (Chicago, 1899). Although used originally to mean practical or nonacademic subjects and activities, anti-academic educators liked to turn the meaning around and to use the term against academic subjects. With the question of what to abandon or abolish, anti-academic rhetoric became especially hostile.

"If we have to cut budgets," said President George W. Frasier of the Colorado State College of Education, "as we all have to, we need a scale of values now more than ever before. My scale says music for all is vastly more important than Latin for a few. Art for all beats alge-

35. H. T. Steeper, "Economies in the High-School Program," *Clearing House* 8 (May 1934), 559–61.

36. Paul D. Collier, "Preservation of the Ideals of Secondary Education," *High School Quarterly* 22 (April 1934), 131.

37. Paul Y. Anderson, "Congress Studies Relief," *Nation* 136 (Jan. 18, 1933), 59–60.

bra for a few. Health education for all must stay when ancient and medieval history are discontinued." Making cuts, said Frasier, was the work of an expert, and he appealed to the citizens of America to let their superintendents rather than their tax leagues do the job. The frills, argued a professor at the University of Wyoming, were not what people had thought of as frills but rather "some parts of the history, mathematics, Latin, and English which were once regarded as fundamentals." H. H. Ryan, principal of the University of Wisconsin high school, asked rhetorically, if the aim of education was the good life, which was the frill, "algebra or speech training? Latin or home economics? Ancient history or music?" High school students joined the outcry, at least two of them at Bay View High School, Milwaukee, who argued for retaining domestic science, music, art, and manual arts, which they said 1,527 students at their school were enrolled in and 1,300 more planned to take in the future.[38]

So far as costs were concerned, academic subjects on the whole were cheaper, and more could be saved by cutting out the practical subjects. An inquiry in Fresno, California, reported the average cost per student per semester hour for industrial arts at $10.45, homemaking $10.43, commercial $8.46, and art $7.86, contrasted with English at $6.28, social studies $5.96, and mathematics $5.87. There were, however, some interesting crossovers, such as foreign languages $8.41 and physical education $3.36, both probably reflecting class size.[39]

It was by no means clear that the practical subjects were getting cut more than the academic. True, home economics was the subject abandoned by the largest number of approved schools in the North Central Association in 1933–34. Foreign languages, however, were dropped by more schools than were manual training, bookkeeping, and agriculture combined. Advanced algebra was a favorite victim for budget cutters and was dropped to about the same extent as physical education.[40]

38. "Education in a Time of Crisis," *NEA J* 21 (June 1932), 174; L. R. Kilzer, "Cinderellas of the Curriculum," *School Executives Magazine* 54 (Jan. 1935), 143; "The Teaching and Learning Situation in Junior High School Classrooms," *Proceedings of the National Department of Secondary School Principals*, 1933, p. 142; William Jenrich and Gordon Lisota, "Frills?" *Wisconsin Journal of Education* 66 (Jan. 1934), 216–17.

39. W. B. Munson, "Research Report from the Fresno City Schools," *California Journal of Secondary Education* 10 (Feb. 1935), 181.

40. H. G. Hotz, "Trends in the Development of Secondary Schools," *North Central Association Quarterly* 9 (Oct. 1934), 247.

IV

The most obvious victims awaiting the budget slashers, however, were not programs but human beings, the teachers and other members of professional staffs. Even when subjects and programs were the ostensible targets, these were the real victims. Besides getting rid of teachers, money could be saved through salary cuts and even in some instances, although not by intent, through not paying teachers at all. Teacher welfare, a precarious matter even in the golden days of prosperity, became in the period of depression a domain of disaster.

Teachers got plenty of sympathy, if little else, from the public. Even Mencken commiserated with them and acknowledged that they had shared little in the rising costs of schools. "The money that has been frittered away," he said "has not gone into their bead-bags but into the pockets of the gaudy Cagliostros who stood over them. . . . But now it is the ma'ms who are thrown to the wolves."[41]

In actuality, the teachers' troubles, like those of school-budgeting as a whole, developed slowly after the market crash. An NEA survey of thirty-seven cities showed that with salaries and purchasing power of 100 base for 1928–29, comparable figures for 1931–32 were 101.8 and 121.9. Thus the first days of depression were for teachers days of relative prosperity. By 1934–35, however, the same figures were 88.1 and 104.9.[42] Although still with slightly more purchasing power than they had had in 1928–29, teachers were obviously shaken and demoralized by the downward plunge in their incomes since 1931–32. Teachers got their severe cuts in a period when averages for other workers had begun to rise.

Again, the averages conceal the extreme hardships suffered in certain localities. In some instances school boards filled teaching positions and superintendencies by selecting from the lowest bidders, and one report from North Dakota cited teaching jobs going on this basis for as low as $30 a month. According to this report, one North Dakota system had seventy applicants for the superintendency. The board had planned to pay $125 a month, but with so many applicants lowered its figure to $100.[43] Such conditions reflected the oversupply of teachers, accentu-

41. "What Is Going On in the World," *American Mercury* 28 (April 1933), 386–87.

42. "The Teacher's Economic Position," *Research Bulletin of the National Education Association* 13 (Sept. 1935), 239.

43. Clarence G. Gludt, "The Auctioneers in Education," *School Executives Magazine* 54 (Jan. 1935), 152.

ated as it was by the cutting of programs and jobs and by the annual floods of new graduates and new applicants. Some 23 percent of the college graduates (first degrees) in 1936 had studied to teach.[44] Under the circumstances of the times, many of these, including some of the ablest, were permanently lost to the schools.

Chicago contributed the most spectacular story of late payment and postponements of teachers' salaries, one that began in April 1931 and extended over a period of more than three years.[45] This was injury enough, but to it were added ingenious and exasperating insults such as the piling up of teachers' loads and the cutting out of jobs and programs. During 1933–34, some 85 percent of Chicago's high school teachers were teaching six classes or more, while 87 percent had more than 150 students daily. By way of comparison, only 10 percent of the high school teachers in twenty-four of the largest high schools of the state apart from Chicago had six or more classes.[46] In July 1933, the board adopted a program of cuts that seemed to justify the battle psychology of the educators and to support the popular impression that such cuts were aimed largely at the nonacademic subjects. Ironically enough, in view of previous battles in Chicago, the board also voted to abolish junior high schools. The cuts involved the laying off of some 1,200 teachers.[47]

Even those who might otherwise have favored reductions in practical subjects and abolition of junior high schools were appalled by the ruthlessness of the program. In spite of civic protest as well as that from teachers, it was largely carried through. A mass meeting was held at the Chicago stadium on July 21, 1933, with 25,000 protestors in attendance and a major speech by Judd, but to no avail.[48] For once, however,

---

44. Bess Goodykoontz, "Employment Opportunities in Services Related to Education," *School Life* 25 (Jan. 1940), 101.

45. A Chicago High School Teacher, "Blank Pay Days," *Saturday Evening Post* 206 (July 1, 1933), 16–17, 68–70; "Spasmodic Diary of a Chicago School Teacher," *Atlantic Monthly* 152 (Nov. 1933), 513–26; "News for Chicago Schools," *Chicago Schools Journal* 14 (Feb.–June 1932), 276; "News Note," *J Ed* 117 (Sept. 3, 1934), 375.

46. A. W. Clevenger, "Accrediting Chicago High Schools," *Chicago Schools Journal* 16 (Sept. 1934), 18–23.

47. "Defrilled Chicago," *Time* 22 (July 24, 1933), 30–31; "School Wrecking in Chicago," *Time* 22 (Aug. 21, 1933), 31; "Chicago's Economy Program," *School Executives Magazine* 52 (Aug. 1933), 394; "The Recent Situation in Chicago," *Sch R* 41 (Dec. 1933), 733–36.

48. "Disemboweling Chicago's School System," *Sch R* 41 (Sept. 1933), 483–91.

teachers were militant, and they demonstrated actively throughout 1933 against the board and the Chicago "establishment," even before the budget cuts in July. This was the year of the Chicago World's Fair, an object of great pride on the part of civic leaders. Militant teachers released their wrath in part by pulling down the World's Fair flag in Grant Park and by storming and overflowing four of the biggest downtown banks and the city hall.[49] None of this did any good, apart from showing that teachers could fight back and did not always submit, as did the "ma'ms" described by Mencken, to assaults of the higher command.

Teachers could and did also show, even in these troubled times, a fundamental idealism about and commitment to all aspects of their job. Although there was little enough they could do to alleviate economic distress among the children of the poor, they managed at least in several school systems to accomplish all that human ingenuity could contrive. At the Libbey High School of Toledo, Ohio, the teachers in 1930–31 began a work relief program for students with funds contributed by themselves or raised by them through various projects. In 1931–32 these work relief jobs (typing, paper-checking, assisting of crippled children, etc.) paid a total of $848.07, of which $475 came directly from the teachers.[50]

In the Detroit public schools, the Committee on Social Service in 1934–35 provided hot lunches, shoes, eye glasses, eye examinations, and clothing, costing nearly $100,000, of which slightly less than $30,-000 came from donations made by the teachers. Board of education employees as a whole subscribed over $50,000 to a community fund and led all other groups in the city in achieving the highest proportion of their quota.[51]

Still another kind of activity appeared in the Seattle public schools. Teachers there contributed time and effort toward free afternoon classes for the unemployed. The courses varied from "practical courses like gardening, home economics and shop work, to courses in literature, history, government, music and art."[52]

---

49. "'Walks' in Chicago," *Time* 19 (May 8, 1933), 34; *Atlantic Monthly* 152 (Nov. 1933), 513–26.
50. Mary M. Kelso, "Job Plan Assists Social Adjustments," *Clearing House* 8 (Nov. 1933), 144–48.
51. "President's Column," *Detroit Educational News* 3 (Nov. 19, 1935), 2.
52. "Seattle Teachers Proffer Services to the Unemployed," *Seattle Educational Bulletin* 9 (Sept. 1932), 1–2.

V

Through all this, the high school population continued to increase. Between 1929–30 and 1939–40, the numbers in the upper four years of public high schools went from 4,399,422 to 6,545,991.[53] The rate was no longer one of doubling every decade, but the 50 percent increase during the 1930s produced more than two million additional students. Moreover, whereas the students of 1930 represented slightly less than half the children from fourteen to sixteen, those of 1940 represented two-thirds.[54] The ideal of universal secondary education, urged so eloquently in 1918 by the Cardinal Principles Report, seemed closer to accomplishment, and the depression was apparently a factor. Between 1930 and 1932 enrollments increased by 704,058 students, contrasted with only 488,143 for the period between 1928 and 1930.[55]

There had always been those who felt that increasing enrollments meant lowering student quality. Now the idea was expressed by many that the new students, presumably forced into high school by lack of jobs, would affect that quality more than usual. "Any effective program for meeting this situation," said Albert J. Kaplan of Central High School, Philadelphia, "must be predicated upon the thought that many of these compulsory students can not benefit from the standard curricula."[56] An expert in English, Dora V. Smith, reported hearing from industrial centers throughout the country in 1934 that the teaching of literature had become more difficult because the National Recovery Act was forcing "older boys and girls for whom the present materials are totally unsuitable" to stay in or go back to high school.[57]

Not only was there a suspicious resemblance between these plaintive cries and those expressed earlier about the students of the 1920s (now

53. Off Ed, *Biennial Survey of Education in the United States, 1938–1940, 1940–1942* (1947), vol. 2, p. 11. The survey adds 55,453 postgraduate students to the figure shown here for 1939–40.

54. David Blose, "Current Trends in the Organization of Secondary Schools," University of Pennsylvania School of Education, *Twenty-Seventh Annual Schoolmen's Week Proceedings*, 1940, p. 46.

55. Off Ed, *Biennial Survey 1938–1940, 1940–1942*, vol. 2, p. 11.

56. "The NRA Codes and Secondary School Efficiency," *S&S* 41 (April 6, 1935), 474. Yet a summary of high school populations from 1916 to 1942 showed no decline in IQs. F. H. Finch, *Enrollment Increases and Changes in the Mental Level of the High School Population*, Applied Psychology Monograph no. 10 of the American Psychological Association (Stanford, California), p. 70.

57. "Promising Innovations in the Teaching of English," *EJ* 23 (April 1934), 283.

apparently regarded as a high-standard group), but the proposed remedy was the stock item that inevitably appears in such discussions, namely, more practical or vocational work. "It is safe to assume," said the principal of the Haverford, Pennsylvania, Township High School in 1933, "that the pupil of low ability will perform in life a work more or less mechanical in nature. Therefore we should substitute for academic studies a greater amount of manual work."[58]

Such expressions of conventional wisdom came thick and fast. "In past years," pronounced the principal of the Montpelier, Vermont, high school, "many of those who could not meet high school standards were able to find some sort of work. Now these pupils are forced to remain in school. The crying need of this group is vocational education." Others despaired of the value of any kind of vocational or mechanical work for such students. "Due to the economic depression which has increased the number of pupils of low IQ's who have been forced to remain in school because there is no employment for them," argued a teacher at the Brighton, Massachusetts, high school in 1936, "schools have emphasized social trends and personal use because these pupils are incapable of reaching vocational standards. This is a serious problem."[59]

Here were beginnings of what would later be called life adjustment education and of the categorizing of students into the academic, the vocational, and those neither academic nor vocational. A leading voice in this was that of Commissioner Ernest W. Butterfield of Connecticut, who as early as 1933 identified one-fourth of the students as college bound, one-fourth as headed for skilled occupations, and one-half who would enter jobs requiring little training, such as selling and waiting table, but who would be citizens and have leisure time. "The school," said Butterfield, "must train these pupils in social cooperation, it must guide them in the participatory activities of citizenship, and it must give them many keen and lasting interests."[60]

Another who used the one-fourth, one-fourth, and one-half categories was Henry L. Farr of South Manchester, Connecticut, identifying these respectively as those who worked with their brains, those in the

58. Raymond Schlosser, "How To Take Care of the Student of Low Ability in the Junior High School," University of Pennsylvania School of Education, *Twentieth Annual Schoolmen's Week Proceedings*, 1933, pp. 334–35.

59. Theodore Kambour, "Differentiated Diplomas," *School Executive* 56 (March 1936), 267; Mary Stuart, "Subjectmatter Round Tables," *NEA Proc*, 1936, p. 349.

60. "The New Fifty Per Cent," Superintendence *Report*, 1933, p. 228.

commercial courses, and those in what he called the general curriculum. Those in the latter programs he saw as future laborers but not, apparently, in skilled trades; millions who were born laborers would have to remain so. The superintendent of Seymour, Connecticut, identified three groups, "the college group, the group who will enter skilled occupations, and the general group," but did not refer to their proportions in the student body.[61]

Such rumblings aroused apprehension about assumptions involved, and a Connecticut principal, Gustave A. Feingold of the Bulkeley High School of Hartford, sounded the alarm to the National Council of Education of the NEA in an address on June 30, 1934. A doctrine was gaining ground, said Feingold, "that the bulk of our high school population is moronic and unfit for the profitable pursuit of high school studies, as we know them. We have been hearing of late, for instance, that 50 percent of the high school enrollment is made up of the sons and daughters of conductors, factory workers and scrubwomen, and since they themselves will become motormen, truck drivers, and charwomen, the education of the high school ought to be of a type which will prepare them for that sort of life." He paid his respects to this doctrine by declaring "that never was a more dangerous policy advocated by people of professional responsibility. . . . The spreading of the idea that 50 percent of the high school enrollment is unqualified for the traditional high school studies is nothing less than a libel against the youth of the nation."[62] Of course the doctrines were not new, but at least as old as the century itself.

On the other hand, some argued that the student bodies of the 1930s were at least no worse than those of the past. Superintendent Worth McClure of Seattle, for example, declared in 1932 that "boys and girls and parents were never more interested in school than now." In statistical terms, Edward A. Rundquist of the Cincinnati public schools cited studies of intelligence scores showing that the high school students of 1933 and 1934 in various Minnesota high schools performed somewhat better than had their predecessors of 1920 and 1929.[63]

61. "More Frills," S&S 37 (Feb. 4, 1933), 148–49; Ridgley C. Clark, "High School Serves Three Groups," J Ed 116 (Jan. 16, 1933), 36.
62. "The Basic Function of Secondary Education," S&S 40 (Dec. 22, 1934), 827–28.
63. "Note," Seattle Educational Bulletin 9 (Sept. 1932), 1; "Intelligence Test Scores and School Marks of High School Seniors in 1929 and 1933," S&S 43 (Feb. 29, 1936), 301–4.

VI

Beyond struggling with reduced budgets and swollen enrollments, schools and school people were caught in a public dialogue on individualism and social responsibility. Educators and philosophers had long debated these matters, but the depression made them central objects of public concern as well. Out of it came a restatement by educators of the importance of social goals and a renewed approval of the ideals of social efficiency and control.

Although the dominant culture emphasized social values throughout the 1920s, thereby supporting the social efficiency of schools, by a curious process of reversal in the 1930s the economic and political ideals of the era of prosperity were recast as individualism, particularly as something called rugged individualism. This was supposedly epitomized by the idea of every man for himself and exemplified institutionally by the absence of business and economic restraints. On a more sophisticated level it was identified with laissez-faire and the popular conception of the economic philosophy of Adam Smith. The fact was that no such laissez-faire had existed in American economic and business life during the 1920s. Some of its slogans had been invoked, however, to attack labor unions, child labor laws, and the like. It would have been equally valid to invoke its slogans against protective tariffs, but this was another matter. These slogans were of course discredited in the depression; individualism, which had been the ideology of the culture of protest, was now attacked with Hoover and prohibition as a cause of the depression and other evils of the times and was identified with the dominant culture.

Those who were emerging as critics of progressive education, or perhaps more accurately of the Progressive Education Association, took advantage of this confusion to attack the idea of individualism in education. The evils of the times, said Professor Isaac L. Kandel of Columbia's Teachers College in the winter of 1932–33, were the consequence of the doctrines of individual satisfaction. He called on progressives to "recognize the consequences of their own doctrines and concern themselves not with a new social order but with the removal of those causes of social disorder which were, until recently, inherent in their philosophy of education."[64]

---

64. "Education and Social Disorder," *TCR* 34 (Feb. 1933), 367.

The individualism with which Kandel was identifying the progressives of the 1920s was individualism in education, which meant individuality opposed to excessive social control. The individualism in the social order of the 1930s which the progressives and others attacked was understood as a callous indifference to human welfare. Kandel attacked both. Unfortunately the progressives themselves accepted the terms of the confusion that was being used against them. Much of this emerged in the controversy over reconstructionism generated by Counts and others who were coming to the forefront in the association itself, but some of it reflected a guilt complex even in the older leaders, a fear that in their endorsement of freedom in pedagogy they were giving aid and comfort to those who selfishly exploited people for their own ruthless ends. In one expression of this, *Progressive Education* magazine devoted its entire issue of January–February 1934 to the social aspects of education and to social aims.

The progressives were not the only educators to become heavily involved in the reaction against something known as individualism, although it was not always clear what this something was. Some, perhaps those who feared that they had at one time harbored individualistic impulses, sought to excuse individualism on the grounds that it had once fulfilled a real need, but was now out of date. According to Professor R. L. Lyman of the University of Chicago, individualism had once been "a major American principle," suitable when our civilization was young, but no longer suitable. The depression, he charged, was partly the result of "unrestricted individualism." He saw also as examples of latter-day individualism such phenomena as filth in literature, political corruption, and the multiplication of subjects in schools. Jesse Newlon found that individual worth and success constituted one of the finest traditions of American culture, but concluded "that the old individualism is by no means adapted to the common good in the complexity of our contemporary life."[65]

Great spiritual, moral, and social good had come out of the individualistic tradition of freedom, according to theologian Reinhold Niebuhr, but we were now "in a different kind of world." How, he asked, could we run our kind of complex civilization with individualistic traditions? It was not one to be guided by independence but by interdependence,

65. "Normalizing English Instruction," *EJ* 21 (Feb. 1932), 89–90, 94–95; "The Status of the New School," *TCR* 32 (April 1931), 608.

which he seemed to think was inconsistent with individual freedom.[66]

Most popular in this period, however, was to simply pull out all rhetorical stops in the denunciation of individualism past, present, and future, pedagogical, economic, or otherwise. Were human individuals naturally cooperative rather than competitive, thought Paul F. Voelker, Michigan's state superintendent, there could be a greater place for individualism: "If human society were organized like a colony of honey bees, all of our efforts and activities, both collective and individual, would be in the common service of us all." Since this happy state of affairs did not exist, Voelker called on schools to put social efficiency first and to study each child with a "view to fitting him into his proper place in the social order." John J. DeBoer of Chicago's Normal College condemned the subject curriculum put forth by a North Central committee as "purely individualistic" and "obsolete before it saw the light of day." According to the superintendent of Easton, Pennsylvania, in 1935, the times were witnessing the "last stand of individualism," identified by him as "the economic philosophy of selfishness, brutality, and greed."[67]

Few educators in this period dared to defend individualism. Some tried in strange ways to rescue it from its disreputable connotations. Philip A. Boyer of the Philadelphia public schools defined what he called individualized education as "those individual learnings that tend to make the individual a better member of the social group." This he defended as "a truly social process" and one aimed at "the effective attainment of social goals."[68] What Boyer did was to underscore the truism that individualized instruction in the sense of teaching one person at a time is not necessarily aimed at and does not necessarily promote individuality.

The quest for some kind of desirable balance between individual and social values had occupied both Charles W. Eliot and those who had produced the Cardinal Principles Report, and it was still occupying John Dewey. "Individualism run riot is laid at the door of modern schools,"

66. "The Spirit of Life," Superintendence *Report*, 1930, p. 14.

67. "Schools Should Serve Society," *Journal of Educational Sociology* 8 (March 1935), 406–8, 411; "The New Realism in Education," *Chicago Schools Journal* 15 (Jan.–June 1933), 133; James C. Bay, "Education As a Force for Social Improvement," Superintendence *Report*, 1935, p. 244.

68. "Individual Instruction and Personality," University of Pennsylvania School of Education, *Twenty-Fifth Annual Schoolmen's Week Proceedings*, 1938, p. 259.

he said, but he insisted that such schools were really trying to work out the balance between individual and group. Lucy W. Wilson returned from Palestine with enthusiasm for the educational ideals of the pioneer communities, especially as expressed by Palestinian educator Shlomo Bardin. What these schools sought, said Bardin, was "to develop a new type of man who, possessed by a passionate yearning toward a just society, is independent, self-disciplined, and self-controlled."[69]

Most of the talk, however, was about social aims and the group; this was consistent with theory that had dominated since at least the turn of the century. American life was hardly conducive to individuality in the days of prosperity, and the depression practically annihilated its last defenses in education. It was in this excessive group spirit that an outsider was able to see one of the country's greatest difficulties. American boys seek one another's company for everything," wrote the Spanish writer and social critic Salvador de Madariaga. "Play and prayer, feast and fast, lesson and leisure—all is arranged in common." He noted that this applied even to the most individual enterprises and that America was "the land of 'petting parties'!"[70]

69. "Why Have Progressive Schools?" *Current History* 38 (July 1933), 446; "The Rural Labor Schools of Palestine," *Prog Ed* 11 (Jan.–Feb. 1934), 78–79.
70. "Americans Are Boys: A Spaniard Looks at Our Civilization," *Harper's Magazine* 157 (July 1928), 243.

Chapter 9

The pursuit of change

> "There is simply no place for the conservative."
> —WILLIAM F. OGBURN,
> 1935.

*I*n a letter of February 20, 1935, President Roosevelt expressed his regrets to the members of the Department of Superintendence at not being able to take part in their forthcoming convention and praised their efforts on behalf of a great cause.[1] The theme of the department's convention was education and social change. Education, said Roosevelt as he congratulated the department on its choice, "must light the path for social change." Both Roosevelt and the department were rendering due homage to one of the most pervasive vogue terms and ideas of the times, the idea of social change itself.

Historians and sociologists had long been at work seeking to describe social change and to account for its ways. Educators had sought to relate it to the practices of schools, John Dewey in *The School and Society* for example. The period of the 1930s, however, seemed to call forth the utmost in rhetorical effort as writers and speakers labored to explain social change in compelling terms. Beyond this was the conviction that social change as a process, regardless of its substance, was something to which people should adjust. Attention was therefore directed to the problems accompanying change and to the resolution of such problems. Those known in education as "reconstructionists," that is, those who sought to have schools reconstruct society, viewed social change not merely as something that happened to people but as something that people could bring about or direct.

Much of the rhetoric of social change centered on the effects of

---

1. *School Life* 20 (April 1935), inside front cover.

machine technology, particularly the phenomenon of urbanization and its related developments in habits, mores, and styles of life. Especially popular were repeat performances of Dewey's 1899 description in *The School and Society* of a complex, specialized, industrialized, and urbanized America that had only recently emerged from a primitive, small village, idyllic scene. Dewey's sober presentation of this fantasy was transformed in the late 1920s and early 1930s into far gaudier prose. The fact was that simple environments still existed and the urbanized America was not new. Some who moved suddenly from the still-existing older America to the metropolitan centers undoubtedly suffered the sort of cultural shock that affected Theodore Dreiser and other writers on their first coming to Chicago.[2]

This shock affected educators as well. "I can remember," said President Lotus D. Coffman of The University of Minnesota in 1931, "seeing my own grandmother dip tallow candles; I have seen her card the wool, spin the yarn, knit the socks. My own mother quilted quilts; made clothing for the family; did the baking; while on the farm the reaping was done with the sickle, the cradle and the dropper; we cut our own wood, split our own rails, cleaned our grain, and in a thousand ways found employment from sun-up until dark." In those days, thought Coffman, America had been characterized by personal initiative and willingness to work. From this he went on to note the coming of radio, telephones, and chain stores, all contributing to new patterns in American life.[3]

Sustaining the note of awe-struck wonder at the presumably new developments but deploring such phenomena as the breaking-up of families, Helen Drusilla Lockwood of Vassar College in 1929 dwelt on what all this was doing to the girls then on campus. These students knew the changing culture in terms of "clothes, jazz, movies, radios, automobiles, country clubs, speak-easies, vague notions of self-expression." They expected "pleasure without effort" and wanted it "glamorous." The Vassar tradition, she concluded, demanded that "the bold vision of this new America" be faced. Lois Meek of Columbia's Teachers College was also somewhat breathless in her portrayal of the new world of 1930. "The World War, automobiles, airplanes, radios,

2. Harlan Hatcher, "The Reaction from Naturalistic Despair," *EJ* 19 (Oct. 1930), 611.
3. "Today's Challenge to the College Graduate," *S&S* 34 (July 4, 1931), 1–5.

prohibition, woman suffrage, congested cities, subways, jazz, talkies, rouge and lipstick, short skirts, women's smoking are only a few of the things that have helped to change our lives these last two decades."[4] In the early 1920s such comments had usually carried a tone of disapproval; by 1930, however, there was a tone of adaptation and adjustment.

The idea of adjustment to change was applied with mounting enthusiasm to the schools. Air-minded educators, for example, called on schools to adapt themselves to conditions generated by air-age technology, with emphasis on new curricular content. "At the present time," said the *Journal of Educational Sociology* editorially in January 1930, "aeronautical information is being imparted in one form or another in three hundred public schools of elementary and secondary grade in the United States" (3:261). Coming strongly to the fore was a revival of the idea that schools had new functions arising from changes in home, community, and church. "As the community disintegrates," wrote V. T. Thayer in 1930, "and the home becomes confused, the school serves more and more as the focusing point for influences bearing upon the child. Upon it now rests the responsibility for developing the child's personality and for socializing the individual in the interests of the future. To meet this new responsibility the school itself is undergoing transformation."[5] The NEA agreed, directing its efforts, however, to showing why schools had to cost more than before. "The organization of society in the twentieth century," declared the *NEA Journal*, "is responsible for the fact that the home and the church have found it impossible to carry on the kind of training that these institutions gave youth before the beginning of the century" (19 [March 1930], 78).

At times the prophets of change were weighted down by gloom. The decline of traditional authority had plunged the America of 1930 into uncertainty and confusion, according to one professor at the Ohio State University. "The meaning of life," he said, "is not so clear to the present generation as it was to our fathers and grandfathers. Traditional authority provided them with many ready-made solutions for the vexatious problems of life." On the whole, those who took the long view tended, like him, to be more solemn in their pronouncements. Harold Rugg described social change since 1700 in two stages: the first—that of

4. "The Meaning of Euthenics," *Educational Record* 10 (April 1929), 72–73, 93; quoted in "Teachers College in the News," *TCR* 31 (Jan. 1930), 371.
5. "School and the Shifting Home," *Survey* 64 (Sept. 1, 1930), 457, 486.

machines—he placed from 1700 to 1900, but the second—that of power—after 1900, with accumulated momentum after 1920. With this ingenious device he combined long-range perspective with immediate alarm, seeing one possible road to the future as leading to "social chaos," the other "to the era of the great society."[6]

Although New Dealers, as might have been expected, showed considerable preoccupation with the notion of change, the first massive document on the subject in this period appeared as one of the last contributions related to the administration of President Hoover. It was the two-volume report of Hoover's Research Committee on Social Trends, appearing in January 1933 (New York) and entitled *Recent Social Trends in the United States*. Leading social scientists took part, among them William F. Ogburn of the University of Chicago, an outstanding student of social change particularly as it is affected by technology.

In his foreword to this report, Hoover said that since the committee had been given the task of examining change, the result was emphasis "on elements of instability rather than stability in our social structure" (p. v). The general tone of the report was one of alarm at the problems brought about by change. "The first third of the twentieth century," the committee declared, "has been filled with epoch-making events and crowded with problems of great variety and complexity" (p. xi). It would be negligent of them to "gloss over the stark and bitter realities of the social situation and to ignore the imminent perils in further advance of our heavy technical machinery over crumbling roads and shaking bridges. There are times when silence is not neutrality, but assent" (pp. lxxiv–lxxv).

The depression itself was social change or a reflection of it, and the New Deal was a complex enterprise aimed at resolving or mitigating the problems it brought on. The New Deal supported the national preoccupation with social change, especially from the point of view of adapting, a major point in defending such measures as the National Recovery Act. New Dealers became identified, at least briefly, as the major ideologues of change. So strong was the appeal to social change that educators, whether formally identifiable as New Dealers or not, were at least briefly drawn into the stream.

---

6. D. H. Eikenberry, "How Can the Unit Courses and Curriculum Commission Develop Its Plan of Curriculum Construction To Serve Best the School Systems in the North Central Association?" *North Central Association Quarterly* 5 (Dec. 1930), 407; "The Educator in the Great Transition," *TCR* 37 (Nov. 1935), 111–18.

Early in July 1933, for example, only some three months after the first recovery measures had appeared, Professor Thomas H. Briggs of Columbia's Teachers College proclaimed the need for school instruction "regarding the principles underlying the momentous economic, political and social changes that are taking place in our country." Already, he feared, there was selfish opposition that might defeat the wisest planning by the President and his advisers. New York University's Philip W. L. Cox beamed his appeal especially to secondary educators, warning them that "radical thinkers" would hesitate to support high school teachers who were "social ignoramuses." High schools in particular, argued Cox, needed to foster support for "such clearly approvable community undertakings as the Tennessee basin project of the national program for economic recovery, for the elimination of child labor, for sanitary labor conditions, for better housing conditions, for richer recreational opportunities, for international understandings, for well-conceived barter plans, and for similar worthy community experiments."[7]

Also explicit and direct was the call in September 1933 from Vierling Kersey, state superintendent in Hoover's own California, to public schools to assist in realizing the aims of the National Recovery Act, partly through combating unemployment themselves (for example, by reducing class size) and partly through explaining the purpose and nature of the act to students. New York City's superintendent Harold Campbell joined the bandwagon by calling on the high schools of his system to explain the National Recovery Act, with emphasis on its aims. So eager were some schoolmen to convert schools into major voices for New Deal policies that the National Recovery Administration, embarrassed by such allies, declared itself against the use of schools for propaganda purposes.[8]

Probably the most ardent expression of all came not from a professional educator but from the new governor of the Territory of Hawaii, Joseph B. Poindexter, in his annual report for 1934. (There may have been an educator behind it.) In any case, he declared that students could not be prepared for active citizenship in 1934 by staying with the subject matter of the past. Social change was demanding new subject

7. "Fascism or Democracy in the United States?" *S&S* 38 (July 15, 1933), 86–88; "The Crisis in Secondary Education," *Clearing House* 8 (Sept. 1933), 6.
8. "Public Schools and the National Recovery Act," *California Schools* 4 (Sept. 1933), 290; "High Schools Teach the National Industrial Recovery Act," *Sch R* 41 (Nov. 1933), 644–45; "NRA in Schools," *School Life* 19 (Nov. 1933), 49.

matter. "A new social order," he declared, "is in the making. In the field of politics, it is called the New Deal. . . . It has revitalized the social studies. . . . It has made the school more aware of the injustices of society."[9] Not all would have agreed that the New Deal had in fact revitalized the social studies, but many educators of diverse political persuasions would have agreed that it should have.

II

Social change was in the air, and conservatism was out of style. Among many intellectuals, conservatism was tagged as virtual stupidity. Professor Richard LaPiere of Stanford, for instance, at a meeting of the California Society for Secondary Education in August 1933, castigated his audience of principals for their views and for perpetuating them in their students. "Have you been liberating your students," asked LaPiere, "from the principles and prejudices of the Middle Ages that they might experiment, however unsuccessfully, with the warp of our culture? You have not! You are, most of you, as old-fashioned mentally as your great-grandparents. I know; for year after year I receive the products, the selected products of our public school system. A more highly conventionalized group of people than the children which you send to me cannot be found." In conclusion, LaPiere said he had tried "to crack the metal shell" of his audience's medieval minds.[10]

To Professor William F. Ogburn of the University of Chicago and Hoover's committee on social trends, a conservative was a social liability. "There is," he said in 1935, "simply no place for the conservative. I don't see how a society can tolerate the conservative—the traditional conservative. He is in the way, he is an enemy of society, and the duty of everybody is to fight him." Ogburn hastened to add that he was not in favor of wild radicals or of radical proposals. What we needed, he thought, were "self-critical radicals with scientific training."[11]

To what extent were teachers and other educators of this period conservative or radical? The question of radicalism emerged more

9. Territory of Hawaii, *Annual Report of the Governor to the Secretary of the Interior* (Washington, D.C., 1934), p. 40.

10. "Social Change and the Function of the School," *California Quarterly of Secondary Education* 9 (Jan. 1934), 136.

11. "How Is Social Reconstruction Achieved?" *Proceedings of the Middle States Association of Colleges and Secondary Schools,* 1935 pp. 31–32.

explicitly as an aspect of the controversies over reconstruction and indoctrination that occupied educators during the 1930s. For the most part, however, teachers did not stand out sharply either way. They were perhaps low-key conservatives who preferred not to strike postures at all. A review of studies of teachers' attitudes since 1922 led to the conclusion in 1937 that teachers were less conservative since the depression than before, although much conservatism remained.[12] Few identified themselves explicitly with conservatism as a cause—or, indeed, with any cause.

Communism, or "Bolshevism," had been the favorite bogey since the great red scare immediately after the World War, a scare that had involved teachers, particularly through New York state's Lusk laws. Neither then nor later did educators come out for communism, although some visited Soviet Russia and made observations about Soviet schools. Some avowed communists contributed articles on education in pedagogical journals, but the articles were expressions of personal opinion.

After the middle 1920s, prosperity took over and the red scare abated. There was a brief flurry in education in 1928, when Secretary James W. Crabtree of the NEA protested against the listing of his organization in a pamphlet from the Daughters of the American Revolution on groups called "sympathetic with communist ideals." His protest apparently led the DAR to withdraw distribution of the pamphlet. On the whole things were quiet in those last days of prosperity, and one magazine editorially noted that the market for attacking the red menace looked "right poorly."[13]

The market was better, however, in the 1930s, when rapid social change and controversy over the New Deal generated antired rhetoric. Even the stodgily anti-academic report of the Society for Curriculum Study entitled *A Challenge to Secondary Education* (New York, 1935) was subjected to the accusation of having been written by a bunch of reds.[14]

A new round of loyalty oaths and provisions like the widely publicized "red rider" of the District of Columbia Public Schools was aimed directly at teachers (and in some cases at other public employees). The

12. M. H. Harper, "Social Attitudes of Educators," *Social Frontier* 3 (Feb. 1937), 145–47.

13. "Secretary's Report," *NEA Proc*, 1928, pp. 1147–48; "Sad Days for Red Hunters," *Outlook and Independent* 152 (July 10, 1929), 416.

14. Forrest E. Long, book review, *Curriculum Journal* 6 (May 22, 1935), 15.

rider was attached by Congress in 1935 to the appropriation bill for the District forbidding payment of salaries to teachers and other employees found to be teaching or advocating communism. Efforts to repeal it were begun in 1936 and dragged their weary way to a crescendo of background controversy into the following year, culminating in conference committee and in the signing of a repeal by the President on May 28, 1937.[15] This two-year tragicomedy in the nerve center of the nation's political affairs undoubtedly fostered increased preoccupation with and controversy about the alleged communist leanings of teachers.

Although fascism was generally frowned on and disparaged, it had a measure of quasi-respectable advocacy based on the idea that Mussolini had saved Italy from mob rule, and reinforced in the minds of some educators by admiration for the work and writings of the philosopher Giovanni Gentile. One writer in 1930 praised educational "reforms" in Italy, attributing these to Gentile and identifying them with self-realization, joy, and freedom. Another, Professor S. B. Clough of the history department of Columbia, in defending Italian education in 1931 emphasized the role of fascism in curbing disorder in Italy, and acknowledged Gentile's philosophical contributions and the Gentile "reform" expressed in educational decrees. Later in the decade, a high school teacher at the Evander Childs High School of New York City also expounded Gentile on lofty grounds. "He attacked the old system," she said, "which had as its ideal a storing up of facts which did nothing to develop the soul. His aim was to raise the standard of culture and to develop intellectual and moral ideals in the pupil."[16]

The main line intellectual defense of fascism for education came not from educators but from Lawrence Dennis, Harvard graduate and businessman, in his book *The Coming American Fascism* (New York, 1936). Schooling, said Dennis, served the function of developing right attitudes toward the prevailing social order, with right defined in a

15. "News Note," *Nation* 141 (Dec. 4, 1935), 635; "The Repeal of the 'Red Rider,'" *NEA Proc*, 1937, p. 879; Ellen Thomas, "Sequelae of the 'Red Rider,'" *Prog Ed* 13 (Dec. 1936), 606–8; Paul W. Ward, "Washington Weekly," *Nation* 142 (March 25, 1936), 371–72; Caroline Williams, "Congress Legislates Character," *Social Frontier* 3 (Jan. 1937), 107–10.

16. Fredericka Blankner, "Education in Italy," *S&S* 32 (July 5, 1930), 21–23; "Education under the New Regime in Italy," University of Pennsylvania School of Education, *Eighteenth Annual Schoolmen's Week Proceedings*, 1931, pp. 362–70; Emma Menna, "The Gentile Reforms in Italian Education," *EA&S* 22 (Oct. 1936), 552.

relative sense and depending upon the purpose. All rational schemes, according to Dennis, were social or collectivist, and right attitudes would help make these work. Educating individuals rather than citizens was impractical and vicious. "The school," he declared, "must be one of the instruments of government of the group culture. The group culture should be the expression of the will of the dominant element of the elite whose values are validated by the power to enforce them." It was up to the elite to condition the people to like this. "Conditioning a people to like what they have and to do their part," concluded Dennis, "is a simple exercise in educational technique."[17]

For the most part, fascism was to American educators and their fellow citizens a totally alarming phenomenon and one that aroused great apprehension. Many Americans in that period were repelled by communism and disagreed with it but were horrified by fascism, especially in its Nazi form. Some were horrified also by what they felt to be the greater probability than with communism that it might be embraced in America. It was not, declared a *Harper's* article in 1934, "a nonexistent peril." The long-time efficiency educator William D. Lewis, formerly deputy superintendent of public instruction in Pennsylvania, in 1936 called for modern social studies materials "to save us from the menace of fascism and perpetuate a constantly improving democracy." Historian Harry Elmer Barnes in 1937 declared that anyone who imagined fascism could not take over in the United States was living in a fool's paradise. Conditions favoring fascism were more prevalent in the United States of 1937, said Barnes, than they had been in the Italy of 1920 or the Germany of 1925.[18]

The sudden appearance in 1933 of technocracy provided a phenomenon that did not fit the conventional terms. It was neither communist nor fascist, radical nor conservative, left nor right, but it was provocative and exciting. Immediately preceding the New Deal, it bloomed quickly and as quickly faded, but educators had seized on it with avidity. According to many it was not even new, but owed its shape and sub-

17. "Education—The Tool of the Dominant Elite," *Social Frontier* 1 (Jan. 1935), 11–15.

18. J. B. Matthews and R. E. Shallcross, "Must America Go Fascist?" 169 (June 1934), 15; "What the Community Should Know about Its Secondary School," University of Pennsylvania School of Education, *Twenty-Third Annual Schoolmen's Week Proceedings*, 1936, p. 74; "The Present Social Scene," Superintendence *Report*, 1937, p. 77.

stance to ideas earlier set forth by Thorstein Veblen in *The Engineers and the Price System* (New York, 1921). Just what technocracy meant was not always clear, but it could be identified with an economy of abundance and consumption based on automated technology and free distribution, all this wrapped in elaborate new terminology for media of exchange that would replace conventional money.

Its advocate in the winter of 1932–33 was an engineer named Howard Scott, hailed by some as savior, denounced by others as fraud. The January 1933 issue of *Harper's Magazine* carried an article under his name and prepared under his supervision entitled "Technology Smashes the Price System" (166:129–42). Favorable comment came from *School Life*, the official magazine of the Office of Education, in the same month (5:86). By the February 22, 1933, issue of the *New Republic* there were six books on the subject for Edmund Wilson to review, one of these by Scott himself (74:50–51). A week later, Scott appeared in person before the Department of Superintendence in Minneapolis.[19] Still another technocrat, Wayne Parrish, appeared before the Philadelphia regional conference of the Progressive Education Association. He deplored the fact that technocracy had become a fad, but defended its main ideas of advanced technology and a reconstructed price system.[20] Over the summer, technocracy disappeared—the New Deal was too strong a competitor—but in its brief hour, it had demonstrated the hunger of many Americans, including many educators, for thoroughgoing, even radical, reformulation of the assumptions underlying their economy.

III

In the drama of social change played out on the national stage, educators worked up subplots of their own. Two of them—reconstructionism and indoctrination—were exciting enough not only to provide educators with new controversies, but to occasionally make the public media and attract notice outside the immediate domain of the schools.

Reconstructionism called on schools and teachers to take the lead in the creation of social change, to do more than adapt and follow, even to the extent, with some of its advocates, of building a new social order. The idea was one of the oldest in teaching. Even the up-to-date ter-

---

19. "The Imminence of Social Change, the Impact of Technology on Price System of Production," Superintendence *Report*, 1933, pp. 20–26.

20. "The Engineer Looks at the Depression," *Prog Ed* 10 (March 1933), 129–34.

minology used for it in the early 1930s was a decade or more old. The secretary of the Pennsylvania State Teachers Association in 1921 had described the work of state superintendent Thomas E. Finegan as "leadership in the movement toward a new social order."[21] The idea and the terms, however, remained dormant until the late 1920s, when George S. Counts, in his book *Secondary Education and Industrialism,* asked whether the high school could fashion or have fashioned for it "an educational and social philosophy which exalts all forms of socially useful labor and which accepts the challenge of the fundamental social reconstruction of society in the light of a rational ideal" (New York, 1929, p. 64).

Interest picked up rapidly in the new decade. The 1930 summer meeting of the NEA's National Council of Education devoted a great deal of time to a list of questions written by John Dewey at the request of the council's Committee on Objectives in Education, one of the questions asking whether criticism of the existing social order should be permitted in schools.[22] In 1932, the National Council devoted much of its winter meeting to education and social planning. At the session of February 20, Counts presented a series of theses with running comments on social planning, educational leadership, and freedom in relation to culture.[23] The discussion involved Dewey, Boyd Bode, and Ross Finney, as well as many other national leaders in the field.

These were busy February days for Counts, possibly the most packed-together sequence of events in his long and most active career. On February 18, two days before the National Council meeting, he had startled the Progressive Education Association at its Baltimore convention with an address entitled "Dare Progressive Education Be Progressive?" Counts had contended in this address that a group claiming the domain of progressive education was obligated to relate itself to political, social, and economic progressivism as well. He had expressed doubt, however, that the progressive schools, "handicapped as they are by the clientele which they serve and the intellectualistic approach to life which they embrace" could become progressive "in the genuine social sense here suggested."[24]

21. J. H. Kelley, "Fitting for Leadership," *Pennsylvania Journal of Education* 69 (April 1921), 431.
22. "Secretary's Minutes," *NEA Proc,* 1930, pp. 242–45.
23. "Freedom and Culture, Freedom and Social Planning, Freedom and Leadership," *NEA Proc,* 1932, pp. 249–51.
24. *Prog Ed* 9 (April 1932), 257–63.

One writer called Counts's address of February 18 "electrifying," another termed the response to it "yeasty."[25] The annual business meeting of the association on February 20 responded to Counts's challenge by instructing its board of directors to create a committee for the study of world economic and industrial problems. This Committee on Social and Economic Problems was created that spring with Counts as chairman.[26] Its report to the Chicago convention in March 1933 was discussed by that body with the recommendation that the committee be continued with a final report to come later.[27] The executive board discussed the report and returned it to the committee for further study.[28] It was published subsequently under the title *A Call to the Teachers of the Nation* as a separate venture of the committee itself and was somewhat skeptically reviewed in *Progressive Education*.[29]

In April 1932 Counts assembled the materials from his February addresses to the National Council and to the Progressive Education Association, and from another made on February 23 to the Department of Superintendence,[30] into a separately published booklet with the new and even more provocative title *Dare the School Build a New Social Order?* (New York, 1932). "That the teachers should deliberately reach for power and then make the most of their conquest is my firm conviction," said Counts in one of the most frequently quoted sentences. The teaching profession, he assured his reading audience "has at its disposal, as no other group, the knowledge and wisdom of the ages" (pp. 28–29). So far as individualism and collectivism were concerned, there was no longer a choice. There was only one choice, that between a feudal collectivism fostering the interests of "a privileged class" and a democratic collectivism "devoted to the interests of the people" (p. 49).

25. "Editorial Review," *School Executives Magazine* 51 (Aug. 1932), 512; Beulah Amidon, "Teachers Look at Education," *Survey* 68 (April 15, 1932), 78.
26. "Notes on the Convention," *Prog Ed* 9 (April 1932), 289; *ibid.* (May 1932), 330*n*.
27. Minutes of Chicago Convention, March 4, 1933, in Teachers College Library, Columbia University, New York City.
28. Minutes of Executive Committee, Progressive Education Association, March 4, 1933, in Teachers College Library, Columbia University.
29. James Truslow Adams, "Can This Bring about the New Society?" *Prog Ed* 10 (Oct. 1933), 310–11.
30. "Education through Indoctrination," Superintendence *Report*, 1932, pp. 193–99.

It was mainly through this pamphlet, far more overwhelming in its totality than a mere sum of the three addresses comprising it, that the issue of reconstructionism burst upon the profession as a whole. The question was no longer simply one of saving the soul of the Progressive Education Association. There has been some tendency to identify reconstructionism too much with the association and its internal tensions. Counts was more widely known throughout the profession on his own merits than as a spokesman for or gadfly of progressive education. Also, the issue of reconstructionism had been developing on a wider front, especially in the National Council of Education and the NEA, before Counts startled the progressives with his bombshell.

A narrow identification of the adversaries in these controversies tended to fasten not on the Progressive Education Association but on a relatively small group of professors at Columbia's Teachers College. Involved here, of course, is the question of the extent to which the so-called professionals, especially those from Teachers College, had taken over the association and absorbed it unto themselves. The group at Columbia (Kilpatrick, Rugg, Counts, Childs, and others) actually came to identify themselves and to be identified by others as "frontier" thinkers, a symbol that carried over into a book edited by Kilpatrick entitled *The Educational Frontier* (New York, 1933) and the establishment by this group in 1934 of the magazine *The Social Frontier,* later called *Frontiers of Democracy.* It was "frontiersmanship," especially as centered in this Teachers College group, that became the adjunct of or synonym for reconstructionism. After all, what could a new social order be if not a frontier?

In the far-flung ramifications of these discussions, reconstructionism acquired both friends and foes, and it would be difficult to say which had the greater influence. The significant thing, however, was the degree of interest and involvement generated in the problem. For a brief time it had the overwhelming impact of other bandwagons such as vocational education or project method. Even the NEA had a Committee on Social-Economic Objectives, and in 1932 the chairman, a staff member of the Office of Education, declared that "a new or radically changed social order was coming" and that the NEA was calling on teachers to take part in building it.[31]

31. Fred J. Kelly, chairman, "Report of the Committee on Social-Economic Objectives," *NEA Proc,* 1932, pp. 208–10.

Strong advocacy evoked opposition, but the volume of criticism of reconstructionism was in itself a kind of tribute to its pervasive appeal. David Snedden paid his respects to the idea in 1935. Granting some core of reality beneath "romantic nonsense" about reconstructionism, he went on to pour ridicule on the idea itself. The underlying core of reality, thought Snedden, was that America was sick, giving rise to prophets and panaceas. "There are sincere, even if romantic spirits among us," he declared, "who honestly believe that if the million teachers in our schools would or could unite on political or other social programs, they could not only speedily cure our societies of their diseases but even purify and elevate to new levels our entire civilization. These Utopians are able to have sober articles published under such titles as 'Dare the Schools Reconstruct the Social Order?'" Warming to his assignment, Snedden found the dreams of having schools take part in social reconstruction not only visionary, but subversive of "civic decency."[32]

Also in a tone of sarcasm, Professor Edgar W. Knight of the University of North Carolina in 1935 referred to professors who had become "apostolic" in their approach to the new social order. "Just as the hot July and August days of other years seemed the most suitable season for getting religion in the old-time revivals," wrote Knight, "so have the pedagogical revivals of recent years been staged in the hot summer session days. Recent summer session preaching on the ills of the old social order differs but little from that which a century ago called sinners to the mourners' benches." Professor Isaac L. Kandel of Columbia's Teachers College was less inclined to such playfulness. Expressing himself against reconstructionism in 1935, he observed the coincidence of proposals for tenure and challenges to build a new social order, and concluded that what was sought was "the right to conduct propaganda in the schools and to have tenure protected while conducting it."[33]

Superintendent Harold Campbell of New York City was another who attacked reconstructionism, pouring vitriolic scorn on the idea that education would lead to a new social order, "whatever that might mean." He denounced what he called the notion that general education

32. "Social Reconstruction, A Challenge to the Secondary School," University of Pennsylvania School of Education, *Twenty-Second Annual Schoolmen's Week Proceedings*, 1935, pp. 48–51.

33. "Academic Freedom and Noblesse Oblige," *TCR* 37 (Dec. 1935), 184–85; "Academic Freedom for Teachers," *ibid.*, 191.

must change because the market had crashed and a new party had come into power in Washington. Still more embittered in his criticism was a leading member of the Progressive Education Association, Burton P. Fowler of Tower Hill School, Wilmington, Delaware, a former principal of Cleveland's Central High School. Directing his comments specifically against "frontier thinkers" who called on teachers to lead America into the promised land, Fowler urged teachers to believe "in orderly change as opposed to revolutionary reforms by violence" and to regard skeptically what he called "short cuts to social efficiency."[34]

Dramatically hostile toward reconstructionism, Dean William F. Russell of Columbia's Teachers College seemed in his utterances to be repudiating part of his own faculty. In 1937 he chose the New Orleans convention of the Department of Superintendence from which to launch his attack. After describing mass demonstrations of rightists and leftists he had seen in France on Bastille Day two years before, he declared that the images of Utopias set forth by educators played into the hands of both communists and fascists. He specifically referred to Counts's challenge of 1932 as a demand for Utopia. "The period of curriculum construction," said Russell, "was followed by the period of Utopia construction, and I think this period has run its course." Counts in his reply the next day expressed his realization of the fact that Dean Russell and other administrators were under heavy fire. In answer to the accusation that he was building Utopias, Counts said, "I gladly admit the charge. A map of the world that does not contain the land of Utopia is not worthy of mankind."[35]

Although Russell's criticism was partly ideological, he was appealing to the practical school man as well. The term *Utopian* popularly meant a dream-world that could not come true. What alienated the school man from reconstructionism was precisely its lack of prospects for success. "Those of us who have not taken leave of our senses," wrote the superintendent of Allentown, Pennsylvania, in 1939, "know that the schools and schoolmasters are not generally going to be permitted *to take the lead* in changing the social order, nor in conducting experiments likely to lead to a radical redefinition of the aims of that order."[36] Reconstruc-

34. "Modern Preparation for College," *High Points* 19 (May 1937), 7; "Completing the Picture of America," *Prog Ed* 14 (April 1937), 232, 234.

35. "Education for the Middle of the Road," Superintendence *Report*, 1937, pp. 102–10; "The Prospect of American Democracy," *ibid.*, p. 144.

36. William L. Connor, book review, *School Executive* 59 (Dec. 1939), 31.

tionism was visionary romanticism, and the voice of the school man in the land in the late 1930s proclaimed that it wouldn't "work."

IV

Indoctrination was a question closely related to reconstructionism, but reconstructionists were not necessarily indoctrinators. Neither were all indoctrinators in pursuit of reconstruction. Still, there were reconstructionists who advocated indoctrination as the way of achieving their goals; but indoctrination did not necessarily mean manipulation of personality that reduced or eliminated freedom of choice. The term could mean intensive advocacy or persuasion without behavioral engineering techniques of the kind that had been advocated since the period immediately following the World War.

Indoctrination and reconstructionism were identified partly because of Counts's advocacy of both.[37] On indoctrination, Counts's thinking had elements of social efficiency, particularly in its advocacy of attitudes and beliefs as aims. Such advocacy in 1932, for example, came from Principal Lloyd N. Morrisett of the Classen High School, Oklahoma City, before the social studies section of the NEA. He called for the development in students not only of understanding but of ideals for a better economic and social order. Some, he realized, would call this indoctrination, but why not? "Why should not high school students have emotionalized attitudes and ideals for a better social order, a better and more just economic order, an improved political order, and a world characterized by brotherly love, mutual understanding, peace, prosperity, and happiness."[38] Faced by such good things as these, opponents of indoctrination had no easy task.

Another argument for indoctrination from a social efficiency background came from Professor Charles C. Peters of Pennsylvania State College. Three weeks after listening to a debate on the subject before the Department of Superintendence, Peters said the only question involved was that of good versus bad indoctrination, with the goodness and badness apparently residing not in the process but in the substance. Good indoctrination was indoctrination for good things; bad, for bad

37. For his explicit advocacy of indoctrination see his "Education through Indoctrination," Superintendence *Report*, 1932, pp. 193–99.

38. "The High School in the Age of Depression," *Historical Outlook* 23 (Oct. 1932), 275.

things. In a manner consistent with his investment theory of education, Thomas H. Briggs of Columbia's Teachers College stood ready also to accept indoctrination for what was right. The right things, he concluded, were those wanted in and by the culture. He called on the adult population as a whole to decide what social order it wanted and on schools to bring such a social order to pass. The aim of indoctrination "should be that which is determined by the ideals of democracy."[39]

Even many with academic commitment were drawn into the indoctrination camp. A teacher at Julia Richman High School, New York City, for instance, believed in it but shrank from the idea of permitting teachers to indoctrinate for what they saw fit. He proposed following not agreement in the culture at large but agreement among scholars in each particular field. In social studies as in algebra, he felt, there were good and bad answers.[40]

Among the major opponents of indoctrination were William H. Kilpatrick and Superintendent Willard Beatty of the Bronxville, New York, public schools. Arguing before the Georgia Educational Association in April 1933 for education that would "help usher in a regime of plenty instead of the present want and uncertainty," Kilpatrick sternly declared, "Again no indoctrination. We do not tell what to think. We help to study." Beatty editorially declared in 1935 that progressives in education by the very nature of their ideas were "opposed to indoctrination in the teaching of the social studies or in any other area of thought." Kilpatrick and Beatty were both heavily involved in the association, and their utterances indicated the extent to which the indoctrination issue apparently split the progressives. Progressive Agnes De Lima was caustic indeed, rejecting both indoctrination and Counts. As she saw it, Counts was calling for something like the old anti-alcohol campaign.[41]

Anti-indoctrinators, like their opponents, came from various walks of pedagogical and intellectual life and represented various schools of feeling and thought. Howard Odum of the University of North Caro-

39. "Character and Democracy Education," University of Pennsylvania School of Education, *Nineteenth Annual Schoolmen's Week Proceedings*, 1932, pp. 213–14; "The Philosophy Which Must Guide Secondary Education Today," Superintendence *Report*, 1935, pp. 102–3.

40. Abraham Geduldig, "Should We Indoctrinate?" *High Points* 15 (Oct. 1933), 32.

41. "Education Face-to-Face with the Social Situation," *High School Quarterly* 21 (July 1933), 164; *Prog Ed* 12 (Feb. 1935), 71–73; "A Communication," *New Republic* 71 (Aug. 1932), 317–18.

lina and the report *Recent Social Trends in the United States* urged English teachers to direct their work in writing to industrial-economic problems, but warned against the temptation to set up propaganda for social dogmas. Rudolph Lindquist of Ohio State University charged the pro-indoctrinators with lacking faith in the exercise of intelligence. Literary critic Joseph Wood Krutch recoiled from indoctrination on the grounds that it assumed the revelation of truth in final form. A teacher at the Samuel J. Tilden High School, New York City, warned that indoctrination could be used to preserve the existing order, a perfectly obvious point, but one that did not seem to occur to those who thought of it as a weapon for social change.[42]

V

Apart from the Progressive Education Association, two other groups became heavily involved in dialogue over reconstruction, indoctrination, and social change: the American Historical Association with its Commission on the Social Studies in the Schools, and the Department of Superintendence through efforts which culminated in the establishment, with the NEA, of the Educational Policies Commission in 1935.

The Commission on the Social Studies in the Schools predated the depression and was a 1929 outgrowth of the most recent in a string of association committees dealing with school programs. It was known as the Krey Commission from its chairman, Professor August C. Krey of the University of Minnesota. Krey was a historian who had become deeply committed to the cause of social studies in high schools, partly because he felt that traditional course work was not suited to what he called "mass education on the present scale." After searching back in 1926 for a function common to all high school social studies, he had come up with the education of youth for social efficiency. Increasingly Krey sounded more like an educationist than did the educationists themselves, especially in repeating the contention that high school students of 1929 were not going to college at the presumed rate of 1899.[43]

42. "The New Setting for English Teaching," *EJ* 22 (Nov. 1933), 718–19; "Freedom—For What Purpose?" *Phi Delta Kappan* 17 (Dec. 1934), 50–51; "On Academic Freedom," *Nation* 140 (April 17, 1935), 449–50; Louis A. Shucker, "Indoctrination: Much Ado about Nothing," *High Points* 16 (March 1934), 17.

43. "History and Other Social Studies in the Schools," *Historical Outlook* 18 (March 1927), 111; A. C. Krey to Jesse H. Newlon, April 23, 1926, A. C. Krey Papers, University of Minnesota Archives, Minneapolis; "Thirty Years after the Committee of Seven," *Historical Outlook* 20 (Feb. 1929), 64–67.

With a $50,000 grant from the Carnegie Foundation, the commission in 1929 turned toward the heroic task of reorganizing high school social studies, including history. The membership of the commission was broadly representative of historians and social scientists, with some people from education. Over its five years of official existence it involved, in its membership of sixteen, historians Avery O. Craven, Guy Stanton Ford, and Carlton J. H. Hayes and social scientists Isaiah Bowman, L. C. Marshall, and Charles E. Merriam. The educationists among its members were a fascinating selection indeed, including George S. Counts, Ernest Horn of the University of Iowa, Jesse H. Newlon, and Superintendent Frank Ballou of the Washington, D.C., public schools. Charles A. Beard was unclassifiable although perhaps the most important member of all. Besides these, the enterprise drew in large numbers of people as members of subcommittees and as consultants.

True to logic and convention, the commission turned to formulating objectives. It had a subcommittee on this subject, but increasingly looked to Beard to provide a statement as a basis for criticism and discussion. The statement Beard presented was extensively discussed in a meeting of the commission in October 1930, and it received both praise and blame. Guy Stanton Ford called it the philosophy of "a many-sided personality," an expression that later appeared in the commission's documents almost as a leitmotiv. Harold Rugg, an outside member of the subcommittee on objectives, praised Beard's document for its statement that social reconstruction must come through educational reconstruction.[44] In July 1931 Krey announced that Beard and the subcommittee had agreed on the statement in tentative form.[45] It finally appeared in 1932 as the first official publication of the commission, *A Charter for the Social Sciences in the Schools* (New York, 1932), with the notation that it had been drafted by Charles A. Beard.

This charter, accordingly, played a major role in the first round of the commission's efforts. Here appeared the idea of creating rich and many-sided personalities, identified in a section heading (p. 93) as "the supreme purpose in civic instruction." If this seems to have anticipated the rhetoric of life adjustment education, it managed at the same time to escape a heavy-handed note of social control. "All instruction in the schoolroom," said the report (p. 94), "must turn on the individual

44. "Proceedings of Meeting at Briarcliff Manor, New York, October 16–18, 1930," A. C. Krey Papers, University of Minnesota Archives.

45. "Report of Progress in the Investigation of the Social Studies in the Schools," *Historical Outlook* 22 (Oct. 1931), 264.

pupil; its results must inhere in the individual, even though some ideal-
ized scheme of social arrangements may be the controlling motive in
the organization and imparting of learning." In a changing society, individuals could not be cast into "typical grooves" but must be prepared
for the making of difficult choices (pp. 95–96). From this, the report
outlined aims involving information, skills, habits, attitudes, and such
qualities as will power and courage.

Early in 1932 the commission outlined a list of volumes it intended
to sponsor for publication, and it set about the task of finding authors
for them, in some cases commission members, in others not. From this
part of the enterprise came works of enduring value, such as Merle
Curti's *The Social Ideas of American Educators* (New York, 1935),
Counts's *The Social Foundations of Education* (New York, 1934), and
Beard's *The Nature of the Social Sciences* (New York, 1934). The latter
aroused a good deal of controversy on the commission itself, since
Beard by this time had become increasingly skeptical about the scientific character of the so-called social sciences, a skepticism he cautiously
set forth in this volume. Of special interest was the fact that his book
carried the subtitle *In Relation to Objectives of Instruction*, indicating
the continuing preoccupation of Beard and the commission with that
topic.

The commission's message was fully unveiled, however, with the
publication of *Conclusions and Recommendations* under its collective
authorship (New York, 1934). This volume had been underway with
a special committee since October 1932 and had undergone numerous
discussions, rewritings, and reappraisals, with a good deal of controversy
along the way. The last revised version by the executive committee was
sent to the membership of the commission for signatures late in February 1934, after the life of the commission itself had formally ended in
December of the preceding year. Here further conflict broke out. Eventually all signed except Superintendent Ballou, Professors Charles E.
Merriam and Ernest Horn, and Edmund Day of the Rockefeller Foundation. Geographer Isaiah Bowman signed with reservations (p. 144).
Since the volume covered a great variety of matters, such as "a frame
of reference," philosophy and purpose, materials of instruction, method
of teaching, tests and testing, the teacher, and public relations and
administration, there were obviously many opportunities presented for
controversy and attack.

Much of the outside attention, however, was centered on the statement of philosophy and purpose. Especially provocative in this were statements on the nature of society and the social order. The commission observed, for example, that "the age of individualism and *laissez faire* in economy and government is closing" and that "a new age of collectivism is emerging" (p. 16). It was convinced "by its interpretation of available empirical data" that the integrating economy of 1934 was "the forerunner of a consciously integrated society in which individual economic actions and individual property rights will be altered and abridged" (p. 17). Although recognizing the emergence of such a society, the commission came out against "goose-step regimentation in ideas, culture, and invention" and urged retaining the largest possible individual freedom in "the realms of personal and cultural growth" (pp. 22–23).

This volume (hereafter referred to as the report) whipped up an immediate storm in the general press and then settled down to continuing and long-term controversy in pedagogical publications and books. Some forty-nine pages of press comments were assembled, with many of the editorials and stories giving the impression that the professors had announced a new age of collectivism. A few papers enthusiastically praised the report, notably the Daytona Beach *News* of May 16, 1934, and the New York *World-Telegram* of the same date. One paper, the Syracuse *Herald* of the same day, took the commission to task, not for its presumed radicalism but for what it called bad thinking in proclaiming that although individualism was doomed we had to keep individualism.[46] One might charge this editor with careless reading, for the report made quite clear its distinction between the economic individualism it thought was doomed and the personal and cultural individualism it thought should prevail.

Professional opinion ran off in many directions. In an early editorial response, *School and Society* (39 [May 26, 1934], p. 682) applauded the commission's efforts to meet the demands of a collectivist social order "without submerging the individual as a helpless victim of bureaucratic control." Much of the professional opinion was critical, especially that from Franklin Bobbitt in two major statements in the summer of 1934. Bobbitt had worked as a consultant to the commission, especially in relation to the *Charter* volume, but he now turned fiercely against

46. This collection, "Press Comment on Conclusions and Recommendations," dated August 15, 1934, is in the A. C. Krey Papers, University of Minnesota Archives.

the general report, finding in it a tone "of the revolutionary hysteria that grips all the collectivizing nations" and the notion that "integrators" would "think and plan for the masses." In his second statement, Bobbitt accused the commission of rejecting the democratic tradition and of writing with "what seems to be a deliberate vagueness," thus permitting everyone to read into the report what he liked.[47] Bobbitt apparently was able to read into it what he disliked.

These attacks evoked some defense of the report by educators, for example Philip W. L. Cox of New York University. Great Britain and the Scandinavian countries, said Cox, were moving toward collectivism, and the term did not need to be associated solely with communism or fascism. He regretted, however, that the commission had used the term *masses*, since some might confuse this with the proletariat. Professor Percival W. Hutson of the University of Pittsburgh disagreed with Bobbitt's presumed implication that collectivism and democracy were irreconcilable. Hutson did not think so, and he believed that the commission was urging collectivism as a way of preserving democracy.[48]

Besides Bobbitt, those who vented their displeasure with the report included Boyd Bode, Chicago's Judd, and Dean Melvin Haggerty of the School of Education, University of Minnesota. Bode found it a threat against freedom of choice, a struggle "not for the right of the individual to settle basic questions for himself, but for the privilege of possessing and exploiting the pupil's mind." He acknowledged the commission's expressed opposition to goose-step regimentation, but considered this inconsistent with what he interpreted to be their desire to have their frame of reference inculcated in the schools.[49]

Judd said sarcastically that the commission went off on topics beyond its legitimate "purview" and left to the imagination of the reader the question of what to do about social studies in the schools. Minnesota's Haggerty, Krey's colleague, compared the report to the movement for evangelical religion of the 1890s. The commission, he charged, used feelings as substitutes for facts, and the report offered not a philosophy but a creed. "The teacher's world," said Haggerty, "is not to be made

47. "Questionable Recommendations of the Commission on the Social Studies," *S&S* 40 (Aug. 18, 1934), 205, 208; book review, *Sch R* 42 (Sept. 1934), 548–49.
48. "Are the Conclusions and Recommendations of the Commission on the Social Studies 'Startling' or 'Alarming'?" *S&S* 40 (Oct. 27, 1934), 554–57; "Collectivism and Democracy," *S&S* 40 (Sept. 15, 1934), 354–55.
49. Editorial comment, *Phi Delta Kappan* 17 (Nov. 1934), 1.

safe for intellectual adventure and liberty of mind; it is to be made safe for the particular social creed approved by this commission." Finally, he declared, the report offered little in the way of help to the classroom teacher on the job.[50]

It was on this last point that the report got its most adverse judgments, and they came from teachers and practical educators. The problem was illustrated by letters from a sympathetic school man, the supervisor of secondary education in Little Rock, Arkansas. On May 23, 1933, he asked whether the commission had formulated any conclusions on grade placement of material for social studies in elementary, junior high, and senior high school. About three weeks later he wrote to Krey thanking him for a letter received in the meantime but noting that his question had not been answered. He had the three books already published by the commission, said this supervisor, but they did not tell him what he wanted to know, namely, what the commission recommended be taught in junior high school, whether the trend in seventh grade was toward European backgrounds or early American history, and whether the commission agreed with the recommendations for social studies in the Fifth Yearbook of the Department of Superintendence. The head of social studies in the Washington, D.C., public schools had only acid comment, criticizing the report for failing to make usable recommendations and for its "glittering generalities" (a popular expression of the day).[51]

On such questions as to what to teach, the commission strove to clarify its position in the *Conclusions and Recommendations* report. It did not believe in one body of material, one way of organization, or one method of teaching. Moreover, it added with a spot of petulance, it had not been "instructed to provide a detailed syllabus and set of textbooks to be imposed on the school system of the country" (p. 145). Nevertheless it would suggest some next steps, one of them to expect textbook writers to "revamp and rewrite their old works in accordance with this frame of reference" and "makers of programs in the social sciences" to recast their syllabuses and schemes (p. 147). The com-

50. "Difficulties Involved in Introducing Socio-Economic Problems into the Curriculum," Superintendence *Report*, 1935, p. 263; "The Low Visibility of Educational Issues," *S&S* 41 (March 2, 1935), 273–77, 283.

51. Charles F. Allen to American Historical Association, May 23, 1933, and Charles F. Allen to A. C. Krey, June 10, 1933, A. C. Krey Papers, University of Minnesota Archives, Minneapolis; George G. Jones, quoted in Frank W. Ballou statement, *S&S* 39 (June 2, 1934), 701–2.

mission also recommended improvement in the education of teachers (pp. 147–48). Finally, as if to reassure itself, the commission repeated what it understood to be its task, to provide a frame of reference "rather than a bill of minute specifications."

Not all the negative response from teachers came from those who wanted to be told what to do. One of the bitterest reactions was that of Julian Aronson, a classroom teacher in the New York City Schools, who expressed resentment over what he felt was the unrealistic appeal of the commission for bold actions teachers would not be permitted to take. "There is the danger," he said, "that some innocent soul out in Iowa may take the Commission's advice seriously." The ammunition was stacked in favor of the powers that were. "Why, then," asked Aronson, "in the face of all these tremendous obstacles, should the Commission expect from social science teachers the intellectual courage of Giordano Bruno?" The threat to livelihood could not be brushed away. "Consider please, Mr. Beard," he concluded, "that we can't all follow you into successful authorship, when we leave our positions for our principles."[52]

After this, the commission perhaps appreciated all the more a kind word from one school man, Superintendent F. H. Bair of the Shaker Heights city school district in Ohio, who called the report, "the most significant pronouncement in its field that has appeared or is likely to appear in many years." He earnestly recommended it to teachers, but especially to administrators and board members, a way perhaps of meeting some of the points raised by Aronson. To Bair, the report was the outcome of "unassailable scholarship, of extraordinary courage, and of bold and forward-looking social imagination."[53]

One aspect of the enterprise which was often overlooked and was not particularly apparent in the published works, although it ran as a theme through part of the correspondence, was the cooperative involvement of educationists and academicians, especially on the commission itself. Since this involved some of the most dynamic personalities of the time in both camps, the effect was sometimes more electrifying than soothing. If nothing else, the project as a whole contradicts the myth that academicians neglected secondary education before the mid-1950s. Krey was a pure academician, and while his zeal may not always have

52. "The Pedagogues Sound the Toscin," *S&S* 41 (Jan. 19, 1935), 95–97.
53. Book review, *School Executives Magazine* 54 (Oct. 1934), 54.

been informed, no one in this period displayed more than he for the cause of secondary schools.

VI

Since every local superintendent confronted, grappled with, or even helped to bring about social change in his own community, it was inevitable that the Department of Superintendence in the 1930s would as an organization reflect the national concern about social change. Like the culture in which it was imbedded, the department struck various postures with regard to ideological challenges and demands, and like the pedagogical domain of which it was also part, went through a succession of attitudes toward the idea of social reconstruction through the schools. As frightened by events as the rest of the American people, the department made radical sounds in 1933 and 1934, turned somewhat ambivalent in 1935 and 1936, and by 1937 and after looked itself and the future in the face with more self-reliance and aplomb. From the middle 1930s on it became concerned with arriving at some agreed-upon bodies of common sense on the social role of the schools, a goal that it pursued through the Educational Policies Commission, its joint venture with the NEA.

Throughout the 1930s, one of the matters of great interest to the public press and of concern to the superintendents was the high visibility of and the presumed domination by what was known as the Teachers College crowd, partly in the sessions of the department's conventions, partly in other groups meeting in the same cities and at the same times. At their Atlantic City meeting in 1935, the department was beaten to the punch by an unlisted meeting sponsored by "the Social Frontier Magazine group" on the Sunday afternoon before the official start of the convention itself. The highlight of this informal session was a speech by Charles A. Beard. According to *Time*, this meeting of 600 people, identified not only with the *Social Frontier* but also with Teachers College, attacked William Randolph Hearst as chief bogeyman and greeted Beard's speech with yells and cheers (25 [March 11, 1935], 28, 30).

The main issue of this convention accordingly became academic freedom versus William Randolph Hearst, whose papers had been critical of so-called radical teachers. Stimulated by the unofficial session held in advance, the department passed a resolution in favor of academic freedom but voted down a rider calling for specific aid to teachers whose freedom might be attacked. This failure to pass the rider aroused the wrath of columnist Heywood Broun, who then used his scheduled appearance before the convention to scold it for not putting teeth into its declarations.[54] Subsequently, in a bitter article on the convention for the *Nation*, Broun used as his title "The Little Yellow Schoolhouse" (140 [March 13, 1935], 309).

Two years later, in its New Orleans convention, the department found itself in other difficulties. Black delegates were seated in separate parts of the hall, and the participants representing the Julius Rosenwald Fund withdrew in protest. The convention started its Sunday evening proceedings with a pageant, "The Glory of Dixie," given by students in the New Orleans public schools. "An interested audience," said the reporter of this event, "sat on the edges of the seats as Negro voodoo dancers raised the primitive note of the Congo amidst the gentle refinement of old planation life."[55] Festivities continued on Monday morning with the distribution to members of the convention of ten thousand "gorgeously colored camellias" by "gay-costumed girls from the parochial, private, and public high schools of New Orleans." On Wednesday morning, the superintendents took part in "a Creole breakfast under the famous Old Dueling Oaks in City Park," including make-believe duels and presumably genuine Negro spirituals. Wednesday evening's program featured more Negro spirituals, these from three hundred students of "the elementary, high, and normal colored public schools of New Orleans."[56]

Since 1937 was the one-hundredth anniversary of the creation of the Massachusetts State Board of Education, the convention made Horace Mann and his crusade part of its ideology and themes. The incongruity of this evoked a critical review from Horace Mann Bond, staff member of the Julius Rosenwald Fund and later dean of the school of education at Fisk University. Bond noted that the call of the convention was to go forward with Horace Mann. "And so," continued Bond, "from Sunday afternoon through Thursday morning, the leaders of contemporary education went forward. They dallied by the way to

54. "The City Room and the School Room," Superintendence *Report*, 1935, p. 168.

55. Belmont Farley, "The Superintendents at New Orleans," *S&S* 45 (March 13, 1937), 354.

56. "Secretary's Minutes," Superintendence *Report*, 1937, pp. 191–93.

devote time to such divertisements as 'Negro voodoo dancers' raising 'the primitive note of the Congo amidst the gentle refinement of old plantation life,' and a mammoth 'morning meal of yellow grits, grillards, hot rolls, orange juice and black, black coffee,' served to 8,000 delegates . . . while imitation Negro 'mammies' furnished incidental entertainment and real Negro 'mammies' did the dirty work. A terminal tribute came in an entire resolution devoted to Horace Mann. . . . There was one final honor reserved for Horace Mann at the hands of the superintendents. They recommended that he be made a postage stamp."[57]

In its 1937 resolutions, the department among other things demanded federal aid to schools as a means of united action against communists, fascists, opportunists, and racketeers; called for clearing out dead wood from the curriculum (as ever!); and, as noted by Horace Mann Bond, requested a commemorative postage stamp for Horace Mann.[58] So far as the speeches and the programs went, the faculty of Teachers College apparently was still in evidence. One participant from Seattle said on returning home that the meeting had been dominated by Columbia men, especially Dewey, Kilpatrick, Russell, and Counts.[59] Another conventioneer from the hinterland, the superintendent of schools at Coleraine, Minnesota, was less awestruck and suggested that the Teachers College "oligarchy" should "be put in the rear seats and muzzled."[60]

The following year, 1938, the department, with its name changed to the American Association of School Administrators, met again at Atlantic City, this time with love and friendship as the keynote ideas. In fact, the Wednesday evening was officially called the friendship banquet, with Superintendent Willis Sutton of Atlanta, Georgia, as toastmaster. One of Sutton's friends, otherwise unidentified, declared this a time "when we can sit around the board and drink in to the very depth of our affection and love for each other." In the final business session, Superintendent Frank Cody of Detroit made a special presentation to

57. "Horace Mann in New Orleans: A Note on the Decline of Humanitarianism in American Education, 1837–1937," *S&S* 45 (May 1, 1937), 607.
58. "Report of the Committee on Resolutions, Adopted February 25, 1937," Superintendence *Report*, 1937, pp. 198–99.
59. E. L. McDonnell, "A Great Convention Held in a Historic Background; Southern Hospitality," *Seattle Educational Bulletin* 13 (April 1937), 3.
60. H. W. Dutter, "Suggestions for Next Year's Convention," *School Executive* 56 (April 1937), 312.

Superintendent Charles B. Glenn of Birmingham, Alabama, a man "whose walk is always a walk down a friendly road."[61]

Whether all this meant consensus on issues was open to doubt, but consensus or at least harmony seemed to be the goal of the late 1930s. Symbolic of this was the Educational Policies Commission, a joint venture of the department and of the NEA. Among its eleven appointed and four ex-officio members at the time of its creation in 1935 were President Lotus Coffman of the University of Minnesota, Chicago's Judd, Atlanta's Willis Sutton (the friendship toastmaster of 1938), Superintendent John Sexson of Pasadena, and Chancellor Frederick M. Hunter of the Oregon State System of Higher Education, who in the early 1920s had been the celebrated socially efficient superintendent of the Oakland, California, public schools.[62] General applause welcomed the creation of this group, tempered by the critical observation made by *School Executive*[63] and *Social Frontier* both that most of its members were too old. Could such a group, asked the *Social Frontier,* be equal to the task of moving into an era of "reconstruction" and profound change? The *Social Frontier* seemed to doubt it, and shed a bitter tear.[64]

The Educational Policies Commission held its first meeting in January 1936 (and its last thirty-two years later in 1968), with Superintendent A. J. Stoddard of Providence, Rhode Island, as chairman. In presenting the work that had been planned to the Department of Superintendence that year, Pasadena's Sexson emphasized the slowness of recovery in school support compared with general recovery in the economy and, appealing to the psychology of battle, said that the Educational Policies Commission could "serve as a unifying agency about which the embattled forces of public education may rally." Among other tasks, he saw that of establishing the desired relationship between education and social reconstruction.[65]

First of many volumes from the Educational Policies Commission came *The Unique Function of Education in American Democracy*

61. "Friendship Dinner," American Association of School Administrators, *Official Report*, 1938, p. 130; special presentation, *ibid.*, p. 160.

62. "Educational Policies Commission: A Statement Concerning Its Organization," *NEA J* 24 (Dec. 1935), 304.

63. "Policies Commission," 55 (Jan. 1936), 165.

64. "An Educational Policies Commission," 2 (Jan. 1936), 99–100.

65. "The Educational Policies Commission," Superintendence *Report*, 1936, pp. 172, 174–75.

(Washington, D.C., 1937). "Educators who fail to read it," said *School Executive*, "will find themselves outdated." Moreover, "years hence the historian will refer to it as marking the beginning of that era in which the relationships of education and society were clearly and courageously defined that all might read and understand."[66] A writer in *Social Frontier* found it quite otherwise, declaring that it consisted of five chapters restated from Beard (hardly surprising since Beard had written the first draft himself), a chapter on objectives "full of pompous idealistic expressions and threadbare axioms," and a concluding chapter that was "a shallow and spineless analysis that bodes ill for the Commission's future efficiency on the greatest job in the history of American education."[67]

Next came a volume on purposes alone, *The Purposes of Education in American Democracy* (Washington, D.C., 1938). In the advance publicity for this volume, Superintendent Sutton declared that the statement of the seven aims of the Cardinal Principles Report (or as he called them, the "Seven Cardinal Principles") was not enough. Frederick M. Hunter saw the effort as "an amplification and interpretation" of the seven aims.[68] The volume actually reduced the seven categories to four—self-realization, human relations, civic efficiency, and economic competence. Undoubtedly the amplification was understood to lie in the accompanying discussion.

The fires of controversy about reconstructionism and social change were dying away in the late 1930s. Probably the efforts of the Educational Policies Commission had little directly to do with this. Educators were becoming fascinated by a new controversy, one over the control of American youth. It was to this and related matters that the attention of the commission itself began to turn. By the late 1930s the question of whether the school dared to build a new social order had little meaning. Neither teachers nor their fellow citizens had much of an idea what such a thing might be.

At its 1940 convention in St. Louis, the American Association of School Administrators presented a musical revue entitled *On Our Way*,

---

66. "Educational Policies," 56 (April 1937), 285.
67. Norman Woelfel, "The Policies Commission Muffs the Ball," 3 (April 1937), 216.
68. "Report of the Educational Policies Commission," *NEA Proc*, 1937, p. 851; "Enlightened Public Support for Education As a Professional Responsibility," *NEA Proc*, 1939, p. 157.

with some eighty-five students from nearby public school systems as orchestra, chorus, and cast. Each of the four acts was devoted to one of the four broad aims stated by the Educational Policies Commission in its *Purposes* volume. According to the report of it, the revue had "catchy tunes, "graceful dancing," and a sound philosophy of education. Economic efficiency was presented "thru the adventures of Fay and Bob, just graduated and deeply in love, who face life haunted by nightmares of employers, advertisers, and loan sharks. But education comes to their aid, and the scene ends optimistically and tunefully." The revue ended with a tableau of youth "affirming their loyalty and dedicating their services to the principles of American democracy."[69]

69. "On Our Way," American Association of School Administrators, *Official Report*, 1940, pp. 118–19.

Chapter 10

Experimental projects

"Educationally we are going to swap horses, and I intend to ride the new horse."

—RUTH MARY WEEKS,
1937.

*P*reoccupation with social change fostered an environment which encouraged continual curriculum revision. Among the groups involved during the 1930s were the Progressive Education Association, the National Council of the Teachers of English, and the NEA Department of Secondary School Principals, known after 1939 by its pre-1928 name, the National Association of Secondary School Principals. The commission on Social Studies of the American Historical Association was also active, but it worked in the loftier elevations of educational statesmanship and not directly with curriculum.

Clearly the most youthful and effervescent agency for curricular change at this time was the Progressive Education Association, chiefly through its Commission on the Relation of School and College and the enterprise known as the Eight-Year Study (1933–41). The Eight-Year Study, however, did not get underway as a project aimed directly at curricular reform. It started with a latter-day revival of issues that had burned fiercely in the period 1890–1910 and involved admission to college. Expressions of concern about college admission began appearing in progressive circles in the late 1920s. One articulate spokesman was Morton Snyder, the association's executive secretary, who declared in 1927 on the basis of visits throughout the country that "without exception, progressive secondary schools are, to varying degrees, compromising with their ideals in their efforts to meet college requirements." According to Snyder, the colleges were receptive to what progressive secondary schools might agree on as procedure satisfactory to themselves.[1]

The question, to an editorial writer in *Survey*, was one that jointly involved students, teachers, and parents in progressive schools. Much had been gained, thought this writer, in the way of creativity and freedom. "But as the first crop of new school children advances into its teens," he continued, "parents and teachers are faced with a grave problem of what to do next. Most of the children want to go to college, but to pass entrance examinations they must be forced into the regimented routine of conventional high and preparatory schools."[2] Especially affected by entrance examinations were students hoping to enter colleges that were members of the College Entrance Examination Board.

Writing in 1928 in a symposium on the problems of progressive secondary schools, Margaret Pollitzer of the Walden School also saw the question in relation to its impact on parents. "There is no doubt," she said, "that at present the experimental work of a free high school is hampered by college demands. It is more hampered, however, by parents' worry over the college bugbear."[3] Advertisements of private secondary schools in *Progressive Education* bore down hard on preparation for college and showed that the governing boards of these schools were by no means unaware of the stakes involved.

The initiative for events leading to the Eight-Year Study was provided by the headmaster of a progressive private school, Wilford M. Aikin of the John Burroughs School, St. Louis, who was also a member of the executive board of the Progressive Education Association. In his campaign against conventional practices in college admission, Aikin protested that he was not calling for lowered standards. "We want," he said early in 1930, "to send to the colleges young men and women knowing how to work effectively, eager in search of knowledge and understanding, with minds alert and curious."[4]

Varying accounts of the first steps have been given, but according to the contemporary documents, the executive board of the association on April 19, 1930, acting on a recommendation made by Aikin two weeks before and on a motion made by Harold Rugg, appointed a committee

1. "Progressive Education—Progress and Prospect," *Prog Ed* 4 (July 1927), 194.
2. "The Common Welfare," 57 (Feb. 15, 1927), 623.
3. Quoted in "Problems of the Progressive Secondary School: A Symposium," *Prog Ed* 5 (Oct. 1928), 312.
4. "The Prospect in Secondary Education," *Prog Ed* 7 (Feb. 1930), 31.

"to enter into a thorough study of college entrance requirements, examinations, and of the whole relationship between schools and colleges."[5] It was in this action that the famous Commission on the Relation of School and College had its origin. Among the fifteen members originally appointed were such leading figures as Jesse H. Newlon, Harold Rugg, and Goodwin Watson, all of Columbia's Teachers College; Superintendent Willard Beatty of the Bronxville, New York, public schools; and Burton Fowler of Tower Hill School, Wilmington, Delaware. Aikin was made chairman.

The committee, known variously in this period as the Committee on the Relation of School and College and the Committee on College Entrance and Secondary Schools,[6] began its work in the fall of 1930 and was quick to identify the major lines it would pursue. Aikin reported in April 1931 that it had asked a number of colleges whether they would be interested in accepting experimentally some students who did not meet the usual requirements and that almost all these colleges had made favorable replies.[7]

In 1932 the committee, now promoted to its permanent title as the Commission on the Relation of School and College, held five regional conferences with college representatives on proposals for experimental admission of students who did not meet conventional requirements. Drawing on the ideas of these representatives, the commission suggested a plan under which colleges would accept students from a cooperating group of secondary schools, without stipulation of subjects and without subject examinations.[8] The college response again was "almost unanimously favorable,"[9] and the commission hoped to find at least

---

5. Minutes of the Executive Board, Progressive Education Association, April 5, 18–19, 1930, manuscript, Teachers College Library, Columbia University; "Editorial," *Prog Ed* 7 (June 1930), 252.

6. Note the varying early designations thereof: Wilford M. Aiken, "Committee on the Relation of School and College," *S&S* 33 (Feb. 21, 1931), 274–76; Wilford M. Aikin, "Report of the Committee on College Entrance and Secondary Schools," *Prog Ed* 8 (April 1931), 318–20. Minutes of the Board of Directors, Progressive Education Association, May 16, 1931, also refer to it as the Committee on College Entrance and Secondary Schools (Teachers College Library, Columbia University).

7. *Prog Ed* 8 (April 1931), 318–20.

8. Wilford M. Aikin, "A Proposal for Better Coordination of School and College Work," *S&S* 35 (June 18, 1932), 842–44.

9. Wilford M. Aikin, "Progressive Reports of Committees: The Relation of School and College," *Prog Ed* 9 (Oct. 1932), 444.

twenty secondary schools interested in the proposed arrangements.

From a list of some two hundred and fifty secondary schools suggested by educational leaders throughout the country, the Directing Committee (a new mechanism created by the commission to handle the college study) managed by the spring of 1933 to sift out a group of twenty-seven for the experiment. That spring also Aikin announced completion of the arrangements, with some two hundred colleges having agreed to accept students from these schools.[10] The program began in September 1933 with students who would enter college three years later, in September 1936. It was to continue for five subsequent college-entering classes, the last of these to have its freshman college year in 1940–41.[11] With this timetable, the project now came to be known as the Eight-Year Study.

Another numerical identification, "the thirty-school study," was a source of confusion. The original list was of twenty-seven, and the later number of thirty was reduced to twenty-nine by one withdrawal. It was confusing also to have some city systems counted as one school each although enrolling several. These and other anomalies tend to upset the neat formula sometimes given that the group had equal numbers of private and public schools. According to one count of the twenty-nine schools, so-called, there were ten public schools or school systems. The systems were those of Denver, Des Moines, and Tulsa. The schools were Altoona Senior High School, Altoona, Pennsylvania; Bronxville High School, Bronxville, New York; Cheltenham Township High School, Elkins Park, Pennsylvania; Eagle Rock High School, Los Angeles; New Trier Township High School, Winnetka, Illinois; Radnor High School, Wayne, Pennsylvania; and Shaker High School, Shaker Heights, Ohio. Among thirteen private schools were the Dalton of New York City; Francis W. Parker, Chicago; John Burroughs, St. Louis; and Tower Hill, Wilmington, Delaware. Six schools were of the laboratory type connected with universities: Lincoln and Horace Mann, both of Columbia's Teachers College; the University of Chicago High School; the University of California's University High School, Oakland; the University School of Ohio State University; and the Wisconsin High

10. "The Relation of School and College," *S&S* 37 (June 17, 1933), 771–72.
11. "The Commission on the Relation of School and College Launches Its Project," *Sch R* 41 (Oct. 1933), 570–73.

School of the University of Wisconsin. These, then, were the "thirty unshackled schools," as they came to be known.[12]

Would the graduates of these schools, once they made it into college, constitute good advertisements for freedom? The commission was increasingly challenged to show not just how well these students did but how well they did in comparison with graduates of so-called conventional or shackled schools. These challenges involved the larger issue, one that more and more divided the faithful in the association itself on how much and what kind of reliance should be placed on quantitative or "scientific" research.

This question was discussed sympathetically by Dean Max McConn of Lehigh University. Late in 1933 he chided the measurements experts for failing to understand the attitudes and aims of progressives, but added to this a reproach to progressives for not recognizing the need in an experiment to provide for measurement of results. "Neither the schools in general nor the colleges," said McConn, "will take much stock in generalized claims of achievement or personal qualitative appraisals; but they can be convinced, even against their prejudices, by comparable measurements."[13]

Spurred by such pronouncements, the Directing Committee created a new group, the Committee on Records and Reports, one that fatefully in 1934 obtained the services of Professor Ralph Tyler of the Bureau of Educational Research, Ohio State University, as research director of a team of experts known as the Evaluation Staff. In 1936 Tyler recommended the selection of four colleges as centers for comparing 150 graduates of the cooperating schools with an equal number from other schools.[14] The executive board of the association gave its approval to this venture, one that expanded ultimately into twenty-five colleges and involved some 3,600 students in the experimental and control groups.

12. See Wilford M. Aikin, "Our Thirty Unshackled Schools," *Clearing House* 11 (Oct. 1936), 78–83. For the original list of twenty-seven schools see "The Relation of School and College," *S&S* 37 (June 17, 1933), 771–72; for what was presumably the final list of twenty-nine schools see Wilford M. Aikin, *The Story of the Eight-Year Study* (New York, 1942), unnumbered front pages. Further discussion of the shifting sands of this question is available in Frederick L. Redefer, "The Eight-Year Study: Eight Years Later," (Ed.D. Diss., Columbia University, 1951), pp. 44–45.

13. "Measurement in Educational Experimentation with Special Reference to the Progressive Education Association Project," *S&S* 39 (Jan. 13, 1934), 36.

14. Minutes of the Executive Board, Progressive Education Association, April 17, 1936.

Midway in the process, Tyler left Ohio State to succeed Judd as head of the Department at the University of Chicago, a move that gave visibility to the project not only with progressives but with the scientific educationists who had long worshipped at Judd's shrine.

Early indications of the outcome were announced during 1939–40, the seventh year of the schedule, and they remained basically unaltered by the later and final returns.[15] On the big question, the result was a draw. Graduates of the experimental and the control schools did about equally well on college grades. Beyond the main outcome, much was made of a supplementary finding that graduates of six schools judged the most experimental of the cooperating group did better than those of six schools judged the least so.[16] According to a *Time* article "2000 Progressive Guinea Pigs," the promoters of the Eight-Year Study had staked their reputations and possibly the future of progressive education on the results (36 [Nov. 25, 1940], 72). These results, said *Time*, constituted a verdict, but neither *Time* nor the results made clear what the verdict really was.

It was clear, however, to some of the enthusiastic opponents of traditional college admission. What they claimed was victory. Max McConn, for example, predicted a period in which "a student who has completed *any* coherent four-year program in a school of good repute, who has a satisfactory rating on a scholastic aptitude test, and who is definitely recommended by his principal or headmaster may gain admission to any college in the land."[17] This was a bold prediction indeed, but one that was never realized.

According to McConn, the original problem of college admission in the Eight-Year Study had almost been lost in the discussion and study of the aims and curricula of the schools.[18] This was probably an exag-

15. Herbert S. Hawkes, Report to the Association of American Colleges, January 10, 1940, in Aikin, *Story*, pp. 147–50; Minutes of Board of Directors, Progressive Education Association, May 5–7, 1940. For what were presumably the final and authoritative figures see Dean Chamberlin et al., *Did They Succeed in College?* (New York, 1942), pp. 27, 166.

16. The published reports of the Eight-Year Study did not give the names of these schools. In March 1969 Paul Diederich, onetime member of the Eight-Year Study Evaluation Staff, identified the Dalton School of New York City as having been one of the six most experimental. See his article, "You May Not Agree, but Progressive Education Should Continue," *Today's Education* 58 (March 1969), 18–19.

17. Preface to Chamberlin, *Did They Succeed*, p. xxii.

18. *Ibid.*, p. xviii.

geration, but from the point of view of those who sought radical curricular change, the very criteria for judgment in the college study, namely grades in conventional college programs, were themselves suspect.

It would not be valid, moreover, to regard the work on aims and curricula as only an afterthought or delayed response. Concessions on college admission, after all, had been wrung not for their own sake, but to encourage experimental work, or at least to make it less risky. What they promised was freedom. This in itself posed the problem of what to do with it. The Directing Committee scrupulously avoided telling the experimental schools what to do, but it did provide the services of three curriculum consultants to meet with the faculties and to discuss with them what might be done.

The executive board of the association went further in the fall of 1933 and created a separate Commission on Secondary School Curriculum, available to the experimental schools but not limited to them. With V. T. Thayer of the Ethical Culture School as chairman, this new commission launched a variety of ambitious projects and produced a comprehensive literature both on secondary school curriculum as a whole and, in the form of separate volumes, on the roles of the major instructional fields in general education.[19] What developed in the cooperating schools, then, was not a uniform pattern of experimentation, but at least some preoccupation with loosely defined categories and types. According to semi-official pronouncements from the Directing Committee, there were three of these: culture epochs (such as "medieval civilization in Western Europe"); broad fields; and individual interests and needs.[20]

Meanwhile one of the experimental schools, the Wisconsin High School, was developing a newer pattern, or at least one not readily classifiable in the preceding categories. It was a pattern of functional units, a term and an idea evolved earlier by the Commission on Unit Courses and Curricula of the North Central Association. The idea was simple but startling. It consisted in organizing courses not around bodies

19. For creation of the commission see Minutes of the Executive Board, Progressive Education Association, September 30, 1933. As examples of publications see V. T. Thayer, Caroline B. Zachry, and Ruth Kotinsky, *Reorganizing Secondary Education* (New York, 1939) and Committee on the Function of English in General Education, *Language in General Education* (New York, 1940).

20. Wilford M. Aikin, "Report of Commission on Relation of School and College," Department of Secondary School Principals, *Proceedings*, 1934, pp. 174–85.

of content or skills but around broad aims, in this case the North Central's four aims of health, citizenship, vocation, and leisure, each called a "constant." As described by Principal H. H. Ryan early in 1936, the four constants at Wisconsin High School occupied about half the time of the student, with free electives for the other half. The work in health used two to three hours a week, community living one to three hours, leisure one to five hours, and vocation one hour. Vocation was a combination of guidance and occupational trends, plus study "of the prominent colleges of the country and their several special virtues." Among topics under leisure were fall sports, the opera *Il Trovatore*, and excursions into the world of music, drama, and literature.[21]

Ryan sometimes alluded to the four constants as making up the "core curriculum,"[22] an expression rapidly coming to the fore in discussions about the Eight-Year Study. As used by Ryan and others in the early period the term did mean just that, the constants or the common and required work, this to counteract the divisive effect of differentiated courses of study or "curriculums." What began to emerge as new was the combination of the common subjects into a broad-fields class, usually covering several periods in the daily schedule, and known as a core class. From this came a next step, that of a core class representing not common subjects but common "experiences" and common aims, an idea closely related to homeroom lessons and activities aimed at common needs not ordinarily dealt with in the subjects.

Such development of the core idea from earlier broad-fields types was illustrated in the program for Denver as described in 1938. At East High School, wrote one of the teachers, core as combined English and social studies was being replaced by a new program of three-period classes reflecting the needs of students and organized around units in personal development and family relations in grade ten and around larger political, social, and economic problems in grades eleven and twelve.[23] The core at Manual Training High School, according to another member of the Denver staff, was centered "in a sequence of

21. "An Experiment in Building a Functional Curriculum," *Curriculum Journal* 7 (Feb. 1936), 4–5; "The Experimental Curriculum at Wisconsin High School," *Clearing House* 10 (Jan. 1936), 301–7.
22. "Some Principles behind the Core Curriculum," *California Journal of Secondary Education* 12 (Jan. 1937), 14–16.
23. T. D. Rice, "A High School Core Program," *Curriculum Journal* 9 (May 1938), 201–3.

problems based upon the needs and interests of pupils rather than on specific subject matter fields."[24] Denver's central-office director of research and curriculum also emphasized the idea of moving away from and beyond correlation, and said that a new pattern was taking the program "beyond such correlated work," including in this, however, some of the special interest electives as well as the core.[25]

Tulsa also moved with this expanding idea of core, relating it to general education. "The core portion of the curriculum," wrote one of the teachers in 1939, "which is referred to as General Education, the Tulsa teachers believe, should be based upon functional needs and significant life problems. Since it is concerned with the solution of problems rather than with subject-matter content, it should cut across all subject matter and departmental boundaries." Core classes in Tulsa met for three, two, and one hours respectively in grades ten, eleven and twelve. Problems studied were those of "personal development, immediate social problems, broad social problems, social-political relationships, and economic relationships."[26]

Not all the curricular ventures in the Eight-Year Study, however, involved new patterns or types. Some were centered directly on changes within subject organization and within traditional subjects. A Latin teacher at the Baldwin School, Bryn Mawr, Pennsylvania, one of the private cooperating schools, reported changes in the teaching of Latin that had formerly been precluded by college admission definitions requiring the study of particular books. "We have always maintained at the Baldwin School," she wrote, "that the chief aim of the Latin Department is to teach a technique of translation which will enable the student to read Latin at sight." This in an age that took for granted the translation of Latin as decipherment of an enemy code was no mean or unworthy aim. According to the teachers at Baldwin School, it involved broad reading of Latin literature rather than the concentration on passages from Caesar, Cicero, and Virgil allegedly called for by the college entrance tests. Under the freedom of the Eight-Year Study, the five-

24. Prudence Bostwick, "A High School Core Program," *Curriculum Journal* 9 (May, 1938), 204–7.

25. C. L. Cushman, "Conference Appraises Denver Secondary Program," *Curriculum Journal* 9 (Nov. 1938), 316–17.

26. Lavone Hanna, "The Plan of the Core Curriculum in Tulsa," *Curriculum Journal* 10 (Dec. 1939), 350–52; also Lavone Hanna, "The Operation of the Core Curriculum in Tulsa," *Curriculum Journal* 11 (Feb. 1940), 66–68.

year program in Latin at Baldwin School did include broad reading in many books.[27]

Further concern about curriculum in the Eight-Year Study was fostered by the work of Ralph Tyler and the Evaluation Staff. This group devised and helped teachers to devise evaluation instruments for the "intangibles" such as attitudes, qualities of thinking, social sensitivity, and the like. Some of these intangibles also figured in the College Study, but received less notice than did the comparisons of grade-point averages. In the experimental schools many teachers were eager to develop means of evaluating these so-called newer outcomes. From this work (involving in part the famous summer workshops in curriculum and evaluation sponsored by the association) came paper-and-pencil tests for the identification of students' interests and for the measurement of such skills in thinking as the application of principles and the interpretation of data. All this of course involved much study and discussion of curriculum and aims. In their insistence on objectives defined behaviorally,[28] the Evaluation Staff was indeed prophetic of what would remain for at least forty years a major preoccupation in curricular planning and theory.

The Eight-Year Study officially ended in the school year 1940–41, although the college agreement was extended until 1943 to cover students who had started high school under the program. Most of the published reports appeared in 1942, our first year in the war, a condition that obviously blunted the thrust of these volumes as indicated in the relatively low sales reached up to July of 1951.[29] Yet these do not tell the whole story. Almost from the very beginning, the project had attracted widespread attention not only for itself but for the association,

27. Evelyn Spring, "An Adventure in Latin Teaching," University of Pennsylvania School of Education, *Twenty-Third Annual Schoolmen's Week Proceedings,* 1936, pp. 503–7.

28. Ralph Tyler, "Evaluation: A Challenge to Progressive Education," *Prog Ed* 12 (Dec. 1935), 552–56; also Ralph Tyler, "Appraising Progressive Schools," *Educational Method* 15 (May 1936), 412–15.

29. The final report of the College Study, *Did They Succeed in College?* (Dean Chamberlin, et al, New York, 1942), sold only some 2,500 copies. *Thirty Schools Tell Their Story* (New York, 1943), a composite report in which each school presented its own pattern of experimentation, reached only 1,775 copies. Aikin's summary volume, *The Story of the Eight-Year Study* (New York, 1942), and the report by Eugene Smith and Ralph Tyler, *Appraising and Recording Student Progress* (New York, 1942), did better with about 7,500 copies each. These sales figures appear in Redefer, "The Eight-Year Study: Eight Years Later," p. 208.

plus much comment, favorable and unfavorable, in the pedagogical press. Part of this resulted from publicity about its financial support, massive, indeed, for the times. From the General Education Board alone, this not including the earlier and smaller grants from Carnegie Corporation, the Commission on the Relation of School and College had some $620,000 in grants. Beyond this the General Education Board had granted some $350,000 to the Commission on Secondary School Curriculum and $220,000 to the Commission on Human Relations.[30] These were for the 1930s stupendous sums for educational projects, and they left the rest of the pedagogical world gasping in envy and respect.

As the Eight-Year Study drew to a close, its record and its publications were variously reviewed. Journalist Dorothy Dunbar Bromley presented it from a "layman's" point of view to the upper middle class audience of *Harper's* early in 1941. She told the story accurately and well, duly noting the results in the six most and six least innovative schools, but concluding that colleges would continue to resist changes in their requirements. A professor of chemistry at the University of Colorado reacted sharply against the tone of approval in the Bromley article. Progressive educationists, he said, were "crowing lustily" over the results, but all the study showed, in his opinion, was "that the colleges have climbed down to meet the steadily increasing deterioration of high school graduates."[31]

Criticism from another direction was expressed in 1939 by Catherine Nutterville, psychologist of the Butte, Montana, public schools, who asked what meaning the study had for non-college-bound students, since the emphasis was placed on success in college work. Experiments, she argued, were needed with programs "for the home, community, and vocational adjustment of those who do not enter college." A professor at Wisconsin also expressed disappointment that the study had not identified criteria applicable to the non-college-going student.[32] Such reproaches were keenly felt by the progressives, and the association's board of directors early in 1940 proposed and attempted to get funds

30. Redefer, "The Eight-Year Study Eight Years Later," p. 38.
31. "Education for College or for Life?" 182 (March 1941), 407–16; G. Wakeham, " 'Education for College or for Life?' " *S&S* 54 (July 5, 1941), 12.
32. "The Progressives' Eight-Year Experiment with High School Counselors," *Education* 60 (Oct. 1939), 100; J. Kenneth Little, "The High School of Tomorrow," *Wisconsin Journal of Education* 74 (May 1942), 421–25.

for an all-youth project.[33] They were too late. The General Education Board was in process of winding up its financial support of educational projects, and the enterprise never came off.

More comforting was the development of regional and state projects involving school-and-college agreements modeled on those of the parent Eight-Year Study. In 1937 one of the major regional accrediting groups, the Southern Association of Colleges and Secondary Schools, launched such a project involving three high schools from each state in its territory. There was also the program of the California Committee on Cooperating Schools, motivated in part by the state department of education. The California project was less explicitly modeled on the Eight-Year Study, but it did give much attention to curricular ventures along the lines of Social Living (unified English and social studies) and of core. Another "little" Eight-Year Study was that of Michigan, involving the state university, other universities and colleges, and a large number of cooperating high schools in what became known as the Michigan College Agreement.[34]

The core increasingly came to symbolize the curricular side of the Eight-Year Study and to attract responses beyond those in the cooperating schools. The spread of core in the late 1930s, while probably not a direct result of the study, did tend to reflect the importance it had achieved therein. Schools not in the Eight-Year Study developed core reputations of their own, for example, the McKinley High School of Honolulu as early as 1933. According to the principal, the McKinley core classes were organized around "the real problems of boys and girls." He dwelt particularly on their relationship to the idea of the home room. The core classes, he said, had become "genuine home rooms," with the study of large social and of immediate personal-social problems. Examples of these included "Is Japan within Her Rights in Manchuria?" and "How Can I Spend my Leisure Time More Wisely?"

33. Minutes of Board of Directors, Progressive Education Association, February 22, 1940.
34. "News Notes," *Curriculum Journal* 8 (Dec. 1937), 335–36; California State Department of Education, "Programs of the Cooperating Secondary Schools in California," *Bulletin of the California State Department of Education*, no. 3, 1939; Paul T. Rankin, "Experimental Study To Discover and Evaluate Modifications in Secondary School Program," *Michigan Education Journal* 14 (Jan. 1937), 223, 225, and J. Cecil Parker, Wilmer Menge, and Theodore Rice, *The First Five Years of the Michigan Study of the Secondary School Curriculum 1937–1942* (Lansing, 1942).

Another school with a national reputation for core was the "new unit" launched at the Evanston Township High School, Illinois, in 1937. This experimental unit at Evanston was noteworthy for its attempt to include a cross section of the entire student body, with some 60 percent planning to go to college and 40 percent not so planning.[35]

Core was later to fall into disrepute, but a faithful remnant of core enthusiasts survived as an organization, the National Conference of Core Teachers, into and throughout the 1960s. This might be interpreted at least in part as one of the long-term survivals of the Eight-Year Study. Professor Roland Faunce of Wayne State University, writing for this group in 1966, referred to the 1930s as the golden years,[36] and so they were, for those who believed in the ideas involved.

What remains is the sense of excitement that was communicated by and through the Eight-Year Study. There had been nothing like it in secondary education in the United States since the controversies surrounding the report of the Committee of Ten in 1893. Most of the people identified with core and the Eight-Year Study were innovating spirits indeed, and they were young. For at least two decades after its conclusion, the Eight-Year Study persisted as the Saint Crispin's Day of American secondary education, and many there were who regretted having lain in bed while it was going on.

II

Equipped with a curriculum commission of its own since 1929, the National Council of Teachers of English worked throughout the 1930s at revising what could be identified as its field of study. This commission centered its attention on elementary and high schools and in fact attracted an audience of those concerned with secondary education as a whole. This resulted not only from the pervasive nature of English, working its way into every nook and cranny of the school program, but from the qualities of the chairman, W. Wilbur Hatfield of the Chicago Normal College, a worthy successor of James F. Hosic in his breadth

35. Miles E. Cary, "Purposeful Activities in the McKinley Senior High School, Honolulu," *Education* 53 (Jan. 1933), 261–68; Samuel Everett, "An Experiment in Community School Education," *Educational Record* 18 (Oct. 1937), 523–47, and Charles MacConnell et al, *New Schools for a New Culture* (New York, 1943).

36. "Core Curriculum: Yesterday and Today," in *Core Curriculum: the Why and the What*, Proceedings of the 13th National Conference of Core Teachers, October 14–16, 1965 (Milwaukee, Wisconsin, 1966), pp. 54–75.

of interests and his persistence in advancing the causes to which he gave commitment. In this instance, however, although Hatfield served as chairman of the commission, he had not created it. That was the work of a classroom teacher, Ruth Mary Weeks of the Paseo High School, Kansas City, Missouri, who in 1929 was president of the National Council.

The commission was an unwieldy conglomerate with a central steering committee of twenty-two members (including Hosic), subcommittees for various aspects of English, and representatives from cooperating organizations such as the North Central and Southern Associations, the national associations for teachers of journalism and of speech, and the American Association of Teachers Colleges. These cooperating organizations used the idea of the commission in dealing with general curriculum as well as English. The membership was broadly representative of classroom teachers and people in teacher education, but also included some English professors from universities and colleges. With so many working classroom teachers involved, the commission in its utterances suggested a down-to-earth quality that had been noticeably missing from those of the Commission on Social Studies.

Prophetic messages about the direction of the commission began coming from Chairman Hatfield in the early 1930s. The commission, he declared to the annual convention of the National Council in 1932, would seek to correlate, or unify, English with other subjects. As elements for the proposed courses, the commission was proposing not facts, materials, habits, or skills, but "life-experiences" carrying "beyond the traditional boundaries of the English department."[37] This idea of curriculum as "experience," accompanied by references to something called the "experience curriculum," was rapidly becoming one of the vogue movements of the times. Derived partly from Dewey's preoccupation with the nature of experience, the idea was indeed challenging and refreshing, but also somewhat vague. This vagueness gave rise to the usual hair-splitting about definition and meaning.

One of the advocates of an experience curriculum for the field of English was Walter Barnes, a veteran of many a campaign about curriculum in the National Council. Barnes started out by speculating on the possibility of an inherent contradiction between curriculum, with its

37. "The Curriculum Commission: A Report of Progress," *EJ* 22 (March 1933), 234–35.

rationalism and rigidity (as he saw it), and experience, with its emotionalism and freedom. Apparently he succeeded in resolving this for himself, since he went on to define a curriculum of experience in literature, which he described also as a grand tour of literary adventures. The idea could be used for many things. An editorial writer in the *English Journal* saw in it the possibility of redeeming the "unit" from its allegedly bad connotations in Morrison's method. A unit in English, he suggested, could be understood as "simply an experience, or a group of experiences, in meeting a common type of social situation, with the guidance and assistance of the teacher to assure success." This idea could also be used in describing the relation of English to other subjects. With the trend toward integration of all subjects into "a single dynamic whole," the "guided-experience unit" would be particularly desirable.[38]

It was hardly a surprise, then, that the report of the commission carried the title *An Experience Curriculum in English* (New York, 1935). Loaded with hundreds of suggestions for materials and activities, the report was indeed a boon to classroom teachers looking for something to do. The commission protested most anxiously that it was providing illustrative material but not imposing a curriculum. Nevertheless, it was the wealth of tangible illustrative material rather than the ideological banners that stood out in the report.

The relatively brief discussion of curriculum theory, on the other hand, left no doubt as to the commission's intent. Curriculum was defined as a series of guided experiences paralleling "present and future out-of-school experiences," that is, situations in real life (p. 9). Hatfield was careful to avoid the idea of curriculum merely as life in the raw; it was, admittedly, a body of contrived circumstances designed so that, for teaching purposes at least, it would be superior to life as it was really lived. In a prepublication speech early in 1935 to the Department of Supervisors and Directors of Instruction of the NEA, Hatfield had referred to these guided experiences as "fairly representative of the wide range of activities in life: conversing, telephoning, discussing, writing reports, writing letters; re-living (thru literature) tragedy and comedy, philosophical reflections and lyric emotion; reading to find information, to solve problems, to secure directions for action; and a

38. "A Curriculum of Literature Experiences," *EJ* 21 (March 1932), 191–99; "What Should a 'Unit' in English Be?" 22 (Dec. 1933), 844–45.

number of others."[39] To clinch the point, the commission insisted in the report itself that everything in the outline of materials and activities was to be read with the idea that the curriculum consisted of these guided experiences. (p. 9).

The activities and materials that the report suggested were on two levels, one for kindergarten through grade six, the other for grades seven through twelve, and they related to such categories as literature, reading, creative expression, communication, corrective teaching, and electives. At one end of the spectrum was a unit on "the literary achievements of the Victorian age, 1832–1890" (pp. 76–79) and at the other a study of the techniques of telephone conversation, including as an objective, "When calling a friend, to converse briefly with another member of his family who answers" (p. 163). Some of this reminds us of the scorned "life-adjustment" activities of the 1950s, but they were not invented by the Commission on Curriculum. English teachers had been happily reporting such at least as far back as 1920 and continued doing so after 1935, with or without the blessing of the commission's report.

The report was widely distributed, and its sale of 25,000 copies by 1940 far outstripped sale of the Eight-Year Study. It was judged to have had "unmistakeable influence" on textbooks and courses of study and been responsible for the "almost universal reference to English as experience."[40] Even William C. Bagley, by this time suspicious of anything that smacked of progressivism, gave it good marks and found in it "a model in curriculum construction." He could not resist adding that it followed the prevailing fashion with "unprecedented discrimination and common sense." New York University's Philip W. L. Cox called it a great advance, but feared that the commission was "trying to save a subject rather than to serve youth."[41]

It was the idea of the experience curriculum that most clearly identified projects of the National Council of Teachers of English. What did the English teachers themselves think of all this? Ruth Mary Weeks, the founder of the Commission on Curriculum, felt that modern developments were inevitable and that it was up to her and other English

39. "Activities of the Curriculum Commission of the National Council of Teachers of English," *NEA Proc*, 1935, pp. 629–30.

40. Harold A. Anderson, book review, *Sch R* 48 (May 1940), 389.

41. "The Report of the Curriculum Commission," *EJ* 25 (Feb. 1936), 169, 172; *ibid.*, 174–75.

teachers to make the required adjustments. "The whole intellectual temper of society," she wrote in 1937, "has shifted in the last twenty years." Here, then, was more tribute to change. Part of this change, she felt, was the idea of an activity or experience curriculum. Whether one liked it or not, to oppose it would be futile. She proposed, therefore, to work with "this new philosophy" for the greatest good and with "the least possible misery." Teachers of English were in the position of riders who had worn out old horses. "Educationally," she concluded, "we are going to swap horses, and I intend to ride the new horse."[42]

To Wilson Follett, writer and critic, it was a process of decay. English was becoming an inspirational subject, said Follett, commenting on a variety of developments in the field, one about which everything was to be felt and nothing known. English teaching was drifting into a false liberalism. "Pupils," he wrote, "who cannot be trusted to give a plural subject a plural verb are now coached in the tricks of dramatic construction, the aesthetics of literary criticism, the canons of the short story, and the composition of free verse, all in the name of 'self-expression.' "[43] It should be noted, however, that even the commission's report had a substantial section on "corrective" teaching for those students who had not learned, among other things, to give plural verbs to plural subjects (pp. 241–56). Moreover, it even referred to "correct forms to be established" (p. 246).

III

Less exotic than the Progressive Education Association or even the National Council of Teachers of English was the NEA Department of Secondary School Principals. It was also more externally conventional in its national project, undertaken in 1932 through its Committee on the Orientation of Secondary Education and its report on issues and functions. Both the department and its report were heavily committed to the social efficiency ideal, and it is noteworthy that by the 1930s this ideal, aimed as it was against the academic tradition, had become so widely accepted as to appear traditional itself.

The chief mover of the issues and functions project was Thomas H. Briggs of Columbia's Teachers College. Although the Committee on Orientation, with Briggs as chairman, was authorized by the department

42. "Content for Composition," *EJ* 26 (April 1937), 295–296.
43. "The State of the Language," *Atlantic Monthly* 159 (Jan. 1937), 56–57.

in 1932, he had already introduced the main ideas in two chapters contributed to the Seventh Yearbook of the Department of Superintendence, *The Articulation of the Units of American Education* (Washington, D.C., 1929). In the first of these chapters (chap. 10, pp. 182–95), Briggs had stated ten issues in secondary education and in the second (chap. 11, pp. 196–207) ten special functions. These covered much the same ground as the later reports of the Principals' Committee.

Equipped with a modest subsidy of $9,000 from the Carnegie Foundation, Briggs and the committee successfully began to popularize the issues and functions approach to the study of secondary schools. Like many another group, this one warned its potential audience not to expect too much. "The only embarrassment that the committee has so far felt," wrote Briggs in 1934, "is over the apparent expectation in some quarters that its deliberations will result in the immediate revolution of secondary education."[44] In the fall of that year, the committee brought out a limited edition of 1,500 copies of the issues for criticism and discussion. Early in 1935 it began to work on functions.

The revised version of the issues, with only minor changes from Briggs's statement of 1929, was officially promulgated by the committee in 1936. Universal versus selective secondary education, differentiated curricula versus a common curriculum, and vocational training versus general education were among the issues considered. In addition, a broad statement of background and definitions was presented. Education, for example, was defined as implying "every phase of the process by which society as a whole, or any of its agencies, consciously seeks to develop socially significant abilities and characteristics in its members." The term *consciously* was used, explained the report, in order to avoid defining education as synonymous with all of life. Secondary education was set forth as something for those no longer finding a satisfactory environment in elemetary school but not yet ready for college or participation in society "unguided by the school."[45] Accompanying the statement of each issue in this version was an explicit statement of the committee's position.

44. "Second Annual Report of the Committee on the Orientation of Secondary Education," *Proceedings of the Department of Secondary School Principals*, 1934, pp. 205–6.
45. "Issues of Secondary Education: Report of the Committee on the Orientation of Secondary Education," *Bulletin of the Department of Secondary School Principals* 20 (Jan. 1936), 24–25.

Some fascinating by-products came from the committee's discussion of its own positions. It found the famous Cardinal Principles Report, for example, sadly wanting in its views on social aims. The Cardinal Principles Report, said Briggs's Committee, was an admirable document, yes, but "a characteristic product of the era of individualism in education." It was, concluded the committee with regret, "consistent with a philosophy of individualism." The bias against individualism here was not just the usual view of social efficiency, but incorporated the attitudes of the New Deal era toward so-called economic "rugged individualism." Where the Cardinal Principles Report erred, according to the committee, was in discussing citizenship in political and ethical terms "with almost no hint of an economic application."[46]

In the "functions" side of its project, the committee meant the responsibilities they believed the secondary school should assume. For the most part, the 1937 statement ran close to Briggs's listing in 1929. These functions were set forth in ten categories or areas: integration of the students; satisfaction of needs; revelation of the racial heritage; exploration of students' interests, aptitudes, and capacities; systematization of knowledge; establishment and direction of interests; guidance; use of methods fostering independent thought; provision of differentiated curricula; and the retention of students until operation of the law of diminishing returns or the transfer of the student to a higher institution, with the elimination of those who could not or would not profit from further study.[47]

Like the Eight-Year Study, the Committee on Orientation evoked a variety of criticisms. Some of the most bitter were aimed at the statement in function ten about eliminating students who could not or would not profit from further study.[48] Among the first to react against this was Superintendent Ernest R. Caverly of the Brookline, Massachusetts, public schools. The Briggs Committee was Jacksonian on universal acceptance and admission; Caverly carried Jacksonian beyond this by insisting on universal retention, with a corresponding obligation on the part of the school to find what each student could do, thus completing the circle around to the Jeffersonian views of Charles W. Eliot. Caverly

46. *Ibid.*, p. 138.
47. "Functions of Secondary Education: Report of the Committee on the Orientation of Secondary Education," *Bulletin of the Department of Secondary School Principals* 21 (Jan. 1937), pp. 5–226.
48. *Ibid.*, p. 209

commented acidly on the fact that "a man in the field," namely himself, clung to the ideal, while those in the theory of education were willing to give up because of practical difficulties. John M. Brewer, a guidance expert of Harvard, strongly supported Caverly. He accused the Committee on Orientation of giving aid and comfort to high schools that did not choose to educate all youth. "I wish," wrote Brewer with vehemence, "I had the pen of Alexander Inglis to answer this proposal to eliminate children."[49]

Others criticized the committee for the alleged triviality of its material. Philip W. L. Cox, who in this period appeared to be shifting away from social efficiency to more dynamic positions on social and economic problems, was particularly critical, calling the issues tweedledee-tweedledum and claiming that the real issues were untouched. Cox poured equal scorn on the Educational Policies Commission and the American Youth Commission and in this period seemed to write the high school itself off as practically worthless. "Character and good conduct according to the school stereotype," he wrote, "are almost synonymous with conformity and docility. Protest, challenge, argument, boldness, invention, criticism are adjudged bad manners or even defiance."[50] Along the same lines, Professor E. B. Taylor of the University of Rochester called the functions statement "oversolicitous in tone," with an attitude toward the student suggestive of the "oversolicitude of a slightly neurotic mother."[51]

In the end, what probably saved the issues and functions project from being just a warmed-over serving of social efficiency was the personal commitment of Professor Briggs, who along with his adherence to such doctrines as the investment theory of education, stimulated many workers in secondary education to focus on educational values rather than administrative machinery. The future historian of education (a figure often appealed to), declared Briggs in 1936, would give little space to those who invented "non-glare blackboards," "dustless chalk," and "cumulative record cards," but would laud those who "have seen education steadily and seen it whole."[52]

49. "'Elimination' . . . Sinister?" *Clearing House* 13 (Sept. 1938), 27–29; *ibid.*, pp. 26–27.
50. "Are These the Real Issues?" *Social Frontier* 3 (Dec. 1936), 88–89; "Must the High School Survive?" *Educational Forum* 2 (Nov. 1937), 32.
51. "The Special Functions of Secondary Education," *Harvard Educational Review* 7 (Oct. 1937), 496.
52. "The Issues of Secondary Education," Superintendence *Report*, 1936, p. 41.

Running alongside the issues and functions project was an enterprise known as the Cooperative Study of Secondary School Standards. This was a joint venture of the major regional associations of colleges and secondary schools, originating in 1932 as a resolution of the National Association of Officers of Regional Associations. The project was designed to coordinate regional efforts at school evaluation and accreditation. With Professor Walter Crosby Eells of Stanford as national coordinator, the project developed evaluative criteria represented in a checklist of more than one thousand items on curriculum, guidance, school services, and student activities. Ratings of individual schools were expressed through a device called the "educational thermometer," a graph for summarizing data gathered through visits and questionnaires.

In 1939, the Cooperative Study brought out *Evaluation of Secondary Schools* (Washington, D.C.), the main volume of its six-volume report, presenting criteria that had survived a validating process in schools known as good, bad, and presumably indifferent. Some two hundred schools were involved in this validation. The regional associations that carried on accreditation (by this time all except New England) continued to define and maintain their own standards, but with increasing use of the questionnaires and forms of the Cooperative Study.

This project lit no fires, but in many parts of the country it was impossible to ignore. Teachers in schools being evaluated were called upon to fill out the many forms, as of course were the administrators. Probably more school people became involved in this than had been involved in the Committee of Ten, the Eight-Year Study, and the Cardinal Principles Report. Thus it was demonstrated again that, in the domain of pedagogy at least, the race was rarely if ever to the swift.

IV

Throughout the 1930s, then, school people and patrons were bombarded by a great variety of ideas and events, including the major facts of depression and the controversies over the New Deal as well as the conflicting doctrines in pedagogy itself. Little wonder that the statewide programs and those of city systems breathed a spirit of eclecticism, or perhaps merely a mixture of ideas old and new. There were many ideologies and terminologies from which to choose in making an assortment for state or local use.

The outstanding state program and the prototype for others was that of Virginia. Although the Virginia program accepted the vogue innovations and created some of its own, it appeared concerned at the outset not with the cosmic theory of curriculum but with the ancient dichotomy of going or not going to college. As a major problem to be worked on in high schools, for example, the state superintendent's report in 1931 listed "adapting the high school offering more effectively to the needs of the non-college-bound boys and girls."[53]

Officially, the Virginia program was started in July 1931 with a directive from State Superintendent Sidney B. Hall to the Division of Instruction. Many meetings of teachers for orientation and in-service education were held in 1931–32, when the emphasis shifted to the production of materials by major committees. New courses were written in 1932–33, tried out in 1933–34, and published for the most part at the end of 1934. It was a classic example of the step-by-step procedure of curriculum planning, beginning with philosophy and objectives and moving through preparation, exploratory use, and installation of new courses and materials. As this went on, the Virginia enterprise absorbed and interacted with various new movements, particularly core.

What made the Virginia program stand out was its organization of social studies or core classes to combine central direction and teacher initiative. This "social-functions" approach provided a "scope" or set of boundaries based on "major functions of social life," for example, "production of goods and services and distribution of the returns of production," "communication and transportation of goods and people," and "expression of aesthetic impulses." Intersecting these social functions (usually ten or so) were grade level centers of interest, one through eleven in Virginia's seven-four system. The center for eighth grade, for example, was "adaptation of our living through nature, social and mechanical inventions, and discoveries.

The eighth-grade center of interest, then, could be combined with the social function of aesthetic impulses to yield the following unit title: "How do man's natural environment and his inventions provide worthwhile opportunities for the cultivation of aesthetic expression."[54] Not all

53. Commonwealth of Virginia, *Annual Report of the Superintendent of Public Instruction School Year 1930–1931* (Richmond, 1931), p. 26.
54. Virginia State Board of Education, *Tentative Course of Study for the Core Curriculum of Virginia Secondary Schools: Grade VIII* (Richmond, 1934), pp. 16–19. See also Paul R. Hanna, "Social Studies in the New Virginia Curriculum," *Prog Ed* 11 (Jan. 1934), 129–34.

such units would be taught by every teacher, but the charts on which the functions and the centers of interest were mapped did furnish inventories of possibilities.

Just how much the Virginia program affected practice in the state is open to question—always true with state programs where voluntary cooperation rather than enforced compliance is the order of the day. In 1936, one of the consultants in the Virginia program found intensive saturation of elementary school programs with the ideas and materials. Replies from 303 secondary schools showed two-thirds using the new state course for the eighth grade wholly or in part. " 'Where there is smoke there must be fire,' and the smoke of activity is certainly visible in Virginia," he concluded.[55] In any case, the Virginia program came to represent the ultimate degree of achievement in statewide curriculum planning, and it appeared with full-scale treatment in many of the discussions of curriculum in the late 1930s.[56]

Among the large cities, Denver, Los Angeles, and Chicago continued to attract the most attention. Denver's identity, however, tended to merge with that of the Eight-Year Study until near the end of the decade. For better or worse, Denver's high schools, some of them in particular, were leaders in the shift from correlation and fusion to the idea of core based on aims, problems, and needs.

It was quite otherwise with Los Angeles and Chicago, although Los Angeles did have one high school, Eagle Rock, in the Eight-Year Study (a school, however, which for the most part was on its own). If the secondary school curriculum in Los Angeles had a definite symbol it was the social living course, usually a combination of social studies and English but sometimes involving other fields. The term *core* was used, but in the sense of unified studies and sometimes interchangeably with social living. By late 1936, most of the senior high schools in Los Angeles had double-period courses combining English and social studies in grades ten and eleven. True, Eagle Rock, because of its part in the Eight-Year Study, was especially prominent in this, but no more so than Lincoln High School, which was not in the Eight-Year Study. As described by the principal, the term *core* was used at Lincoln to denote

55. J. Paul Leonard, "Is the Virginia Curriculum Working?" *Harvard Educational Review* 7 (Jan. 1937), 66–71.

56. For example, Sidney B. Hall and Fred M. Alexander, "The Core Plan in a State Program," in *A Challenge to Secondary Education*, ed. Samuel Everett (New York, 1935), pp. 13–47.

the total required program, including the two-hour course in social living and a one-hour course (for three of the four years) in man's natural environment.[57]

Controversy in Los Angeles was aggravated by changes in homework and marking, and there were those in the city, state, and region who viewed the schools there as hotbeds of unmitigated progressivism. Central-office leadership throughout this period, however, at least in its published utterances, gives the impression of having been well-balanced and moderate and unusually sensitive to some of the deeper problems involved. Although a strong supporter of core, which in Los Angeles meant social living courses and related programs, William B. Brown realized the dangers of stressing social aims to the detriment of individual values. A required core program he was afraid might itself become a straitjacket, and he recommended in 1938 that at least half the time in junior high school and two-thirds to three-fourths of the time in senior high school be reserved for electives. These would include not only full-length courses, but even short unit courses running for as few as ten weeks. "This plea," he said, "is for a greater variety of electives at all secondary levels, more freedom of choice, and less early specialization of pupils."[58]

Decentralized planning in Los Angeles encouraged great variety in school programs. One of the most interesting was a program in unified studies reported by Vice-Principal Everett Chaffee of the Samuel Gompers Junior High School. Here, guidance was paramount in the approach. It was desirable, argued Chaffee, to use classroom teachers for specific guidance responsibilities, and social studies teachers were in the most strategic position for this, particulary for taking over the group guidance functions of traditional homerooms. The problem, however, was how to manage this under a system where each social studies teacher had five or six separate classes. It was resolved by changing to double-period sections, thus reducing the number of pupil contacts.

"By setting up a basic two-hour course consisting of subject matter formerly contained in separate social studies, English, and related

57. "What's Happening in California Secondary Schools," *California Journal of Secondary Education* 12 (Feb. 1937), 123–26; Helen Babson, "The New Program at Eagle Rock High School, Los Angeles," *Clearing House* 9 (May 1935), 560–64; Ethel Percy Andrus, "General Procedure at Abraham Lincoln High School, Los Angeles," *Clearing House* 9 (Feb. 1935), 334–39.

58. "The Core Is Not All of the Curriculum," *Curriculum Journal* 9 (May 1938), 212.

courses," argued Chaffee in support of this move, "it is possible to cut in half the number of actual classes and pupil contacts a teacher has during the day." This was carried out at Gompers. Since the social studies teachers took on guidance work previously shared by the whole faculty, presumably in homerooms, it was possible to shift some of the teaching load to other departments, making possible the assignment of social studies teachers to two separate groups only, with four periods for classroom teaching and two for guidance.[59] This kind of flexibility in Los Angeles schools could be credited in part to central-office eclecticism.

Chicago, too, was eclectic. Most of its diverse projects and approaches in the latter 1930s, however, originated in the central office, although some came from high schools officially designated as experimental. It had practically everything from the moderate revision of President Eliot to the latest curricular dare-devilment of the times, with the social efficiency movement in between. It was the note of social efficiency that tended to prevail.

Leadership came mainly from a new and controversial superintendent, William Johnson, who was appointed in the spring of 1936. Johnson enjoyed the distinction of being the first Chicago-born superintendent of schools in the history of the system, and he had behind him a long and diversified career in the Chicago schools as classroom teacher and administrator. Perhaps this gave him the confidence to experiment. In any case, with the worst of the financial storms over so far as the school system was concerned, Johnson apparently decided that what the times called for was not a holding operation but an attack. As he proceeded to carry this out, he attracted even more controversy than had William McAndrew, which was in itself something of an achievement.

Johnson's primary influence through the central office, in the late 1930s, had to do with antifailure policy, with the related question of homework and grading; general requirements; student loads; character education and socialization; and vocationalism. These were bound together by the everlasting plaint, not unique to Chicago, about the deteriorating quality of high school students and the needs and demands of mass education. In some of this, the social class factors were only thinly hidden, and organized labor in Chicago, as in the 1920s, remained on these matters a critical and challenging force.

59. "Adolescent Needs and the Social Studies," *Social Education* 3 (Nov. 1939), 545–46.

Failure had long been regarded as a special problem in Chicago and one to which both McAndrew and Bogan had given their attention. In the first semester of 1936–37, the high school failure rate stood at 4.9 percent, with plane geometry at 8.7 percent the worst offender.[60] Johnson launched a comprehensive campaign against failure, including subject selection, revised student loads, and homework policies, plus one feature that might be judged almost surefire in its effect, that of requiring teachers to anticipate failure. "If between regular marking periods," said the superintendent's annual report in 1937, "the teacher feels that the work of a student is likely to be graded unsatisfactory at the close of the period, the teacher is required to report this fact to the office, in writing, giving what seems to him the reasons for the unadjusted situation." The use of these approaches produced or was accompanied by a reduction in Chicago's failure rate, by 1938–39, to an all-time low of 2.3 percent.[61]

Johnson was moderate in his first move affecting student programs, in fact it was practically a direct application of what had been recommended by the NEA Committee on College Entrance Requirements in 1899. What the central office did was to abolish, literally at the stroke of the pen, the twelve four-year "curriculums" or separate courses of study and to replace these with a pattern of constants and electives for all students entering February 1937 and after. Of the sixteen units, seven were stipulated as constants, while nine were left free. The constants were English, general science, United States history, physical education, music, and art, with further provisions within these for options in fulfilling them. Choice of electives was regulated by stipulating three three-year sequences or two of three years and two of two years each.[62] Thus did Chicago repudiate one of the fondest devices of the social efficiency ideal, differentiation by courses of study. Of course it was not alone in this; some systems had done so years before. Still, it was a major victory for the 1899 point of view, to capture a system as large as Chicago and as late as the 1930s.

Since physical education, art, and music were now to be given credit,

60. City of Chicago Board of Education, *Annual Report of the Superintendent of Schools for the School Year 1937–1938* (Chicago, 1938), pp. 239–43.

61. City of Chicago Board of Education, *Annual Report of the Superintendent of Schools for the Year Ending June 11, 1937* (Chicago, 1937), p. 112; William H. Johnson, "Our Schools 1938–1939," *Chicago Schools Journal* 21 (Sept. 1939), 6.

62. Chicago, *Annual Report June 11, 1937*, pp. 103–4.

the load of "major subjects" in the sixteen-unit requirement was lighter by two units. There was also a provision that students in ninth and tenth grades were to take no more than three such majors instead of the traditional four.[63] This fit the antihomework campaign as well, since the student with fewer scheduled class periods would have more study hall time for the unfinished business from classroom supervised study. At the same time it created more crowded study halls and added disciplinary problems with students who had less to do than before. There were, of course, provisions under which students in the first two years could take additional major subjects, but these were complicated and in any case not open to those in the first semester of high school.

The three-major plan turned out to be a real bone of contention, with the Chicago Teachers Union as one of its main opponents although by no means the only one. It was abandoned during the school year 1938–39 to the accompaniment of great rejoicing from the Teachers Union, which congratulated itself for having brought about the restoration of "the normal high school program" of four majors.[64] The plan had clearly misfired, and the Chicago board in this period was not disposed to attempt the saving of lost causes.

Johnson complicated his position during 1938–39 with his statements on vocational education. Evidently he was the victim of misunderstanding fostered not only by his own somewhat contradictory statements but by inaccurate reporting in the press. The word that first went out was that he planned to put 80 percent of Chicago's high school students into what was called trade school education.[65] According to one report, protests from labor (not just the Teachers Union) drew Mayor Edward Kelly into the controversy. Following a session arranged by Kelly between the school board and representatives of unions, Johnson said that his plan had been misrepresented.[66] Chicago, of course, had long had vocational education, and what Johnson and the board did now was to work on an expansion of it without further controversial symbols such as 80 percents.

63. *Ibid.*, p. 104.
64. *News Bulletin of the Chicago Teachers Union* 2 (Sept. 24, 1938), 3; also 2 (May 6, 1939), 1.
65. For references to the 80 percent figure, see "Chicago 'Super' Battles for Trade Schools," *Life* 3 (Dec. 13, 1937), 59–60; "AFT Protests Chicago Plan," *American Teacher* 22 (Nov. 1937), 27.
66. Editorial, *Nation's Schools* 21 (March 1938), 18–19.

The Teachers Union continued to object, especially to the plans for programs in the new Southside Trade School that were designed to supplement the long-standing program at the Washburne Trade School. Specifically, the union protested against the allocation of three years to vocational training, contending that vocational trends called for general education rather than narrow and specialized skills. It also criticized the implication, in the board's statement, that vocational skills would reduce unemployment. "The statement assumes," said the union, "that trained workers create jobs. During all the years of the depression thousands of highly skilled and experienced workers were out of work because local industries did not employ them."[67]

Johnson's somewhat archaic approach to vocational education was reminiscent of pre-1920s social efficiency, as was also his heavy-handed campaign for character education through the social aims. "Education today," proclaimed his annual report for 1938, "means preparation for complete living. Looming ever more important in successful living, the social factor or the capacity for facile social adjustment is demanding increased attention from the progressive educators of the nation. . . . Socialization as a science is far more intricate than many of the more conventional branches of learning." Since students in the evening high schools were older than those in day schools, they were, said the report, "more independent in their thinking," with wider outside contacts, thereby standing "in more urgent need of socialization."[68] The day school programs included student government, clubs, social groups, and other kinds of extraclass activities.

There was, moreover, tangible behavioral evidence on the attainment of the goals. Where 48,089 panes of glass had been broken in Chicago school buildings in 1936 and 48,108 panes in 1937, for the year 1938, the first year of functioning student government, the amount of breakage was reduced to 36,461 panes.[69] At the turn of the decade, Johnson added Americanism to his programs for character and socialization. "Effective Americanism," he wrote, "implies that each individual is willing to subordinate selfish interests in order that he may live in harmony with those about him. The schools of our city have accepted the task of

67. *News Bulletin* 2 (March 4, 1939), 1; *ibid.* (April 1, 1939), 1–2.
68. Chicago, *Annual Report 1937–1938*, pp. 172, 292.
69. William H. Johnson, "Teaching Patriotism in Our Public Schools," *S&S* 50 (Dec. 2, 1939), 705–10.

socializing the curriculum in order that each youthful citizen may come to know his place in the scheme of things."[70]

In some nine or ten experimental high schools, with the number varying from time to time, the programs were less conventional. The idea behind them was conventional enough, that students with "little interest and aptitude in present subject offerings" needed new curricula.[71] At the Greeley Branch of the Lake View High School, the innovation went farther than most, and a program like that of Wisconsin High School's Eight-Year Study, of four functional fields in the ninth grade, was used.[72] Later this program was extended to all incoming ninth-grade students at the Lake View High School, modified by stressing personality development and mental health. Conventional marking was replaced by letters from teachers to parents.[73] Another of the experimental schools was Wells High School, a new school that had opened in February 1935. Located in a neighborhood relatively homogeneous ethnically (mostly people of Polish descent), Wells High School, under the leadership of Principal Paul Pierce, became in a city environment the prototype of a community school, with extensive participation by parents and neighborhood groups.[74]

Most sweeping of all was the program at the Calumet High School, described in *Curriculum Journal* as having "embarked on a curricular experiment in which all subject divisions have been abandoned." According to this report, each student in the experiment worked on a problem chosen by himself, with the school day divided into interest periods rather than subject periods. Involved in this program were 120 freshmen selected at random and placed in four groups, each with a teacher-adviser.[75]

70. "Teaching Americanism in the Chicago Public Schools," *Chicago Schools Journal* 22 (Jan. 1941), 98.

71. James E. McDade, "An Experimental Curriculum Program in Chicago," *Curriculum Journal* 7 (May 1936), 7.

72. "News Notes: Experiment in Integration," *Curriculum Journal* 9 (Jan. 1938), 4.

73. "News Notes: Expansion of Experiment in Integration," *Curriculum Journal* 9 (Nov. 1938), 290.

74. Paul Pierce, "Major Steps in Reorganizing a High School Curriculum," *Sch R* 44 (Nov. 1936), 655–66; Paul Pierce, "Curriculum Reorganization in a Chicago High School," *Curriculum Journal* 8 (April 1937), 156–60; Paul Pierce, *Developing a High School Curriculum* (New York, 1942).

75. "News Notes: Curriculum Experiment in a Chicago High School," 8 (Nov. 1937), 287.

Whether all this had any meaning for Chicago as a whole has long been a matter of dispute. Perhaps Johnson and his regime symbolized the confusion of qualities that was Chicago itself, a city of class and racial tensions, badly scarred by depression, caught in many conflicting and inconsistent currents of social change. Could it reconstruct or only adapt, and did it even adapt very well? Superintendent Johnson was credited, even by his adversaries, with excellent intentions, and modern revisionism had reinterpreted both his leadership and some of the forces that led to his downfall in the mid-1940s.[76] According to one critic, he did right things in the wrong way. Still, in the view of this same critic, Chicago's problem loomed larger than the public relations of the superintendent. "What Chicago can do in the next few years to overcome mass production in education, to substitute democracy for hierarchy and to make the education of its children creative and dynamic is of nationwide concern," he said, perhaps more prophetically than he knew. "It will be an indication as to what an urban society can do to stop the present trend toward a mechanized regimentation that increasingly resembles fascism."[77]

76. J. Stephen Hazlett, "NEA and NCA Involvement in a School Controversy: Chicago, 1944–47," *Sch R* 78 (Feb. 1970), 201–27.
77. John F. Millar, "The Chicago Schools," *S&S* 48 (Oct. 15, 1938), 501–2.

Chapter 11

The enemies within

*I*n the battle psychology that prevailed among educators, there were enemies within and without the gates. Those without in the 1930s were primarily New Deal political leaders suspected by professional educators of wanting to take over the mission of controlling the destinies of American youth. There were also the political conservatives who cut school budgets. Within, among educators themselves, however, were some who espoused that vague entity of disrepute known as traditional education. This was not only enmity, it was treason to the cause.

Such treason assumed tangible shape in the group known as essentialists and articulate expression from a number of individuals. Among the latter were such as William S. Learned of the Carnegie Foundation, Abraham Flexner, Associate Superintendent John L. Tildsley of the New York City public schools, and, most visible of all to the general public, the new and very youthful president of the University of Chicago, Robert Maynard Hutchins. Internal controversy among educators was, of course, nothing new, but the variety that prevailed in the 1930s seemed to have extra notes of acrimony and distrust.

Criticism did not in itself mean treason. There was in fact a stereotyped and approved pattern of criticism that educators could indulge in without risking their professional reputations. Expression of this orthodox criticism was even a means of professional advertising and enhancement. College preparatory courses could be criticized, "formal discipline," Latin, algebra and geometry, uniformity of standards, the study of anything long past and far away, and alleged college domination. In

285

short, the approved pattern of criticism was anti-traditional and anti-academic. Dedicated ideologues of education competed with one another in denouncing the pedagogical merchandise offered by the schools as hopelessly inadequate and out of date.

The object of this approved criticism was to make a case for curricular change, but even Doak Campbell of Peabody, himself an expert in changing the curriculum, sarcastically observed in 1939 that the case had been made and could be allowed to rest. "Time-honored educational practices," said Campbell, "have been held up to scorn. At times the damning process had approached the proportions of a religious crusade. Some of the writers, not to be outdone in their zeal, have demolished the whole curriculum." Assistant Superintendent F. M. Underwood of the St. Louis public schools called this a "mania for change," especially among professors of education who took delight in shocking teachers by setting up and shooting at straw men. "It seems to be the favorite pastime of these professors," lamented Underwood, "to ridicule the 'traditional' school. . . . We realize that times and customs change, but the needed adjustments can be made without exaggerated and unwarranted claptrap." Another critic ridiculed it as a contest among "those making a living out of the educational business" to see who could do the most to tell the people that public education was worthless. "The attacks," he said, "are most numerous and persistent with regard to the Senior High School. Hardly anyone has a good word for that part of our public school system."[1]

The stock criticism, then, still had a ready market. Those who expressed it might at times be written off as bores, but not as heretics and traitors. It was a quite different matter to express criticism that was not approved, which unfortunately also fell into a stock pattern for ceremonial utterance. This anti-anti-academic list included such bogies as lowered standards, coddling, the decline of work (an approved criticism by the end of the decade), fads and frills, trivialities in the curriculum, vocationalism, and practical subjects. This is not to say that the alleged traitors were in agreement among themselves, for treason also

---

1. "Some Modern Trends in Curriculum Thinking," University of Pennsylvania School of Education, *Twenty-Sixth Annual Schoolmen's Week Proceedings*, 1939, pp. 211–12; "Riding 'Hobbies,' " *Educational Method* 18 (Dec. 1938), 129; T. B. P., "Suppose We Stop Tearing Down," *Clearing House* 13 (Nov. 1938), 176. Probably written by Assistant Superintendent Thomas B. Portwood of the San Antonio, Texas, public schools, a member of the editorial staff of the journal.

was marked by internal dissent. Still, the pattern was reasonably clear, and the offense of the traitors was adherence to the academic tradition.

Apart from the work of those identified as high-level and cosmic traitors, the essentialists and people like Hutchins, there was a kind of sustained muttering against modern education (sometimes called "progressive"), heard in a variety of contexts. Occasionally this smoldering body of combustible material would burst into flame and attract national attention, as it did early in 1940 with the publication of an article written by a high school teacher and entitled "Lollipops vs. Learning." Addressing the general public through the columns of the *Saturday Evening Post*, she identified progressive educators as symbols of soft pedagogy and as the villains of the piece.

"I accuse many Progressive educators of preparing their charges for the grim realities of modern life on a diet of lollipops," this teacher solemnly declared. What had set her off, according to her story, was the use by a fellow teacher of a simulated relay race for the teaching of spelling. This kind of gimmickry had been prevalent for many decades and had been denounced as sugar-coating by none other than Dewey himself in 1902 (*Child and the Curriculum*, Chicago). Other lollipops, she said, were the homeroom, which she called an attempt by progressives to socialize the child, and the practice of passing everybody.[2]

Her identification of soft pedagogy with progressive education was typical of the confusion that had developed. It was becoming easy to attach some of these stereotypes to progressive education, perhaps because the stereotypes themselves were simple and dramatic and because progressive education constituted a single target. Educators not themselves progressive, and therefore not directly under attack, understandably tended to become protective about progressive education and to regard all attacks against it as coming under the rubric of criticism disapproved. Thus the progressives, in sustaining unfair injuries from one direction, picked up allies from another, although some turned out to be strange bedfellows indeed. An unfortunate accompaniment to all this was the tendency to use the label *progressive* for all kinds of innovation and for all attacks made against traditional schools.

This apparently was the approach of William Betz, specialist in mathematics in the Rochester, New York, public schools, who in 1937 laudably enough affirmed his faith in the goodness of mathematics as a

2. Ann L. Crockett, 212 (March 16, 1940): 29, 105–6.

school subject. Lined up against mathematics he saw pragmatic opportunism, incoherent curriculum revision, mechanistic views of the mind, and—progressive education. "At present," he said, "those educators who subscribe either to the policy of 'social reconstruction' or to the creed of the child-centered school represent very powerful pressure groups." Mathematics was out of favor with these educators because it did "not fit into the philosophy of planless and effortless education."[3]

Similarly, a professor of education at Union College denounced progressive education for the alleged softness it had brought to elementary schools by catering to children's interests. Changes in family and community life, he contended in this revival of a hoary utterance, had removed work from the home life of children, and it was up to educators to put work into their school life. Progressives were making school play instead of work. This was an interesting variant of the argument from social change and one that must have astonished Dewey if he saw it. A Harvard professor of government, after visiting Lincoln School, concluded that progressive education was suited only for those destined to lead lives of leisure and comfort, not for those who would have to live and make their way in the real world. From an anonymous teacher in the Midwest came applause for the Harvard professor. The vast majority of teachers, she declared, agreed with him and welcomed his statement of what they dared not say for themselves.[4] If she was right, leading educators were up against not only the visible traitors, but a whole fifth-column of those undisclosed in the teaching force.

II

Advocates of social efficiency were presented with a real dilemma in this confusion about progressive education. On one hand, their values and ideals ran counter to those of the progressives, but on the other they shared with progressives a predilection for change. Even though social efficiency was by now an old story, its proponents saw much that remained to be done, and academic tradition clearly remained the object of attack. This was explicit in the issues and functions reports of the

3. "Mathematics As a Universal and Permanent Element in Education," *TCR* 39 (Nov. 1937), 133.
4. Franklin C. Chillrud, "Is Our Elementary Education Too Soft?" *Social Education* 5 (Oct. 1941), 438–41; Carl Joachim Friedrich, "This Progressive Education," *Atlantic Monthly* 154 (Oct. 1934), 420–26; Letter to the editor, supplement, *Atlantic Monthly* 155 (April 1935), p. 52.

Briggs Committee. From such a point of view progressive education, as a catalyst creating circumstances favorable to change, needed protection.

What the social efficiency leaders did was to break in various directions. Jessie H. Newlon and George S. Counts made common cause with the progressives and in fact joined them. Reconstructionism was a platform broad enough for some progressives and some advocates of social efficiency as well. Perhaps this accounts for the desperation with which Counts sought to win the association over to a more political-social approach. The more this was resisted by progressives themselves, the less tenable his effort seemed to be, but it was a magnificent effort on his part. Other attempts in the same direction were less lofty: to merge the usual attitude of the efficiency educators toward preparation for college with the rebellion in the Eight-Year Study against traditional requirements of admission; or in the realm of curriculum, as in the development of functional units at Wisconsin High School, to merge life activities aims with the movements toward core based on problems and needs.

Another possibility was to praise the receptiveness of progressive educators toward change, but to express what might be called an approved pattern of criticism of progressive education. Progressive educators, moreover, could be gently chided for their impracticality.[5] In this line of approved criticism, progressivism was viewed as appropriate enough for well-to-do private schools, but not for the rough-and-tumble of public schools except in suburbs like Winnetka. Progressives could also be reproved for inefficiency and waste. Using the term *activity movement* rather than progressivism, Professor Alonzo Grace of the University of Rochester scoffed at modern elementary schools for their obsession with what he called orange crate creativity, with "great gobs of messy paint . . . smeared on a ten-foot strip of wrapping paper."[6] In a controversy about progressive education in the public schools of Roslyn, New York, much was made of an alleged instance in which a class had spent a whole day learning to make nut bread.[7]

There was always the possibility of not temporizing with progressive education at all, but making open war upon it. Here would be no sym-

5. I. N. Madsen, "How Practical Is 'Progressive Education' for Public Schools of Today?" *EA&S* 19 (April 1933), 249–59.

6. "Some Expensive Fallacies in American Education," *EA&S* 19 (March 1933), 195.

7. "Joy and Happiness Schools," *Time* 31 (March 21, 1938), 32.

pathetic criticism of erring brethren, but rather denunciation of pedagogical misdeeds, of presumed softness and a breakdown in the learning
process itself. This criticism was not approved, and the efficiency educators who espoused it were suspect. David Snedden, nevertheless,
accused the progressives of concentrating on method and of avoiding
the task of determining educational aims scientifically. According to
him, progressivism had limited value, mainly in the education of very
young children. Once the most formidable of all the anti-academic
educators, Snedden now found himself written off as a traditionalist
who dragged his feet against change. He realized, however, that the
preoccupation of the progressives with method, especially as it related
to qualities of thinking, was akin to the older movement for mental
discipline.[8] It was the loose identification sometimes made between
progressive education and social frontiersmanship, too, that tended to
alienate political and economic conservatives like Snedden.

Among the efficiency educators (and others) were some who
regarded progressive education as a passing phenomenon and looked
forward to its early demise. Ernest W. Butterfield, superintendent at
Bloomfield and former state commissioner in Connecticut, poked fun
at progressives in 1939 for their resemblance to a religious cult and
declared the movement to be in its last stage of autumnal glory.
Although this may have been wishful thinking, there was no doubt that
by the late 1930s the progressive image was not only blurred but tarnished. The modifier *progressive*, in relation to education, said the
superintendent of Montgomery, Alabama, was beginning to have the
same effect as *quack* to medicine, *shyster* to lawyers, and *hypocrisy*
to religion.[9]

Those who predicted the end of progressive education were adept
prophets, at least so far as the association itself was concerned. At the
end of the 1930s, however, progressivism and the association were still
far from dead. The Eight-Year Study, for example, was riding high in
apparent triumph. Progressives could still bask in the warmth and glow

8. For Snedden's attacks see his "Purposes vs. Methods in the 'New' Education,"
S&S 30 (Nov. 9, 1929), 632–35; "Functional Approaches to the Study of Educa-
tional Purposes and Values," *S&S* 33 (June 13, 1931), 777–81; *Toward Better
Educations* (New York, 1931).

9. "Progressive Education Is Dying? Hail: Saltatory Education," *Clearing House*
14 (Dec. 1939), 202–4; Clarence M. Dannelly, "Finances and Philosophies,"
School Executive 61 (Oct. 1941), 25–26.

of being modern. Their eccentricities were condoned, their enemies deplored.

III

Although the term *essentials*, especially in the form and sense of *minimum essentials*, had been in use for several decades in education, the term *essentialism* denoting an explicit doctrine did not appear prominently before the appearance of the essentialist platform in the spring of 1938. Like the progressivism it purported to oppose, essentialism had various facets and did not always lend itself to capsule definition. It did have the advantage of being centered in a realtively small group of people, the seven members of the Essentialist Committee for the Advancement of American Education, created in the winter of 1938 several months before the appearance of the platform.

The most visible essentialist was William C. Bagley, who had been sternly denouncing progressivism since the early 1920s and could be counted upon for antiprogressive utterances on about every topic that arose.[10] Bagley personified the conflict in styles between progressivism and social efficiency and did not seek any accomodation of the two bodies of doctrine. In his book *The Educative Process* (New York, 1905), he had been one of the first to use the term *social efficiency* and had proclaimed it as the standard by which all practice in education should be judged. He was regarded as less anti-academic than other proponents of social efficiency, but this was partly because of a shift in the identification of the academic tradition itself. Like other social efficiency experts, Bagley did not reject subject matter. In fact, he believed firmly in the body of subject matter that could be selected and proved for attaining social aims. What social efficiency rejected was subject matter that could not be so proved, and the idea that mental discipline involved the form of subjects rather than their substance. From this arose contempt for Latin as a formal subject that sought to make its case on disciplinary, not substantive, grounds. By the 1930s it was the neodisciplinary tendency among progressives that seemed anti-academic

10. For his career see Isaac Kandel, *William Chandler Bagley: Stalwart Educator* (New York, 1961); Erwin V. Johanningmeier, "William Chandler Bagley's Relationship between Psychology and Education," *History of Education Quarterly* 9 (Spring 1969), 3–27.

in its disparagement of content and Bagley who seemed pro-academic instead.

Much of what occupied Bagley's attention in his attacks against progressivism was the notion of "softness" in what he was calling in 1929 the "freedom theory" of education. "I told you sixteen years ago," he declared to the superintendents at Cleveland in 1929, "that we could not build our democratic structure on the shifting sands of soft pedagogy. That statement still holds. There must be iron in the blood of education and lime in the bone." Four years later during the deepest depression, Bagley again addressed the superintendents, this time at Minneapolis, to spell out the defects of what he called the dominant American educational theory of the time. They were, he argued, defects of pupil initiative versus teacher planning, pupil experience versus race experience, and immediate interest versus adult need. Resulting from these defects was an education "effeminate," weak, and enfeebling.[11]

Bagley's antiprogressivism evoked acrimony on all sides, and he found himself isolated from other leading figures on the American pedagogical scene. His followers were not necessarily outnumbered by the progressives, but he was outnumbered among people with status, whatever that may have been worth. Perhaps as partial compensation for this isolation (although he seemed to glory in it), Bagley accepted the development of the Essentialist Committee for the Advancement of American Education, a group that apart from him was led largely by Michael Demiashkevich of George Peabody College for Teachers. The other five members were Walter M. Ryle, president of the Kirksville, Missouri, State Teachers College; librarian Louis Shores of Peabody; M. L. Shane, professor of modern languages at Peabody; Guy M. Whipple, formerly of the University of Michigan; and F. Alden Shaw, headmaster of the Detroit Country Day School. According to one recent account, it was Shaw who first suggested the committee to Demiashkevich.[12]

The essentialist's platform appeared for discussion at the Atlantic City meeting of the Department of Superintendence in 1938 and was

11. "Some Handicaps of Character Education in the United States," Superintendence *Report*, 1929, p. 146; "Modern Educational Theories and Practical Considerations," *ibid.*, 1933, pp. 45–51.

12. Gurney Chambers, "Michael John Demiashkevich and the Essentialist Committee for the Advancement of American Education," *History of Education Quarterly* 9 (Spring 1969), 46–56. For another recent overview of the work of the committee, see F. Alden Shaw, "The Existentialist Challenge to American Education," *S&S* 99 (April 1971), 210–14.

published under Bagley's name in April of that year.[13] Three of its four sections were discussed at Atlantic City and the fourth added for the published article. In the opening two sections, the platform restated Bagley's oft-delivered conclusion that public education in the United States was "appallingly weak and ineffective," and it reviewed the social and economic factors presumably involved. There was the usual cast of immigrants and those who had moved from urban to rural environments within the United States. On the other hand, the report considered states with the "heaviest burden of immigration from backward countries to assimilate" to be the most advanced from the point of view of civilization (pp. 241–44).

Section three made use of paired opposites such as freedom and discipline, individual and society, and play and work. American education, according to Bagley, had sought to rationalize "the loosening of standards" and "the relaxation of rigor" by espousing the freedom-individual-play halves of these pairs. This was transmitted through the abandonment of rigorous standards for promotion, disparagement of system and sequence in learning, the activity movement, the discrediting of exact and exacting studies, emphasis on social studies, use of the lower schools to establish a new social order, and the curriculum revision movement and its vagaries (p. 245).

With the unfurling of the banner of democracy in section four, the platform specified the need for informed and intelligent citizens and "a community of culture" with a common core of "ideas, meanings, understandings, and ideals." The essentials in this common core were reading, computing, "at least a speaking acquaintance with man's past and especially with the story of one's own country," creative art, "health instruction," and the elements of natural science (pp. 252–53). The latter part of section four was mainly rhetoric and exhortation. Both in biological and social evolution, it declared, struggle and competition, selection and rejection were often cruel, but on the whole they were "primary factors of progress." The clear duty of organized education was to recognize change and to develop a theory that would be "strong, virile, and positive, not feeble, effeminate, and vague." Quoting Huxley (without reference) to the effect that what had been ordained among the prehistoric protozoa could not be altered by Act

13. "An Essentialist's Platform for the Advancement of American Education," *EA&S* 24 (April 1938), 241–56. Subsequent references appear in text.

of Parliament, the platform added that neither could it be "by the wishful thinking of educational theorists" (pp. 255–56).

Today there seems little in the essentialist platform that would arouse anyone to either fury or ecstatic applause. Certainly the warmed-over Social Darwinism might have been irritating, but hardly enough to warrant the fury that allegedly exploded at the Atlantic City convention. Some claimed, however, that the press gave it undue prominence and created an exaggerated impression of conflict. The story in *Newsweek* headed "Essentialist Group Urges Pupils Be Coddled Less and Taught More" observed that the platform constituted the first organized plea in twenty years for a return to traditional teaching. *Newsweek* doubted, however, that the platform would halt the "steady trend of the modern method" (11 [March 14, 1938]: 26–27).

Other reactions were noncommittal. Perhaps "establishment" educators thought it best to ignore it or to play it down. In his annual quasi-official report on the superintendents' convention, Belmont Farley of the NEA gave the essentialists only one paragraph in fourteen closely printed pages, plus a brief quotation from Dorothy Thompson's column about an incipient revolt of parents against progressivism.[14] Comments in the general press revealed no great sense of excitement.[15] The pedagogical press was not quite sure what it thought. An editorial in the *Nation's Schools* (22 [July 1938]: 12) expressed the view that the conflict would contribute to progress, and told its readers that the association had been founded by followers of John Dewey and the scientific movement in education.

What did the practical schoolman on the firing line make of all this? Superintendent John A. Sexson of Pasadena, California, called it rival sensation-mongering and spotlight-grabbing. Reporting on the essentialist's platform to the Pasadena teachers in their local school paper, Sexson called it the usual annual sensation magnified by a tabloid press. According to him, the progressives were already discredited and in retreat and the essentialists were trying to capitalize on the "present wave of conservatism"—an interesting observation for the year 1938. Fortunately, Sexson concluded, Pasadena teachers had never worn labels but had gone about their work. "Pasadena children can read,

14. "The American Association of School Administrators," *S&S* 47 (March 12, 1938), 331.

15. "The Press Views Education: Progressives versus Essentialists," *School Executive* 57 (May 1938), 416–17, 447.

write, and spell. They are mannerly. Their language is acceptable and effective."[16] Whether this was because Pasadena had profited from progressivism or had escaped it he did not say.

The long-term impression among educators, such as it was, tended to be like Sexson's. Without explicitly defending progressivism, they seemed to regard the essentialist's platform as something inappropriate, possibly in bad taste. Bagley converted no multitudes to his cause. He had been isolated before; he seemed to be isolated still. In his address to the annual Teachers College dinner at the superintendents' convention in 1938, shortly after the platform had been released, Bagley faced the new loneliness against which he had been warned. He recalled his earlier stand against determinism, declaring, "I had no companions then." It was better, in any case, "to be right than respectable."[17]

In the late summer of 1938, just months after the appearance of the platform, the death of Michael Demiashkevich deprived Bagley of able and scholarly support for his position. Demiashkevich had been born, reared, and given his undergraduate general education in imperial Russia, later taking his doctorate at Columbia (1926). He had served with distinction at Peabody since 1929.[18] Apart from Demiashkevich and Guy M. Whipple, Bagley's other associates on the committee were not widely known. Strangely enough, back in the early 1920s Whipple had been one of Bagley's major opponents on the question of determinism and intelligence. By 1930, however, he and Bagley made common cause against ineptitudes in the movement for curriculum revision. Whipple characterized the movement as "amateurish, trifling and a sheer waste of time—nay, worse than that, an injection of pernicious confusion into what should be orderly progress," comparable to inviting "a group of practical electricians to redesign a modern power plant."[19] By the time the essentialist's platform was published, Whipple was no longer active and did little more than lend his signature to the document and his name to the cause.

16. "What Are the Essentialists?" *Pasadena School Review* 10 (March 1938), 1, 8.
17. "Some Relations of Education to the Status Quo," *S&S* 47 (April 30, 1938), 562–65.
18. For a review of his career see "In Memoriam: Dr. Michael John Demiashkevich, 1891–1938," *Educational Forum* 3 (Nov. 1938), 125–29.
19. "Educational Determinimism: A Discussion of Professor Bagley's Address at Chicago," *S&S* 15 (June 3, 1922), 599–602; "What Price Curriculum-Making?" *S&S* 31 (March 15, 1930), 367–68.

Bagley therefore had no choice but to go it alone. He did it so well that apparently few who discussed essentialism in the period following 1938 realized that he himself was just about the whole movement. This is not to say that Bagley was bereft of sympathizers or allies, but for the most part he never offset the idea that in some way he was disloyal to education. Unfortunately he remained a prisoner of the same assumptions that bound his opponents, particularly on such matters as mass education. He and his opponents shared the belief that an increase in numbers meant a decline in ability. Relaxation of standards, he felt, was therefore inevitable, but he objected to making this presumed necessity into a virtue.[20]

On occasion, Bagley was rewarded by outbursts of applause in print. In 1941, for example, a professor at the Ypsilanti, Michigan, State Normal College, stated his belief that strong doses of essentialism would turn out students with greater mastery of the English tongue. Such "exact learning of subject matter" and mastery of fundamentals, he felt was especially important for students planning to go to college. Good orthodox social efficiency dualism, this. Herbert A. Tonne, a professor of business education at New York University, stepped in to defend essentialism against the charge that it favored tradition. It was the progressives, argued Tonne, who were really the traditionalists, since they would be willing to accept any subject, even Latin, if it were taught along progressive lines. Essentialism, argued Tonne, would mean teaching only essential subjects and would eliminate "mere learning for the sake of learning."[21] Tonne was correct, but he had little chance to offset the popular impression of essentialism as a way of turning back the pedagogical clock.

Some have seen in the academic resurgence of the late 1950s and early 1960s a kind of delayed victory for the essentialist point of view.[22] If essentialism is taken solely as meaning hard pedagogy versus soft, some of the pedagogical styles of the academic resurgence might seem very essentialist indeed. Apart from this the resemblance tends to be obscure, especially in relation to curriculum. Certainly the emphasis on

20. "An Essentialist Looks at Foreign Languages," *EA&S* 25 (April 1939), 245.

21. H. H. Jordan, "Speaking of Essentialism," *EA&S* 27 (Sept. 1941), 453–58; "Is Essentialism Synonymous with Traditionalism?" *S&S* 53 (March 8, 1941), 311–12.

22. Gurney Chambers, "Educational Essentialism Thirty Years Later," *S&S* 97 (Jan. 1969), 14–16.

method and inquiry in the science projects seems more akin to the Committee of Ten subject reports of 1893 than to the essentialist's platform.

In the end, what essentialists probably found most objectionable about progressivism was its commitment to electivism, options, and choice. To the essentialist there were of necessity things that everybody should know or be able to do. To progressives there were few if any such things, a position consistently maintained throughout his professional career by the first honorary president of the association, Charles W. Eliot, who had also back in 1892–93 served as chairman of the NEA Committee of Ten. During the Eight-Year Study, some progressives, in pursuing core, began to waver on this point. Nonetheless, it was a progressive resolution of the core problem to define the common elements as needs, processes, and human concerns rather than as common subjects or even common subject matter apart from subject boundaries.

IV

It was not necessary to have signed the essentialist platform to qualify as one giving aid and comfort to the enemies of education. William S. Learned of the Carnegie Foundation for the Advancement of Teaching was eligible through his identification with and his pronouncements on the Pennsylvania Study. Learned, who earlier in his career had been a professor of education at Harvard, had gone through some doctrinal shifts himself. Writing on secondary education for the Vermont Survey made by the Carnegie Foundation in 1914, he had recommended the abandonment of Latin except for those who needed it for college entrance and except in schools large enough to offer it "as a widely administered elective." In the 1920s Learned, still writing for the Carnegie Foundation, but now as a staff member, had aroused apprehension by comparing unfavorably the academic accomplishments of students in American secondary schools with their counterparts in Europe.[23]

The Study of the Relations of Secondary and Higher Education in

23. Carnegie Foundation for the Advancement of Teaching, *A Study of Education in Vermont*, bull. no. 7 (New York, 1914), p. 101; Carnegie Foundation for the Advancement of Teaching, *The Quality of the Educational Process in the United States and in Europe*, bull. no. 20 (New York, 1927).

Pennsylvania, known more briefly as the Pennsylvania Study, was a project of the Carnegie Foundation, undertaken in 1926 at the request of the Joint Commission of the Association of Pennsylvania College Presidents and the State Department of Public Instruction. Among other things, the study carried on a massive testing program, beginning with 27,000 graduating high school seniors of the state in 1928 and followed by retesting in 1930 and 1932 of those in the group who went to college. Data released from these tests throughout the 1930s tended to show a low level of learning in college and aroused criticism of what was referred to as the course and credit system.[24]

In the summary volume for the study, *The Student and His Knowledge* (New York, 1938), Learned and his co-author, Ben Wood of Columbia's Teachers College, argued for the validity of knowledge as an outcome of the educational process and for using this as the main object of their testing program. Knowledge was not to be identified, however, with a "mass of crammed and undigested information" recalled for semester tests and then abandoned (pp. 4–7). It was to be viewed as a matter of understanding and of relationships, and one of the main instruments for testing it in the study was a test in general culture with a maximum score of 600.

On this general culture test, the average score of 254 for college sophomores seemed dismal enough, but the 314 for college seniors was even more dismal, with a difference of only 60 points over two years of college. More devastating still was the overlap in the distribution of the high school and the college groups. Some 22 percent of the high school seniors, for example, had higher averages than college sophomores, while 10 percent had higher than college seniors (p. 21). Many of the high school graduates who did not go to college were better equipped for it than many who did go (p. 61). Earlier identification of capable students through a program of intensive and continuous testing, therefore, was strongly recommended, along with greater financial aids for those who otherwise could not go to college (pp. 61–62).

Among those who responded with consternation and alarm to the data in the study was the historian and sociologist Harry Elmer Barnes. Fully a quarter or more of the college students in Pennsylvania, lamented Barnes, "were incompetent time-servers without the mental

---

24. John R. Tunis, "Human Waste in the Colleges," *Scribner's Magazine* 96 (Sept. 1934), 138–44; "The Menace of 'Education,'" *Nation* 139 (Sept. 5, 1934), 257–58.

ability to qualify them as intelligent and worthy college students." Stanford's Lewis M. Terman referred to the findings as "appalling facts" and feared that the pace in college work was being set by dull minds. He urged scholarships ranging from $500 to $1,500 a year for students from the top deciles in intelligence, presumably as measured by his Stanford-Binet Test.[25]

Educators who responded defensively to the study tended to suggest that the affair was unfortunate in providing enemies of education something to shoot with. The focus on knowledge in the testing program was condemned as traditional and academic, but the contrast being made was no longer with the traditional aim of mental training. Instead it was with personality characteristics and personal-social qualities. Goodwin Watson in *How Good Are Our Colleges?* (New York, 1939), for example, declared the findings immaterial if one were interested not in knowledge but in "self-confidence, joy of living, ability to cooperate, and range of friendships." The *Clearing House* review of his book agreed with him and accused the study of concentrating on erudition. The results, said the reviewer, "gave much comfort to the educational Jeremiahs," obviously so since it emphasized those aspects that surprised "the supporters of naive stereotypes regarding erudition as education."[26]

Abraham Flexner was another whose reputation was tarnished over the years by identification with disapproved kinds of criticism. Once an innovator who had helped sponsor Lincoln School at Teachers College, Columbia, and who had ridiculed the survival of Latin in the high school curriculum, Flexner next turned his ridicule on the kinds of trivialities later stereotyped as life adjustment education. His main work of castigation, *Universities: American, English, German* (New York, 1930), came at the start of the decade, but it guaranteed his reputation throughout. In this book he spared really no one, but reserved his main invective for American secondary and higher schools. When he published his autobiography in 1940, Flexner felt no compulsion to smooth over these attacks, but he did reveal what was perhaps a guilt complex for his attitude toward Greek and Latin at Lincoln School. He had proposed their omission, he said, to allow leeway for experimentation and to provide enough time for the modern subjects. "To my surprise," he

25. "The Responsibility of Education to Society," American Association of School Administrators, *Official Report*, 1939, p. 140; "The Gifted Student and His Academic Environment,"*S&S* 49 (Jan. 21, 1939), 70–72.
26. *Clearing House* 14 (Dec. 1939), 245. Watson quoted in review.

added, "I found myself denounced as an 'enemy' of the classics. . . . My critics forgot, if they ever knew, that Greek had been my favorite study" (*I Remember* [New York, 1940], pp. 251–52). It is unlikely that his denunciation as a presumed enemy of the classics matched in fury what he got in 1930 and after as an enemy, also presumed, of modern education.

The fall from grace of Associate Superintendent John L. Tildsley of New York City came in the middle and late 1930s. Tildsley had been known as a competent large-city schoolman who made most of the approved sounds about the need for curriculum revision. He had called for universal secondary schooling. By the middle 1930s he was beginning to reconsider his earlier enthusiasms. Proceeding from the base of social efficiency (specifically by invoking Briggs's investment theory), Tildsley feared the lowering of standards "to keep pace with the lowered intelligence, will power and character of the median high school pupil" and recommended that students judged not equipped for high school be kept in special schools staffed by selected elementary principals and teachers.[27]

His Inglis Lecture of 1936, *The Mounting Waste of the American Secondary School* (Cambridge, Mass.), therefore, should not have come as a surprise and probably did not to those who had closely followed his statements in New York; it was, however, his first major national expression of these views. The message was clear: close the high school against those who come poorly equipped. In reviewing the published lecture, A. H. Lass, a teacher at the Abraham Lincoln High School, New York City, praised Tildsley for his honesty and sincerity, but correctly predicted for this Inglis Lecture "an existence of violence."[28]

According to an unsigned review in the official *Bulletin* of the Department of Secondary School Principals (20 [May 1936]: 73–74), Tildsley's lecture struck the low-water mark of the Inglis Lecture series. The reviewer doubted that many would read it through, observing that those who did not would miss little, since its contribution could be rated "near zero." Among the presumed defects in the address, the reviewer listed faults in logic and intemperate language and predicted that educators would be amused by its ranting.

Undeterred by the response to his Inglis Lecture, Tildsley later denounced reconstructionism and frontiersmanship, receiving for this a

27. "Planned Education," *High Points* 17 (June 1935), 5–20.
28. *High Points* 18 (March 1936), 76–78.

counterdenunciation of himself.[29] In this latter period he seemed also to be shedding at least the social control aspect of the social efficiency ideal, expressing at the height of the defense movement in late 1940 the idea that students should not be drafted for total war and that war should not be a dominating factor in the school. The only hope for a good society, he declared at this time, lay in the growth of the individual child, and school people should oppose "any crusade, cause, movement which interferes with that child's right to growth or with the teacher's right of promoting that growth free from needless interruptions and distractions."[30]

V

Still, after the essentialists had come and gone and Learned, Flexner, and Tildsley had acquired reputations for treason, there remained one clear and undisputed champion of heretical views, one whose personality stood out most sharply with the public and who was himself regarded by educators as the most dangerous of all suppliers of aid and comfort to the enemy. Robert M. Hutchins had not always had this reputation, but had been hailed at the time of his appointment at thirty to the Chicago presidency as dynamic, innovative, and young in spirit as well as years. The pedagogical community had great expectations for Hutchins, not only because of his work at Yale Law School but also because of the progressive reputation of his father, William Hutchins, as president of Berea College, Kentucky.

In his first major utterance at Chicago after his appointment, the commencement address in 1929, but before his assumption of duties, Hutchins stirred his audience with an eloquent affirmation of faith in thinking as the major aim. "My view of university training," he said on this occasion, "is to unsettle the minds of young men, to widen their horizons, to inflame their intellects." The purpose of education, he went on, is not to teach facts, theories, or laws, not to reform people or to amuse them, but "to teach them to think, to think straight if possible, but to think always for themselves." Hutchins moved quickly at Chicago

29. "Why I Object to Some Proposals of the Frontier Thinkers," *Social Frontier* 4 (July 1938), 319–22; Simon S. Olans, letter to the editor, *Social Frontier* 5 (Oct. 1938), 31.
30. "Shall the Schools Be Conscripted for Total War," *High Points* 23 (Jan. 1941), 5–13.

toward breaking the lock-step and toward greater flexibility and freedom for the student.[31] Credit-counting went off the books and comprehensive examinations were substituted. Liberals hailed him in all quarters,
and it was the liberal *Nation* that put him on its honor roll (132 [Jan. 7,
1931]: 8) for his efforts at Chicago "to put routine in the background
and bring education and enlightenment to the fore."

Gifted in mental ability, personal presence, writing, and speech,
Hutchins appealed mightily to the generosity and hopes of those who
viewed modern education as a cause. His early actions were no mere
flash in the liberal pan. Appearing before the Department of Superintendence at Washington, D.C., in 1932, Hutchins added what was then
his friendly voice to the idea of greater freedom for high schools. Each
level of the educational system, Huchins argued, should be free of
restrictions from other levels. "It must devote itself to meeting the needs
of its students rather than to meeting the demands of some other organization. . . . It follows that the public schools must have this freedom.
The forces of experiment and progress latent in them can never be
released if they are compelled to think chiefly of meeting the requirements imposed upon them by institutions of higher learning. If one
thing is clear it is that the primary purpose of the high school is not to
prepare students for the colleges and universities."[32]

At the NEA convention of 1934, Hutchins called for universal secondary schooling, with varying programs and opportunities, until the
age of eighteen or even twenty.[33] He argued for this again in 1934 in
the Stearns Lecture at the Phillips Academies. "If existing schools and
colleges are not adapted to the needs of all these students (and they
certainly are not) we must establish new ones for them. If existing
methods of selection and instruction can not be employed we shall have
to invent others."[34] Specifically, he urged secondary schools to carry
students through what had been regarded as the first two college years,
and he was already identified as a champion of the public junior college.

31. Quoted in *J Ed* 110 (July 1, 1929), 17n; Robert M. Hutchins, "The
Reorganization of the University of Chicago," *High School Conference*, 1930
pp. 53–56; Hutchins, "The Higher Learning in America," *Journal of Higher
Education* 4 (Jan. 1933), 1–8.
32. "The Interdependence of Educational Institutions," Superintendence *Report*,
1932, pp. 148–50.
33. "The Teacher, the School, and the National Life," *NEA Proc*, 1934, pp.
17–22.
34. "The Educational Function of New England," *S&S* 40 (Aug. 25, 1934), 235.

There was, however, a fateful note in this 1934 address. In considering what the preparatory schools might do with students carried through the sophomore college year, he suggested a general education based on ideas. Since ideas were usually found in books, he proposed for this period a course of study consisting "largely of books, great books."[35] At this point the orchestra, had there been one, might well have sounded a *leitmotiv* of doom, for Hutchins had doomed himself to his subsequent role as an enemy of modern education. This obviously did not happen all at once, but it was the beginning of his end.

Why should books, especially "great" ones, have given so much offense to the community of modern pedagogy? This question has never been answered and in fact is rarely asked. It has almost been taken for granted that books are in some way offensive, even to those who write and publish them. The answer may well be the degree to which books symbolize academic education and become offensive to those with the anti-academic point of view. In any case, as Hutchins developed this idea he attracted most vigorous and most negative response.

With the publication of two articles based on his Storrs Lectures at Yale in 1936, later incorporated in his book *The Higher Learning in America* (New Haven, 1936), Hutchins made the break complete. There were, he said, three sources of confusion in modern education: the love of money, an erroneous notion of democracy, and an erroneous notion of progress. The third of these put its faith in evolution and consequently in adjustment to environment, with an accompanying empiricism in place of thought and a resulting anti-intellectual university. He recommended, instead, the fostering of scholarship and the single-minded pursuit of intellectual virtue.[36]

It was in the second of these articles that he uttered five trenchant sentences destined to carry far as his intellectual trademark. "Education," said Hutchins in this memorable passage, "implies teaching. Teaching implies knowledge. Knowledge is truth. The truth is everywhere the same. Hence education should be everywhere the same."[37] This may have been foolish, although behind it lies a truth that education doesn't always have to be different, but it remains a fascinating prob-

---

35. *Ibid.*, 240.
36. "The Confusion in Higher Education," *Harper's* 173 (Oct. 1936), 449–58; "What Is General Education?" *Harper's* 173 (Nov. 1936), 602–9.
37. *Harper's* 173 (Nov. 1936), 603.

lem to explain the wrath it has aroused among proponents of the pedagogically modern.

Meanwhile Hutchins continued to seek support from the academic community or segments of it. At this stage (1937) he seemed to be trying to repair the breakdown in communication by explaining himself repeatedly and at length, particularly from the point of view of building a doctrine to support his great books. In an address before the New York City Association of Teachers of English on January 30, 1937, he sought this doctrine in what he called the liberal arts, namely, grammar, rhetoric, logic, and mathematics. This was evidently the trivium plus the four traditional items of the quadrivium subsumed under mathematics as a blanket category. These liberal arts would be conveyed through the great books: "An education which consisted of the liberal arts as understood through great books and great books understood through the liberal arts would be one and the only one which would enable us to comprehend the tradition in which we live."[38]

Hutchins avoided trapping himself in a demand for the universal study of Latin and Greek. In his opinion, the traditional teaching of the great classics had degenerated into philological tricks. "I do not wish," he told the New York English teachers, "to return to the study of Greek and Latin for all pupils in the public schools. I do not wish to impose the liberal arts as they were understood in the Middle Ages upon them. I do wish to get whatever of value Greek, Latin, and the liberal arts had for the American boy and girl today." This obviously would have to be done in translation, and Hutchins therefore saw the English teacher as a source of the tradition in American schools.[39] In reviewing Hutchins's address for *High Points* (19 [October, 1937]: 73), teacher A. H. Lass of New York City attacked it as showing "cruel disregard" for the "underprivileged" in the schools by cutting off at least 75 percent of the students. There is no direct suggestion of this in the printed text of Hutchins's address. What Lass apparently did on this occasion was to fall into the old social efficiency notion that the so-called masses were incapable of handling academic schooling.

The pace of controversy continued, with Hutchins usually giving as good as he got. Most of his adversaries breathed the spirit of indignation when they discussed him and his views, although Porter Sargent, the nonconformist publisher of handbooks on private schools and himself an object of controversy, good-humoredly sought not to condemn

38. "Tradition in Education," *Harvard Educational Review* 7 (May 1937), 312.
39. *Ibid.*, pp. 312, 305.

Hutchins but to explain him. Sargent found his explanation (as have many since) in the purported influence of Mortimer Adler, Aristotelian and Thomist, on Hutchins. Still, Sargent thought, Hutchins could be redeemed. "If he could only get away from his medievalists," concluded Sargent, "if Adler could be sent off on a sabbatical, if Hutchins could get time to read some good modern books, he might come out, right side up, face forward."[40]

Instead of redeeming himself, however, Hutchins provoked further alienation by carrying his appeal to the "masses" themselves, and in the columns of the much-scoffed-at *Saturday Evening Post*. Hutchins ran four articles in the *Post* beginning in December 1937 and running into February 1938.[41] In part he expressed what would have passed as orthodox criticism of higher education. "You will be filled with countless useless facts, 60 percent of which you will have to repeat to pass countless tests," he said in his January article, addressing prospective college students. On the other hand, he scored college presidents for having in one of the innumerable surveys of such matters ranked mental discipline number twenty-two in a list of twenty-five possible aims and below even personality and good manners (pp. 16, 72). These articles evoked some nine hundred letters from *Post* readers, one-sixth of which disagreed with him violently.[42] Journalist Milton Mayer of Chicago called this the largest response to nonfiction material in the *Post*'s experience. Mayer tended to support Hutchins's views but was afraid they had been presented poorly. In his view, the pedagogical issues were by now hopelessly obscured by emotional controversies involving Aquinas and Adler.[43]

Criticisms of Hutchins did not always reach the higher plateaus of expression and thought. Hutchins gleefully referred to an unidentified educator who told his audience that the Hutchins theories had come from Germany and were considered so bad there that even the Nazis had kicked them out.[44] Another kind of observation came in 1940 from Dean William Russell of Teachers College, Columbia, in the course of

40. "What's the Matter with Hutchins?" *Clearing House* 12 (March 1938), 396.
41. "We Are Getting No Brighter," 210 (Dec. 11, 1937), 5–7, 98; "Why Send Them To School?" 210 (Dec. 25, 1937), 10–11, 30–31; "Why Go To College?" 210 (Jan. 22, 1938), 16–17, 72–74; "What Can We Do About It?" 210 (Feb. 19, 1938), 27–28, 73–75.
42. "Hutchins Answers Hutchins," *Saturday Evening Post* 211 (Sept. 24, 1938), 23, 34, 36.
43. "Hutchins of Chicago," *Harper's* 178 (Feb. 1939), 344–55; (April 1939), 543–52.
44. *Saturday Evening Post* 211 (Sept. 24, 1938), 23.

pursuing the old standby relating so-called traditional education to the saving of money. Russell said that the breakdown of the doctrine of formal discipline had raised the cost of American education by requiring broader, richer, and more practical programs in the schools. "The easiest way to finance education in New York State," said Russell, "would be to bring President Hutchins and Stringfellow Barr of St. John's College, Annapolis, here, and have them introduce the classical system, narrow the curriculum, and go back to the old methods of teaching." As a presumably crushing conclusion, Russell observed that "no vast expenditures" had been made "for ships like the Normandie or the Queen Mary in the days when we believed the world was flat."[45] It should be noted that Hutchins was not trying to save money and that he consistently advocated the spending of more scholarship money for the talented poor.[46]

The entire controversy about Hutchins was more significant to educational doctrine than were the responses to other presumed traitors. Hutchins was no ordinary critic. Even vitriolic observers like H. E. Buchholz, publisher of educational journals, who slammed away at NEA leadership and the drives for federal school funds,[47] did not attract the intense response that Hutchins did. Neither did Bagley and the essentialists (whom Hutchins, incidentally, had declined to join). There was evidently something special about Hutchins's offenses that could outweigh the man's personal attractiveness and charm.

Again the conclusion seems inevitable that his troubles came from advocacy of a mainly literary education. Perhaps he could have gotten away with championing great books for their supplementary value to the central objectives of education, but the reading of books, great or otherwise, for their intrinsic and internal values could win neither acceptance nor toleration in the pedagogical scheme of things in the United States of the late 1930s. It is not that Hutchins's schemes were beyond reproach. Friendly critics like Milton Mayer could, however, discuss them objectively and point out where they could be corrected and improved. For others, Hutchins was not only a traitor but a most dangerous heretic. To take part in the numerous burnings of President Hutchins had become an act of pedagogical faith.

45. "A Century of Teacher Education," *TCR* 41 (March 1940), 489.
46. *Saturday Evening Post* 210 (Jan. 22, 1938), 16.
47. For Buchholz's fulminations see his "More Money for Less Education," *American Mercury* 16 (March 1929), 271–78; *Fads and Fallacies in Present-Day Education* (New York, 1931); "The Pedagogues Leap To Save Us," *American Mercury* 26 (July 1932), 328–45.

Chapter 12

For the control of youth

"Our last minority group is Youth."
—RUTH BENEDICT,
1941.

So far as educators were concerned and the general public also, to judge from press and radio, the main problem of the 1930s was the problem of youth. Herein was expressed for the adult generations the sense of collective guilt for depression and for social and economic injustice in the American way of depression life. The result was a love affair of American society with its youth, one that crossed the thin boundary into hate during the agonizing years that marked the decade's end. Youth served as both the victim and the alleged perpetrator of the chaos of the times.

Deeply involved in the problem of youth was the American high school. To those educators who at least as far back as the World War had envisioned the high school taking over the responsibility for all American youth, the times seemed propitious indeed. The vision of universal custodianship had faded somewhat in the brightness of prosperity but stood out clear and sharp in the murky despair of the depression. Now, if ever, was the time for the high school to come into its own. Educators took up this task with particular zest, especially since it fit so well into the movement for social reconstruction and the perennial drive to free the high school from domination by the college.

The task, moreover, was one that enlisted educators of varying persuasions, even though the initiative in 1919–20 had come from the doctrinaires of social efficiency. For the progressives, at least by 1930 for many in the Progressive Education Association, the appeal was in meeting the needs of adolescents, a movement that had earlier developed as an aspect of the child study crusade. Among the ancestral voices of progressivism on this point was that of G. Stanley Hall, with his massive two-volume work *Adolescence* (New York, 1904). The obvious impact of the depression on the lives of those defined as adolescents by their ages served to bring the progressives into a common cause for youth and into pushing for an expanded role for the high school in relation to this cause.

As a rallying cry, the Progressive Education Association (and others) fostered the term *needs,* and since youth were the ones involved, the popular expression became that of *the needs of youth* or *adolescent needs.* Just as Ralph Tyler symbolized the work on evaluation in the Eight-Year Study, so the association's work on adolescent needs came to be identified with Caroline Zachry, director of the Mental Hygiene Institute of the State Teachers College, Upper Montclair, New Jersey, whose services were obtained by the Curriculum Commission as director of research.

In spite of Hall's volumes and mountain ranges of other research, Miss Zachry and her associates took the position that little was known about the subject. "When we undertook the study of adolescents," she wrote in 1935, "one of the healthiest experiences of our group was our frank admission that we had little reliable first-hand information about adolescents. We realized that much that has been written on the subject is based on adults' opinions about adolescents and very little on careful observation and study of adolescents themselves." Also a limiting factor, she said, was the curriculum based not "on the needs of adolescents, but on traditional material that has little or no relation to their individual needs or to the social problems which confront them."[1]

Miss Zachry's Committee on the Study of Adolescents, a subgroup of the Curriculum Commission, attempted particularly to relate the needs of adolescents to the strains and conflicts of the contemporary culture. "Restlessness among young people and their sense of futility," wrote Miss Zachry in 1938, "their tendency to identify themselves with anti-democratic movements, widespread neurosis and crime testify not only to a lack of personal satisfaction; they suggest further that democratic society is undermining itself by failing to realize the potentialities of this period—neglecting to direct young people into channels of social usefulness."[2] This has been a familiar enough theme from that day to our own. It served, along with much discussion of the strains of depression

1. "A Progress Report on the Study of Adolescents," *Prog Ed* 12 (Nov. 1935), 484.
2. "Some General Characteristics of Adolescence," *Prog Ed* 15 (Dec. 1938), 591.

society, as the basis for the comprehensive report by Miss Zachry and the committee, *Emotion and Conduct in Adolescence* (New York, 1940), a volume that sold some thirteen thousand copies[3] and received much applause.

With the applause came a dissenting note from a staff member of the Institute of Child Welfare of the University of California, who in an otherwise favorable review found the book too sombre and patronizing. "I felt like a wise and weary mother who had just pulled a whole universe of biosocial offspring through an epidemic of highly toxic adolescence and couldn't quit worrying about them," she wrote. Although granting the need for a sensitive approach to adolescence, she warned against "a perverse maternalism which regards adolescence, if not as a neurosis, at least as a grim business."[4]

II

Yet the facts of depression life for youth were grim enough and were reflected in scores of surveys, especially of employment, but also of recreation, family living, education, and health.[5] Employment, however, was the hard-core problem from which others tended to arise. Besides the technical studies, there were general and popular books on the problems of youth, including Kingsley Davis's *Youth in the Depression* (Chicago, 1935), Maxine Davis's *The Lost Generation* (New York, 1936), and Bruce L. Melvin's *Youth—Millions Too Many?* (New York, 1940).

Beyond the local and regional surveys and the popular books were the studies, pronouncements, and reports of the American Youth Commission, an enterprise created in 1935 under the auspices of the American Council on Education. Few commissions had had so many members prominent in a variety of backgrounds and careers. The original group of seventeen included the chairman, Newton D. Baker, onetime secretary of war; Ralph Budd of the Chicago, Burlington, and Quincy Railroad; Robert M. Hutchins, president of the University of Chicago; Lotus D. Coffman, president of the University of Minnesota; the novel-

3. Frederick L. Redefer, "The Eight-Year Study: Eight Years Later" (Ed.D. diss. Columbia University, 1951), p. 208.

4. Jean Walker McFarlane, *Prog Ed* 17 (Oct. 1940), 432.

5. See Carl A. Jessen, "Surveys of Youth," *School Life* 21 (June 1936), 273–75.

ist Dorothy Canfield Fisher; Chester H. Rowell of the *San Francisco Chronicle*; Matthew Woll of the American Federation of Labor; and Owen D. Young of General Electric Corporation. Changes came through the deaths of Coffman and Baker and the resignations of Hutchins and Budd. Owen D. Young succeeded Baker as chairman. The first director was Homer P. Rainey, former president of Bucknell University, who resigned in 1939 to become president of the University of Texas and was succeeded by Floyd W. Reeves. In its first major report, *How Fare American Youth?* (New York, 1937), written by Rainey, the commission took a national view of youth's problems, including employment.

The facts on jobs were plain and bitter. Youth sixteen to twenty-four made up one-third of all the unemployed although these nine years comprised only one-fifth of a working lifetime (p. 34). About 40 percent of youth available for and wanting work were unemployed, a figure rising in some communities, such as Newark and Denver, to more than 50 percent (p. 35). In its next major report, *Youth Tell Their Story* (Washington, D.C., 1938), written by Howard Bell, data were presented on 13,000 youth in Maryland, a sample of youth sixteen to twenty-four years old, one-fifth of whom were in school, one-eighth homemakers, slightly less than half employed, and about one-fifth unemployed, neither homemakers nor in school (p. 275).

From such bodies of data came the question of whether or not high schools had failed in preparing or providing for youth. Few would have doubted the value of the schooling, but many were beginning to doubt the value of the vocational enterprise therein, at least in the orthodox form inherited from the Smith-Hughes Act of 1917. Roosevelt himself gave the vocationalists a tongue-lashing in the message accompanying his approval of the 1938 appropriation bill for the Department of the Interior. Declaring that he had signed the bill with "much reluctance," Roosevelt centered on the allocation of nearly $14,500,000 for vocational education, some $10,000,000 more than he had recommended. He especially condemned what he called the pressures exerted on Congress for the additional funds. "Much of the apparent demand," he said, "for the immediate extension of the vocational education program under the George-Deen Act appears to have been stimulated by an active lobby of vocational teachers, supervisors and administrative officers in the field of vocational education, who are interested in the emoluments paid in part from Federal funds."[6]

Those who were prepared to compromise with vocationalism insisted on a revised version of it. Broad general programs in industrial, agricultural, and business education were highly extolled, with the idea that students so prepared could more effectively adapt to retraining. General education was also looked on with favor, particularly from the point of view of developing personality and adjustment.[7] Anti-vocationalism was not necessarily pro-academic. In fact it was possible in this period, by espousing this kind of general education, to be anti-vocational and anti-academic at the same time.

It was with general education in mind that the high school was now being pushed as a custodial agency for all youth. The argument for it reflected in part a belief in a long, possibly permanent, future of unemployment for the young or for all in America, a fear being voiced by national leaders, economists, and social planners. "What are we to do," asked Joy Elmer Morgan of the NEA staff in 1934, "with our youth up to the age of eighteen or twenty when the best technical engineers and industrial experts are agreed that they cannot be used in the industry and agriculture of the future?"[8] One writer claimed that 4,433,022 could be removed from the labor market simply by a universal requirement for completion of high school.[9]

Not everyone advocated the custodial function simply to get unwanted youth off the labor market. Some felt a sense of responsibility for youth who in any case would be unable to find jobs, while others sincerely considered the high school the best place for all youth to be. "In the reorganization of secondary schools," declared the President's Advisory Committee on Education in 1938, "a central place should be given to their major task of preparing all youth to the age of at least 18

6. Quoted in *Phi Delta Kappan* 20 (Oct. 1937), 75–76.
7. Walter V. Bingham, "Abilities and Opportunities," *Vocational Guidance Magazine* 12 (Feb. 1934), 9.
8. "Why the Public Should Support Its High Schools," *NEA Proc*, 1934, p. 490. See also Harold F. Clark, "What Is New in Jobs?" University of Pennsylvania School of Education, *Twenty-Fourth Annual Schoolmen's Week Proceedings*, 1937, 364–69; William G. Wilson, "News," *Chicago Schools Journal* 21 (Jan. 1940), 175–76; "The Fortune Quarterly Survey," *Fortune* 17 (Jan. 1938), 83; "Permanent Unemployment," *Saturday Evening Post* 207 (Feb. 2, 1935), 26.
9. Roy C. Woods, "Education, A Cure for Unemployment," *Literary Digest* 119 (Jan. 26, 1935), 32.

for useful, self-sustaining membership in American society." Professor J. K. Norton of Columbia's Teachers College stressed the responsibility of the schools to all youth. "The obligation is not met," said Norton, "if a youth withdraws from school before he is equipped for full-time employment. There should be no 'out-of-school unemployed youth' for federal agencies to educate." Others, including Strayer of Teachers College and Hutchins of Chicago, explicitly reached out for the period beyond eighteen and up to twenty years of age.[10]

What all this meant in the way of changing the high school was eagerly spelled out by a variety of contenders for innovation. Such a role in serving all youth, said the President's Advisory Committee in its report, called for "far-reaching modifications of secondary education, new curriculums, new courses, and, possibly, new methods of instruction" (p. 16). In its resolutions for 1938, the American Association of School Administrators (until shortly before called the Department of Superintendence) called for education in "creative citizenship, satisfying personal relationships, appropriate use of leisure, and vocational competence." Old contentions were dutifully refurbished and presented to do service for the cause. Professor J. Paul Leonard of Stanford (formerly of William and Mary College and the Virginia curriculum program) called for "a clean break with the academic tradition," meaning, he said, "renouncing allegiance to college preparatory curriculums." High schools, declared Leonard, needed to be reoriented around the problems of youth with remapped vocational programs and an adequate system of guidance.[11]

This was the situation when Charles A. Prosser, whose service to the cause went back at least as far as 1905, delivered the Harvard Inglis Lecture of 1939, *Secondary Education and Life* (Cambridge, Massachusetts, 1939). Prosser still defended what might be called traditional vocational training, but stipulated that it should not begin before sixteen. The views of Homer P. Rainey, director of the American Youth

10. *Report of the Committee* (Washington, D.C., 1938), p. 16; "The Civilian Conservation Corps, the National Youth Administration, and the Public Schools," *TCR* 43 (Dec. 1941), 179; George D. Strayer, "Changing Conceptions of Educational Administration," American Association of School Administrators, *Official Report*, 1939, pp. 47–48; Robert M. Hutchins, "The Teacher, the School, and the National Life," *NEA Proc*, 1934, p. 17; Hutchins, "The Junior College," *Educational Record* 19 (Jan. 1938), 5–11.

11. "Report of the Committee on Resolutions," American Association of School Administrators, *Official Report*, 1938, p. 191; "Unifying the Secondary Curriculum around the Problems of Youth," *NEA Proc*, 1939, p. 622.

Commission, were closer to the newest attitudes on vocationalism. His conclusion was that for most youth, "the high schools need not be concerned primarily with specific vocational training in a strict sense, but would profit most by emphasis upon general education basic to vocational training as well as to other functions of secondary education. The high schools should concentrate their vocational training upon a program of generalized vocational education which would be applicable to a family of occupations."[12]

Some feared the intrusion of other agencies if the high school should fail in its custodial duties. George S. Counts warned that if this happened, the high school would be reduced to the offering of the old Latin school with the possible addition of modern languages.[13] Prosser also foresaw a possible loss to other agencies but did not seem afraid. "Some new agency," he pointed out in his Inglis Lecture of 1939, "similar to the Boy Scouts, CCC, or NYA, to illustrate, may be created to which would be assigned the duty and responsibility for giving neglected youth the sort of life education which the high school refused to provide" (pp. 86–87). In his report to the American Youth Commission, *Secondary Education for Youth in Modern America* (Washington, D.C., 1937), Harl Douglass of the University of North Carolina suggested experimentation with a variety of institutions, including versions of CCC camps, modified Danish folk schools, and vocational schools of junior college grade. A year later he was even more skeptical about the high school and urged more consideration of part-time school-and-work programs for many youth.[14]

Few of any persuasion went as far in their custodial impulses as E. George Payne, an educational sociologist at New York University, who argued that the period of what he called education should extend to the age of twenty-five. He did not state to what age this should be compulsory. Like other advocates of custodianship, Payne expressed concern about the traditionalism of school people and their lack of awareness of revolutionary change. Still, he felt, it would be better to make use of educators than not, and presumably better to center at least the coordination of this long-term education in schools. The schools would need

12. "The Needs of American Youth: What the American Youth Commission Has Found," *NEA Proc*, 1938, p. 351.

13. "The Challenge to the Secondary School," American Association of School Administrators, *Official Report*, 1942, pp. 253–57.

14. "Youth and the Schools," *High School Journal* 21 (Oct. 1938), 204.

to be reconstructed, and part of this education might be carried out in camps "where a complete communal life will be provided and where young people will learn to cooperate and live together."[15]

III

From all this ferment there was bound to be a report, and one did indeed come in 1940, a slender but portentous paper-backed volume put out under the auspices of the American Youth Commission, although not written by them. The report was given the less-than-modest title *What the High Schools Ought To Teach* (Washington, D.C.), and was one of the most vigorous expressions ever made on the subject of secondary education in the United States. It may also have been the most anti-academic of any major report. Even in the portions which seemed less so, the report was fully consistent with the ideals of social efficiency and control.

What the High Schools Ought To Teach was written by a special committee appointed especially for this by the American Youth Commission. Three city superintendents, one high school principal of an independent district, one director of a private vocational school, and five professors of education, one of whom had recently been a city superintendent, made up the committee. The city superintendents were Pittsburgh's Ben Graham, chairman of the committee; Denver's Alexander Stoddard, who when he was in Providence, Rhode Island, had given wholehearted central-office support to a guidance program both intelligent and humane; and Atlanta's Willis A. Sutton. Oscar Granger was principal of Haverford Township High School at Upper Darby, Pennsylvania. The director of the private vocational school was Charles A. Prosser. Interestingly enough, in view of the malevolent influence long ascribed to him by academicians, this was Prosser's first and only appearance on a major national committee. The professors of education were Thomas H. Briggs of Teachers College and of the investment theory; Will French (recently superintendent at Tulsa and at Long Beach, California) and George D. Strayer, both of Teachers College; Harvard's Francis T. Spaulding; and Chicago's Ralph Tyler of the Eight-Year Study, possibly representing progressive education.

This was a remarkable group. Also remarkable was the dispatch with

15. "Education, the War, and After," *Journal of Educational Sociology* 15 (Oct. 1941), 91.

which it handled its job. Appointed in January 1940, it had its report ready by the end of June. In publishing the report, the American Youth Commission, by this time directed by Floyd Reeves, expressed its "great approval of the main conclusions and recommendations, although reserving the right to disagree on details," and pronounced it a document "as sound as it is stimulating and original" (p. vi). The committee's chairman, Ben Graham, in his transmittal of the report, said that it had received unanimous adoption in the committee itself. The report opened by asserting that "the change in pupil population is compelling secondary schools to modify their curricula," that pupils now came from "every level of society" and that "the program of instruction which may possibly have been appropriate when the pupils were few and selected does not fit at all the needs of the great majority of those now in secondary schools" (p. 7). It attributed the increase in high school population to compulsory attendance laws. It observed, more accurately, that the growth of mass unemployment among youth, especially in the depression, was also a major factor (pp. 8–9).

At this point the report expressed concurrence in the growing sense of disillusionment with vocational education, especially as specific job training. "The fact is," it said, "that a large proportion of the workers in America are engaged in routine jobs that require relatively little skill or training" (p. 10). The committee therefore advocated general education and in accordance with this argued for reading as a high school subject. This concern with reading was good essentialism, not inconsistent with social efficiency, and in itself neither academic nor antiacademic. The committee also repudiated what it called a tendency "to decry the use of books as a means of education" and called for more libraries and more free reading (p. 14).

The second major concern of the committee reflected what was becoming a popular criticism of American youth, that they did not know how to work. Some looked upon this as the fault of the school, a notion that found favor with essentialists. The committee, however, went beyond the general idea of work to emphasize physical and manual work in an almost mystical way. And of course it saw value in paid work as a means of helping youth gain a sense of self-support (pp. 15–21).

On the other hand, the committee also recommended unpaid work projects in the schools themselves, cleanup campaigns for example. School-related work experience in the community, some for pay, was also recommended. The committee discussed and leaned toward but did not specifically recommend compulsory national work service, still at this stage of a nonmilitary character. "If all young persons," it said, "were mobilized to do service for the country for a reasonable period during adolescence, a long step would be taken in the direction of solving some of the most urgent youth problems of the present time." It added that there was no "factor of general education" more important than that of work (p. 19).

After calling for more social studies in the curriculum and for a course in personal problems, the report turned its criticisms on what it called the "conventional subjects" English, mathematics, foreign language, history, and science. English composition was accused of having degenerated into "formal exercises in the course of which pupils are drilled in the trivialities of verbal expression" (pp. 27–28).

Inevitably, criticism of mathematics centered on the two-year sequence of algebra and plane geometry, and the committee recommended that those general principles "which are the bases of all precise thinking" be extracted from the courses. "Everyone ought to know how to translate a table of figures into a graph which shows trends at a glance," said the report, for example. The rest of algebra and plane geometry could be eliminated (pp. 28–29). General language was recommended as a substitute for a foreign language. The recommendation for history was that the work be shaped around "the achievements of civilization in inventions and the spread of democratic ideals" (p. 29).

Further explication of the anti-academic ideal appeared in another section headed "Vicious aspects of the ninth grade." It was necessary, said the committee, to concentrate attention on the one level in secondary education "which is perhaps more vicious than any other." What was vicious about the ninth-grade was that the courses had no direct appeal to the students and that every course was designed to prepare for what would come later. The vicious elements in the ninth-grade curriculum were required English composition, required algebra, and the presumed stipulation of two courses from the three fields of foreign language, science, and history, with foreign language commonly insisted on and with the history as ancient history. "It would be difficult," judged the committee, "to design a more uninviting year's study for adolescents," and it feared that large numbers of youth were "turned away from the pursuit of learning" by it (pp. 31–32).

IV

The amount of response was moderate, certainly nothing like that evoked by the report of the Committee of Ten or even by the Cardinal Principles Report. Perhaps the intensity of the national defense drive in the latter half of 1940 muffled this report, much as our entry into the war a year and a half later muffled that of the Eight-Year Study. It may have suffered from being regarded as indisputably correct. Even the discussion of work was a revival of impulses from the end of the First World War and the NEA convention of 1919.

Nevertheless a few did stop to note their approval or disapproval. One commentator paid it what he evidently considered the highest of compliments by finding it consistent with the seven aims of the Cardinal Principles Report. Academicians who might have dissented apparently gave it little attention, although several anguished objections were expressed. A. H. Lass, the teacher at Lincoln High School, New York City, who had struck out at Hutchins earlier, now turned his anger on the report, calling it "a mischievous document, an incredibly arrogant and misleading attempt to tell all in thirty-six pages." He apparently objected less to the doctrine of the report than to the accuracy of its conclusions about the shortcomings of high schools in relation to the doctrine. A faculty member in English at the University of Pennsylvania reacted against the anti-academic tone of the report specifically, expressing the fear also that the committee sought to reduce English composition to business letters and reports on economics.[16] *School and Society* reported that resolutions censuring the report had been passed in April 1941 by the executive council of the Modern Language Association of America and by the Classical Association of New England (53 [Feb. 1, April 19, 1941], 143, 500–501).

The American Youth Commission continued to support its committee and their report. In its later publication, *Youth and the Future* (Washington, D.C., 1942), the commission expressed its particular desire in view of some of the discussion to "reaffirm its belief in the soundness of the major recommendations made in the report" (p. 118). What the report expressed more than anything was the shift away from the passions of social reconstructionism and toward a kind of utilitarianism which in the long run was more consistent with social efficiency. With

16. George E. Shattuck, "What Lies Ahead for Secondary Education," *Secondary Education* 10 (Oct. 1941), 209–10; book review, *High Points* 10 (Dec. 1940), 71; MacEdward Leach, "Logical Articulation," *EJ* 30 (Nov. 1941), 754–64.

vocationalism temporarily in disrepute, the task was one of converting general education to practical use.

This emphasis was bolstered by anti-academic expressions in the pedagogical press, allegedly from students themselves. Since these eventually took shape as a letter from one named John Jones, it may for convenience be referred to as the story of the John Jones Letter, a fascinating one indeed in mass communications and an example of the way the wheel so often turns. One of its earliest appearances came in 1936 in an article by Lloyd Morrisett, at that time assistant superintendent in Yonkers, New York. According to the article, this was "a letter from an alumnus to his high school principal." The presumed alumnus castigated his former principal for having run a traditional and unreal school that had failed to teach the practical concerns of everyday life, such as painting houses, figuring mortgages, and taking care of babies. Morrisett used this to argue for a high school curriculum related to life, contending that high schools in 1936 were dominated by a college preparatory curriculum although the great majority of students, according to him, would never enter college.[17]

Nearly two years later, the principal of a high school in California quoted portions of this document, referring to them as "the words of an actual high school student."[18] A similar letter appeared in *Progressive Education* in November 1938, signed by "A High School Student." This "student" complained of the time squandered in school on dead languages and dead kings and queens. "Why not," asked this letter, "have a course in personality in high school? This should be a course in which boys and girls are taught to dance, talk interestingly, dress with good taste, and get along with each other" (15, pp. 565–66).

According to an unsigned editorial in *School Executive*, February 1940 (59, p. 18), the letter had been written by a dissatisfied young graduate from a high school in Washington, D.C., six years before, but had recently been made public by Assistant Superintendent Chester W. Holmes of that system. Holmes, however, denied that it had been written by a graduate in Washington, D.C., and cited as his source for the letter none other than Lloyd Morrisett's article on the subject four years before. "We do not yet know," said *School Executive*, faithfully cling-

17. Lloyd Morrisett, "The Curriculum and Life," *Clearing House* 11 (Sept. 1936), 3–10.
18. Harry Gross, "Designs for Living and Learning," *Prog Ed* 15 (Jan. 1938), 10–11.

ing to the cause, "from what high school the letter-writer did graduate" (59 [April 1940], 20). So far as can be determined, no one ever has.

Nevertheless the letter has continued to thrive. It turned up in a major textbook, *Principles of Secondary Education* (New York, 1941, pp. 425–26), by Rudyard K. Bent and Henry H. Kronenberg. Nearly three decades later the letter turned up in a nationally-syndicated article on the desire of youth for information on how to spend their money wisely. Here John Jones spoke again: "I want to know why you teachers did not tell and teach about life and the hard, critically-practical world. . . . I wish I had been taught more about family relations, child care, getting along with people, interpreting the news, paying off a small mortgage . . . how to budget and live within the budget, the value of insurance, how to figure interest" (*Wisconsin State Journal*, March 21, 1970). Perhaps John Jones' letter has become one element of stability in an ever-changing pedagogical world.

V

On April 7, 1933, the first enrollee signed up for what was to become the Civilian Conservation Corps, and the first camp opened ten days later, April 17, at Luray, Virginia. These were the beginnings of what developed into a major conflict between schoolmen and the New Deal over the custody of youth, but at the outset there was little sign of the rivalry to come. The CCC in this early phase was an agency of conservation and of work relief.

Schoolmen in fact applauded the first exploratory efforts of the CCC to organize programs of education in the camps. This phase of the CCC started in January 1934 with the appointment of nine major educational advisers, one for each of nine corps areas. Dean Clarence S. Marsh of the University of Buffalo School of Business Administration became the educational director, and by mid-February 1934, advisers were rapidly being appointed to fill out the total of one to each of 1,468 camps.[19]

For some, the CCC was a major project in educational and social reconstruction. "The Civilian Conservation Corps," wrote one advocate, "is the first practicable step toward building a sound future society. In the camps we are trying out those social principles which have heretofore existed only in men's minds or upon paper." Moreover, the camps

19. "Education for 300,000," *School Life* 19 (Feb. 1934), 117, 130.

championed the doctrine "that group training is more worthwhile than that of the individual" and that "the sentimentally democratic worship of individualism would ruin camp morale." The camps, he contended, should be regarded not as emergency measures but as permanent institutions in American life.[20]

The educational adviser of the Atlanta area advocated the development of a universal and compulsory CCC to be entered at eighteen and to include military, civic, and vocational training. It would remove, the writer pointed out, one million youth annually from the labor market and provide William James's moral equivalent of war. Another writer applauded these sentiments but added that the camps should enroll women as well as men. Even Commissioner John Studebaker, as late as 1937, was recommending or at least accepting a permanent CCC, although not necessarily on a compulsory basis. "The responsibility is definitely at hand," said Studebaker, "to help plan the work and activities of the camps so that they will be closely integrated with American institutional life."[21]

Further work relief came for youth in the summer of 1935 through the creation of the National Youth Administration. With Aubrey Williams as director and an initial appropriation of $50,000,000, NYA started out by providing up to $6 a month for high school students, $15 a month for college students whose families were on relief, and comparable aids for older youth who were out of school. High schools and colleges were called upon to develop the work projects under which youth could render service for their allotments. The resulting beautification and landscaping projects undoubtedly stimulated some of the thinking about work experience as part of the curriculum.

Rivalry between New Dealers and schoolmen apparently began with the NYA. Plans for it had originated with Mrs. Eleanor Roosevelt, Secretary of Labor Frances Perkins, and several industrialists concerned with youth, David Sarnoff of the Radio Corporation of America and Owen D. Young of General Electric for example, the latter serving later as chairman of the American Youth Commission. The plans were adopted at the same time that President Roosevelt rejected a youth

20. Henry L. Farr, *S&S* 40 (Sept. 22, 1934), 386–88.
21. C. A. Edson, "What's To Become of the CCC?" *Forum and Century* 93 (April 1935), 245–47; Henry Goddard Leach, "Education for Patriotism," *ibid.* (May 1935), 257–58; "Possibilities for Education through the CCC," *Phi Delta Kappan* 19 (May 1937), 297–98.

plan submitted to him by Commissioner Studebaker. As a way of providing for two million unemployed youth, Studebaker's plan envisioned the creation in each community of a guidance and adjustment center from which youth would be assigned to various kinds of paid work. Such centers were to function through community-wide councils organized under the Office of Education and a National Advisory Council for Youth.

Why Roosevelt turned down this plan in favor of the NYA was not clear.[22] The NEA had backed Studebaker's plan, but concealed any resentment it may have had of the outcome by passing a resolution at its July convention in 1935 praising Roosevelt for the NYA, adding, however, a wish that the money might be spent under Studebaker's direction.[23] In any case school people felt rebuffed by Roosevelt, a feeling that became chronic with his repeated avoidance of conventions held by the NEA and the Department of Superintendence.

The NYA was launched through programs developed by the state directors. "I think I left Washington on about the seventeenth of August," wrote one of these five years later, "to get back to Minnesota and get a program going by the third of September." In Texas the program was gotten underway with efficiency and enthusiasm by a twenty-seven-year-old former teacher named Lyndon B. Johnson. This youngest of the state directors had a booming program within a few weeks, one that, according to one account, was rated by Aubrey Williams as the best in the entire country.[24]

For innovators, pedagogical and general, the NYA seemed more attractive than the CCC, possibly because of the semimilitary style and administration of CCC and possibly because of the greater variety of school activities for which youth could get relief and work under NYA auspices. To conventional schoolmen, however, both the CCC and the NYA came to present a threat. Columbia's George D. Strayer sounded the alarm on NYA in the summer of 1935.[25] "The time has come," fulminated *School Executive* in November, "for our profession to act, and

22. For a comprehensive and penetrating account of these matters, see George Philip Rawick, *The New Deal and Youth* (Ph.D. diss., University of Wisconsin, 1957), pp. 171–84.
23. "Report of the Committee on Resolutions," *NEA Proc*, 1935, p. 208.
24. C. B. Lund, "National Youth Administration Methods: In the State of Minnesota," *North Central Association Quarterly* 15 (Oct. 1940), 185; *Encyclopedia Americana*, int. ed., s.v. Johnson, Lyndon B.
25. "The Federal Youth Program," *School Executive* 55 (Sept. 1935), 10–11.

to act vigorously—to demand that the educational activities of the federal government be placed under the control of educational authorities, under the control of the United States Commissioner of Education, and of the educational authorities in the states and localities" (55:84). By the summer of 1936, according to a report in *Time* (28 [July 27, 1936], 260), a major reaction among educators was developing against the NYA.

Some educators preferred to chide their own colleagues for sins of omission presumably responsible for the creation of the New Deal agencies. This usually involved the traditional criticism of the high school itself as academic. According to the president of Southern Illinois Normal University, the existence of NYA and CCC constituted a reproach against the conservatism of professional educators. "The fine sweep of imagination which conceived the idea of camps in which socially useful in itself highly educative work, education, and subsistence would be combined, would, I fear, have been quite beyond us," he said with special reference to the CCC. "We would have been able to think of nothing much more original than to invite the idle boys to come back to high school to flunk beginning algebra once more."[26]

As the decade wore on and Roosevelt showed little enthusiasm for the many bills for general federal aid put up by the NEA, it became fashionable to explain this as his displeasure with the traditional and academic character of the schools. "New Deal leaders," confidently asserted the superintendent of Montgomery, Alabama, "doubtless including the President, himself, feel that the 'cultural' education which largely characterizes the work of the public schools is too conservative and not sufficiently practical. They hold that Federal money released to the present public school systems would simply purchase more of the book-type, the fundamental type, the non-technical type, the college-preparatory type of education, which they claim has not proved sufficient unto present-day needs."[27]

The New Dealers themselves, however, did not express these views, at least not in public. Aubrey Williams, on the contrary, spoke most warmly of college education and took satisfaction in the NYA's having made it possible for many youth who might otherwise not have been

26. Roscoe Pulliam, "The Influence of the Federal Government in Education," *S&S* 47 (Jan. 15, 1938), 71.

27. Clarence M. Dannelly, "Finances and Philosophies," *School Executive* 61 (Oct. 1941), 25–26.

able to attend. He proudly announced results of a survey of 62,000 NYA students in 666 colleges, which showed among other things that the NYA students in 80 percent of these colleges ranked higher in scholarship than their fellow students. Furthermore, two-thirds of the NYA students ranked in the upper halves of their classes.[28] According to a survey made at the Indiana State Teachers College, one-fifth of the students at that school in 1940 were there by virtue of their NYA jobs. Consistent with the findings of the larger survey, these students were "the most outstanding single group of students on the campus, so far as grademaking is concerned."[29] The NYA was apparently fostering the academic scholarship that New Deal leaders were supposedly discounting. Schoolmen clung nonetheless to their interpretation of New Deal hostility. Their main fault, as they saw it, was that they had not succeeded in showing Roosevelt how anti-academic they really were.

Roosevelt simply perplexed the schoolmen and dismayed them. He appointed Studebaker, then apparently ignored him. Although cool to general federal aid, he supported the spending, largely through the Public Works Administration, of over $400,000,000 in buildings for libraries, colleges, and schools. He could and did make the appropriate rhetorical pronouncements on behalf of education, but pointedly avoided the NEA. When cornered he came up with the right answers, graciously agreeing with President Agnes Samuelson in 1936 that all national efforts in education should go through the Office of Education and be channeled through state departments and local school boards. If and when, he added, the federal government entered matters purely educational, "it shall be my purpose to avoid all division of responsibility" and to put educational agencies entirely in charge.[30]

With the swing, after 1940, into the cycle of defense, events moved rapidly toward a showdown between the New Dealers and the schoolmen. The NYA for several years had been adding to its original function by setting up institutions that looked suspiciously like schools themselves. There were some six hundred "resident centers," for example, involving by early 1940 some thirty thousand young men and

---

28. Reported in "NYA Students Continue To Surpass the Average in Scholarship," S&S 51 (April 20, 1940), 509–10.
29. A. C. Payne, reported in news note, Clearing House 15 (Nov. 1940), 178.
30. "A Letter to the President and His Reply," NEA J 25 (March 1936), 77. See Morris L. Appel, President Roosevelt and Education (Ph.D. diss., Ohio State University, 1947) for overview of the topic.

women. In a resident center, each day's eight-hour program was equally divided between work projects and related training, with enrollees, of course, receiving the usual NYA payments.[31]

Some of these were fairly ambitious enterprises, such as the one at Clarkesville, Georgia, established early in 1938 through the joint efforts of the NYA and the county school board. It was set up on a 325-acre site with buildings formerly used by an abandoned district agricultural and mechanical school. The 240 enrollees ranged in age from seventeen to twenty-four, including some high school graduates. Among fields of instruction offered were agriculture, home economics, handicrafts, radio, ceramics, metal, art, music, commercial, and plumbing, with related work in English, mathematics, and social studies.[32] Other centers discussed in the press were the NYA Camp Roosevelt for girls at Ocala, Florida, and the South Charleston, West Virginia, project for the skilled metal trades (*Life* 8 [April 15, 1940]: 77–83).

In the summer of 1940, Studebaker took the initiative in forcing a definition of the respective domains of his Office of Education and Aubrey Williams's NYA. A document entitled "Definition of the Respective Functions of the United States Office of Education and the National Youth Administration" was agreed to by Studebaker, Williams, and a group of state school officers and state directors of vocational training. "Briefly, then," said this document, "the function of the U.S. Office of Education is to secure the development and operation of educational or training programs for all youth and the function of the National Youth Administration is to organize and administer programs of work for needy or selected students." It was stipulated two months later in an appropriation act by Congress that all training programs for youth in the NYA should be under the control of state boards of vocational education.[33]

The agreement raised peculiar difficulties of its own. It proved difficult in practice to draw the line between work for the sake of training and work for the sake of work. Bickering therefore continued, with Williams seemingly making the greater effort for conciliation. In an

---

31. Kenneth Holland, "Work Camps for America," *Curriculum Journal* 11 (May 1940), 224–27.

32. Claude L. Purcell, "An NYA Residential Project," *Curriculum Journal* 11 (Nov. 1940), 325–27.

33. John W. Studebaker, "Training Projects and Work Projects," *School Executive* 60 (Feb. 1941), 13–14.

address to the North Central Association in March 1941, he emphasized the massive service of NYA in enrolling some four million youth over a period of five and one-half years, about half-and-half in-school and out-of-school youth, but insisted that the NYA had been honoring its agreement. As he explained it, the NYA did no class teaching, but he admitted the possibility that training might come as a by-product of job experience.[34]

Various straws in the wind began to appear in the form of proposals for new administrative organization of youth services. Although the American Youth Commission tried to remain loftily above the frictions between NYA and the schoolmen, it recommended late in 1940 that NYA and CCC be combined under the Federal Security Agency.[35] By 1941, the schoolmen were ready to attack. The NYA and CCC were now spending $400,000,000 a year, or one-sixth as much as the entire public school system, and the superintendents who gathered for their convention in that year heard Harvard's Francis T. Spaulding proclaim this development as the third pedagogical revolution in American history—the academy had been the first and the public high school the second. They helped, therefore, to create a National Committee on Coordination in Secondary Education, with Spaulding as chairman, to deal with the problem. This committee soon proclaimed that the lesson of NYA and CCC, the importance of work experience, had now been learned, and it called on public schools to take over the NYA, to start work camps, and to supervise the CCC.[36]

It seemed to educators at this point that the country was ready for the total youth program envisioned since the end of the War. Now, with victory in their grasp, the ideologues of social efficiency faced the loss of all this to the extraschool agencies of the New Deal. They were not necessarily against the New Deal, and even those whose latter-day resentments were based on fear viewed some federal part in the enterprise as legitimate. There were attempts, accordingly, to formulate comprehensive approaches that would rise above the unedifying note of jurisdictional conflict.

---

34. "The Relation of the Program of the National Youth Administration to the Work of the Schools," *North Central Association Quarterly* 16 (Jan. 1942), 238, 241.

35. "A Proposal to Combine the CCC and the NYA," *S&S* 53 (Jan. 4, 1941), 14–15.

36. "The Third Revolution," *Time* 37 (March 10, 1941), 69–70.

A major statement appeared in May 1941, written by Stanford's J. Paul Leonard and proposing a new youth commission charged with a three-year task of designing "a complete program for the total welfare of youth from ages approximately 13 to 21," involving public schools, federal agencies, state agencies, and private agencies.[37] All youth thirteen to eighteen would be encouraged to work without pay for one year, not necessarily in one continuous period, on state, community, or national projects. The program was to include "an adequate guidance clinic and counseling service" to which youth would report for diagnosis and service. Relief payments might be made to youth under eighteen. Those unemployed at eighteen and not going to college were to be given public work employment at regular pay (p. 267). Public school systems were to have local supervisors "to assist in reorganizing the school curriculum, doing away with subject divisions, and establishing, instead, a program of individualized education to meet the diversified needs of youth" (p. 272).

Leonard's proposal was never taken up. Meanwhile the Educational Policies Commission was busy formulating its own scheme for youth, expressed in its book *The Civilian Conservation Corps, The National Youth Administration, and the Public Schools* (Washington, D.C., 1941). It recommended the use of federal money with state and local control. During periods of unemployment, the federal government should provide jobs for youth on public works, but not with the aim of training. On the immediate issues, the report went straight to the point. As soon as NYA and CCC completed their emergency assignment in defense work, they should be abolished. Their educational functions should be transferred to state and local school authorities and their public works functions to a federal agency of public works (pp. 3–7).

The report revived the old grievance of educators over Roosevelt's rejection of the Studebaker plan back in 1935 (pp. 18–19). It reviewed violations or alleged violations of the Studebaker-Williams treaty of 1940 (pp. 37–39). The $720 a year cost for each enrollee in the resident centers was contrasted with $200 a year in public high schools for eighteen- and nineteen-year-olds and $160 for sixteen- and seventeen-year-olds. Included in the $720 NYA cost, however, were $360 for wages. Wages were the same in the CCC, but the total cost per enrollee

---

37. "Proposal for a Concerted Youth Program," *California Journal of Secondary Education* 16 (May 1941), 265. Subsequent references in text.

ran from $950 to $1050 (p. 61). In its inventory of values to come from a new youth program, the Policies Commission stressed the four aims in their report on purposes, plus those of special education, continuous guidance, work experience, job placement, and supplementary education (p. 71).

This was a declaration of total war against the New Deal programs. Still, the anti-NYA and anti-CCC forces did not have it all their own way, even among educators. Harl Douglass of the University of Colorado was especially vigorous in his denunciation of the Policies Commission, defending the NYA for having given more than a million students the chance to stay in school. Douglass accused the commission of aligning itself with conservative Republicans, tory Democrats, Roosevelt-haters, *Liberty Magazine*, and the *Chicago Tribune*.[38] On the need for NYA relief, Douglass was right. As late as 1942–43 in the first flush of wartime prosperity, the average annual income of families whose children received NYA assistance through the high schools was $765.[39]

Victory for the educators in the end came not so much from the cogency of their arguments as from the wartime drive to cut nonwar spending. First to go down was the CCC. It ended in June 1942 with the deletion by the House Appropriations Committee of an item of some $75,000,000 that would have kept it going for another year. Over two million youth had gone through the camps, but by 1942 only some eighty thousand were still enrolled. The same committee cut the NYA from $150,000,000 to $50,000,000 for the coming fiscal year.[40]

A year later NYA was given $3,000,000 to wind up its affairs and go out of business. According to *School Review*, the Republicans in the House tipped the balance against the NYA. Political opponents used the arguments of educators as justification for their stand. "Educators did not kill the NYA," said the magazine, "but many of them helped" (51 [Oct. 1943], 455). Having beaten off what appeared to be flank attacks from CCC and NYA, educators could now turn to the custodianship of all youth and prepare to fulfill the anti-academic destiny of the American high school.

---

38. "The Mysterious Stranger—The Policies Commission's Stand," *Frontiers of Democracy* 8 (Dec. 15, 1941), 77.
39. "End of the NYA," *Sch R* 51 (Oct. 1943), 455.
40. "End of CCC," *Time* 39 (June 15, 1942), 10.

VI

New Dealers and schoolmen not only fought over the destiny of youth, but they and others in American society were absorbed in the pastime of explaining to themselves and sharing explanations with others as to what the youth of the times were really like. The generation under scrutiny ranged from those born about 1916 to those born about 1926 and embraced ninth-grade entrants at both ends of the 1930s decade. Today these people range from the mid-forties to the mid-fifties in age.

The notion of a generation gap, usually referred to in the 1930s as a rift, prevailed then as now. To make the country youth-conscious, thought the *Saturday Evening Post* in 1936, was a good thing if it meant finding jobs for youth and providing better guidance. If it meant creating antagonism between youth and other age groups, warned the *Post*, it was merely pernicious. The *Post*'s genteel competitor the *Atlantic Monthly* showed its sympathy with so-called legitimate youth protest by opening a special department of the magazine for letters from people under thirty. A youthful commencement orator at the Lincoln School of Columbia's Teachers College in 1937 concluded with the following peroration aimed at the teachers and other adults: "We used to look to you so eagerly, for you were so old and strong, and we were so young and helpless. And now we dare to think that you are old and helpless, and we are young and strong. We who are about to live salute you!"[41]

Among those who saw the rift as an antiyouth movement sponsored by the adult world was a Wisconsin public official writing under a pseudonym. He called the matter of youth versus age the new class struggle predicted long before by the sociologist Edward A. Ross. The old held the power, and the United States was a country ruled by "old men whose mental processes have been solidified in the grooves of mediaeval theology." America's youth were neurotic and frustrated as a result and could turn to fascism as a way out. "What a pity," he concluded, "that the United States should risk a period of fascist darkness because a few thousand old men accidentally established in high places by a decadent social order should continue to rule us with beclouded minds." Anthropologist Margaret Mead saw youth frozen into a minority group and cast in the role of democracy's scapegoat. Perhaps this

---

41. "Youth-Conscious," 209 (July 4, 1936), 22; "Under Thirty," 161 (June 1938), 840–43; address by Donald Barr, quoted in "Youth Addresses the Teacher," *Curriculum Journal* 8 (Nov. 1937), 325.

idea was popular among anthropologists, for it was expressed also by Ruth Benedict, who declared that "our last minority group is Youth." In her defense of youth, she felt that the older generation could learn from them "how it too would have behaved if it had been bred to the extra-materialistic dream of the twenties and then cut loose without a sou to earn."[42]

Like other groups, minority or majority, youth bore a variety of reputations. It was mainly an inquiring, restless, intellectual force, to Superintendent Frank D. Boynton of Ithaca, New York, at the beginning of the decade. "Today," he said late in 1929, "our young people are asking why. They want an explanation. They question authority. . . . No other generation of youth ever used its intelligence as the youth of today is using it." The young impressed many as profoundly idealistic. Richard R. Brown, the assistant director of the NYA, for example, saw this idealism as youth's contribution to the new order. "We must try," he declared to the NEA Department of Classroom Teachers at Portland, Oregon, in 1936 "to regain youth's idealism, enthusiasm, and straightforwardness. . . . Youth must be taken into the council chambers and listened to respectfully. There must be no clinging to outworn creeds, no forcing of set patterns of ideals upon youth, no feeding it predigested opinions and theories."[43]

This attitude of respectful awe toward the presumed idealism of youth persisted nearly to the decade's end. As late as February 1938 school people were still indulging in it. "These boys and girls," said the principal of the New Utrecht High School of New York City to his faculty, "bring to us an idealism which is beautiful—an idealism which is surging through their being. We must harness that marvelous spiritual force, we must use it for their greater good."[44]

On the other hand, there were those who agreed with Yale's Frank E. Spaulding that the young were for the most part soft and lazy. Spaulding blamed it on a breakdown of high school standards; in the old days the high school had been a place of hard work, but it had now become one of "recreation and mild endeavor." So bad did he con-

---

42. Paul Niven, "Youth versus Age: A New Class Struggle," *Social Frontier* 31 (Jan. 1938), 120; "Democracy's Scapegoat: Youth," *Harper's* 182 (Jan. 1941), 127–32; "Our Last Minority: Youth," *New Republic* 104 (Feb. 24, 1941), 271–72.

43. "Trumansburg," *S&S* 31 (Feb. 1, 1930), 143; Richard R. Brown, "Youth and the New Order," *NEA Proc*, 1936, p. 209.

44. Maurice E. Rogalin, quoted in Bella M. B. Chase, "Character Training in the Public Schools," *High Points* 20 (Feb. 1938), 18.

sider the high school on this point that he joined those who were giving up on it and suggesting that many youth would be better off working. He did not, however, insist on physical labor, as did the report *What the High Schools Ought To Teach*, and educators like President T. W. MacQuarrie of San Jose State College, California, who prescribed a one-semester high school course in "window-washing, ground-tending, and janitor work."[45]

The doctrine of physical labor for youth now began to expand into a cause, with a proposal from Eleanor Roosevelt of compulsory work camps for all youth. Some young idealists themselves felt guilty on the matter and through the International Student Service organized some forty work projects in the summer of 1941, but they disagreed with Mrs. Roosevelt, their sponsor, about the desirability of making such service compulsory.[46] She disagreed herself with the accusation that youth were soft, or if they were, that it was their fault. "Well," she pointed out in an address to a vocational service group in New York City, "if youth has gone soft, we've gone soft too, and we've let them go soft. Perhaps we all need to change a little."[47]

In the eyes of some, the softness was moral and not physical, and revealed itself in youth's apathy and indifference. It was popular to blame the culture of the times. American youth, cried out the dean of women at the University of Michigan, suffered from the absence of a cause. Russian youth showed courage for their cause, but American youth were simply not interested in any cause whatsoever. This state of affairs seemed to bring out her generosity and desire to help. "Like a parent who yearns to give his child some of his own strength and understanding," she confided to the NEA in 1936, "we wish to help this new and struggling group of college students." The journalist Bruce Barton was shocked to learn that when youth formed discussion groups they talked not about religion and politics but about marriage and jobs. "We need to give young people a crusade," he said; "not to the Holy Land, or to the capital, but against the slums of their own towns, the waste and inefficiency of their own community governments, the labor

---

45. "The Progressive Debilitation of the Secondary School," *Harvard Teachers Record* 4 (June 1934), 120–36; quoted, *School Executive* 57 (Nov. 1937), 144n.
46. "Boys and Girls at Work," *Time* 38 (Aug. 25, 1941), 58–59.
47. "What Can We Do for Youth?" *Occupations* 19 (Oct. 1940), 10.

relationships in their stores and factories, the social injustices of their own little political units."[48]

The question of moral indifference came up especially in connection with the military draft. Opposition to it and to other aspects of national defense from youth in 1940 evoked a veritable concatenation of abuse directed at youth for their presumed moral indifference. Adult commentators blamed youth, but also found satisfaction in blaming themselves, even in competing with one another for shares of the blame. Archibald MacLeish started much of this by claiming the main guilt for himself and his fellow writers, including Hemingway and Dos Passos. They had, he declared, misled an entire generation of youth on the subject of war and peace. In another expression of this, he included scholars and scientists as well. Mortimer Adler, believed by many to be the evil genius of President Hutchins's unpopular views, wanted instead to take the blame for educators, particularly in relation to doctrines of moral relativism.[49] Hutchins himself also disliked moral relativism, but he did not join the chorus engaged in the denunciation of youth.

Bruce Bliven of the *New Republic*, famed as a liberal, charged the whole society with sins of omission, especially the omission of indoctrination. Going back to the mid-1930s controversy about indoctrination in schools, Bliven expressed regret that so many educators had been opposed to it. "Our indoctrination for democracy," he concluded sorrowfully in September 1941, "at least for the past few generations, has been so feeble that it has been practically non-existent. We should have known that the alternative to effective indoctrination on our part is anarchy, or, worse still, secret indoctrination by the enemies of our way of life."[50]

VII

Criticism about apathy seemed strangely unrealistic in relation to those youth who involved themselves, excessively so according to some critics, in the major political and ideological issues of the times. It was this involvement that distinguished youth of the 1930s from their flam-

48. Alice C. Lloyd, "Two Generations Facing a Mutual Problem—Cooperation," *NEA Proc*, 1936, p. 224; "Address," *NEA Proc*, 1938, p. 398.

49. "Post-war Writers and Pre-war Readers," *New Republic* 102 (June 10, 1940), 789–90; "The Irresponsibles," *Nation* 50 (May 18, 1940), 618–23; "This Post-war Generation," *Harper's* 181 (Oct. 1940), 524–34.

50. "Russia's Morale—and Ours," *New Republic* 105 (Sept. 1, 1941), 275.

ing predecessors of the decade before, according to Frederick Lewis Allen. During the thirties, he said, "daughters of patrician families were horrifying their staid parents, not by advocating companionate marriage but by marching to the aid of striking cafeteria-workers." Youth were excited about share-croppers, Veblen, and the CIO, not psychoanalysis and James Joyce.[51]

Young people were condemned on one hand for apathy, but on the other hand accused of radicalism and subversion for their expression of social concern. A YMCA official in Minneapolis, for instance, while doubting that violent social revolution could succeed in America, feared serious riots and disorders from "radical propaganda and teachings." Disloyal teachers and students, particularly students in radical organizations, had to be fought. The head of the English department at Stuyvesant High School, New York City, saw what he considered to be a new breed of students in high schools. Such students tended to be "glib talkers" and make themselves felt in English classes. No longer did high school students come selected from good homes and eager to learn. "We have crowded schools," he warned, "made up of strangely assorted elements." The answer was to stop coddling such students.[52]

Some high-school principals in New York City agreed with this teacher about not coddling students. After several peace strikes in the schools in 1935 and 1936, Principal Gabriel Mason of the Abraham Lincoln High School, while declaring himself in favor of the peace movement, strongly voiced his disapproval of the means used by some of the students to express themselves in it. He asked officials of some hundred leading colleges whether they wanted notations on transcripts for students who had taken part in the strikes. The overwhelming majority of the college officials asked for such notations, many of them expressing their opinion that character was as important or more important than scholarship for admission to college.[53]

Mason concluded that such notations should be made. Evidently some high-school principals in New York City did make them, for Cox of New York University made some sharp and sarcastic references to

51. "Since Yesterday: The Social Climate of the Nineteen-Thirties," *Harper's* 180 (Dec. 1939), 48.
52. William Kelty, "Is It Misguided Patriotism?" *S&S* 41 (June 1, 1935), 735–36; Frederick Law, "Let Us Reorganize the Teaching of Literature," *EJ* 28 (Feb. 1939), 107.
53. "What Every College Wants To Know," *High Points* 18 (Sept. 1936), 30–37.

the practice. This drew angry protest from one of the principals, not identified, who ascribed to the school board the original ruling about putting such notations on the transcripts. Apparently he agreed with the practice, however, for he said that "it would be a calamity to have our graduates leave our schools with a feeling that whenever they wish to defy authority vested in the school, the college, the police, or the courts, it is all right for them to do so." Cox apologized for his sharpness, but stuck to his point, characterizing "protest and challenge" as "too precious to a democracy for the public school to treat them other than sympathetically."[54]

With such ferment at home and European examples before them, many in the United States began asking whether we too had a youth movement. Skepticism was indicated by the frequent use of the modifier "so-called." One writer, after searching for a youth movement in the United States in the spring of 1934, concluded that there was no such thing. If we ever did have one, he said, the politicians, clergy, university presidents, and commencement orators who were calling for one (presumably in the campaign against "apathy") would not like it.[55] In the opinion of Thomas Minehan, author of a popular book on youth called *Boy and Girl Tramps of America* (New York, 1934), there were many barriers to a genuine youth movement in this country, including what he called "vested youth interests" that sought to do things for youth without involving them as partners.[56] An unsigned editorial in *Progressive Education* was sure there was a youth movement "scarcely out of its swaddling clothes," and saw in it a genuine desire to investigate the American social and economic machine. The writer based his conclusion in part on a reported membership roll of some 240,000 youth in one organization alone (12 [April, 1935]: 217).

Whether or not youth organizations added up to a youth movement, there is no doubt that they made their presence felt in the depression culture. Most prominent in the public eye and in discussions among educators were the American Student Union and the American Youth Congress, both organized early in the decade, and the orthodox and

54. "Must the High School Survive?" *Educational Forum* 2 (Nov. 1937), 32; quoted in P. W. L. Cox, "A Letter—and an Apology," *Clearing House* 13 (Sept. 1938), 52–53.
55. William E. Berchtold, "In Search of a Youth Movement," *New Outlook* 163 (June 1934), 49.
56. "Youth and the Depression," *Social Studies* 26 (March 1935), 149–50.

approved National Student Federation. The AYC started as an annual meeting bringing together a variety of youth organizations. The first was held in New York City in July 1934, and ultimately forty-eight organizations were involved. Paralleling the annual American Youth Congress was the World Youth Congress, the first held in Geneva, Switzerland, in 1936, and the second at Vassar College in 1938, with an opening rally at the New York City Sports Stadium.

Tension among youth built up enormously after the outbreak of the European war in September 1939. John Chamberlain of *Fortune* magazine, reporting late that year on interviews with youth throughout the country, observed that the seeds of skepticism had taken root. "Everywhere," he said, "the isolationist strain ran deep."[57] An outbreak of antiwar resolutions and memorials from college youth, especially from those at the Ivy League colleges and universities, excited particular apprehension among adults. Professor Paul Cram of Harvard discussed one hundred unsolicited letters from students received by the *Atlantic Monthly*, most of them against American intervention although in favor of material aid to Great Britain. To Cram this anti-interventionism was a result of having replaced the Bible and the classics by modern studies, especially in the sciences. He got in a sideswipe at President Eliot by attributing the difficulty in part to the doctrine of equivalence of subjects, a term used during the 1890s, not necessarily with accuracy, to represent Eliot's point of view.[58] An indication of high school sentiment came in June 1941 with the report of a direct vote taken by 283 graduates of the Mansfield, Ohio, senior high school, in which only 9 percent favored direct intervention by the United States.[59]

Inevitably, tensions over the European war began to involve the American Student Union and the American Youth Congress. The ASU in its fifth annual convention held at Madison, Wisconsin, late in 1939 voted 322 to 49 against condemning the Russian attack on Finland. According to the *New Republic*'s report, most of the members at the convention were noncommunist but had been impressed by the argument that a condemnation of Russia was part of a drive toward American intervention in the war.[60]

57. "American Youth Says Keep Out," *New Republic* 101 (Dec. 20, 1939), 253–54.
58. "Undergraduates and the War," *Atlantic Monthly* 166 (Oct. 1940), 410–21.
59. "Life Goes to a High School Graduation," *Life* 101 (June 30, 1941), 98–101.
60. Irwin Ross, "The Student Union and the Future," 102 (Jan. 8, 1940), 48–49.

Next came the winter Citizenship Institute of the American Youth Congress beginning February 9, 1940, in Washington, D.C. The main concern of the Institute was to foster the most recent version of the perennially unsuccessful American Youth Act. Unfortunately events pushed it (and the AYC) into collision course with President Roosevelt. Addressing some five thousand participants and others, Roosevelt referred to their attitudes against Finland as twaddle and based on ignorance. This was greeted by boos, just how many and how long becoming a matter of dispute. Leslie Gould's account in *American Youth Today* (New York, 1940, pp. 11–13) differed with press reports. According to Gould, there were only two who booed and they were quickly hushed.

Regardless of the number of boos, they were apparently deeply felt by the President, who in his private expressions, according to some reports, became quite critical of youth. This experience, said one correspondent, "lifted his dander higher than most people realized." At a press conference in June 1940 Roosevelt spoke favorably of the perennial proposals for compulsory youth service. When asked what he thought of a recent editorial in the *New York Times* calling for a military draft, Roosevelt assured the press that he had not meant military training. Still, the impression remained, and it was not undone by Roosevelt's remark to the effect that youth who had been in the CCC were not among those full of isms. "The President," the *Life* correspondent concluded, "is fed up with unrestrained youth."[61]

It was about this time that Roosevelt answered a letter from Roger G. Merriman, a Harvard faculty member and master of Eliot House, in which the latter had complained about the peace-at-any-price students and referred to them as "shrimps." Roosevelt thanked Merriman for his sentiments and said that he liked the word. "There are too many of them," he said, "in all the Colleges and Universities—male and female. I think the best thing for the moment is to call them shrimps publicly and privately." Most of them, he added, would "get in line," however, if conditions, presumably in the European war, became worse.[62]

This was not, however, the absolute end to the love affair between the New Deal and youth. The end came a little later when the American Student Union repudiated Eleanor Roosevelt for her endorsement

61. Robert Sherrod, "Roosevelt on U.S. Youth," *Life* 9 (July 1, 1940), 7–8.
62. Letter dated May 20, 1940 in Elliott Roosevelt, ed., *FDR: His Personal Letters*, 4 vols. (New York, 1950), 2:1028.

of compulsory youth camps. According to *Time*, the separation took place by mutual consent. The *New Republic* called it a sad leave-taking, for Mrs. Roosevelt had been the major champion of youth in the New Deal Administration.[63] Although she gave up on the American Student Union, however, she did not give up on youth, transferring her affection to the International Student Service instead.

Perhaps those who condemned youth in the 1930s could not have known how many of these same youth would soon be enrolled in the most terrifying of all mankind's wars. Many of those drawn into the war were still in high school at the decade's end. Considering the times through which they had passed and the prospects ahead, their wishes or demands seem moderate indeed. In November 1940, Teachers College's L. Thomas Hopkins reported on over one thousand interviews he had conducted with high school seniors during the preceding seven years. Some of what he picked up sounded like a composite John Jones Letter and showed concern with jobs, leisure time, family life, and personal problems. The seniors interviewed, according to Hopkins, came out for the abolition of all requirements and of "all homework and other disagreeable chores and artificial incentives." This may have sounded soft to some. These were youth, however, who were finishing high school and were in no position to satisfy themselves personally from any presumed lowering of standards. They also asked for a larger student share in the responsibility for managing and running the schools. Most poignant of all, and what seems to bear out their kinship with youth of more recent times, they were worried in the words of Hopkins, himself an adult, "over the rigid controls which adults have over life that prevent them from being themselves."[64]

63. "Divorce Week," 37 (Jan. 13, 1941), 38; "Have the Young Gone Sour?" 104 (Jan. 13, 1941), 39. See also James R. Kearney, *Anna Eleanor Roosevelt: The Evolution of a Reformer* (Boston, 1968), pp. 23–29.
64. "Seniors Survey the High School," *TCR* 42 (Nov. 1940), 119–22.

Chapter 13

A change of climate

"This year emphasis is on defense."
—CLEARING HOUSE,
DECEMBER 1940.

*A*s the educators engaged themselves in settling affairs with NYA and CCC, they were also occupied by the massive national defense effort suddenly demanded of them. They took up their new task with zest, largely because of patriotic impulses, possibly also because it was tangible enough to provide welcome relief from such vague tasks as leading in social change, although the defense program in itself was a change of social and pedagogical climate.

Hitler's invasion of France and the Low Countries had jolted Roosevelt's attention to questions of war production and industrial mobilization for the United States, with the announcement on May 29, 1940, of committees to work under a National Defense Advisory Commission. John Studebaker, Commissioner of Education, assumed for the schools the responsibility of preparing 1,250,000 workers for defense industries, and early in July worked out a program to this end with the school officials of most of the states. Six hundred schools were made ready to give ten-week courses of forty hours per week to 150,000 youth and unemployed older people, potential defense workers. Roosevelt quickly approved an appropriation of $15,000,000 for this purpose.[1] By November 1940, some fifty-five educational organizations had come together to form a National Coordinating Committee on Education and Defense to devote attention not only to job training but to other aspects of the defense program.[2]

1. "Double and Triple Shifts," *Time* 36 (July 8, 1940), 38–39.
2. George F. Zook, "Coordinating Committee for the National Defense," *School Executive* 60 (Nov. 1940), 9–11.

At the general session of the superintendents' convention at Atlantic City in February 1941, Studebaker triumphantly reported on the progress of defense training. By July, he claimed, nearly one million defense workers, in addition to workers regularly trained in vocational schools and classes, would have been trained. Over half of these had been taken from the rolls of public employment and the Works Progress Administration, and more than 60 percent of those finishing the courses were already at work. School programs for this ran in double and triple shifts. They were carried on in high schools, special vocational schools, engineering schools, junior colleges, and any institution where they could possibly be accommodated.[3]

On July 1, 1941, just about a year after the program had started, a letter was sent to President Roosevelt from the executive secretaries of the American Association of School Administrators, the American Vocational Association, and the NEA proudly pointing out that in fact 1,500,000 persons had been trained through the combined efforts of 10,000 schools. In 500 communities the schools had adopted the motto "We Never Close." According to the letter, half of all the workers hired in the expanding aircraft industry had been trained in the school defense program and at an average cost of only twenty-one cents per man-hour.[4]

At the convention of the American Vocational Association in December 1941, Studebaker declared that the program had by that time trained 1,776,000 for defense jobs, twenty-nine times the number turned out in the First World War, and this in a period of just seventeen months. Half the country's vocational schools were by then running twenty-four hours a day.[5]

One of the most completely dedicated school systems in the country was the Cincinnati system, which from May 28 to June 8, 1941, presented an Industry and Defense Exposition occupying six thousand square feet of space in the city's public music hall and featuring a complete machine shop, a transportation laboratory, and seven other exhibits. At work in Cincinnati were the nine regular vocational schools, five of them occupied in the national defense training program. Three of these schools, Automotive, Aviation, and Mechanical, ran three shifts each for a round-the-clock twenty-four-hour program. Two schools,

3. "An Educational Program for the Common Defense," American Association of School Administrators, *Official Report*, 1941, p. 19.
4. "School Aid to Defense," *School Executive* 60 (Aug. 1941), 18.
5. "Training Front," *Time* 38 (Dec. 22, 1941), 48.

Building and Electrical, ran on twelve-hour programs. Since July 1940, over a thousand students had finished the defense courses and a thousand more were in training in the spring of 1941.[6]

The more than a million defense workers generated by this crash program proved to be a massive morale booster for the schoolmen of America at that time. Accustomed to public castigation from both "leading educators" and their own constituencies, superintendents and principals could bask briefly in a deluge of congratulation and applause. Naturally they were grateful to the vocational educators on their staffs who made this possible and for the vocational aim now so widely acclaimed as vital to the national welfare. Vocational educators came back into their own after nearly a decade of denigration and defeat. "Never again," proclaimed Dean Edwin A. Lee of the School of Education of the University of California at Los Angeles, "will American schoolmen be superficially critical of vocational education." Jesse H. Newlon also saw a new day for vocationalism, but with somewhat more guarded enthusiasm. "We may expect," he pointed out early in 1941, "a great extension of vocational education, probably in the upper reaches of an extended secondary school. This job must be well done, but not at the price of a well-rounded general education for every individual."[7]

Yet the very success of the program suggested doubts about the need for widespread and intensive specialized training in the schools. If workers capable of handling the machinery of advanced technology could be turned out so readily, why then have long-term vocational programs in high schools at all? Might it not be more practical to add short-term intensive programs to normal high school programs of general education? Obviously the defense training program was turning out workers with minimal skills only, but for the most part this was all that industry needed in any period, war or peace. And according to the national director of defense training in the fall of 1941, an unskilled hand could be trained to run a lathe in six to eight weeks, whereas it took two years to make a machinist.[8]

6. "Cincinnati's Schools Participate in Ohio's 'Defense Day,'" *School Executive* 11 (July 1941), 8–9.

7. "Vocational Education and the Offense Program," American Association of School Administrators, *Official Report*, 1942, pp. 139–42; "Education in the New Year," *School Executive* 60 (Jan. 1941), 11.

8. *Time* 38 (Dec. 22, 1941), 48.

"It is the semi-skilled type of operator and no one else," said Professor William E. Warner of Ohio State University in July 1941, "who is now being prepared in the defense training classes of our schools under the provisions of Bill 812 and other acts which have given the U.S. commissioner of education approximately $75,000,000 to use for this type of rifle-barrel specialized training and for which he reports there will have been between 800,000 and one million workers trained by July 1."[9] The skilled workers who were not being trained in the defense program made up in normal times only one-tenth of workers in manufacturing. None of this, then, justified conventional industrial training of an advanced nature for large numbers of students. Even in the midst of plaudits for vocational educators, general education began to seem more important after all. Possibly the belated reaffirmation of the prevailing skepticism of the 1930s toward intensive long-term vocational training prepared the ground for life adjustment education at the end of and after the war.

II

Defense, and later war, took over more of secondary education than was represented by vocational training, however. Not only the vocationalists but also the indoctrinators got a lift from defense. Indoctrination could be bad or good, according to Samuel Berman, principal of the Ludlow School, Philadelphia, but he expected that schools would be called upon to accept their assignments with loyalty and understanding. The social studies program, said Superintendent Ben Graham of Pittsburgh (chairman of the committee that had written *What the High Schools Ought To Teach*), should teach what was right with America, not what was wrong with it. Since 1920 there had been too much debunking in history, and he called for a program that would "eliminate the 'debunkers' of American history, cast out the defeatists among our social studies authors, and make democracy and strength the keynote of our teaching." The principal of the Wildwood, New Jersey, high school, was especially prolific in offering suggestions, laying out a complete program of patriotic music, patriotic exercises, club programs,

9. "Bottlenecks," *North Central Association Quarterly* 16 (July 1941), 20–21.

homeroom programs, flag ceremonies, and field trips: "Indoctrination? Yes; and if that be pedagogical treason," he concluded, "find a better way in a time of crisis."[10]

Still, as was pointed out at the time, the response of the American people as a whole and of educators in particular was a great deal less frenzied than it had been only a little more than two decades before, with the important exception of the treatment of Americans of Japanese ancestry on the Pacific Coast. "Many of us," said Superintendent G. Derwood Baker of Boulder, Colorado, "anticipated a general wave of reactionary hysteria as the war crisis grew more acute at home and abroad but we have been surprised and pleased at the degree of tolerance which has prevailed. Our prophets of doom have so far been wrong. Apparently the great American public did learn something from the last war and its aftermath; something to be avoided. Apparently the work of our schools during the past twenty years stressing the civil liberties and the virtues of tolerance has not been in vain." The historian Merle Curti also felt "far less hysteria and undue emotional hatred." He warned, however, that it might develop as the war went on."[11]

Schools nevertheless were taken up with a variety of proposals on how to gear themselves for the war, ranging from policy suggestions for condensing the high school course to two and two-thirds years, to exhortations to efficiency; the central office of the New York City schools, for instance, asked teachers to save paper by giving fewer written examinations and requiring less rewriting of unsatisfactory work. In between appeared a variety of curricular devices and adaptations. As far back as 1937, a mathematician at the University of North Carolina had anticipated a new demand for his field in such a context, giving as an example of a meaningful problem the calculations needed by a Chinese aviator dropping a bomb on a Japanese flagship in Shanghai harbor. "With all the wars and rumors of wars that are current in the world today," he concluded, "some of us may be sol-

---

10. "Mobilizing Our Educational Forces," *School Executive* 60 (Oct. 1940), 12; "Education and the National Defense," American Association of School Administrators, *Official Report*, 1941, p. 125; John P. Lozo, "Indoctrinating for Democracy: A Program for High Schools in Wartime," *Clearing House* 16 (March 1942), 390.

11. "When Parents Ask," *Prog Ed* 18 (Dec. 1941), 430; "Immediate Problems of the Schools," *TCR* 43 (March 1942), 435.

diers sooner than we expect, and we look to the college man to take the lead."[12]

Mathematics was an obvious field for wartime attention. In November 1941, mathematician William L. Hart of the University of Minnesota submitted a progress report of his Subcommittee on Education for Service of the War Preparedness Committee of the American Mathematical Society and the Mathematical Association of America. In junior and senior high schools, suggested Hart, all boys and girls with mathematical aptitude should be urged by advisers "to observe that the study of mathematics through the stage of trigonometry and some solid geometry may serve as a distinctly patriotic action." He (and presumably his group) did recommend curricular divisions in mathematics, but based on intelligence, not on the expectation of going or not going to college. Substantial mathematics, he advised, would also be better than specific mathematics for military use.[13]

On the other hand, one publishing house advertised a new one-semester textbook for geometry with an introductory unit in algebra, calling it the geometry of current events, "a practical geometry book for today's young people." The advertisement printed the following questions, among others, in bold-faced type: "How do naval gunners determine the range of an enemy ship? How do army engineers estimate the width of a river for a pontoon bridge? How do artillerymen find the elevation of an enemy battery on a mountainside?"[14]

Some educators were comprehensive in their suggestions for militarizing not only mathematics but other subjects as well. In English, for example, "written compositions might interpret military and naval orders which are concrete, meaningful, and to the point. . . . Bulletins are available from the United States War Department dealing with terms and abbreviations used in military nomenclature." For commercial classes, the same man suggested "basic principles of military correspondence, forms for written combat and field orders, correct filling out of quartermaster requisition and supply blanks."[15]

12. Paul E. Elicker, "Accelerating Students in Secondary Schools," American Association of School Administrators, *Official Report*, 1942, pp. 52–57; "Schools for Victory," *Clearing House* 16 (March 1942), 398–401; Edward T. Browne, "Mathematics: A Living Science," *High School Journal* 21 (Jan. 1938), 7-23. Address to students at Duke University, Nov. 9, 1937.

13. "Mathematical Education for Defense," *School Science and Mathematics* 41 (Nov. 1941), 783.

14. *Clearing House* 16 (Feb. 1942), 377.

15. A. H. Bryan, "The High School in Wartime," *NEA J* 31 (Feb. 1942), 60.

States and regions organized themselves to incorporate a variety of wartime adjustments and provision into the work of the schools. The New York State Department of Public Instruction's "7-Point Mobilization of State's Teachers" was aimed not only at those in school but at parents, out-of-school youth, and the foreign born, to "prepare them morally and physically for the war for existence now facing America." All teachers were asked to volunteer at least four hours a week for the various activities, including instruction in American ideals for the foreign born, agricultural and homemaking education, and physical fitness.[16]

Physical education, like vocationalism, again enjoyed a place in the sun and became one of the main enthusiasms of those who sought to adapt the schools to war. Much of this was straight physical training motivated by scare campaigns arising from rejection statistics in the draft. Jesse Feiring Williams, a professor of physical education at Columbia's Teachers College, however, attempted to put it into a broader framework, aruging that fitness was more than just physical, but emotional and mental as well. "Treason," warned Williams, "may occur among persons physically fit, but never among those emotionally educated." He made a variety of recommendations, emphasizing the possibilities of school camps "to promote national solidarity, to give reality to democratic ideals and to insure, especially for urban children, essential experiences that come only from close contact with nature."[17]

Much was said, also, about citizenship education for those in and out of school. It was interpreted particularly as the development of democratic understanding, values, processes, and skills, with the accompanying understanding of the war as an ideological conflict. It did not neglect the more conventional historical treatment, and the newer media were used. Even before our defense program was started, World Book Company offered records with the voices and utterances of such leading figures as Chamberlain, Daladier, and Hitler. "Here is a new teaching instrument," said their advertisement, "which in addition to supplying a vivid account of a world crisis, brings to the study of history a new realism and significance." The Motion Picture Project of the American Council on Education early in 1940 announced its Current Bibliography No. 1 of a series with the meaningful and still favored title "Films on War and American Neutrality." Among the films listed were *The*

16. "Schools for Victory," *Clearing House* 16 (Feb. 1942), 336.
17. "Fairy Tales and Reality: An Essay on the Relation of Physical Fitness to National Defense," *S&S* 53 (Jan. 11, 1942), 34, 38.

Expansion of Germany, Lessons of the War in Spain, The League of Nations, and *Germany Invades Austria.*[18]

In the Los Angeles city schools, the curriculum department sponsored a unit on national defense taught in the forty high schools of the city during the last month of the school year 1940–41. It was taught largely in Senior Problems, a required course in most of the city's high schools. "The purposes of the unit," said William B. Brown of the curriculum department, "were to build and stengthen loyalty to American ideals and institutions, to give seniors a review picture of the geography and resources of our nation, and to provide some understandings of the things being done to defend this country and its way of life."[19]

Interestingly enough, there was no great development of military training, as such, in the high schools. Some expansion of the ROTC program had taken place in 1938 and 1939, overlapping in part the outbreak of the European war but preceding our own campaign for national defense. There were local conflicts over the introduction of ROTC, such as the one in Kenosha, Wisconsin, in 1938 when ROTC was defeated in a city-wide referendum by a vote of 9,085 to 4,685.[20] A national dialogue on the matter began early in 1938 between Edwin C. Johnson, secretary of the Committee on Militarism in Education (a peace organization) and Ralph C. Bishop, secretary of the Civilian Military Education Fund, with the statement by Johnson that the War Department was seeking to introduce ROTC in more high schools. Bishop denied this but said he would have approved it had it been true.[21] Enthusiasm for ROTC varied among school systems, Chicago providing an example of extreme dedication with 9,000 students enrolled.[22]

Life magazine gave much attention to the ROTC program of the Thomas Jefferson High School, San Antonio, Texas, in a photographic

---

18. *Prog Ed* 17 (Jan. 1940), 3; "War Films," *ibid.,* p. 6.

19. "National Defense: A Timely Unit for Los Angeles Seniors," *Clearing House* 16 (Oct. 1941), 71.

20. "Knitting Warrior," *Time* 16 (April 18, 1938), 28, 30. The caption refers to Mary D. Bradford, the former superintendent of the Kenosha Public Schools, who took a leading part in the fight against the ROTC. See also Edwin C. Johnson, "Main Issues in the Junior ROTC Controversy," *Harvard Educational Review* 9 (Oct. 1939), 469–81.

21. "Mr. Bishop *versus* Mr. Johnson," *Clearing House* 12 (Jan. 1938), 281–83.

22. W. F. Morrison, "Developing Leaders," *Chicago Schools Journal* 20 (May 1939), 224–27.

essay it did of the school in 1938. This perhaps reflected the visual appeal of the ROTC and its auxiliary of girls more than it did a desire to promote ROTC in the schools. In a subsequent issue, the magazine printed a letter from a high-school student (not at the school in question) objecting to the emphasis placed in the article on the work of the ROTC.[23]

When the defense boom came in 1940, there was no attempt to capture the student population either for military service or for work; they were left free from solicitation and exhorted to stay in school instead. This word came in the late summer of 1940 from none other than the President himself. In a letter addressed to the administrator of the Federal Security Agency dated August 14, 1940, Roosevelt said that he had heard of college students and prospective college students who were planning not to attend during the fall and to join the armed forces or work in shipyards instead. "Such a decision," he said "would be unfortunate." Youth should continue with their education; they would be promptly notified if needed "for other patriotic service."[24]

Almost a year later Commissioner Studebaker repeated this idea, expressing some concern for the labor market. "As this is written," he said in June 1941, "we are still at peace. We still have a huge reservoir of unemployed workers. Labor shortages as yet exist only in a few highly skilled defense occupations. . . . Except for those who have received specific pre-employment vocational training for skilled mechanical occupations, withdrawal from school to enter the labor market would only result in continued unemployment of older workers."[25] This note implying competition among age groups for defense jobs appeared also in a variety of comments to the effect that youth were underrepresented in the new and growing labor force.[26]

Military service, of course, was a different thing, but nevertheless authorities urged youth not to enlist but to wait their turn, especially if they were in school or college. School people themselves reacted to the draft with some confusion. It had come quickly, from the first tentative proposal in the spring of 1940 to national registration in October of

23. "One American High School, the Thomas Jefferson of San Antonio: Here 2394 Young Texans Get an Education and a Lot More Besides," 10 (March 7, 1938), 22–29; William Melnick, 10 (March 21, 1938), 2.
24. Quoted in "Public Schools," *Phi Delta Kappan* 23 (Sept. 1940), 26.
25. "Youth's Duty To Remain in School," *School Life* 26 (June 1941), 257.
26. "Training for Defense," *New Republic* 104 (April 21, 1941), 520.

that same year, and had caught educators and others unprepared. As late as the summer meeting of 1940, the NEA was still trying to avoid taking a direct stand; it favored the emphasis on defense but said the danger could be met without interruption of normal education, an expression from which Roosevelt may have taken his cue about advising youth to stay in school.[27]

After the draft came, some educators found in it what they apparently were willing to accept as virtues. New York University's John Carr Duff, for example, felt that army training would do for many youth what high schools had failed to do, make them feel important. Such training had specific purpose, in contrast with the vague purposes of schools. If youth indeed were soft and lacking in discipline, he reflected, what they needed was not more homework or examinations, not more quadratic equations or ablative absolutes, but real chores instead of academic ones. The failure of high schools, again, lay in their academic tradition and the dead hand of preparation for college, and it was "tragic irony" that military service should offer youth their first "realistic opportunity" in relation to American life.[28] Such expressions as these were not promilitarist; they were merely new versions of the old anti-academic complaint.

III

Educators had to adjust not only to the military draft but to a whole complex of matters relating to the contrasting styles of war and peace. In spite of protestations to the contrary, the national mood after May 1940 did turn upside down many of the values held during the 1930s, and called for praising what had been condemned and condemning what had been praised. Not the least affected was the long-standing organized movement of education for peace, one shared by educators with many of their fellow citizens.

Under isolationism, peace had been patriotic, with the *Saturday Evening Post* in 1933 declaring that if war came in Europe we must "refuse to be drawn into it on any pretext." True to its militant isolationism, the *Post* even then had urged a high level of preparedness and defense.[29]

27. "NEA on Preparedness," *Time* 36 (July 15, 1940), 55.
28. "What Discipline for American Youth?" *Clearing House* 15 (April 1941), 471–73.
29. "Once Burned," 21 (Nov. 18, 1933), 22.

The bias against participation in any overseas war, however, was very strong in all quarters through the middle thirties, and educators were involved in a host of peace organizations, conferences, and movements. On July 4, 1935, the summer NEA convention responded favorably to a general session speech by Senator Gerald P. Nye of North Dakota on the dangers from the munitions industries and the crucial necessity of education for peace.[30] Actually, educators were committed on these matters before the popular isolationism of the 1930s and at least as early as the period after World War I. Moreover, the approach they made through international organizations had even run counter to some of what might be called the ideology of isolationism itself.

Of course this rendered all the more wrenching the adjustments that educators now began to feel they had to make. The first reactions to the outbreak of war in Europe were inevitably mixed, as, for example, those in an entire issue of *Frontiers of Democracy* dedicated to the question. Some of the contributors declared that it was not our war, but Newlon insisted that the interests of democracy everywhere demanded the defeat of dictatorships. Newlon saw no reason at this time (fall of 1939) for the entrance of the United States and hoped it would not be necessary, but he advocated "everything short of war" in aid for Great Britain and France.[31]

The views expressed shortly after at the winter meeting in St. Louis (February 1940) of the American Association of School Administrators were also mixed. In one of its formal resolutions, the association urged the government to make every effort to keep us out of the war, but at the same time to provide "a reasonable and practical program for adequate defense." It also identified the public schools as defense agencies, since our ultimate defense lay in the loyalty, morale, and character of our people. Speaking for himself, Dean William F. Russell of Columbia's Teachers College came out strongly for defense preparation and asserted that the only way to keep out of war was to be strong. "We need," he said, "the armor of military power, of physical health, of religious belief, and of abiding love in our country and in the American dream."[32]

As the tumultuous events of the spring and summer of 1940 began

30. "The Munitions Investigation," *NEA J* 24 (Sept. 1935), 185–92.
31. "The Weakness of Isolationism," 6 (Dec. 15, 1939), 78.
32. "Committee on Resolutions," American Association of School Administrators, *Official Report*, 1940, p. 189; "Education for National Defense," *ibid.*, p. 146.

to change the appearance of all things, the board of directors of the Progressive Education Association took up earnest consideration of the attitude toward the war that might be assumed by progressives. At its September meeting it discussed at length a report by its executive secretary, Frederick L. Redefer, dealing comprehensively with many aspects of the problem.[33] Revised on the basis of this discussion and published in November, the report aroused great interest as a quasi-official utterance of the association itself. Like the majority of statements, this one supported the need for national defense but warned that patriotic exercises and vocational training were not enough. "The times call for bold action," said the report, "but we must be wary lest in preparing for defense we walk unknowingly into the camp of the enemy." Anticipating questions that might be raised about the appropriateness of scholarship during such a period of crisis, the report asked, "When has there ever been a greater need to develop real scholarship among students, adults and in the community to avoid superficiality, glib generalities and easy solutions?"[34] The report contained much discussion of democratic values and the importance of preserving them in periods of war and defense.

Reaching beyond the limited progressive domain were the views of the Educational Policies Commission, which in September 1940 issued its statement on war and defense. With totalitarianism gaining dominion over most of Europe and Asia, the American people, said the statement, should be prepared to stand as guardians of freedom. Defense was not only military, but economic and moral as well, economic because it involved occupational preparation, and moral because it involved understanding and commitment to the goals of democracy.[35]

Leading educators as individuals also testified to their awareness of the changing times. Newlon moved toward intervention in a summer session address at Teachers College, presenting his audience with what *Time* magazine called a large dish of crow. In this speech he dismissed as fallacies the idea that wars never settle anything and the notion that World War I had been brought about by munitions makers. He referred

33. Board of Directors, Progressive Education Association, Minutes of Meeting September 27–29, 1940, Teachers College Library, Columbia University, New York City.

34. "Democratic Education: Suggestions for Education and National Defense," *Prog Ed* 17 (Nov. 1940), 453, 457.

35. Educational Policies Commission, "Education and the Defense of American Democracy," *NEA J* 29 (Sept. 1940), 161–68.

to peace education as a sentimental program and feared that propaganda analysis had been carried too far. George S. Counts also spoke up. His statement, published late in August, offered a ten-point program to make America strong. In the world of 1940, felt Counts, a nation had to be strong or perish. He advocated the maintenance and advancement of education, a comprehensive program of vocational training for a sound economy in an age of changing technology, the fostering of democratic values, and the guarding by schools of the "humane and intellectual heritage of the race."[36] Pronouncements of educators reflected sensitivity to the values for which the war was presumably being fought, in a way that they had not in World War I.

In some quarters, however, there was a tendency to regard peace education as having been largely a mistake. "The peace education program which has been an emphatic feature in New York City schools for some years," *Clearing House* commented late in 1940, "is being altered and revised, if not put away in a closet. This year emphasis is on defense." At the meeting of the Middle States Association of History and Social Science Teachers, Atlantic City, November 23, 1940, an exchange developed between Arthur E. Bestor, Jr., of Columbia's Teachers College and Phillips Bradley of Queens College. "Opening the morning session," declared the report on this meeting, "Arthur E. Bestor, Jr., of Teachers College, Columbia University, declared with some reservations that social studies teachers in recent years have overemphasized peace as an objective of national policy. He described the elimination of military history as a dangerous attempt to escape from reality." Bradley, on the other hand, insisted that "schools should do all in their power to prepare children for a warless society."[37]

In the midst of the defense campaign, the National Council of the Teachers of English brought out under the auspices of its Committee on International Relations a report entitled *Educating for Peace* (New York, 1940). The committee granted that a book on this subject might seem futile and ironic, and a sympathetic reviewer added "if, indeed, it does not incite to riot." According to this reviewer, the book took a long view of the matter and proposed that we continue education "in the slow, hard process of intelligence," in contrast with many educators,

---

36. "Newlon's Confession," *Time* 36 (July 22, 1940), 48; "Educators in This Crisis," *New Republic* 103 (Aug. 26, 1940), 268–69.

37. "School News Digest," 15 (Dec. 1940), 244; report signed A.E.B., "Middle States," *Social Education* 5 (Jan. 1941), 58–59.

"including university presidents," who thought that intelligence and understanding could wait until after the war. It might well turn out that what we did with Hitler in 1940 was less important than how we prepared for the decades ahead.[38]

Others responded to the report less sympathetically. James K. Pollock, professor of political science at the University of Michigan, for example, gave it short shrift indeed in his discussion before the Commission on Institutes of Higher Education of the North Central Association on March 27, 1941. In fact, he saw it as an example of the inability of English teachers to deal with social problems. He called it "balderdash," adding that if it was typical, "then one can understand why so many of our students are being misguided politically and socially."[39]

Throughout most of 1941, the issue before educators and other Americans was no longer the need for defense but that of intervention. One of the earliest declarations for it from educators had in fact been made the year before when Dean Henry W. Holmes of the Harvard School of Education called upon the United States to oppose Hitler and his philosophy "even if war is the result." In the spring of 1941, twelve of the fourteen members of the board of editors of *Frontiers of Democracy* wrote a statement that was circulated for discussion throughout the summer schools of the nation. This was a statement from so-called educational frontiersmen, and its signatories included William H. Kilpatrick, Newlon, Harold Rugg, Ruth Benedict, V. T. Thayer, and John L. Childs. "We advocate," it said, "full responsible participation on the part of the United States in the democratic struggle against the Axis to the extent, if necessary, of actual entrance into the war."[40] Included in the issue of the magazine where this was published were expressions of agreement and disagreement. There were many letters on both sides, and they reflected the seriousness and tragic cruciality of the question under discussion.

With Pearl Harbor, interventionists and noninterventionists alike realized that a new era in American history had begun. When it had

38. Leon Svirsky, in *Harvard Educational Review* 11 (Jan. 1941), 131–32.
39. "Higher Education in a Democracy," *North Central Association Quarterly* 16 (Oct. 1941), 160.
40. "American Teachers and the Present Crisis," *Educational Method* 20 (Oct. 1940), 8; Board of Editors, "This War and America," *Frontiers of Democracy* 8 (Oct. 15, 1941), 10.

begun was less clear. In retrospect the turning point seemed to have come with the outbreak of the war in Europe in September 1939, or at least no later than the spring of 1940 with the fall of the Low Countries and of France. Youth who had suffered from depression were now called upon to take their part in war. The literary critic Malcolm Cowley commented on how precisely the decade of the 1930s fit the events that defined its framework. "It is a neat pattern that we have to consider," he said: "a decade that actually lasted for nine years and ten months, that began on October 29, 1929 . . . and ended on the early morning of September 1, 1939."[41] For more than two years following that morning in September, youth and others lived in the uncertainty that was resolved for them in December, 1941. In these two years the American people returned in part to the mood, values, and concerns of the First World War and lost some of what had been gained during the preceding decade.

Lost were the perennial ideals represented by progressive educators and some others in the period since World War I, views of human relationships and the nature of human life. Progressives believed, perhaps naively, that human beings could want to do the right things without fear or force and that they had intelligence capable of use to determine what these right things were. While the ideals of progressive education had not been widely practiced, the discussion of them had made status, authority, and force unpopular, at least as words. Under wartime pressures these bad words and the ideas they stood for once more became reputable. When one was no longer supposed to reason why and when force again became a respectable approach to human affairs, progressive education had no choice but death. Humane culture had nothing that would be heard; its transmission through the schools in this context had little relevance or point.

There was, however, a postwar world to be built and planned for. Practical life activities called for by the John Jones Letter would go on and in a suitable environment of education for social control. The efficiency educators could plan for the realization of doctrines proclaimed two decades before at the end of the First World War. Progressive education had no foreseeable future. What also could not then be foreseen was that the pedagogical grapes being eaten by these fathers would some day set the teeth of their children's children on edge.

41. "A Farewell to the 1930s," *New Republic* 101 (Nov. 8, 1939), 42.

Notes on Unpublished Sources

ELLIFF PAPERS. Correspondence of Professor Joseph D. Elliff of the University of Missouri, a state chairman of the North Central Association for Missouri. Includes the period 1915–23. Western Historical Manuscript Collection, State Historical Society Manuscripts, University of Missouri Library, Columbia.

JUDD PAPERS. Correspondence and other unpublished documents of Professor Charles Hubbard Judd of the University of Chicago. Mainly for the period 1927–37. University of Chicago Library.

KREY PAPERS. Correspondence and other unpublished documents of Professor August C. Krey of the University of Minnesota in his capacity as chairman of the Commission on Social Studies of the American Historical Association. Mainly for the period 1929–34. Includes correspondence with some of the leading figures of this period: Charles A. Beard, George S. Counts, Jesse Newlon, Guy Stanton Ford, and others. University of Minnesota Archives, Minneapolis.

NATIONAL ARCHIVES. Papers on deposit in the Office of Civil Archives, Social and Economic Branch, largely in Record Group Number 12. Includes general correspondence of the Commissioner of Education and other staff members of the Bureau (or Office) of Education, 1870–1932, various subject files, and Historical Files of the Bureau (or Office) 1870–1953. National Archives and Records Service, Washington, D.C.

O'SHEA PAPERS. Correspondence and other unpublished memoranda and documents of Professor Michael Vincent O'Shea of the University of Wisconsin. Covers the period 1897–1932. State Historical Society of Wisconsin, Madison.

PROGRESSIVE EDUCATION ASSOCIATION. Minutes and records of the Board of Directors, Executive Board, and Advisory Board for the period 1924–26. Teachers College Library, Columbia University, New York City.

PROGRESSIVE EDUCATION ASSOCIATION. Correspondence and other documents of leading figures in the association, mainly for the period 1930–50. This collection was developed through the efforts of Professor Archibald Anderson of the University of Illinois and is now on deposit at the University of Illinois Archives, Urbana.

RAINEY PAPERS.   Correspondence and other documents of Homer P. Rainey as director of the American Youth Commission 1935–39. Western Historical Manuscript Collection, State Historical Society Manuscripts, University of Missouri Library, Columbia.

REPORT CARD COLLECTION.   Hundreds of report cards from schools 1851–1940. On deposit in the Educational Archives, College of Education, Ohio State University, Columbus.

Index